TERMITES OF THE STATE

What role do democratic governments play in market economies? And what role should they play? Using a multidisciplinary approach, yet still based on economic theory, this book answers these questions by presenting a detailed and profound analysis of the economic role of the state in modern economies and in democratic societies. It shows how urbanization, technological developments, globalization, and the growing complexity of systems – the "termites of the state" – have been creating growing stress for societies and for economies. Populism and growing income inequality are just two recent manifestations of this stress. Written by internationally recognized economist Vito Tanzi, this book should be of keen interest to any instructor, student, or general reader of economics and public policy.

An economist of international renown, Vito Tanzi served for twenty years as Director of the Fiscal Affairs Department of the International Monetary Fund in Washington, DC, with which he was affiliated for nearly three decades. Dr. Tanzi is the author or editor of more than twenty-five books, including *Government versus Markets* (2011) and *Public Spending in the 20th Century* (2000, with Ludger Schuknecht). A former Undersecretary for Economy and Finance of the Italian government, he was President of the International Institute of Public Finance (IIPF) from 1990 to 1994. Dr. Tanzi is known for the Tanzi effect, or Olivera-Tanzi effect, which refers to the diminished real value of tax revenues in periods of high inflation due to collection lags. He has served as a consultant to the World Bank and the United Nations and previously taught at George Washington University and American University.

TERMITES OF THE STATE

Why Complexity Leads to Inequality

VITO TANZI

CAMBRIDGE
UNIVERSITY PRESS

CAMBRIDGE
UNIVERSITY PRESS

One Liberty Plaza, 20th Floor, New York, NY 10006, USA

Cambridge University Press is part of the University of Cambridge.

It furthers the University's mission by disseminating knowledge in the pursuit of education, learning, and research at the highest international levels of excellence.

www.cambridge.org
Information on this title: www.cambridge.org/9781108420938
DOI: 10.1017/9781108355681

© Cambridge University Press 2018

First published 2018

Printed in the United States of America by Sheridan Books, Inc.

A catalogue record for this publication is available from the British Library.

Library of Congress Cataloging-in-Publication Data
Names: Tanzi, Vito, author.
Title: Termites of the state : why complexity leads to inequality / Vito Tanzi.
Description: New York, NY: Cambridge University Press, 2018. |
Includes bibliographical references and index.
Identifiers: LCCN 2017043719 | ISBN 9781108420938 (hardback)
Subjects: LCSH: Economic development – Political aspects. |
Economic policy. | Free enterprise. | Equality.
Classification: LCC HD87.T3763 2018 | DDC 339.2–dc23
LC record available at https://lccn.loc.gov/2017043719

ISBN 978-1-108-42093-8 Hardback

Contents

Acknowledgements   *page* vii

Introduction   1

PART I   CHANGES IN THE ECONOMIC ROLE
OF THE STATE IN THE TWENTIETH CENTURY

1   The Age of Laissez-Faire   15

2   The Economic Role of the State between the World Wars   22

3   The Coming of the Welfare State and Reactions to It   31

4   When Economists Thought They Had Found
     Nirvana: Welfare Policies   40

5   When Economists Thought They Had Found
     Nirvana: Stabilization Policies   55

6   Barbarians at the Gates: Challenges to Nirvana   60

7   General Rules to Guide Governments   69

8   Giving Markets More Freedom   76

9   A Minimum Economic Role for the State?   89

PART II   COMPLEXITY AND THE RISE OF TERMITES

10   Implications of Excessive Government Withdrawal   105

11   The Growth of Termites   110

12   Termites in Regulatory Activities   123

13   A Brief Inventory of Government Tools   132

14   A Closer Look at Regulations   144

15   Modernity and Growing Termites in Market Activities   153

16   The Allocation Role of Modern Governments   163

17   Public Goods, Quasi-Public Goods, and Intellectual Property   175

18   The State's Economic Objectives and Its Institutions   187

19   The State and the Distribution of Income   191

20   Market Operations and Income Distribution   202

21   Poverty, Inequality, and Government Policies   216

22   Market Manipulations and Economic Outcomes   226

23   Termites in the Stabilization Role   236

24   Modern Government Role and Constitutional Guidelines   247

25   The Quality of the Public Sector and the Legal Framework   263

26   The Quality of Public Institutions   287

PART III   FOCUSING ON EQUITY

27   Synergy between Wealth Creation and Government Role   305

28   Recent Concerns about Inequality   315

29   How Should Governments Intervene?   324

30   Intellectual Property and Income Distribution   341

31   Historical Background on Intellectual Property Rights   355

32   Tax Rates, Tax Structures, and Tax Avoidance   367

33   Summing Up Past Developments   383

34   Why Worry about Income Distribution?   393

Bibliography   401
Index   427

Acknowledgements

This book was written over a three-year period, mostly between 2014 and 2016. Parts of it were written during a research visit at the Center for Economic Studies (CES) at the University of Munich, Germany, in 2016. I would like to thank the Center and its director at the time of the visit, Professor Hans-Werner Sinn, for the kind invitation to spend time in the beautiful, productive, and pleasant environment offered by the splendid city of Munich and by the CES at the University of Munich. The time spent there could not have been more pleasant and more conducive to the work on this book.

This book is based on a lot of reading, a lot of thinking, and a lot of observing. It is impossible for an author, and especially for one at an advanced age who has spent many years in a full and busy professional life, not to be influenced by his or her past work. As a consequence, consciously or subconsciously, it is difficult not to plagiarize one's own past work. Therefore, this book has been influenced in various places by my two previous books on the economic role of the state, and by many academic papers, published over a half-century, dealing with what governments do or try to do in the economies of countries. Some but not all of these papers have been cited in the book. The two previous books, from different perspectives, dealt with the economic role of state. They were *Public Spending in the 20th Century: A Global Perspective* (Cambridge University Press, 2000), coauthored with Ludger Schuknecht; and *Government versus Markets: The Changing Economic Role of the State* (Cambridge University Press, 2011).

I must thank first my wife, Maria, for the continuous support that she gave me with her presence and her companionship during the many months of writing, and for assuming many house chores that should have been my responsibility to deal with, such as preparing the annual income tax declarations and paying bills, and for assisting me with frequent computer problems. At times I became so absorbed with this work that she must have felt that she was living with a zombie. My son, Alex, an economic reporter at Bloomberg Net, discussed with me various current US economic issues and, occasionally, provided me with useful statistical information, or called my attention to pertinent articles. My thanks go to him. My son, Giancarlo, a PhD in biology, helped me better understand some issues related to the medical and pharmaceutical industries. I also wish to thank two longtime friends, Professor Christopher Clague and Dr. George Iden, who were both my classmates at Harvard in the early 1960s, for reading earlier versions of the manuscript and giving me useful comments that helped improve the presentation. Naturally, they are not responsible for any remaining errors, or for the views expressed.

Finally, I would also like to thank the International Monetary Fund (IMF), the institution with which I was associated for twenty-seven years: twenty as Director of its Fiscal Affairs Department, and seven as Head of its Tax Policy Division. The IMF gave me an ideal vantage point from which to observe and evaluate directly the policies and the economic performance and behavior of many countries' governments. Those twenty-seven years, coupled with the years I spent as Undersecretary for Economy and Finance in the Italian government, in 2001–2003, and a couple of years working for the US Congress, together with much consulting work over many years for various international institutions, completed my professional preparation and gave me a uniquely broad "hands-on" experience, rarely if ever available to public finance economists. Added to my academic preparation at two top universities under some of the world's top public finance experts at the time, and to my university teaching, that hands-on experience should be a guarantee that the views expressed in this book, whether they may be right or wrong, and whether shared or not shared, have not come from just armchair theorizing, but from direct observations of how the real world truly operates.

Introduction

The economic role that states, or more narrowly governments or public sectors, in all their aspects, play or should play in democratic countries with market economies is a topic of great importance to countries, economists, political scientists, historians, and anyone else interested in economic policy and in economic development. It might be considered *the most important topic in economics*. As Jeremy Bentham put it three centuries ago, "the chief task of economists ... is to distinguish ... the Agenda of Government from Non-Agenda; and the companion task of Politics is to devise forms of Government ... which shall be capable of accompanying the Agenda" (cited in Keynes, 1926, p. 40).

This topic has interested and fascinated me for a long time, at least since the years spent in graduate school, at Harvard, in the early 1960s; or, perhaps, without the full awareness of the importance of the topic, even earlier, while I was living in post–World War II Italy in the 1950s, during a highly politicized period. In those years there were frequent, heated debates among high school students. On one side of those debates were ignorant leftist students, some of whom, who called themselves socialists or communists, saw private property as theft and wanted to nationalize all the means of productions. They saw the elimination of private-sector activities and of private property as the obvious and simple solution to the Italian economic problems of the day. On the other side of these debates were equally ignorant students with centrist or rightist views and, in some cases, even with Fascist-inspired views, who did not believe in socialism or communism.

In those years, not long after the fall of the Fascist regime in Italy and the end of World War II, there were still many individuals around who were nostalgic about the Fascist period during which, they believed, order had prevailed, rules had been observed, and trains had arrived on time. There were also leftists, inspired by the strong political propaganda being disseminated by the then important Italian Communist

Party, a party that, in those years, was still strongly influenced by developments in Russia. Those developments had attracted and influenced many Italian and European intellectuals who had come to believe that the Soviet experiment, with central planning and the elimination of the private market, was pointing to a better future and a more equitable society, a society in which the *basic needs* of individuals would be satisfied by the state and everyone who could work would have a decent, government-provided job.

A few years later, in a very different environment and place – when I was a graduate student in economics at Harvard, during the exciting years of the Kennedy administration, and when the "Keynesian Revolution" was raging and reaching a peak in popularity in a place that was very much at the center of both of those events – Harvard – the question of what governments should do in the economies of countries that were not centrally planned and retained a market economy was receiving a great deal of attention, both inside and outside the classrooms.

At that time (early 1960s), the economic, scientific, and ideological challenges that were coming from the Soviet Union, then seen as a great military power and believed by many as having created a well-functioning and vibrant "centrally planned," or "socialist," economy, were strongly felt, especially after Russia had launched Sputnik into space, had shot down a high-flying American spy plane, and had exploded a hydrogen bomb, while also attempting to place missiles on the Cuban soil.

Before going to Harvard, and while a student at the George Washington University in Washington, DC, I had been lucky to have studied under a top public finance scholar, Professor Gerhard Colm. He was one of the many refugees from Hitler's Germany and, at that time, was the director of the National Planning Association in Washington. I had also spent six months working as a research assistant in a study group nested within the Joint Economic Committee of the US Congress. That group had been set up to prepare a report for the US government on the economic challenges coming from the Soviet Union. The study group had assembled among its staff several well-known academic economists and was led by a dynamic, young, and brilliant Harvard professor, Otto Eckstein, another refugee from Hitler's Germany. At that time Professor Eckstein, one of the youngest full professors at Harvard, was considered among the rising stars in the economics profession. The task of the congressional commission was to advise the American government on how to respond to the economic challenge coming from the Soviet Union. The commission produced an important study that was reported (by T. Sorensen, a Kennedy adviser and later biographer of Kennedy) to have played a significant role in influencing the thinking and policies of the Kennedy administration.

I had also spent another two years working for a Congressional-Presidential Commission (the Outdoor Recreation Resources Review Commission) that was tasked with determining the optimal use for the extensive public land owned by the US federal government. This commission produced several reports that set the stage for the future use of public land.

During the years I spent at Harvard, in the first half of the 1960s, some of the leading economists of the time – Paul Samuelson, Robert Solow, Simon Kuznets, Kenneth Arrow, Franco Modigliani, Wassily Leontief, Kenneth Galbraith, Robert Dorfman, Alvin Hansen, Otto Eckstein, James Duesenberry, and several others – were in the Boston area, either at Harvard or at MIT. Richard Musgrave, who was then considered the leading public finance economist in the United States, would come to Harvard a little later and would be the second reader of my doctoral dissertation; I thus completed my public finance preparation under a third refugee from Nazi Germany.

From different perspectives, all of the aforementioned economists were addressing the question of what the role of the state should be in a market economy with democratic institutions. They were trying to identify circumstances that would require, or justify, the intervention of the government in the operations of the economy, and how that intervention could take place without damaging, or replacing, the market and without excessively restricting individual freedom.

After the Great Depression, which had left many scars in the US society, it was a period when laissez-faire policies – policies that until the late 1920s had required relatively little governmental intervention in the market, and when laissez-faire thinking had been still dominant in many circles and in several countries – no longer seemed acceptable to an increasing number of economists and citizens. At the same time socialist economic planning was not considered a desirable alternative by most US economists.

A search was on, in those years, for a theoretically based, "normative" role of the state, a role that would recognize and respect the property rights of individuals and the work of the free market but that would also recognize and address the existence of market failures and the social needs of communities, as well as the special needs of individuals who faced temporary or permanent economic difficulties. It would be a new economic role that would be played by governments, guided by, presumably, *benevolent* and *competent* policymakers and implemented by efficient and honest bureaucrats. The new role would replace the very limited one that the state had played and had been expected to play in the past, and that in the United States had continued to be played in the 1950s by the Republican Eisenhower administration, in spite of the changes brought by the New Deal, when the laissez-faire, conservative thinking of earlier years had been challenged by the policies of the Franklin D. Roosevelt administration.

The work of most, though not all, of the aforementioned economists reflected an optimistic view that the government could do more and better than it had been doing in the past in the economic sphere, and that, with its action, it could improve the lives and the welfare of many citizens. Some of the aforementioned economists, especially Kenneth Arrow, had raised some fundamental questions about the difficulties that would need to be dealt with, if the government increased its economic role, to promote social welfare. The identification of what was the "public interest" or "social welfare" was a particularly difficult enterprise. Nevertheless, the optimistic view had become the prevailing view in Cambridge, Massachusetts, both at Harvard and at MIT. It was one of those times in history when different ideologies were colliding in the market of ideas and influencing the formulation of economic policies. This was also happening in Europe and especially in countries such as Sweden, France, the United Kingdom, Italy and several others.

The Eisenhower administration, which had been in power during much of the 1950s, had come under sharp criticism by an increasing number of economists for its conservative policies and for not doing more for the welfare of the citizens and the performance of the economy. As a convinced Keynesian (James Tobin) put it, in an article written in 1958, "Orthodox fiscal doctrines have ... dominated our policies during the five years since 1953, and ... have brought the nation to the brink of catastrophe" (published in Tobin, 1966, p. 57). He had added that "increased taxation is the price of growth" (ibid., p. 87), a statement that at that time would have been endorsed by many of the economists in the Boston area but that was challenged by others, especially at the University of Chicago. That view would continue to be challenged by more economists in future years, starting in the 1970s and would prevent in the USA the increase in the level of taxation that would characterize many other advanced countrues in future years.

I wrote my PhD dissertation under the supervision of Otto Eckstein (with Richard Musgrave as the second reader), on the impact of the individual income tax on economic growth in six major countries. A revised version of it was published as a book in the United States and in Japan and played some role in the supply-side revolution in the late 1970s, when it was cited by some proponents of that approach. After leaving Harvard, and for the following half-century, I continued to be interested in the question of the economic role of the state, while observing how that role, in the United States, other Western countries, including in Europe, and developing countries, was changing and generally growing.

In 1974, while a professor of economics in Washington, I took advantage of a sabbatical year and a research grant from the Bank of Italy to return to Italy. I spent a good part of a year reading the extensive Italian literature on the economic role of the state – literature that goes under the name of "Scienza delle Finanze" – and observing closely Italian economic developments when Italy was fast transforming itself into a welfare economy, at a time when the first oil crises hit the Western economies.

The Scienza delle Finanze is a particular school of thought developed by Italian economists, somewhat independently from the rest of the world, mainly in the period between 1850 and the 1930s, until the Fascist regime of Benito Mussolini made it more difficult for scholars to express views that did not coincide with those of the regime. Linguistic limitations had prevented that literature from influencing more than it did the English-language literature on public finance, the literature that would come to dominate the field of public finance in the decades after World War II. Richard Musgrave and Alan Peacock had reported some of that literature in a book they had edited in 1958, and James Buchanan played some role with his writings in bringing it to the attention of economists of what became the School of Public Choice.

The Scienza delle Finanze developed in a period that had not been an easy one for the Italian economy, and during which not all Italians had seen the government of the recently unified Italy as necessarily a benevolent one. In 1861, Italy had been unified and had created a national, legal entity from the aggregation of seven separate states that, until that time, had had different laws, different institutions, and, to a large extent, even different spoken languages. After it was unified, Italy had experienced some problems in some ways similar to those that the European Union and the European Monetary Union have been experiencing in recent years (see Tanzi, 2012, 2013a). Perhaps as a consequence of those difficulties, the Scienza delle Finanze had reflected a more realistic and more down-to-earth aspect compared with the Anglo-Saxon literature, which, until the School of Public Choice had come into existence, had seemed more detached from reality. A similar comparison could be made to the literature that had developed in Germany and in Scandinavia, where the state had been seen more often as a truer representative of the interests of the community.

The Italian School had developed during a period, and within a historical context, when the Italian government had not been seen as representing truly and fairly the whole community (see Tanzi, 2012). In an article published in 1958, James Buchanan, one of the founders of the School of Public Choice, after he had returned from a long visit to Italy and had been exposed to the Italian School, had written that the Italian Scienza delle Finanze had been an "eye opener" for him, and had significantly influenced his thinking on the economic role of the state. Through the work of Buchanan, and to a lesser extent that of Richard Musgrave and Alan Peacock, the Scienza delle Finanze had had some influence on the development of the School of Public Choice (see Buchanan, 1960; Tanzi, 2000b, chapter 1).

The sabbatical year that I spent in Italy in 1974 coincided with the beginning of the oil crisis, which required some governmental response, especially in a country, such as Italy, that imported all of the petroleum it consumed. The policies the Italian government adopted at that time influenced my thinking and helped create some initial skepticism about the simplistic and then fashionable view, held by many, of Keynesian, counter-cyclical policy, a view that many Italian economists were pushing, as well as about some aspects of an activist government's policies. At that time the Italian government was in the process of creating a public health system and other welfare programs that would require much more public spending and was dramatically increasing taxes and creating large fiscal deficits. Those policies would lead to the creation of a large public debt that in future years would become a permanent weight on the Italian economy and a continuous worry for future Italian governments.

The solution to the economic crisis that had been created by the sharp increase in the price of petroleum, and which many economists were recommending at that time, was to increase government spending, especially for investment, even though the crisis was clearly structural in nature and caused not by a fall in aggregate demand, but rather by a fall in aggregate *disposable* income. The increase in the price of an important import, petroleum, had obviously made the Italian population, and the populations of other countries in similar conditions, poorer. It had acted in the same way as would have acted a heavy tax on the economy to be paid to foreigners. It seemed strange to argue that such a problem could be solved, or alleviated, by higher public spending. It should not have been surprising when the higher public spending led to high fiscal deficits and to higher inflation, in Italy and in several other countries at that time, and not to the expected higher economic activity.

When I returned to Washington, after the sabbatical year in Italy, I accepted an invitation to join the IMF as head of the Tax Policy Division, one of the important divisions in the Fiscal Affairs Department of the IMF. I went to the IMF, on leave from my university position, on a two-year contract, but ended up spending the next twenty-seven years working for that organization and dealing with government policies in all parts of the world. Twenty of those years were spent as director of the Fiscal Affairs Department, a department that had the largest concentration in one place in the world of professional economists specialized in public economics.

The positions that I occupied at the IMF gave me a privileged vantage point for observing directly how different governments operated around the world, and how different economies reacted to various policies, including those that increased public spending. It also allowed me to check how the actual actions of governments and the reactions to them were consistent with the theories that public finance economists had developed and continued to develop over the years about how governments operated and how economies reacted to their actions. These were invaluable lessons that complemented the previously acquired academic knowledge.

Over a long and active professional career that has stretched for more than a half-century, I published many books and hundreds of articles dealing in various ways with the economic role of the state, and worked in many different countries, either developed, developing, or in transition, on issues related to what governments do. In 2013, I published a book and in 2015 some articles on the ongoing debate, in the United States and in European countries, on whether, in order to deal with the recession that followed the financial crisis, the governments should adopt policies aimed at what was called *growth* or *austerity*, and on how governments had reacted, or should have reacted, to the crises that affected many countries (see Tanzi, 2013, 2015a, 2015d). That debate reminded me of the ones I had observed in 1974, in Italy, and again in 1997–1999, during the financial crisis in Southeast Asia (see Tanzi, 2008a).

After leaving the IMF at the end of 2000, and after spending a couple of years in the Italian government, at ministerial rank, I had more discretion in the use of my time. In the years that followed, I spent increasing amounts of time reading or, in some cases, rereading and meditating over some of the classic works on the economic role of the state, and especially on works that presented different perspectives on what governments, or states, should do in their economic roles. These works included the writings of Adam Smith and of other famous philosophers and political scientists of the past, such as Thomas Hobbes, John Locke, J. J. Rousseau, Edmund Burke, and Alexis de Tocqueville, and also of classical French economists of the nineteenth century, as well as more recent works by F. A. Hayek, John Maynard Keynes, Richard Musgrave, Milton Friedman, James Buchanan, Kenneth Arrow, Amartya Sen, Robert Nozick, and others.

The aforementioned works were always illuminating, but I had the feeling that today's world had become different from that of the past, especially, but not only, because of the growth in the frequency and importance of negative externalities, and because of the impact of globalization and new technological developments on economic activities and on the power of national states. National governments have continued to try to control well-defined territories, while the borders of those territories have become much more porous to peoples, money, pollution, and various other, not always legitimate, activities. Urbanization has also created government functions that had attracted less attention in the past, when the need for those functions had not existed, or had not been felt as much.

As mentioned earlier, my long professional career, concentrated mostly on aspects of public economics, had required working closely and frequently with different kinds of governments around the world. This experience had given me an unusually broad perspective and an experience rarely found among economists, to consider some of the questions of what governments should do in the economies of their countries, how well they do it, and what obstacles and difficulties they encounter or can encounter in their actions.

In addition to the academic training acquired in a top graduate school, where I had had the fortune of working with some of the best minds in economics at that time, I had taught graduate courses in income theory and in public finance for about ten years, before benefiting from the twenty-seven years all spent in senior positions at the IMF. After leaving the IMF, I spent two years, 2001–2003, in the Italian government, as Undersecretary for Economy and Finance. These two years allowed me to observe, *from the inside* (as opposed to from the outside, as I had done in previous years), the messy ways in which policies are made and implemented by public sectors that tend to be far more fragmented than economists assume them to be (see Tanzi, 2015a, for a description of that experience). This experience made me appreciate the famous maxim that "if you want to continue to eat sausages, you better never go to the room where they are made."

In conclusion, unlike most of those who write about the economic role of the state or of the governments, I have had the chance of not only appreciating and enjoying the theorizing by academic economists, about what governments should or should not do in the economic sphere, and of telling governments, from outside, what they should or should not do, but also of observing closely, *from the inside*, what they actually do.

While I have remained convinced that a reasonably well-functioning government is essential and can be a force for the good, and a necessary condition for the welfare of communities and citizens, as Adam Smith believed, with the passing of time, I had become more aware than I had been earlier about the difficulties and the pressures that governments face, especially when their economic roles become too ambitious, and when they deal with economies that have become more complex, as most modern economies have become. These pressures inevitably distort their role from the optimal path that they should follow or may wish to follow. Complexity often ends up damaging the role of governments, perhaps more than economists realize. The more complex that role becomes, the less likely it is that it will remain optimal.

I also became more aware of problems that develop *within* the public sectors, problems that can reduce (at times by a great deal) the effectiveness of governmental actions. Many public finance scholars seem to have a *unitary* and centralized view of the public sector (see Tanzi, 2006a). They believe that there is a nerve center where all or the most important decisions are made and, once made, those decisions are smoothly and clearly transmitted to those who must carry them out. However, even in countries that do not have a federal structure, the public sector is made up of many components that do not always operate in a harmonious way, as would a good orchestra under the guidance of a good conductor. Ron Suskind's 2011 book, *Confidence Men*, provided some interesting information on this issue within the early years of the Obama administration. The more actors there are within an administration, the greater the likelihood that problems among the principal agents will develop, and the greater will become the difficulties and the lack of harmony within the government's operations.

Some difficult problems originate outside the governments that would make the work of *any* government difficult. Other problems develop inside the governments and inside the broader public sectors. The relevance and the severity of the problems change with time, and tend to vary in different countries. However, there are similarities in these developments. This book tries to highlight some of them. The problems depend to some extent on how ambitious the role becomes that governments attempt to play, and on the choice of the instruments used. The greater and more ambitious the role, the more likely it is that complexity will grow, creating unanticipated problems.

In recent years, in most countries, both the problems and the difficulties of solving them seem to have grown, making an observer more pessimistic about the future, and more skeptical about some of the simplistic solutions that one hears from both economists and politicians.

This book has tried to avoid what could be called the trap of *current, fashionable thinking*. It is easy to fall into the trap that is created when the most recent writing is assumed to reflect the final word on a topic, a word that is believed to incorporate and to be built on all the knowledge accumulated in the past. This assumption of a perfect market of ideas and of progress in thinking may be realistic in science. It is not often realistic in economics. If one believes in an efficient market for ideas or knowledge, one may feel that it is a waste of time to read anything that is more than a few years old. Many economists today feel that way, and some read only the latest articles in good economic journals.

However, as Gunnar Myrdal wrote in a brilliant essay first published in 1929, "we cannot pretend to understand completely, or even to define logically, the economic-political speculation of recent times except in the perspective of historical evolution" (p. x). Myrdal pointed out that in economics "the number of authentically recognized general truths is ... very small" (ibid., p. xiii). And, he added, while in science the "warfare of ideas usually leads to some definite result," "in economics *all* doctrines live on persistently. No new theories ever completely supplant the old" (ibid., p. xiv; italics in the original). Under the influence of Myrdal, I have made a special effort in this book to place the issues discussed within their broad historical contexts.

The book covers various areas not covered by other books. It provides arguably the most detailed anatomy of the public sector available, and it does so while avoiding the use of unnecessary technicalities, to make the book accessible not only to economists but also to individuals from other disciplines and even to the educated public. The terms *state*, *government*, and *public sector*, in most cases, have been used as synonyms, although, of course, one could attribute to each of them precise, individual meanings. The terms have been used in their precise, individual meanings only when necessary.

Finally, the book is divided in three distinct parts, each interesting in its own way. The first part, consisting of nine chapters, provides a description of how the basic economic ideology that guided governments' actions in their economic role changed during the course of the twentieth century.

The second part, consisting of sixteen chapters, describes how the larger role assumed by governments during the twentieth century – promoted by changing ideology, by the growing urbanization of the population, and by the growing complexity of the market – became progressively more difficult to monitor and to control. The third part of the book, consisting of eight chapters, deals with the highly relevant and controversial topic of income distributions that have become progressively more unequal within many countries and that are giving rise to potentially dangerous populist reactions. These chapters discuss some of the factors that have contributed to this situation and what governments can do about it. Some of these factors have not attracted the attention they should have in the relevant literature.

Universal opulence ... extends itself to the lowest ranks of the people ... [in a] *well-governed society.*

Adam Smith (italics added)

What civil policy can be so ruinous and destructive as the vices of men? The fatal effects of bad government arise from nothing, but that it does not sufficiently *guard* against the mischiefs which human wickedness gives occasion to.

Adam Smith (italics added)

PART I

Changes in the Economic Role of the State in the Twentieth Century

CHAPTER I

The Age of Laissez-Faire

The twentieth century witnessed major changes in what governments do and in what they are expected to do for their countries' economies and for promoting the welfare of their citizens. At the beginning of the century the *actual* economic role of the state was still significantly influenced by the (qualified) laissez-faire economic philosophy that had dominated, or influenced, the actions and the policies of governments during much of the second half of the nineteenth century. That philosophy had survived in spite of increasing challenges coming from socialist thinkers, who had little sympathy for markets and for private property, and, especially in the latter part of that century, from workers' demands for better pay and working conditions in the new, large industrial enterprises in which they worked and that the Industrial Revolution had created. Many of these enterprises had at that time much monopolistic power. In the last decade of the nineteenth century, some governments, such as that of Germany, had started to abandon timidly the strict laissez-faire policies of earlier years.

Laissez-faire thinking had limited government intervention on the working conditions of the workers and had called for and justified low levels of taxation and public spending. It had limited the direct interference by governments in the activities of specific enterprises and markets, even though, in some countries, including the United States, governments had occasionally assisted some economic activities and some enterprises by providing protective tariffs, by building important infrastructures, and in other ways.

Governments had to some extent a *developmental role* within economies with free markets. Import duties had been used to promote the developmental objective, while also providing governments with limited fiscal revenue. In the words of Richard Musgrave (1969), import duties had provided a useful "tax handle" in some countries and especially in the United States, where the federal government had relied on those revenues for many of its limited revenue needs, until the federal income tax, introduced in 1913, provided it with an important, alternative revenue source.

As measured by the shares of taxes and public spending in the countries' gross domestic products (GDPs), and by the impact that governments had on the lives of most citizens, by the end of the twentieth century the economic role of the state (and, it should be added, the governments' capacity to promote that role) had increased a great deal in all industrial countries, in some more than in others. During the twentieth century the role of the state underwent many significant changes. During the first half of the century, the changes were less noticeable, *in a purely statistical sense* (see Tanzi and Schuknecht, 2000, table 1.1, pp. 6–7). Those who look mainly at the levels of taxes and public spending as shares of GDPs, in judging the economic roles of states, might easily miss the important economic and social changes that were taking place in those years in several countries.

At the very beginning of the twentieth century, there was growing globalization of economic activities, combined with still relatively little direct involvement by governments in the economies and in the lives of most citizens. It was a period of increasing trade and capital movements among countries and of fast economic growth, promoted by changing policies and technologies. However, it was a period of still relatively limited *direct* governmental interference in the activities of markets and in the lives of citizens.

The growth of the economies had been spurred by the deepening impact of the Industrial Revolution (see Gordon, 2015), which had introduced major new technologies (railroads, electricity, steamships, cars, indoor plumbing, new ways of producing clothes, machines to produce many manufactured goods, petroleum as a source of energy, and so on) that were changing the world in truly radical ways. That revolution required huge investments, and was accompanied by an accelerating process of urbanization. It was fed by large migratory movements, both *within* countries (from rural areas to the new urban centers, where the industrial enterprises were being set up) and *between* countries, toward new and still largely underpopulated countries.

Machines had been replacing human muscles in the production of old and new products, making industrial workers enormously more productive (see Gordon, 2015). The negative social side of the revolution was that the machines were replacing the activities of many self-employed artisans, thus harming the latter's economic conditions and creating economic difficulties for many of them and for their families, at a time when there were no social safety nets except those provided by extended families and some charities. These effects generated, at times, violent reactions and stimulated attempts by workers to organize and to oppose the changes, causing some governments to begin to intervene.

New sources of energy were becoming available with the spreading use of electricity and the growing production and use of petroleum and coal. The large migratory flows at that time, often limited to mostly male workers, meant that those who migrated often left behind their families, their communities, and their traditional ways of life. They moved to new, alien places, where they often felt isolated and disconnected from their traditional communities and from their families. In the new places they had jobs, and generally higher incomes, but little social support.

Trade among countries increased rapidly in the decades before World War I. It was facilitated by the availability of new large steamships and by railroads, and was made possible by policies that were more favorable to trade. The gold standard facilitated large movements of capital. In the interior of the United States, in Australia, in Argentina, in Brazil, and in other countries, newly accessible agricultural lands had created large local surpluses in some basic commodities. These surpluses could be transported by rail, by canals, and by roads to nearby locations, from where they could be exported to distant countries that needed these commodities. Economies were being transformed and industrialized at a rapid pace, with the assistance of the new technologies, new workers, freer markets, and new industrial organizations (see Porter, 1992; Gordon, 2015).

The latter part of the nineteenth century, the period after the American Civil War, the German and Italian unifications, and other important political events, until the beginning of World War I, could be described as the period closest to laissez-faire, in terms of economic policies, that the world had known. Of course, this characterization may not be appropriate for all countries, and does not imply that countries' governments completely abstained from influencing and interfering with private economic activities. Some governments had continued to play, or occasionally played, significant roles in promoting, in various ways, particular industries, at times by assisting them with specific regulations, by building needed infrastructures to help some industries, by restricting imports, or by promoting the industries' investments in other countries, at times even with the assistance of military interventions. Some countries, including the United States, continued to impose taxes on some imports for revenue and protection reasons. This period saw "the rise of big business" in the United States and in several other countries (see Porter, 1992). Large enterprises that hired thousands of workers became common in various countries. Many of these enterprises had monopoly power and because of their wealth acquired much economic and political power.

In several countries and especially in Bismarck's Germany, there was the beginning of important movements toward the creation of some rights for industrial workers; the creation of governmentally financed educational opportunities for children (see Cipolla, 2002); the stipulation of a minimum age at which children were allowed to work; and the setting of limits to the number of hours that industrial workers could be made to work during a week (often sixty hours). It was also a period when various social and political reforms, such as those that allowed an increasing number of individuals, including women, to vote, were introduced in some countries. Some of these reforms were so important that a British historian called this period the Age of Reform, in a monumental study dealing with the United Kingdom (Woodward, [1938] 1962).

An American author, writing on the US experience, stated that in the period between 1865 and 1901, when "a nation of farms was ... becoming a nation of cities and factories," "the [dominant] doctrine of laissez-faire was [being] subjected to a determined attack" (Fine, 1964, p. 373). Similar changes were underway on the European continent, some pushed by what was called "Catholic socialism," and some by nonreligious "socialists" (see Nitti, 1971). However, as Fine put it, while the doctrine of laissez-faire was under attack, "laissez faire [had been] woven into the fabric of the law during the years from 1865 to 1901" (see Fine, 1964, p. 127). In the United States, it would take the Great Depression for a strong attack to begin to be made on that laissez-faire ideology. In some other countries totalitarian governments were also interfering with the free market for political reasons.

Several governments, for example, those of Italy and the United States, had been interfering with a pure form of laissez-faire in the operations of the market by occasionally using import duties, credit allocations, and some regulations, in ways that might not have been consistent with a pure form of laissez-faire economic ideology. In the United States, in the new century, first Theodore Roosevelt and later Woodrow Wilson, during what came to be called the *Progressive Era*, introduced legislation directed at restricting the power of monopolies and reducing some abuses. They reduced import duties and introduced regulations on some monopolies, aimed at curbing the enormous economic power that some enterprises and individuals had acquired. They also introduced other controls on the operations of enterprises, some aimed at increasing the safety and the bargaining power of workers whose organizations were becoming progressively more active.

In 1913, the United States created the Federal Reserve system and introduced the income tax. The former was introduced after a deep financial crisis had hit the country; the latter was initially introduced to compensate for the revenue loss due to the reduction or the elimination of import duties. These developments would have important economic ramifications in future years. Perhaps not unrelated to these developments, and indicating how the world was changing at that time, in 1912 an Italian statistician, Corrado Gini, had proposed a way to measure income inequality in countries. The use of the so-called Gini coefficient, which soon became a popular statistic, may indicate that income inequality had become a serious social concern by that time.

Workers' associations and labor unions were being created in various countries and were pushing for more rights and better working conditions for workers. Some of the labor unions would acquire increasing political and economic power with the passing of time, especially, but not only, in Europe. This was in part a reaction to the power that was held by the owners of the enterprises and to the growing evidence that workers were often abused and exploited. Accidents in some industrial sectors were common, and there was little if any compensation for the injured workers or for their families, nor were there pensions for those who became disabled.

Strikes were becoming increasingly common and occasionally turned violent, like the one in the United States that led to the killing of workers and to the May 1 labor-day holiday in Europe to honor workers. With the passing of time, the labor unions became politically powerful, perhaps too powerful for laissez-faire economies. By the 1920s, in some countries, including the United Kingdom, labor unions had become so powerful that, in 1926, Keynes would write, "the *Trade-Unionists*, once the oppressed, [have] now [become] the tyrants, whose selfish and sectorial pretensions need to be bravely opposed" (published in Keynes, 1933, p. 341). Both the power of the labor unions and the growing influence of economic planning, which had found a real-life application in Russia after the revolution, and which was attracting an increasing number of followers in Europe, made the period between the two world wars less consistent with laissez-faire principles than earlier decades had been. In the United States and in other countries, the period before World War II was a period of great economic and social change.

During the second half of the nineteenth century, many economic reforms had been aimed at increasing the *rights of workers* vis-à-vis the *excessive power* of the *owners* of the enterprises. They had not been directed at creating *citizens'* or *workers'* economic rights vis-à-vis *the state*. However, the late nineteenth century and early twentieth century saw the beginning of policies aimed at creating a greater and more direct economic role for the state, first in its relations with *workers* and later in its relations vis-à-vis *citizens* in general. Not surprisingly, these policies accompanied increasing democratization, including the increasing share of the populations that could vote in many countries. In Great Britain it was only in 1928 that women could vote. In Italy they had to wait until after World War II. Some of the new policies and changing intellectual winds would lead to the creation of "welfare states" in the second half of the twentieth century.

Policies that would lead to the welfare states had been introduced first in Germany, a country that the German economist Hans-Werner Sinn has defined as the first welfare state. They had started with the labor reforms introduced by Bismarck during the last two decades of the nineteenth century. Bismarck may also have been the first policymaker to make use of what today is called "fiscal policy." The reforms that he introduced in Germany would spread to other European countries (see Ritter, 1996). With his encyclical letter *Rerum Novarum*, issued in 1891, Pope Leon XIII had given his blessing to social reforms and to developments that dealt mainly with the relations between employers and workers; the right to association of workers, a right that was still controversial at the time; the importance of and obligation of charity in assisting those in need; and collaboration between different classes. Property rights were defended in the pope's encyclical. However, it was stressed that those rights *must be accompanied by social responsibilities*, a theme that has continued to dominate Catholic thinking and that influenced some modern constitutions. That theme has been strongly debated in recent decades.

In spite of the aforementioned trends and reforms, in *relative* terms and in relation to the *spending* and *taxing* role of governments, the developments in the second half of the nineteenth century – until World War I in Europe and the Great Depression in the United States and in some other countries, such as the Scandinavian countries – could be described as still broadly respecting (qualified) laissez-faire principles, while, at the same time, giving more-deserved attention to the rights of workers. In 1913 the share of public spending into GDP for most industrial countries still averaged only about 13 percent (see Tanzi and Schuknecht, 2000, table I.1, p. 6).

Those laissez-faire principles were still guiding the teaching of economics in universities and the views of most mainstream economists in the 1920s. For example, writing in 1929, months before the stock market crashed, the Swedish economist Myrdal could state that "a very uncompromising laissez-faire doctrine dominated the teaching of economics in Sweden" (published in Myrdal, 1954, p. vi). The same was true of the economics that was taught in the United States, the United Kingdom, and other European countries, even in the 1930s. In 1926 Keynes would write a famous essay that called for "the end of laissez faire."

CHAPTER 2

The Economic Role of the State between the World Wars

The laissez-faire doctrine that had prevailed in earlier years started to be challenged, in Europe, before and after World War I and, in the United States, especially during the Great Depression, in 1933–1938, when the administration of Franklin D. Roosevelt introduced the New Deal and important regulatory reforms. A few economists also started revising their teaching and their thinking on what role the state should play in the countries' economies.

The changes in thinking and in policies would transform, in later decades, the government role, from the "night watchman" and largely observer-oriented (but qualified) role played in the past, into an important, direct agent of, presumably, the interests of the majority of citizens. Up to that time the changed attention of the state had been directed mainly at promoting workers' rights versus powerful employers, as it had been after the Bismarck reforms introduced in Germany and in some other countries. In some sense, the changes that occurred would aim at transforming the government into a general insurer of the citizens, or an "ultimate risk manager" (see Moss, 2002).

In the decades before World War II, when some governments had started to increase their involvement in the economies, they had done it less by increasing public spending and taxes and more by increasing their direct interference in some market decisions (as they had done during the mercantilist period criticized by Adam Smith).

As mentioned previously, important regulations and policy changes were introduced in the United States by the Roosevelt administration during the New Deal, but the level of taxation and public spending had increased little. The same was the case in other countries. This regulatory intervention was administratively and politically easy because it did not require many public resources. However, it did require increasing numbers of public bureaucrats, thus contributing to creating what some would call a "bureaucratic state." A bureaucratic state would allow the government to expand its regulatory role in the economy.

In some European countries, the laissez-faire ideology that had pre-vailed until that time had started to be replaced by an ideology based on greater, direct interventions in economic decisions. Authoritarian govern-ments that had taken power in Italy, Germany, Spain, and some other countries had found it politically expedient to shift the actions of the governments away from laissez-faire and toward policies that gave them more political control over the citizens. The direct actions did not require much public spending, thus keeping low the need to impose unpopular taxes. Nonauthoritarian governments also found it convenient to use, to some extent, these direct controls in the pursuit of their political objec-tives. Many enterprises that had run into difficulties during the Great Depression were nationalized. The most extreme changes were those intro-duced of Russia which had replaced the existing market economy with an extreme form of central planning.

In several countries governments relied more on the use of regulatory powers, on credit allocations, on controls over the prices of some basic goods and services, and on controls over organized labor. They tried to influence the wages of workers by requiring more government authoriza-tions for various economic activities, and by using other direct or indi-rect controls over particular economic activities. As mentioned earlier, some regulations of labor market activities, especially those directed at the protection of dependent workers, had started in the previous century, to reduce abuses by employers, for example, with respect to child labor and working hours. Labor unions had become more important, and some of their leaders had developed sympathy for socialist ideologies, which aimed at reducing the role of private property and at increasing the nationaliza-tion of important enterprises. Control of unions by some nondemocratic governments, for example, by the Fascist government of Italy, gave those governments more power. Some of these actions created difficulties for market economies.

Until World War I, government spending and tax levels had remained low in most countries. For example, the average public spending for nine-teen advanced countries in 1913 was still only about 13 percent of GDP (see Tanzi, 2011, p. 9). The highest levels, around 17 percent of GDP, were in Belgium, France, and Italy. In 1910, social transfers accounted for less than 2 percent of GDP and often much less (ibid., p. 10). Some increases occurred during World War I, when several of the countries at war, includ-ing the United States, sharply increased military spending.

In spite of some increases in tax rates, during World War I, tax levels increased less than public spending. Most governments were reluctant to raise taxes and preferred to finance the war largely with borrowing (see Ferguson, 2007). Strong and, at times, ethnically motivated appeals to patriotism (an early form of "nudging") had been used by the countries at war, including the US government, to sell public bonds. In France, the appeals were used to elicit donation of gold to the government.

In what turned out to be a lucky coincidence for that country, the United States had introduced the federal income tax before World War I, on May 8, 1913, after the Sixteenth Amendment to the US Constitution had been ratified, on February 23, 1913, and after a big political fight. The amendment to the US Constitution empowered Congress "to lay and collect taxes on incomes, from whatever source derived." The Constitutional amendment did not state anything about making the income tax progressive, but the tax was introduced with low, progressive rates from 1 percent to 7 percent on incomes of more than $10,000. By 1918 the rates had been increased to a range from 16 percent to 72 percent, indicating that wars make it easier for governments to tax the rich. After the war the rates would be significantly reduced until 1930, when they would start rising again. In 1944 the rates would range from 41 percent to 94 percent.

The revenue from the newly introduced income tax made it possible for President Wilson to reduce the monopoly power of some enterprises, by reducing the import duties that had helped protect them from foreign competition. As mentioned, shortly after its introduction, the federal income tax would help finance the war, when federal spending rose from $742 million in 1916 to $14 billion in 1918 (see Wolfensberger, 2004). Until that time the level of total *federal* tax revenue in the United States had been only 2–3 percent of GDP, a level that, with the exception of the war years, continued to prevail until the Great Depression. In 1932 total federal revenues were only 2.8 percent of GDP. In 1940 they were still only 6.8 percent of GDP (see US Office of Management and Budget, 2009).

The revenue from the income taxes largely replaced the reduced revenue from the import duties. Given this low tax level, there was not much that the federal government could do with policies that required public spending. Neither President Wilson nor Presidents Coolidge or Hoover had had much interest or enthusiasm in increasing the (non-war-related) spending of the US federal government. Even in Franklin D. Roosevelt's time the increase in public spending by the federal government was modest by modern standards. It rose from 8 percent of the much lower depression GDP in 1933 to about 10 percent in 1939–1940. Only the war years would bring it sharply up. Wilson's own views on the economic role of the state, as they were outlined in a book that he published in 1889, will be described in a later chapter.

When the United States introduced the federal individual income tax in 1913, a tax that the *New York Sun* described as "taxation of the few for the benefit of the many," it did it with the very low rates reported earlier. Most individuals paid no taxes, because of the very high personal exemption, and the average tax rate of most of those who paid any tax (about 2 percent of the population) was only 1 percent of their taxable income. The highest marginal tax rate (7 percent) was applied to the taxable incomes that exceeded a half-million 1913 dollars. Obviously, that rate covered only very few and very wealthy individuals.

Clearly, at least initially, the federal income tax was not intended to be a tax on the masses, or a tax to generate a lot of revenue. In spite of this, it may be of historical interest, and it may help give a good feel for the time, to mention that the then chairman of the Ways and Means Committee in Congress (Cordell Hull, Democrat from Tennessee), in a speech in Congress, declared that the proposed tax would raise more money than the "human mind would conceive to spend" (see Tanzi, 1988). It should also be mentioned that so many lobbyists had descended on Washington, to oppose the tax, that President Wilson is reported to have remarked that "a brick couldn't be thrown without hitting one of them" (Wolfensberger, 2004, p. 6). Showing great foresight, the lobbyists, or those who paid for their services, must have been aware that the tax would create a new powerful instrument that governments could use in the future for social engineering. In its initial version, the tax was a small seed, but in time it would grow to reach enormous size.

During the third and fourth decades of the twentieth century, the idea that some form of *economic planning by governments* could help improve the performance of economies, and increase the welfare of citizens, had acquired currency with some politicians and with some economists in several countries, especially in Europe. That idea received the support of many intellectuals who had some leftist tendencies. These individuals had absorbed the increasingly popular socialist ideas. Since the previous century, socialist thinkers had been critical of the capitalistic form of economic organization, and some of them had pushed for the nationalization of the means of production, and for the replacement of the market with economic planning. However, mainstream economists and policymakers, who continued to endorse the laissez-faire ideology, rejected those ideas as coming from "low radicals."

In the 1920s, economic planning had had its first real-life experience in Russia, when it had been put into practice by the Soviet government, following the Bolshevik Revolution of 1917. The Russian experiment had attracted an increasing number of sympathizers and followers outside Russia, as well as some mainstream economists. With the passing of time, and with the help of well–orchestrated socialist propaganda, the idea of economic planning had started to influence an increasing number of intellectuals and policymakers in European countries. Some of those intellectuals, who had visited Russia in the 1920s, had been taken on well-choreographed and closely monitored tours, and some of them had come to see the Russian experiment as providing a possible roadmap for the societies of the future that, they believed, could promote the welfare of the masses and end poverty.

A detailed, informed, and somewhat sympathetic review of the socialist system and several countries' experiences with it, especially after World War II, was provided by the Hungarian economist Janos Kornai (see Kornai, 1992). An earlier, theoretical defense of an economy based on socialist principles had been provided by Lange and Taylor in 1938. Their book had been much debated in academic circles. The issue of central planning attracted a lot of attention from Western economists in the 1930s, because the Great Depression had created doubts in the minds of an increasing number of economists and others about the claimed merits of the capitalistic system, and especially about the beneficial role of laissez-faire. Central planning offered an alternative that looked feasible and potentially attractive to many.

If followed, economic planning would reduce and, in the extreme Soviet version, eliminate almost completely the private market, in economic decisions, replacing it with decisions made centrally. Directed by government bureaucrats, central planning would replace the free economic agents in making economic decisions on what to produce and on how to distribute what was produced. The planners would presumably focus on producing essential, basic goods, using the resources that had previously gone toward the production of "luxury" or "nonessential" goods. In the process they would aim at satisfying the *basic needs* of citizens and at generating a society with more economic equality and social justice.

As Hayek would point out some years later, in his important and influential book *The Road to Serfdom* ([1944] 2007), the idea of economic planning became popular in the 1920s and especially in the 1930s in major European universities, including in the prestigious Cambridge University in England, where it received the endorsement of several influential economists. It had attracted an increasing number of intellectuals and many workers.

In those years, authoritarian and fascist governments in European countries and elsewhere, such as Argentina, Brazil, Mexico, Japan, and some other countries, would adopt some version of economic planning, which allowed them to increase their *political* power and their *control* over the economy and over the populations, as Hayek pointed out. These controls would, at times, take on aspects of what some today call "crony capitalism." They tended to benefit individuals or industrial groups that were favored by the authoritarian regimes, over less favored ones. For Italian examples, see Carlo Celli (2013); discussions of "corporatism," especially chapters 8 and 9, in Bosworth (2006); and Steiner (1938). For information on Argentina, and the influence of planning on Peronism, see Falcoff and Dolkart (1975). Peron had been a military attaché for Argentina in Fascist Italy in the late 1930s and had assimilated some of the aspects and policies of that regime.

In those decades economic planning contaminated, to some extent, also the actions and the policies of governments that had remained democratic, such as those of France, the United Kingdom, and Germany in the 1920s, before the advent of Nazism, as well as those of other countries. It continued to influence Germany, during Hitler's years, and Italy, during all of Mussolini's years. Mussolini had started his career as a socialist.

By that time the economic role of the state in the market economies had not yet manifested itself mainly in high taxes and large public spending, as it would in later decades. Rather, it had manifested itself mostly through regulations, the nationalization of some enterprises, the creation of national monopolies, the allocation of credit, and various other direct interferences by governments in economic decisions and activities. By that time social legislation had been, or was being, introduced to regulate labor relations and the power of enterprises, and also to give more power to government-controlled, or -influenced, labor unions, and to government-friendly enterprises, or representatives of enterprises (see Steiner, 1938, for Italian examples).

While there were sympathizers, at Cambridge University in England and at other British and European universities, toward the Russian experiment in central planning, and some of the sympathizers saw that experiment as pointing to a potentially attractive economic future without poverty, Keynes's own views were less favorable, but they were still interesting and, thus, are worth reporting. He visited Russia on his honeymoon in 1925, after marrying Lydia Lopokova, a Russian ballerina. On his return from the honeymoon he wrote an essay in which he conveyed his impressions and his views on what he had seen in Russia.

Keynes commented that "Leninism is a combination of two things ... religion and business" (1933, p. 298). He added that "if Communism [with its central planning] achieves a certain success, it will achieve it, not as an improved economic technique, but as a religion" (ibid., p. 305). Furthermore, "any religion ... [has] power against the egotistic atomism of the irreligious" (ibid., p. 306). Keynes's view on the religious side of social-ism was similar to those that, in 1900, had been expressed by the Italian economist Vilfredo Pareto in a review of a book on socialism, written by G. le Bon, a French sociologist, called *Psychologie du socialism*. As Keynes would comment twenty-five years later, Pareto had commented on the religious appeal of socialism. It should also be noted that some aspects of socialism have historically attracted, and continue to attract, the Catholic Church, as can be seen by reading Pope Francis's recent pronouncements and the encyclical letter *Laudato Si'* (2015). See also Nitti (1971) for some interesting historical background on this issue.

Writing in the last decade of the nineteenth century, Nitti, a distin-guished Italian economist and politician, had identified four forms of socialism: religious, anarchic, collectivist, and state socialism. He had also called attention to the *religious* aspect of socialism and to the relationship between the ideals of socialism and those of Catholicism. In his view, what they have in common is restrictions of some individual liberties. Nitti had commented that the relationship between socialism and Catholicism seemed to have been particularly close among German Catholics. Nitti's treatment of this topic later attracted the attention and high praise of A. Schumpeter.

Perhaps more interestingly for our discussion, in his essay, Keynes had compared the ongoing Soviet experiment in the 1920s, with its extreme form of central planning, to "modern capitalism [which] is absolutely irre-ligious, without internal union, without much public spirit, often ... a mere congeries of possessors and pursuers" (Keynes, ibid., pp. 306–307). He had added that because of its lack of religiosity "such a [capitalist] system has to be immensely, not moderately, successful to survive" (ibid., p. 307). His conclusion was, "To-day [capitalism] is only moderately suc-cessful," and "we doubt whether the business man is leading us to a des-tination far better than our present place" (Keynes ibid.). It is clear, from Keynes's other comments in the same essay, that he was comparing the *Russian* experiment with the *American* developments in the 1920s, a decade that would end with the disaster of the Great Depression.

Keynes's pessimism about the future of capitalism, *as it was practiced in the United States in the 1920s*, was obvious. To some extent it anticipated the pessimism expressed by some recent writers, such as, for example, Naomi Klein in some of her books (2007, 2014), as well as several economists, including Piketty in his 2014, bestselling book. In the views of these modern critics and of those who had taken part in the "Occupy Wall Street" movements a few years earlier, modern capitalism is clearly not "leading to a destination far better than our present place" for many people and workers. In the United States and in some other countries workers' wages have stagnated for decades, the income distribution has become less even, and, in the views of these critics, our grandchildren will not live in a world as good as the present one.

In another famous essay, "Economic Possibilities for Our Grandchildren," written in 1930, Kenyes may not have offered as good a forecast of the future as some have interpreted those "possibilities" to offer. In that essay, Keynes worried about the fact that "technical efficiency [has] been taking place faster than we can deal with the problem of labor absorption" (Keynes, 1933, p. 358). He worried that "the love of money as a possession … [is] … a somewhat disgusting morbidity." He also referred to the "distasteful and unjust … social customs and economic practices, affecting the distribution of wealth and of economic rewards and penalties" (ibid., pp. 369–370). The current relevance of these comments can only surprise the modern reader.

One of the reasons for that pessimism today, as it was at the time when Keynes wrote that essay, is what has been happening to income distribution and to real wages in recent decades in the United States and in some other countries. Growth does not seem to be improving the economic situation of *most* of the citizens of these countries (and working hours are *not* being reduced as Keynes had assumed possible). Concerns about the future absorption of labor, because of new labor-saving technologies, are growing. Thus, at least from this point of view, *modern* capitalism does not seem to be leading to a better destination. The incomes of *most* workers are not increasing, or not increasing quickly enough, We shall return to the issue of equity in later chapters of this book and discuss the role that the state is or may be playing in this process.

Keynes, while not endorsing the Russian version of economic planning and while giving that version little chance of success in the long run, was convinced of the need for greater governmental involvement in the economies of Western countries at that time, especially in the American economy (perhaps the same could be said for some other members of Cambridge

University at that time, such as Joan Robinson, Piero Sraffa, and others). As Keynes put it in his essay written in 1925, even though the chance that something good would come out of the Russian experiment was minimal, "even a chance gives what is happening in Russia more importance than what is happening ... in the United States of America" (p. 311).

In 1925 the US economy was probably the most laissez-faire economy among those of advanced countries, having been affected less than the European countries by the Russian experiment; and its concentration of income had become greatly uneven. The stagnation of real wages for many workers in many countries in recent decades and the increasing concentration, in relatively few hands, of the income and the wealth within those countries have made many current observers share some of the pessimism about the future of the capitalist system, *in its present version*, that had been expressed by Keynes ninety years ago.

It ought to be understood and stressed that Keynes's concern was for the *form* that the capitalist system had assumed, *not the system itself.* What could be called "termites" had entered that system in the 1920s, just as many believe that they have entered the system and the operations of the market and governments in the present day. Some of the modern termites are a different kind; still, they are damaging both the market economy and the role that governments play in determining the economic outcomes that the market economy is generating.

One objective of this book is to identify some of these termites in today's world and especially in the United States, to see how they may be damaging the role of the state, and also the legitimacy of the market system and perhaps also of the democratic system. The question will remain whether some of these termites can be stopped and reversed by good policies, rather than the populist policies that some are now promoting.

CHAPTER 3

The Coming of the Welfare State and Reactions to It

Starting during Franklin D. Roosevelt's administration in the United States, in the middle of the Great Depression, and intensifying in later years, after World War II, the economic role of the state, in the United States, the United Kingdom, and several other advanced countries, countries that continued to rely largely on market economies, started to change at a rapid pace, reflecting both changing intellectual winds and economic and political circumstances. Within three decades, that role went from what it had been in the past, mostly a qualified laissez-faire role in which governments (including that of the United States) occasionally used regulations and direct controls in some sectors of the economy, but largely stayed out of major fiscal interventions, to some version of a modern welfare state, characterized by high taxes, high public spending, and growing entitlements for citizens.

Perhaps we cannot do better, in addressing the intellectual winds that promoted the change, than to cite again from another essay by Keynes, published in 1926, appropriately titled *The End of Laissez Faire*. Keynes was not an armchair economist who relied predominantly on theoretical arguments to support or oppose government policies. He was closely in touch with the reality of the market and with the economic viewpoints of the major thinkers and economic operators of his time. He also operated successfully in the stock market and had a close knowledge of how private markets actually worked.

As he put it:

> Let us clear from the ground the metaphysical or general principles upon which, from time to time, *laissez-faire* has been founded. It is *not* true that individuals possess a prescriptive "natural liberty" in their economic activities. There is *no* "compact" conferring perpetual rights on those who Have or on those who Acquire. The world is *not* so governed from above that private and social interests always coincide. It is *not* so managed here below that in practice they coincide. It is *not* a correct deduction from the

Principles of Economics that enlightened self-interest always operates in
the public interest. Nor is it true that self-interest generally is enlightened.
(Keynes, [1926] 1933, p. 312; italics in the original. Keynes was writing in a
period of great intellectual ferment and change. Pope Francis would, probably, strongly endorse Keynes's statement.)

For a description of the policies that would be introduced in the United
States in the 1930s, during the New Deal, the books by Schlesinger, Jr.
(1957, 1958) are good sources. See also Hawley (1966) and Alter (2006). In
the period between 1933 and 1938, in the United States, a dramatically new
economic role was assumed by the US federal government, and numerous
additional regulatory powers were given to both the federal and the state
governments. Because of the effects of the Great Depression, and because
of the new administration that had won the elections, at that time, the
United States would lead other countries in introducing important economic reforms, while it was still operating within the context of a fairly
free market economy. From many points of view, and especially from the
point of view of the growing economic role of the state, the era of the New
Deal was an extraordinary period, even though, as we have shown in the
previous chapter, public spending and tax levels remained low by modern
standards.

During the second half of the twentieth century, many governments,
excluding those linked with the Soviet Union, generally and progressively
reduced their reliance on *direct* interferences in the working of the market and reduced some interventions and economic regulations that they
had used in the past to regulate monopolies. They also started introducing
new forms of regulations on actions by individuals and enterprises that
generated negative externalities, while they tried to leave more scope for
legitimate market forces to operate. At the same time they increased their
reliance on taxes and on public spending to promote social goals, including the promotion of greater equity and the economic safety of citizens.

Over the next three decades, until the 1980s, the net result of the
changes would be the creation, in several advanced countries, of so-called
welfare states, or *quasi* welfare states, within market economies. Especially
in Europe, these welfare states required very high levels of public spending
and taxes. With the passing of time they would also require an increasing number of regulations aimed at reducing negative externalities of
various kinds, and not just at controlling industries and monopolies for
their market power, as they had done in earlier years. These policies would
generate strong reactions on the part of many individuals and enterprises
that felt that their economic freedom was being constrained and reduced,

compared to the case in the past, by the high taxes and by the new kinds of regulations. These reactions have become more intense in recent years.

Until the end of the twentieth century, the *direct* interference by governments in economic decisions that did not generate actual or potential negative externalities, or in operations that did not create monopoly powers (except for those created by patents and by other forms of government protection of intellectual property), would be gradually reduced, though never completely eliminated. At the same time the *indirect* interference, coming from the higher taxes to finance high public spending, and, increasingly, from the aforementioned behavior-changing regulations connected with, and justified by, negative externalities and safety concerns (which were becoming more frequent, because of increased urbanization, increased activities with environmental implications, and technological changes), was increased. It should be added that often there were conflicting views, and inevitable friction, between government agencies and representatives of private enterprises on the existence or severity of the externalities that regulations aimed at controlling.

As the years passed, there was less interest in, and less pressure for, nationalizing enterprises, while many (though not all) of the enterprises that, in Europe, had been nationalized before or soon after the war were returned to the private sector. There was also decreasing interest, at least in advanced countries, in controlling trade in real goods, and in controlling directly the cost of credit to particular borrowers and the prices of some basic goods and services, although some of these actions continued to be frequent in developing countries, and occasionally occurred even in advanced countries. The *consumption* of some goods and services, for example, energy, water, and transportation, continued to receive explicit or implicit subsidies, and there were also *implicit* subsidies for the production of goods that created environmental costs but did not pay for those costs.

In the 1980s and the 1990s, under the political influence of Margaret Thatcher in the United Kingdom and Ronald Reagan in the United States, and under the ideological influence of supply-side economics – an influence that, to some extent, could be interpreted as a return to the laissez-faire thinking of the past (but wearing new clothes) – several European governments and some governments from Latin America and other regions privatized their public enterprises, many of which had been nationalized during the Great Depression or during and after World War II. In some cases, as in Italy, the sale of public enterprises was in part promoted by the need to increase public revenues to finance high public spending when taxes could not be raised, and when countries tried to contain their fiscal deficits and public debts. In some cases, as again in Italy, the joining of the European Economic Union made this necessary, to satisfy the Maastricht rules.

Import duties and import restrictions on goods, in general, were gradually reduced, in part due to trade agreements and the action of the World Trade Organization. Controls over financial market operations were reduced, and financial capital was allowed to move more freely, within and across countries, than in the past. Controls over the use of deposits by banks and other financial activities in general were also reduced. Central banks became more independent from direct political influences. Government controls over wages and over the prices of particular goods and services became rare, and rationing became a policy of the past, except in rare occasions.

Especially in the 1990s, in spite of the high taxes and the new externalities-related regulations, faith in the market returned, and trust in its operations and acceptance of its outcomes reached high levels. As the influential Harvard philosopher Michael Sandel stressed in a 2012 book, the results of the market acquired, for some observers, almost moral or ethical significance. The "moral limits" of the market were progressively extended to areas where, perhaps, they should not have been. As Sandel argued, this extension, promoted and applauded by some prominent economists, including Milton Friedman, Gary Backer, and others, had the goal of crowding out some community, or tradition-based, social norms. Indirectly, it gave more power to individuals who had high incomes, when the scope of what could be obtained with money increased.

Some leading economists, including a few who won Nobel Prizes in economics, advanced theoretical arguments that supported the conclusion that markets required little controls and that market outcomes have moral values. As a consequence, controls on the market ought to be reduced, and the outcomes of the market operations should not be questioned. The range of market activities was progressively extended to areas that had previously been considered off limit. As one example among many, some went as far as to argue that it would be socially desirable if children available for adoption, or some human organs, were sold freely in the market and thus were allocated by the market to the highest bidders.

It was argued that, if free markets were not interfered with, they would generate optimal economic and social results and would justify most of the transactions in which the participants entered freely and with full knowledge of what was being exchanged. Legitimate market transactions were seen as always improving welfare, because both sides gained from them, if they entered the transactions freely and had full knowledge of what they bought and sold. Therefore, the more legitimate transactions that the market promoted, the greater would be the welfare that it generated. As economies developed, the total number of transactions increased dramatically, and the share of incomes that went to those who engaged in transactions increased relative to the incomes of those who engaged in production.

The new thinking became increasingly influential, especially in the 1980s and 1990s. It influenced the policymakers in the previously centrally planned economies of Eastern Europe, the countries that were undergoing a process of transition, from being centrally planned to becoming market economies. In those countries, trust in the power of the market became so strong as to generate some jokes, such as the one about how many workers would be required to change a lightbulb. The answer was that in a centrally planned economy it would have required three workers: one to do the work, one to supervise the operation, and one to write a report on the operation. In a market economy nobody would be required, because the market would do it! Clearly the market was assumed to have magical power.

Central banks became more politically independent than they had been, reducing the opportunities that governments had had in the past to allocate credit to preferred sectors; occasionally to resort to "inflationary finance" to finance their public spending; or to fix the rates of interest to favor particular sectors. However, central banks became more accommodating to the market with their monetary policies, believing in the rationality and the honesty of those who could get and use easy credit from the banks. The central banks did not believe that there could be "irrational exuberance," or other phenomena that could lead to excessive borrowing and to eventual bursting of bubbles.

In spite of the growth and popularity of what came to be called "market fundamentalism," especially in the United States, the United Kingdom, and some other countries, the levels of public spending and of taxes, as shares of the countries' GDPs, kept rising throughout much of the second half of the twentieth century, until the last decade of that century. An exception was the United States. For a variety of reasons, including growing taxpayer resistance, changed policies, and the increased ability of large corporations and rich individuals who operated globally to avoid taxes, the increase in tax levels came to a stop, in most countries, in the 1990s, according to data provided by the Organization for Economic Co-operation and Development (OECD). However, in various countries, public spending continued to rise, thus contributing to rising public debts (see Tanzi, 2013b). In European countries, high public debts and fiscal deficits would contribute to their economic crisis after 2007.

In the new century, an important new government role began that has accelerated in recent years: the use of *paternalistically inspired* regulations and so-called *public nudges* to promote, on the part of citizens and enterprises, behavior considered socially desirable (see Thaler and Sunstein, 2008). Some of these new regulations, or simply *nudges*, were justified and promoted using results obtained from experiments conducted by a fast-growing new branch of economics called "experimental economics" (see Lewis, 2017). The *nudges* had the virtue of not needing compulsion on the part of the government or (significant) public resources. Therefore, the movement could be considered "paternalistically libertarian," because individuals and enterprises were free to ignore the nudges, at low or no costs.

Some of the new regulations were backed by, and were thus justified by, new scientific results, for example, those related to bans on smoking in public places and to the use of particular chemical substances, and, increasingly, by environmental concerns and the need to maintain biological diversity and to decrease the incidence of some illnesses. Behaviors that had been widely accepted in the past, such as big game hunting, enterprises discharging poisonous substances in rivers, and individuals consuming large amounts of sugar or making load noises in public places, came increasingly under some government controls and attracted some new regulations, making libertarian-inclined citizens feel that individual freedoms were being reduced by governmental action.

As a consequence of the aforementioned changes, the *direct* governmental interference in the working of the economy (associated in earlier decades with various aspects of economic planning or direct interventions) was, with some exceptions, progressively reduced over the years, while different, often *indirect* kinds of interferences (justified by externalities, by security concerns, by health concerns, and by presumed irrational behavior on the part of individuals) were increased. The latter inevitably led to complaints, by conservative economists and by politicians, that the power of the government had grown excessively and unnecessarily. In countries with federal governments it led to conflicts between national and subnational governments. Questions were raised about the scientific evidence used to justify some of the new regulations, and about the relation between the costs and the benefits of new regulations.

Some argued that free markets and new technologies could in time deal with some of the negative externalities and with the associated problems, therefore reducing the need for governments to intervene. Some pointed out that past predictions of environmental disasters had at times proved wrong, and that despite predictions of scarcity in some basic commodities, the prices of various commodities generally had gone down rather than up over the years.

An almost "religious" trust in the capacity of the market to solve problems seemed to play a role in the attitudes of particular individuals, showing that economists are not immune to quasi-religious influences of different kinds. See, for example, Greenspan (2004) and his trust in the market. The market was assumed to have almost magical powers to solve many of the problems encountered by humans, if only the government would stay out of its way.

In some ways the attitude toward the market was similar to the one related to the role of religion in socialist economic thinking, to which Pareto and Keynes had called attention a long time ago. It should be added that, on the other side, there are also many who believe, with similar "religious" zeal, that almost any social problem should and could be solved by government intervention and by public spending. And, of course, any society has numerous social problems waiting for solutions. They could justify increasing governmental intervention until little is left of the free market.

Some of the societal, economic, and technological changes that have taken place over many years, including globalization, new market relations and organizations, changes in the structures of taxes, changes in political attitudes, migration, and others, have inevitably affected the distribution of income and the perception of what is equitable in democratic society. In today's societies, the view that some individuals have a right to privileged positions because of the families in which they were born is no longer accepted, as it may have been for individuals considered "nobles" or "aristocrats" in the past. The present view is that all are equal before the law, even when their wealth may be different. But, of course, in reality wealth opens many doors for rich individuals that are closed for other individuals.

Especially during the decades immediately after World War II there had been a major change in the *instruments* that governments used to pursue the objective of equity. However, in the 1980s and 1990s interest in income distribution had become less intense than in the previous decades, because of changing political winds, greater concern for economic efficiency and for growth, and, as mentioned earlier, greater acceptance of market results. To some extent market results had replaced results based on birthrights. In those two decades the pursuit of economic efficiency became the more-important objective, in the view of many economists and in the actions of some policymakers.

In this connection, it might be mentioned that a Nobel Prize winner in economics, Robert Lucas, who had become very influential in that period, has been reported to have stated that, "Of the tendencies that are harmful to sound economics, the most seductive, and … the most poisonous, is to focus on questions of distribution" (cited in Surowiecki, 2015, p. 32). It may have been a coincidence, but well-researched lists of super rich individuals and of billionaires started becoming available in 1982, when *Forbes* started publishing one. It was later followed by a list prepared by *Bloomberg Net*.

In more recent years there has been a growing perception and growing evidence that the market, in its recent globalized version, while still by far the most efficient instrument that we know to produce good economic outcomes, has been generating what many consider to be less desirable results in terms of the distribution of income, especially for the middle classes and for many workers. There have been also increasing questions as to whether the market has been generating the kind of economic growth that would make everyone better off, as some economists had claimed it would. In some sense, modern concerns about the market are similar to those that Keynes had expressed in his 1926 essay, cited earlier.

As a digression, and going back to a discussion of the economic instruments used by the government, it is not always appreciated by economists that regulations and other kinds of direct government controls can, to some extent, replace, in their economic effects, purely *fiscal* tools (taxes and public spending) to promote objectives broadly similar to those that can be pursued with taxes and spending (see Tanzi, 1998b). Those controls can create a "shadow fiscal policy." Objectives such as the allocation of resources, the redistribution of income, and even the stabilization of the economy can be pursued not just with the use of taxes and public spending – as one might assume from public finance textbooks – but also with a well-planned shadow fiscal policy, promoted through well-selected new regulations and changes in existing regulations.

However, the traditional public finance instruments (taxes and public spending) are generally more transparent, though often more expensive in terms of public resources. Often, though not always, they are also more efficient than the shadow fiscal policy in promoting the objectives of governments, and the results of the shadow fiscal policy are at times more difficult to identify. For this reason shadow fiscal policy may at times be a preferred choice for corrupt governments, or for governments that prefer to be less transparent in their actions.

According to this interpretation, in some sense, governments have always relied on "fiscal policy," even before they started to make more use of taxes and public spending in the twentieth century. Mercantilist governments were in fact using shadow fiscal policy to benefit some individuals or groups. They chose the regulatory instruments because these instruments were less transparent and cheaper to use. Shadow fiscal policy can be related to the concept of *fiscal illusion*, which had been analyzed by the Italian economist Amilcare Puviani more than a century ago, in 1903. Fiscal illusions are often easier to create with regulations than with taxes and spending.

It can be concluded that, as the twentieth century came to an end, by and large, market forces had been allowed to play a larger role, in many, though not all, of the advanced countries, especially during the last decade of that century, the period of the Washington Consensus and of market fundamentalism, than they had played in earlier decades, in spite of the higher levels of taxes and of public spending in most countries, and in spite of various structural obstacles that continued to exist in the markets of many countries. At the same time the redistributive role that governments had played in the decades immediately after World War II was being reduced, in response to efficiency and incentive concerns that had led to important policy changes, especially in tax policy but also in spending policies such as the welfare reform of 1996 in the United States. This aspect will be discussed in greater detail in later chapters.

In the following chapter we shall go back to the period after World War II when economic trust in the power of governments, to bring desirable changes in the lives of citizens, reached the apex. That period would be followed by one in which trust in the action of the government would be reduced, and there would be a kind of return to laissez-faire thinking characterized by high trust in the operations of the market. That thinking would stop the growth in the level of taxes and spending, but it would not be able to reduce the tax and spending levels reached in earlier years, because of various economic and political obstacles, including the aging of the populations that would require high spending for pensions and health and would create pressures for more social spending, especially in the health sector.

CHAPTER 4

When Economists Thought They Had Found Nirvana: Welfare Policies

The period after World War II, especially the 1950s and 1960s, was one of great optimism on the part of many economists and politicians with regard to the government's ability to deal with economic problems and to improve the lives and the welfare of citizens. It was believed that these objectives could be achieved with well-planned government programs. The programs would be financed by progressive taxes or, when necessary, by public debt. The war needs had taught many governments how to collect more taxes, and Keynesian, countercyclical policies had taught economists how to keep the economy close to full levels of employment. Progressive income taxes and well-targeted "tax expenditures" would promote the consumption of "merit goods" and equity; and necessary regulations would prevent damaging externalities and control monopolies.

While the 1980s and 1990s would later be seen as pro-market decades, the 1950s and 1960s were definitely pro-government decades, for economies that in both periods continued to be market economies. In the 1950s and 1960s even a newly elected Republican president in the United States, Dwight Eisenhower, in his first State of the Union address, had thought desirable to mention the word "government" almost forty times, while the heads of big corporations would show interest in collaborating with the government to solve particular problems. These attitudes were different from those that would develop and prevail in the late 1970s and early 1980s, when another Republican president, Ronald Reagan, and the prime minister of the United Kingdom would refer to the government as the problem (see Hacker and Pierson, 2015).

The increases in tax rates and tax revenue that had been necessary to finance the large military expenditures of fighting World War II, after the war ended, had given the governments that had fought the war large public resources and new tools learned by tax administrations and budget offices. The US and British economies had not been excessively damaged by the war, so the large war-related tax revenue could be diverted to civilian purposes. For example, in the United States public spending had risen from about 10 percent of GDP in 1940 to almost 44 percent in 1943–1944. The public spending would go sharply down until 1948 (to about 12 percent of GDP). It would then start rising again, to close to 20 percent in future years. Taxes could be maintained at higher levels than before the war, and some of the resources could be redirected from military spending to social programs. However, in the United States social programs would never absorb as many resources as they did in several European countries, and tax levels would not be raised to European levels.

By the end of the war, Keynesian economics was becoming popular, and, for an increasing number of economists, it was becoming the latest religion. By that time, many economists had come to believe that the "Keynesian Revolution" had given governments the necessary tools to fight and to eliminate the feared depressions that, after the experience of the 1930s, had become the ultimate economic danger in the minds of many.

Careful analyses of the functioning of markets by economists in those years had been identifying areas in which the free market was believed to have failed. These analyses had shown where government could and needed to intervene, to make the market more efficient and to increase the welfare of the citizens. By this time the profession of economist had come into the limelight, was attracting many able individuals to it, some with strong mathematical backgrounds, and was acquiring a prestige that it had not had earlier and that, perhaps, it would never have again. It was a time when it became especially rewarding to be a professional economist.

In the middle of World War II, in 1942, William Beveridge, a well-connected and influential professor at the London School of Economics, had published a report (the *Beveridge Report*) that had become immediately famous and an unlikely best seller for a public document in the middle of a great war, when paper was scarce. The *Beveridge Report* generated great expectations on the part of British citizens with regard to what government policies could do to improve their lives after the war. When the war ended, the report had a great influence in shaping the *welfare reforms* that the British government introduced in the second half of the 1940s and that created the British "welfare state."

In its own words (and with the use of government programs and actions) the *Beveridge Report* promised to eliminate the "five great evils" of mankind: "want," "disease," "ignorance," "squalor," and "idleness." The *Report's* recommendations could not have been implemented in 1942 while the war was going on, and while the United Kingdom needed all the resources available to fight it. However, after the war was over, the recommendations were instrumental to the British government in guiding the creation of a nationalized and universal social security and health service in the United Kingdom, in addition to various other welfare programs that the country would introduce before the end of the decade. Having been introduced in an important and politically influential country, as was the United Kingdom, these programs – which created "a taxpayer-funded welfare state and full employment as a national goal" – would be imitated by several other countries (see Wapshott, 2011, p. 227).

Keynes, who at the time of the preparation of the *Beveridge Report* had been spending much of his time on the other side of the Atlantic, thinking about and helping to create the Bretton Woods institutions, had not been directly involved with the recommendations contained in the *Beveridge Report* (see Marcuzzo, 2010). Those recommendations were not directly connected with the Keynesian Revolution, which dealt with the objective of stabilization and full employment and not directly with social reform. The available evidence indicates that "Keynes was not a passionate social reformer" (Skidelsky, 2000, p. 265) and that he would not have welcomed a welfare state that would require a high level of taxation (see Clark, 1964). The British welfare reforms, while popular with the British population, were more controversial with economists (see Peacock, 1955).

After the war the Keynesian Revolution had acquired a dynamic of its own, especially in the United States, where the Great Depression had had a devastating effect on the American economy and on the American society. The Keynesian Revolution, as promoted in the United States by enthusiastic followers of Keynes, such as Alvin Hansen, Lawrence Klein, and others, risked leaving behind its originator. As Wapshott (2011, p. 226) put it, the "gap between what Keynes intended [to do] and what the Keynesians did in his name [was becoming] larger." In later years, conservatives and many general observers would blame Keynes for the growth of public spending in many countries and for the excuse that his theories had given to governments to spend more and to interfere more in the market. However, in fairness to Keynes, it should be noted that his responsibilities were limited, and they were only indirectly linked to these later developments (see also Tanzi, 2015c).

Hayek (who had been highly critical of Keynes's views on countercyclical fiscal policy, even before the *General Theory* was published in 1936) would be unsparing in his criticism of Beveridge and of his welfare recommendations. He was reported to have declared that "[he had] never known a man who was known as an economist and who understood so little economics," as he believed that Beveridge did (cited in Wapshott, 2011, p. 227). In this he may have shared, to some limited extent, Keynes's own view, in the judgment of the architect of the creation of the British welfare state.

The "War on Poverty" in the United States, the social programs that were introduced by President Johnson some years later (in 1964), and similar programs introduced in France, in the Scandinavian countries, and in some other countries were all examples of the ongoing, dramatic changes in economic thinking that had taken place since the 1920s, and of the growing optimism about what could be achieved with government policies.

Laissez-faire was being quickly abandoned and forgotten by many economists as a guiding ideology. Many economists had come to believe that good government policies could eliminate, or at least reduce, poverty and many of the economic risks (unemployment and loss of income due to illnesses, disability, old age, etc.) faced by citizens in modern societies. It came to be widely believed that, with its policies, the government could significantly reduce those risks and increase the well-being of most citizens, without paying a high price in terms of efficiency and in terms of reduction of individual liberties and economic vitality. A growing number of economists had come to believe that democratically elected, *benevolent* governments, with significant public resources, aided by *competent* and *honest* bureaucracies, and advised by *clever* economists, would be able to deliver on this objective. It should be noted that, by this time, the governments of most advanced countries had extended the voting rights to most adult citizens including women.

President Johnson's War on Poverty had, to some extent, delivered on a wish expressed by President Franklin D. Roosevelt a couple decades earlier in a "fireside chat" in January 1944 (the year before his death). The fireside chat might in turn have been influenced, or inspired, by the *Beveridge Report*, of which President Roosevelt would have been aware. In that chat, Roosevelt had proposed a "second Bill of Rights" for the American citizens, one that would focus on *economic* rather than political rights. President Truman, in his inaugural speech in 1949, had also pledged to eliminate absolute poverty in the United States, but had not acted on his pledge.

The US Declaration of Independence had listed "Life, Liberty, and the Pursuit of Happiness" as rights of individuals, and the first ten amendments to the US Constitution, which were named the Bill of Rights, had listed specific rights of US citizens. In the promotion of these goals and rights the US federal government derived its power from the "consent of the governed." These rights could not lead to specific *economic* programs for a welfare state. It should be added that the definition of "consent of the governed" failed to stipulate who were the governed, since most of those living in the United States at that time did not have a vote and could not have expressed their "consent."

Roosevelt's Bill of Rights was detailed. It specified *economic* obligations of the US government towards its citizens. For every US citizen, it promised "a useful and remunerative job," a "decent home," "adequate medical care," "a good education," and "adequate protection, from the economic fears of old age, sickness, accident, and unemployment." Thus, for the *citizens*, it contained all the elements of an ambitious welfare state and a remarkable correlation with the promises contained in the *Beveridge Report*. For *businesspeople*, Roosevelt's Bill of Rights included the guarantee "to trade in an atmosphere of freedom from unfair competition and domination by monopolies." Thus, it contained a promise of a welfare state operating within a well-working private market that would give the government the objective to intervene to eliminate "market failures."

President Roosevelt was promoting ambitious and potentially very expensive welfare policies for American citizens while, at the same time, promising a well-working free market for economic operators. No "crony capitalism" or other threats, including nonjustified interventions by the government in a well-working market economy, would be allowed, and no abuse of power by any group over the market would be permitted. He was implicitly assuming that there would be no conflict between these two objectives and that a well-working private market would tolerate and finance, without creating excessive economic disincentives and difficulties, the high spending that his Bill of Rights was promising for the American citizens.

There was no estimate, and there could not have been any estimate, in Roosevelt's fireside chat of the financial cost of his promises and of how those costs would be covered and allocated among the population. There was also no mention of how the performance of the US economy might be affected, in the short and in the long run, by the creation of the promised programs. The classic *economic problem*, which had always worried economists, namely the existence of too many needs and too few resources, was not acknowledged, or it was downplayed.

The assumptions must have been that the promises could be met with a better and more equitable use of resources. Full employment, which Keynesian policies promised could be achieved and maintained, would contribute to the needed resources. Perhaps, the implicit assumption was that the large public spending, which at that time was being used to fight the war, could be redirected toward more desirable and peaceful uses, once the war was over. The introduction of these welfare policies would also guarantee that the aggregate demand would not fall after the end of the war and once military spending was sharply reduced, which could have plunged the country back into the feared depression. This was a great fear of many Keynesian economists and also of many citizens at that time.

A constant in some of the promises of the kind made by President Roosevelt in 1944, at least in peaceful times, has been that the *economic problem* could be dealt with, or at least alleviated, by making the economy operate at full employment and increasing the tax burden on the rich, while using efficiently the resources so obtained to pay for well-designed and efficiently delivered social programs. Regardless of whether the rich should or should not be taxed more, an issue to which we shall return later, the resources that could be obtained from taxing only the rich would not be likely to be sufficient to cover the costs of all the ambitious programs mentioned by President Roosevelt, unless those programs were delivered at a low, basic, or minimal level.

This aspect was pointed out a few years after Roosevelt's fireside chat by an influential book written by a French author, Bertrand de Jouvenel ([1952] 1990). He pointed out that *the taxation of the rich* could not be sufficient and could not be sustained to finance welfare programs. Roosevelt would have used the war spending, which directly or indirectly (through rationing) was being paid by everyone. The question would have been whether the sacrifices that had been accepted by most American citizens to fight a major war that threatened their way of life would continue to be acceptable by them in normal times, after the war was over, in order to finance Roosevelt's expensive Bill of Rights.

The optimism that prevailed in the years after World War II among liberal policymakers and economists was so great that, in 1958, one of the most famous and influential American economists at that time, J. K. Galbraith, in a book that attracted a lot of popular and economist attention, *The Affluent Society*, would affirm that "the problem of production" had been solved, so that enough could be produced to satisfy everyone's "basic needs." In his view, the remaining problem to be addressed by the US government was that of distribution.

However, while enough might have been produced to satisfy all the basic needs of the citizens, as those needs were perceived and defined at that time, "non-basic" needs still existed, as Keynes had recognized three decades earlier. These non-basic needs could be considered less important by some, but not by all citizens. In later years, some economists would point out that access to non-basic and less essential needs may be necessary to sustain incentives and efforts and thus economic growth. This point would be made forcefully in a 2013 book by the 2016 Nobel Prize winner in economics, Angus Deaton. Furthermore, even basic needs have a way of being elastic and of expanding and changing character with the passing of time, thus increasing the resources needed to produce and satisfy them. What may have been considered basic needs in 1958 would no longer be considered so in 2017. At the same time, non-basic needs tend to be infinite, given the new products and services generated by technological advances and by human ingenuity. Just think of new drugs to fight old and new diseases.

The distribution of income is perhaps the main variable that determines the demand for non-basic goods, goods that may be important for some people to sustain their incentives, and that make at least some of them work harder to acquire them to satisfy their non-basic needs. In turn, that demand tends to define the needs that can be considered "basic," because needs that may not have been considered basic at one point in time tend to become basic in some other era of economic development. Therefore, the distribution of income, together with the average per capita income, determines the level of resources needed to satisfy basic needs.

Furthermore, basic needs, such as health services, adequate shelter, sufficient food, basic education, and so on, may be satisfied at widely different levels. As average income grows, and as the income distribution becomes less even, the satisfaction of basic needs requires more resources. For example, in the United States, public and private expenditure for health care (presumably a basic need) in 1960, at about the time when Galbraith published his book, required 5.4 percent of GDP. By 2017 the expenditure for that basic need had risen to about 18 percent of GDP.

Returning to the issue of the almost "religious" attitude held by some economists vis-à-vis economic theories or ideologies, it might be mentioned that, according to Wapshott, Galbraith's "deification of Keynes" had been so great that, in 1937, on his honeymoon, he had taken his bride to Cambridge, England to seek an audience with the "great man" (see Wapshott, 2011, pp. 164–165). Commenting on the presumed obscurity and lack of rigor of Keynes's *General Theory* (a point that had been stressed also by leading economists at that time, including Schumpeter, Hayek, and others), Galbraith was reported to have commented that, "as with the Bible and Marx … obscurity stimulated abstract debate" (see Clarke, 2009, p. 8). As an interesting anecdote, in a lecture at Harvard in 1962 for the economic theory course taught by Professor Wassily Leontief, in which he was comparing the work of Irving Fisher, an economist that Leontief admired for his clarity, with that of Keynes, whom Leontief did not admire (especially the *General Theory*) because of his lack of clarity, Leontief maintained that Keynes owed part of the success of the *General Theory* to the ambiguity of his writing. In Leontief's view, that ambiguity had forced continuing debates among scholars on what Keynes exactly meant, thus increasing the attention of economists to Keynes's work.

During Roosevelt's years, Keynes's view of the United States had changed dramatically, from the negative view that he had held in 1925, reported earlier, to a new, enthusiastic view, due to the policies that the Roosevelt administration was introducing, which were closer to Keynes's views and recommendations. By the late 1930s he had come to see the United States as "the economic laboratory of the world" (see Wapshott, 2011, p. 164).

Some recent defenders of the welfare states have argued that particular categories of public spending, especially those that free women from household chores such as taking care of small children and aged parents, thus allowing them to join the workforce, might help alleviate the constraints imposed by the *economic problem*. For example, Esping-Andersen, an influential Danish economist and sociologist, in a 2008 book argued that some social programs can increase the size of the labor force, by allowing more women to enter it and work in paid jobs and to pay taxes on their incomes. Therefore, women can raise both the countries' economic output and their tax revenue, to make it easier to finance the social programs. He pointed out that in the Scandinavian countries the labor force participation, and especially the participation by women, is among the highest in the world, thus contributing to the countries' national output and tax revenue. Other defenders of the welfare state have made similar points (see papers in Costabile, 2008).

A problem with that observation is that, often in welfare states such as those of the Scandinavian countries, many of the working women end up working for government programs and doing largely the same, but now paid, jobs outside their houses as they were doing inside the houses, when they were not part of the formal labor force. The difference is that their work is now paid, often by the government, and, being paid, is counted as income in the national account statistics. This raises questions about the comparability of the per capita incomes of countries with widely different public programs (see Tanzi, 2008a). It can still be argued that, by having an income and a paid job, many working women acquire more personal liberty, compared with the alternative of having to attend, unpaid, to dependent family members. Thus, more public spending may lead to more personal liberty!

Social programs, along the lines of those mentioned by President Franklin D. Roosevelt in his fireside chat, and those introduced in several European countries in the years after World War II, in part addressed the problem of the distribution of income, the problem that Galbraith believed was still to be solved in the United States in 1958, before the introduction of President Johnson's War on Poverty. As mentioned, Galbraith seemed to accept the view that the economic problem, the one of too few resources and too many needs, no longer existed, at least with respect to the production of "basic goods." His book was published at a time when the average incomes, in the United States and elsewhere, were a small fraction of what they are today. Therefore, if he had been right at that time, he might be even more right now, when per capita incomes are much higher and available resources are much more abundant.

That leaves out the question of the production of non-basic goods and the role of those goods in creating and maintaining incentives in modern societies. Deaton (2013) argued that the desire to acquire non-basic goods is an important ingredient for economic progress. If that possibility is removed, economic progress will slow down, as it did in centrally planned economies. There is thus a cost in pushing redistribution too far, and there is the question of the level at which the basic needs of individuals and families must be satisfied. The higher is that level, the less non-basic goods can be produced and the greater the negative impact on incentives.

Three implicit and important assumptions backed the optimism about the role of government in the 1950s. The first was that, in redistributing income from the well-to-do to the general population, first through the transfer of taxes to the government and, then, from the government spending back to the citizens, there would be few leakages and few inefficiencies created by the social programs and by the payment of taxes. Therefore, the government's objectives could be achieved at reasonable costs, mainly measured by the tax revenue. There would be no, or minor, deadweights.

The second assumption was that, in a nonwar period, high tax revenue could be raised without generating significant short or long run disincentive effects, or reactions on the part of those who paid them, and also without disincentives on the part of those who were on the receiving end of the public transfers. At that time disincentive effects attracted still relatively minor attention. For example, Samuelson (1947) had dismissed them as a minor issue. It should be pointed out that while public spending had reached 44 percent of GDP in 1943–1944 the level of public revenue had only reached 20 percent of GDP. In other words the war had been financed to a large extent with debt even though revenue had increased a great deal, from before the war.

The third assumption was the already mentioned one, that basic needs are absolute (mostly essential food and shelter) and that once they are satisfied, at a basic level, they make individuals happy or at least satisfied, both presently and in the future, regardless of the distribution of income and the changes in the per capita income levels.

Given those assumptions, the government objectives could have been achieved more easily if two "free lunches" – which some vocal, contemporary, liberal economists believe exist today – had existed at that time: first, the possibility of a great monetary expansion by the monetary authorities without any visible and undesirable short or long run consequences on prices and on the allocation of resources. This expansion would have given governments almost the equivalent of a debit card with free and almost unlimited balances in it. The second was the possibility of a Keynesian fiscal expansion that would increase income and government revenue, also without negative consequences. This latter possibility was clearly understood and was taken into account at that time given the prevailing assumption that there were unused resources in the economy. It had been important in allowing the large increase in military spending to fight World War II and later to counter the Soviet challenge.

In the years after World War II, the US Federal Reserve Bank had been instructed, by the Full Employment Act of Congress of 1948, to promote, as one of its objectives, "maximum employment, production, and purchasing power," while paying attention to price stability. Because by 1948 public spending in the United States had collapsed to 11.6 percent of GDP, there was great concern among Keynesian economists that the Great Depression would return. The confidence that some economists have in the existence of the aforementioned two "free lunches" in today's economies has made it possible to call for large increases in public spending both in the United States and in European countries, in the belief that these increases can be achieved at almost zero costs, while producing great benefits by injecting needed demand in economies facing "great stagnation."

In the early decades after World War II, major goals of economic theory and of the work of economists were, first, to look for and to identify areas in which private markets had failed, or could fail; and, second, to study ways in which governments could intervene and correct the market failures, through public spending, tax expenditures, or other ways. The important goals, besides the stabilization of national income at full employment, were the elimination or reduction of economic risks for citizens; some redistribution of income, in order to achieve a more equitable income distribution; and the maintenance of growth and price stability. These goals were to be achieved with the recently discovered Keynesian countercyclical policies, with the help of new social programs, and with progressive tax systems, while allowing the economies to continue working as significantly free market economies.

Some of the political wishes, such as those mentioned in the *Beveridge Report* of 1942 and in Roosevelt's fireside chat of 1944, became government promises, and the promises were slowly transformed into concrete policies that created "entitlements" or "bills of rights" for citizens. These "rights" required specific programs and new or reformed public institutions.

A transition had been made in the redistribution of income that had occurred, from the traditional and highly focused redistribution that had existed in the past – redistribution within extended families and from charitable institutions to individuals clearly in need, because of infirmities, major handicaps, the death of income earners with families, and other reasons. This assistance had been seen as clear acts of *charity*, by both those who gave and those who received the assistance. Welfare *policies* had been very rare in the past. For example, in the seventeenth century the Dutch Republic had had some programs in support of the poor, mainly to maintain peace, and England had had its Poor Laws, which would be curtailed in 1834, and there had been some other rare examples in the Republic of Venice, directed at sailors, and in Norway, directed at miners.

The government programs came to be seen increasingly as *rights* or *entitlements* on the part of those who received the benefits. In older, traditional societies the redistribution (outside families or not involving charities) that had taken place had generally been from the masses toward those at the top, the aristocrats, nobles, or major landowners, or in some countries toward those who owned slaves. Thus, the concept of a Gini coefficient–inspired redistribution had had almost no meaning historically.

By the 1950s the *entitlements* had started acquiring aspects of "property claims" by some categories of citizens, or, in countries with universal programs, by all citizens against governments and against society in general. As I shall argue later, the claims also tended to become *elastic* in some programs. They tended to grow with time and with the rise of the countries' per capita incomes.

Rising expectations had been created for the citizens of many countries, and in democratic countries the citizens had the power to influence the government through their vote. The citizens would become impatient with the slow and, at times, inefficient delivery of the promised goods and services. They would pressure governments to spend more to create new, improved, and more generous programs, and to extend the programs to progressively larger groups, than the ones that had been intended when the programs had been originally formulated. For the programs that were universal from the beginning, the pressures were simply to make them more generous.

There was at work what I, in other writings, have described as a "law of public expenditure growth." There were always some groups and some political figures and economists ready to support and justify that growth (see Tanzi, 2013b, chapter 14). The assumption, or the hope, was always that the growth of public spending would improve the welfare of the citizens at relatively low or modest costs.

The policymakers of many countries, including those of the United States, had become convinced at that time that, with enough governmental action, and especially with enough public spending, financed by progressive taxes or, when necessary, by public borrowing (at a time when public borrowing had become less threatening and less sinful than it had been considered in the past), the lives of most citizens could be significantly improved and poverty could be abolished. Over the years, the globalization of the financial market would progressively make the supply of funds, which the governments of particular countries could borrow, more elastic, at least until the countries ran into difficulties. This greater elasticity allowed some countries to accumulate large public debts not caused by major wars or catastrophes (see Tanzi, 2016b).

Policymakers also believed that the amount of public spending necessary to achieve the desired goals could be determined with precision, perhaps with the assistance of newly developed econometric models (which, at that time, especially in the 1960s, were becoming increasingly popular) and with the greater availability of relevant statistics. This was the beginning of what came to be called the *scientific* phase of economics, when many economists became convinced that, with the help of mathematics and statistics, economics could become less like sociology and more like Newtonian physics.

At that time economics was attracting an increasing number of individuals whose initial training had been in physics or mathematics. Mathematics became the language preferred by many economists. It gave economics a look of rigor and precision that it had not had in the past. This new approach would ignore a warning issued in 1953 by Gunnar Myrdal that, for economics, "belief in the existence of a body of scientific knowledge acquired independently of all valuations is … naïve empiricism" (see Myrdal, 1954, preface).

Two different approaches were followed by countries in the pursuit of their policy objectives. First, in order to generate more welfare for their citizens, and especially to make the income distributions more equitable (an important, declared objective of some governments), progressive taxes, and transfers focused directly toward *poor* households, were used. "Tax expenditures," a concept introduced in the United States in the 1960s, were also used to reduce the cost of acquiring some desirable goods for tax-payers who paid income taxes. The use of tax expenditures had the political advantage of reducing the level of public spending and taxes in countries, such as the United States, where there was still strong opposition from part of the population to high levels of taxes and public spending. It was a form of the "fiscal illusions" that Amilcare Puviani had written about.

Tax expenditures could encourage the consumption of particular goods, such as homes, health care, education, and others that Musgrave had defined as "merit goods." In countries that introduced value-added taxes the effect of tax expenditures could be achieved in part by using lower rates for the consumption of some merit goods. Tax expenditures are less beneficial to people with incomes too low to require the payment of income taxes or to be subjected to higher income tax rates. They are more beneficial to individuals with incomes high enough to be subjected to significant tax rates. Tax expenditures may have led to excessive consumption of particular merit goods, such as housing in the United States. In the United States tax expenditures were given preference during the Clinton administration in the 1990s, in part because Congress was controlled by the Republican Party in that period. Tax expenditures could be promoted as tax reductions.

In the 1950s and 1960s textbooks on public finance and books on taxation strongly favored the use of direct and highly progressive income taxes, because these taxes were assumed to better reflect the taxpayers' "ability to pay." At that time economists had not yet expressed major concerns about potentially significant disincentive effects that could be associated with high income tax rates (see Musgrave, 1959; Goode, 1976). Progressive income taxes with high rates and the use of tax expenditures lent themselves more easily to the kind of social engineering that policymakers and even citizens wanted to pursue at that time.

Surveys conducted in the United States in those years often concluded that the personal or individual income tax, which had become highly progressive not just in the United States, was an *ideal tax*. As mentioned, potential disincentive effects of high marginal tax rates were ignored, minimized, or questioned in those years. In the United Kingdom, the marginal tax rates became so high in the 1960s that they inspired a song by the Beatles, "Taxman." The song made reference to a marginal tax rate of 95 percent, which was the rate then in use in the United Kingdom. A major issue for tax experts at that time was how to tax *unrealized* capital gains, incomes that escaped the tax net, thus potentially contributing to making some individuals rich by allowing them to avoid taxes and making the tax presumably less equitable.

The use of progressive income taxes (combined with focused transfers and tax expenditures) satisfied directly the objective of making the *after-tax* income distributions more even. It placed less importance on the direct expenditure side of the public budget. This alternative was chosen by the United States and by some other Anglo-Saxon countries (see Tanzi, 1968). In later decades, starting in the 1980s, in reaction to growing theoretical findings by some economists and concerns about potential disincentive effects of high marginal tax rates, the personal income taxes started to undergo major changes. Those changes would reduce their progressivity, especially for those who received incomes from capital sources (see Tanzi, 2014c, and later chapters in this book). In spite of these changes, and broadly speaking, the United States continued to follow the route described earlier. Its tax system continued to be progressive, especially for incomes from labor sources.

Other countries, such as the Scandinavian countries, France, and Belgium, chose the route of higher public spending, combined with higher, but less progressive, tax levels. The higher spending was made necessary by the fact that some public programs (such as the provision of health services, educational services, and social pensions) were made universal and, being universal, were available to *all* or most of the citizens, regardless of their position on the income scale. These countries had to rely on higher tax levels and on necessarily less redistributive tax systems to be able to finance the higher public spending. The tax systems of these countries made more use of indirect taxes and, increasingly, of the newly introduced value-added tax, to finance the public programs and to reduce poverty rates with the spending action of the government. The difference that exists between the levels of public spending and taxes in the United States and those in the European countries is largely explained by the revenue from the value-added tax in the latter. European countries often tax government transfers as income and have lower personal exemptions and tax expenditures. For early empirical evidence of these two approaches, see Tanzi (1968).

With their redistributive policies governments succeeded in improving the lives of many lower-income citizens, in spite of problems that developed, some of which will be discussed later in this book. One must not lose sight of, or ignore, the ways in which the lives of many citizens were improved in various countries over recent decades because of the actions by governments. Lives were improved not only because of the rise in real incomes, due to economic growth and to the technological changes that occurred over the years, but also because of the policies of the governments.

Those actions allowed lower-income citizens to become better educated, to enjoy better health, and to be better protected against life's various difficulties, including temporary or permanent losses of income due to permanent disabilities, to unemployment, or to old age. In many European countries, the actions reduced the wide differences in life expectancy among individuals at different income levels, differences that have continued to be far more significant in the United States. In some countries, minimum social pensions and programs such as allowances for children in large families, subsidies to housing, and other forms of assistance put a floor on the absolute standard of living of most people and reduced absolute poverty for many of them.

CHAPTER 5

When Economists Thought They Had Found Nirvana: Stabilization Policies

The first half of the 1960s was the period when trust in the ability of governments to stabilize economies, using the Keynesian theory, probably reached the highest level. It was a time when the planets were believed to have lined up in ways that were expected to generate the best outcomes for governmental interventions to stabilize economies and to make them grow. That period was helped by the fact that the labor force increased dramatically due to the baby boom after World War II, while the number of people retiring was modest. This development contributed to generating faster growth rates and increasing tax revenue in the 1960s.

The United States provides the best example of this conclusion. In the early 1960s a new administration (the Kennedy administration) had been elected. It was led by a charismatic, cultured, rich, and young individual who had brought with him to Washington the "best and the brightest" individuals, from top universities, and especially from Harvard. These were highly educated, trained, and intelligent individuals who were expected to be able to make wise decisions in the government positions that they assumed, and to make policy changes that would benefit the population, using the latest results from economic analyses. They would introduce new, modern ways for the government to do things. The new president benefited from wide trust, a characteristic that can be considered an important public good because it leads to easier acceptance of new policies. Many expected him to make good decisions and to be a benevolent and wise leader in a country that, at that time, enjoyed wide prestige in the free world.

At that time the American economy was undergoing a fast process of industrialization, a development that made it easier for the government to raise higher taxes from large enterprises and from the high and increasing share of national income that dependent workers were receiving (see Tanzi, 2014c). Some of the complications for tax systems that would come later, associated with globalization, with the activities of multinational corporations, with the growth of difficult-to-tax services, with the communication revolution, and so on, had not yet appeared or been felt.

Another important factor was that the quality of the personnel in the various departments of the government (the public employees and administrators) had become much higher than it had been in earlier decades, and economists had done a lot of good work in previous years to identify market failures and to suggest ways to deal with them. Trust in economic knowledge and in the value of that knowledge had probably reached the highest level that it would ever reach, as had trust in government. There were fewer doubts, compared to today, about the practical value of economic knowledge, and economists enjoyed a far higher prestige than they do today.

Take, for example, the 1962 *Economic Report of the President*. It had benefited from the contributions of many of the leading economists of the time. The Council of Economic Advisors was led by Walter Heller, an economist with enough personal prestige to play regular tennis with the president of the United States. He was widely known to the public, and, when he discussed economic policies, he spoke in a language that normal citizens could understand. The Council of Economic Advisers, which had prepared the *Report*, included among its staff two future Nobel Prize winners in economics (James Tobin and Robert Solow) and had also relied on consultants that included two other future Nobel Prize winners (Kenneth Arrow and Paul Samuelson). The *Report* would attract the kind of attention that could only be dreamed of by the authors of recent reports.

The 1962 *Report* was a clear example of the extent to which the Keynesian Revolution and trust in the government to be able to make policy changes assumed to be beneficial to the citizens had reached their apotheosis, while economists had reached the peak of their prestige. The *Report* expressed no doubts that "the Government can time its fiscal transactions to offset and dampen fluctuations in the private economy" (US Council of Economic Advisers, 1962, p.17). To facilitate that task the *Report* proposed giving the president, when needed, "stand-by authority for prompt, temporary income tax reductions, [and] ... stand-by authority for capital improvements expenditure" (ibid.). Perhaps not surprisingly, Congress, which still included many politicians with conservative views, refused to give the president that power. The *Report* made several other recommendations for policy changes. They included some that would be enacted by President Johnson's War on Poverty in 1964.

In those years the Kennedy administration used a major reduction in tax revenue and in tax rates on personal incomes (from the highest, marginal rate of 91 percent to one of 70 percent) to stimulate the economy. The economy seemed to respond to the stimulus as had been expected. Heller would later explain that the choice of cutting taxes, rather than increasing spending, had been made mainly because there were no laws that could have been used by the government to allow the quick increase in public spending, a policy that had been considered the more desirable option by the Kennedy administration. Enacting new spending laws would have required more time and would have encountered strong opposition in Congress, especially by the representatives of the Republican Party (see Heller, 1966). The proposal to cut taxes, always a welcome policy for businesspeople, had been presented by Kennedy in a speech to mostly Republican businesspeople at the Economic Club of New York in December 1962, and had received a favorable reception (see Stein, 1969, p. 417).

The Kennedy and later US administrations would also benefit from a "landmark document" in regulatory history that would bring important changes in future decades to the government's use of regulations. This document was the *Landis Report* to President-Elect Kennedy, a report delivered in December 1960. The *Landis Report* had been drafted by "one of the bright young men of the New Deal" who had been "a principal author of both the Securities Act of 1933 and the Securities Exchange Act of 1934" (see McCraw, 1980, p. 3). James Landis, the author of the *Landis Report*, "had credentials of expertise in regulatory matters that few Americans, if any, could match" (ibid.). He had been asked "to survey the current state of Federal regulations and report the results" (ibid.). "Landis [had been] the author of ... the most persuasive theoretical treatise in favor of regulations ever written – 'the Administrative Process' ... delivered at the Storrs Lectures at Yale in 1938" (ibid.).

Given the background of the author, the *Landis Report* had come as a great surprise. "It offered harsh indictments of regulatory performance in agency after agency, detailing the inefficiency and cronyism that had invaded nearly all the [regulatory] commissions" (McCraw, 1980, p. 3). Landis had become aware that "the system which he himself had helped to design [in the 1930s] was not working, and might never work" (ibid., p. 4). That system was based on the existence of natural monopolies and had focused the role of regulations on the fairness and reasonableness of rates, fares and other fees in those natural monopolies, while leaving to the monopolies the terms of competitive behavior, including the control over entry into and exit from the industries.

The *Landis Report* argued that there was a need for a new functional form of regulation, one that would focus "on the rights of citizens to a safe and healthy work place, to equal employment opportunities and to a clean environment" (ibid., pp. 4–5). In other words the focus of regulations was to be shifted to the needs and the rights of citizens. This new functional form would open the road to much deregulation in future years and, progressively, also to the introduction of new forms of regulations, which have become common in the past decades.

In conclusion, while in the years that followed the Kennedy administration the role of the government in the United States (and in other countries) would increase in terms of public spending and new social programs, it would decrease and change in terms of the *traditional* regulations, which had been introduced especially during the New Deal, and in terms of direct controls by government in various economic sectors. Sectors such as road and air transportation, telecommunications, and others would be deregulated, and all industries would be progressively subjected to different forms of regulations, more focused on safety and on reducing damaging externalities than on dealing with monopoly power.

Toward the end of the 1960s and especially in the 1970s the economic and political situation would change and become less clear. There would be the beginning of attacks on the certainty and on the trust that peoples had put in Keynesian countercyclical policies and in the benefits that had been expected to come from the larger role of the state in the economy, the role that had been introduced by President Johnson's War on Poverty in the United States and by similar and, at times, more ambitious programs in other, especially European, countries.

In future years some critics would point out that several trillion dollars had been spent fighting poverty in the United States, but, a half-century later, the official poverty rate in that country was still as high as it had been in the 1960s when the War on Poverty programs had been enacted. However, while the officially measured poverty rate in the United States had remained high, after some decline in the first few years immediately following the introduction of the War on Poverty, there are some reasons to believe that particular factors may have distorted the statistical results, thus hiding some of the progress that had been made on that score. Some of these factors were an increasing number of cohabiting couples; the reduction of the size of the average household; noncash benefits that were not accounted for by the poverty statistics; refundable tax credits that were also not accounted for in the official measurement; and the difficulty of measuring correctly price changes. Some have estimated that correcting for these factors would show that the poverty rate was in fact reduced (see, for example, Bailey and Danziger, 2015; Jencks, 2015). However, those estimates concern *absolute* poverty and not *relative* poverty. As I argued earlier, relative poverty may be more important.

In the United Kingdom there were increasing criticisms in the 1960s and 1970s about the "nanny state" that had been introduced by the Beveridge reforms; about the continuing and growing power of unions in several sectors of the economy; and about the very high marginal tax rates, which exceeded 90 percent of taxable incomes. In the United States in the early 1960s, the maximum federal tax rate on the income of individuals had been 91 percent, and "from 1965 to 1980 the permanent maximum rate was 70 percent" (see Pechman, 1987, p. 301). These were the rates for the *federal* income tax. In addition many US states and counties also taxed and continue to tax the income of individuals, some at significantly high rates. Therefore, for many taxpayers, the overall rate was somewhat higher than 70 percent until the Reagan administration, with the approval of Congress, reduced it.

By the late 1970s the intellectual winds had shifted and the ground had become ready for conservative leaders, such as Thatcher in the United Kingdom and Reagan in the United States, to win elections and to bring major policy changes. These policymakers had a less benign view of the role of government in the economy. They tended to view that role more as a problem than as the solution to some of the problems of society. The rest of this book will focus on the challenges to the large role of the state and on changes that in time would introduce what I have called "termites" in that role. The termites would significantly reduce the attraction that the large government role had had in the earlier decades after World War II.

CHAPTER 6

Barbarians at the Gates: Challenges to Nirvana

The happy alignment of stars, described in the previous chapter, that had made possible and had encouraged large and presumably successful interventions by governments in the economies of countries did not go unchallenged for long. Perhaps, it was natural that that happy alignment could not have lasted. There were soon challenges, some ideological in nature, some technical, and some prompted by economic and other developments, especially in the second half of the 1970s.

The challenges gave ammunition to those economists, politicians, and plain citizens who had never felt comfortable with the expanding economic role of governments, but had been in the minority in earlier years. As that role, measured by the levels of public spending and taxation into GDPs, grew, the early optimism and the large consensus that had accompanied and had supported that expansion started to be challenged, especially in the United States and in the United Kingdom, but also in some other places such as New Zealand and Ireland. At first it was challenged by a few isolated, conservative critics, and then by an increasing number of economists, political scientists, and plain citizens.

Among economists, the earlier challenges had come mainly from conservative, or libertarian, pro-market economists, such as F. A. Hayek, Milton Friedman, George Stigler, James Buchanan, Ronald Coase, Alan Peacock, and a few others, and from some politicians and philosophers, such as Barry Goldwater, Robert Nozick, and others in the United States, and some in the United Kingdom and in other countries. These individuals had followed with alarm, suspicion, and growing concerns the expansion of government activities that had taken place in those years. However, until the second half of the 1970s, their voices had had little impact. There had always been a few conservative thinkers in research institutions, such as the American Enterprise Institute in the United States, the Institute of Economic Affairs in the United Kingdom, the Frazer Institute in Canada, and others in other countries who had not been happy with that expansion.

They had been in the minority, and their arguments had not carried much weight with the general public in the previous decades.

As time passed, the critics became more numerous, their arguments more sharp, and they began to be listened to by a growing number of citizens. In the second half of the 1970s, during the oil crisis and the economic recession that followed, the critics attracted a larger popular following, and their views started to influence important politicians, especially in the United States and in the United Kingdom, but also in some other countries. In those years, the rate of inflation had accelerated in several countries, and in some (such as the United Kingdom), it had reached historical records. In spite of the high inflation, the unemployment rates had remained stubbornly high, or had even increased, while the growth rates of the economies had slowed down or, in some countries, had become negative. A prolonged slowdown or recession had taken hold in several economies, contributing to the increase in fiscal deficits and public debts.

The increases in fiscal deficits had come in spite of the positive contributions to tax revenues that the so-called *fiscal drag* – the positive impact that a moderate rate of inflation has on tax revenue, in tax systems with progressive tax rates applied to unchanged nominal incomes – was having (see Tanzi, 1980b). What Ronald Reagan called the "misery index," the summation of the unemployment and the inflation rates, became high, creating political difficulties for some governments and for the prevailing Keynesian ideology.

These developments were seen as direct challenges to the original optimism and to a key postulate of the Keynesian framework, the *Phillips curve*. Supporters of the then prevailing Keynesian orthodoxy (though not necessarily the work of Keynes himself) had assumed that there would be a trade-off between the unemployment rate and the inflation rate. A higher unemployment rate was expected to reduce the inflation rate, and vice versa. This relationship had been called the Phillips curve, named after the economist who had first described it. Keynesian economists had not considered it likely that a relatively high inflation rate could coexist with a high and increasing unemployment rate. Furthermore, large fiscal deficits at that time did not seem to be having the positive impact on economic activity expected from Keynesian countercyclical policy.

Some influential economists, including Milton Friedman and Robert Lucas at the University of Chicago and Robert Barro at Harvard, had challenged the countercyclical fiscal policy with intellectually appealing, theoretical arguments, largely based on the view, then gaining currency, that economic agents are rational in their behavior. The debate that followed was, in some significant aspects and with due changes, a preview of the one that would follow the financial crisis of 2007.

Milton Friedman and some of the economists around him at the University of Chicago (who came to be identified as members of the "Chicago School"), as well as economists associated with James Buchanan in Virginia (the "School of Public Choice"), had found weaknesses not only in the prevailing Keynesian countercyclical policy but also in the view that a growing government role would necessarily promote the public interest and general welfare. They raised pertinent questions about the impact of a larger and growing government role, a role that required high taxes, or increasing public debt, to finance high public spending, and more regulations. That role was based on the assumption that policymakers were benevolent and competent, so the government would make economic decisions that were predominantly consistent with the best available knowledge and in the public interest.

In real life there would be an asymmetry in the pursuit of Keynesian stabilization policies, an asymmetry that would become evident and increasingly important with the passing of time. Namely, governments could be expected to be more prompt and more willing to increase spending when such increase might seem justified by economic conditions, but much less willing or able to reduce spending when reduction was called for, during economic expansions and good times. Over the longer run, it was believed that this asymmetry would inevitably lead to growing public debts and to higher levels of public spending, as in fact was happening.

Some economists also suggested that there were deficiencies in the Keynesian theoretical framework. Hypotheses such as "rational expectation," that is, the rational anticipation by economic agents of *future* economic policies, might reduce the impact of Keynesian *current* policies; and the "Ricardian Equivalence" hypothesis, that is, the "rational expectation" by taxpayers of future tax increases to pay for the current public borrowing that accompanied a fiscal expansion, was proposed and started attracting increasing numbers of, especially academic, followers.

By the early 1980s, some of these theories had acquired an almost religious aspect among some economists. Those who questioned them were accused of lack of faith or, worse, lack of brains. In academia the younger economists who challenged the new theories risked not getting promotions or tenure in academic positions.

The Ricardian Equivalence was not a new hypothesis, in spite of the novel way in which Robert Barro had reformulated it. He had asked whether public bonds represented real wealth. If they represented real wealth, they would contribute to the increase in aggregate demand when public debt grew. He argued that the repayment of the debt would require higher future taxes, and that expectation would reduce the current private spending of rational individuals. The conclusion was that the bonds did not represent real net wealth and that fiscal deficits had less of an expansionary impact on demand than Keynesian economists assumed.

Barro's argument was conceptually similar to the hypothesis that had been suggested much earlier by David Ricardo, in chapter XVII of his book ([1817] 1973). Ricardo had advanced a hypothesis that was plausible for his time, when taxes were paid by very few rich and well-informed individuals, and public bonds, which were largely held by the same people, were expected to be repaid by taxing, in the future, the same individuals who had bought the bonds. It is not the situation that has prevailed in modern time. Ricardo had theorized that a rising public debt would lead the rich individuals to cut their current spending (and increase their savings), in anticipation of the higher taxes that they would have to pay in future years to redeem the higher debt. If Ricardo's intuition was correct, higher *public* spending, financed by public debt, would not have the expansionary effect on the economy that Keynesian fiscal policy had predicted. It would be neutralized by lower *private* spending, due to the anticipation, by the taxpayers, of the higher future taxes.

The "Scienza delle Finanze," the Italian school of thought mentioned earlier, had been aware of, and had discussed, the realism of the Ricardian Equivalence hypothesis, because of the frequent fiscal deficits that had characterized the Italian public finances after the unification of Italy in 1861 (see Tanzi, 2012). The famous Italian economist Vilfredo Pareto had dismissed that hypothesis and had concluded that it was too far-fetched to have much practical relevance. He had expressed strong doubts that individuals would be so rational and so well-informed as to be able to make the needed calculations and to anticipate the future tax payments that would fall on them when the public debt was to be repaid (see the reference to Pareto in Tanzi, 2000a, p. 1).

Robert Barro had resuscitated the Ricardian Equivalence hypothesis and, by giving it a rigorous, mathematical packaging, had made it look novel and more attractive for modern, mathematically inclined, but historically less-informed economists, who believed in rational behavior. In a period when economists had great faith in the rationality of individuals' behavior, and when mathematics had made old hypotheses look "scientific" and believable, the Ricardian Equivalence hypothesis had acquired more plausibility and had been given a central role in much academic work in macroeconomics, in the latter part of the 1970s and especially in the 1980s.

That was a period when public debt was rising rapidly in many countries including the United States and had started to raise concerns in the minds of some observers including James Buchanan. For example, in the early 1980s, a speech given by Jacques de Larosiere, then the managing director of the IMF, at the Annual Congress of the International Institute of Public Finance in Innsbruck, Austria, in which he had called attention to the danger of the fast growth of public debt in several countries, had attracted a lot of media attention.

In the 1970s some economists had also started paying more attention to the writings of economists of the Austrian School, and especially to those of Hayek, von Mises, and other major economists of that school. Some of Hayek's work had originally been published in the United States, where he had spent many years teaching at the University of Chicago. His work would attract particular attention in libertarian circles and, in 1974, would earn him the Nobel Prize in economics, a prize that, interestingly, he would share with Myrdal, the Swedish economist who, with his wife, had been one of the major architects of the welfare states' policies in the Scandinavian countries, policies that had not been welcomed by Hayek. It must have been a clever diplomatic decision on the part of the Nobel Prize committee to share the prize between these two famous and well-deserving economists who had sharply contrasting views on the economic role of the state, at a time when it was still not clear in which direction the world would move in the future.

Austrian economists, and especially Hayek and von Mises, had been early critics of the Keynesian theories on stabilization and had also been skeptics of some of the benefits that many liberal economists expected from the growing spending role of governments. In the 1950s and 1960s, when the enthusiasm for the Keynesian Revolution and for welfare states had reached the peak, the works of these economists had attracted less attention than they would, starting in the 1970s.

In the second half of the 1970s, after he received the Nobel Prize, Hayek's work would attract a large following. Of particular importance would be the fact that Hayek's work had attracted the attention of a major and influential political admirer in Margaret Thatcher (see Ebenstein, 2001, chapter 37; Wapshott, 2011, chapter 16). This politically influential admirer would guarantee that Hayek's work would have political repercussions in future years and would acquire important international popular appeal.

Some economists and political scientists realized that, as had been widely assumed to be the case for markets, especially in the 1950s and 1960s, governments could also fail in various systematic ways, in addition to failures connected with honest, but random, mistakes. These economists started looking for categories of *government failures*, as economists had done for *market failures* in the 1940s and 1950s. The idea that governments could fail was not as new as it might have seemed. It had in fact been central to laissez faire. However, it had been largely ignored in the early decades after World War II.

With some obvious variation due to the different political and institutional context, it was a view that had prevailed for much of the nineteenth century, and it had been reflected, to a large extent, in the Italian economic literature of that period, in the aforementioned Scienza delle Finanze. Among other contributions, that literature had developed the already-mentioned concept of *fiscal illusions*, illusions created by governments to misguide or fool citizens and to induce them to back particular policies. The Italian School had also classified governments into three basic categories: monopolistic, individualistic, and paternalistic (see Tanzi, 2000a, chapter 1).

The *individualistic* category was the one closest to the view assumed by the normative role of the state. The *paternalistic* view would have more in common with what could be called a *tutorial role* of the state, which is a role now pushed by various economists associated with experimental or behavioral economics that uses *nudges* to help individuals make better decisions (see Thaler and Sunstein, 2008). All of those categories, to some extent, rejected the laissez-faire view of the government role that, in some not always correct interpretations, implied that the government should minimize its role in the economy and just let the "invisible hand" do its miraculous work.

According to some historians, the concept of *laissez-faire*, which had come to play such a large role in classical economics and which, in modern versions, would return to play a growing role in the 1980s and 1990s, had been promoted in the nineteenth century not so much as an ideology that espoused the ability and the innate virtue of the free market to achieve desirable outcomes, as many economists had come to believe, but more as a view that reflected the lack of trust that people had at that time in the ability of governments to solve problems with their interventions. If the government was not able to solve problems, it was better if it did not even try to.

The view that a free and unregulated market economy can perform economic miracles is a relatively recent one, in spite of the frequent references to Adam Smith's *invisible hand* over the years. On this important but rarely acknowledged point, it may be worthwhile to cite from an important historical book that discussed in great detail various reforms introduced in the nineteenth century in the United Kingdom. As the author of that book put it:

> A great deal of the talk about *laissez faire* [in the nineteenth century] must be discounted, or at least put into its proper context. In many cases the argument concealed an admission that a problem was insoluble, or that it must be endured, because no one could think of any method of solving it. From this point of view, the policy of *laissez faire* was not the result of a new and optimistic belief in the progress of society through private enterprise. It was rather an acknowledgement that the fund of skill and experience at the service of society was limited, and that, in the management of their common affairs, men would not be able to find the elasticity and adaptiveness [sic] which individuals showed in devising schemes for their own self-interest. The treatment of social and economic questions was more haphazard and empirical than Englishmen were ready to acknowledge. If a practical solution suggested itself, if a tentative experiment could be made, the doctrine of *laissez faire* would be thrust aside, only to be used again after another failure to discover the way out of a difficulty (Woodward, [1938] 1962, p. 16).

This implies that laissez-faire was a kind of frequent, second best approach to be used when what might have been the first best was not expected to be feasible.

Interestingly, Woodward attributed the failures of governments in nineteenth-century England mostly to limited *administrative* capability and not to biases by, or malevolence of, policymakers. He stressed that "there were no properly constituted [public] bodies to provide a substitute for the older mechanism of state regulation. The civil service was small in numbers, limited in function to the executive work of the great departments, and recruited entirely by patronage" (ibid., p. 17). This is an important point that is often ignored. It should be added that laissez-faire was not exactly popular. As an other prominent British historian, G. M. Trevelyan, would put it: "the Industrial Revolution [had] destroyed [Apprendship] …, and [had] substituted [it] with a laissez-faire chaos" (1942, p. 192). He would add that "…Discontent with the spirit of laissez-faire had been growing long before the death of John Stuart Mill in 1873" (p. 558). [Mill] 'had urged the better distribution of wealth by direct taxation, particularly taxes on inheritance; the bettering of conditions of life by social legislation enforced by an effective bureacray...'". (Ibid.) Mill was also in favour of "a complete system of manhood and womanhood suffrage..." and thought that "democracy and bureaucracy were to work together... (p. 558). Pressures for a state with more efficient bureacrats were clearly growing. The bureaucratic state would precede the spending state. Those pressures to create more bureaucratic ability by governments are described in Bayly, 2004, pp. 271–281.

By the second half of the twentieth century, the *administrative capacity* of governments would increase a great deal in many countries, because of the larger numbers of employees recruited in the public administrations and because of the better training and education of those who were hired. Max Weber–type administrators had replaced, to a large extent, the ones recruited by patronage. A presumably competent bureaucratic apparatus had become available for governments to rely upon and for the administration of more efficient and more ambitious policies. The new administrators at that time enjoyed high prestige and social status.

Various public bodies with specific responsibilities had also come into existence. In addition, more precise rules had been created to guide their work activities. Therefore, the government could be expected and could be entrusted to do more than it had in the past. It could be argued that if government failures persist today, they must be attributed to other causes than "limited administrative capability," while the market may still not be able to solve particular social problems through its own operation.

In the United States, an important change that has attracted relatively little attention came during the years of the New Deal when thousands of administrators, including a large number of economists, were hired by the federal government (see Fogel, 2000). As Fogel put it, "Roosevelt established a 'brain trust' of academic specialists to advise him on economic and social policies" (ibid., p. 129). "There [had been] little demand for these specialists in Washington until the onset of the Great Depression" (ibid., p. 130). This was not surprising due to the fact that the budget of the federal government until that time had been less than 3 percent of the US GDP. As Fogel put it:

> There were hardly a hundred economists employed by the federal government in 1931, even if one counted statistical clerks. By 1938 ... the number ... had risen to five thousand. Today [2000] that number stands at over twenty thousand" (ibid., p. 130).

This is a clear indication of the complementarity of policies and institutions. The New Deal not only changed policies in the United States, but it also created some of the conditions that made possible the change in policies. And Kennedy would bring to Washington "the best and the brightest". In some European countries, such as France and Germany, the increase in administrative capability had come earlier than in the United States.

Although it may be seen as an obvious observation, it should be stressed that the efficient use of an active fiscal policy requires several ingredients. They include: (a) policy decisions made by benevolent, informed, and competent policymakers; (b) financial resources needed to finance policies that require spending; (c) capable human resources to implement and monitor the public programs; (d) public institutions to carry out the policy decisions; and, finally, (e) rules to guide and (when necessary) limit the actions of policymakers and public administrators. When any of these ingredients is missing, fiscal policy is less likely to be able to deliver the hoped-for results. Some have observed that in recent years the number of public administrators has generally fallen in the United States and in other countries and possibly their ability has fallen because of higher paying jobs in private sectors' jobs.

CHAPTER 7

General Rules to Guide Governments

Besides being influenced by the quality and number of public administrators, the role played by governments is also much influenced by "a calculable legal system and of administration in terms of formal rules. Without it *adventurous and speculative trading capitalism* and all sorts of politically determined capitalisms are possible" (Weber, 1958, p. 25; italics added). Thus, sufficient and competent administrators, good institutions, good laws, and formal and informal rules and norms are all essential elements for a *well-working government*, even though they may not always be sufficient. As the recent and ongoing debate on developments in Greece and in other member countries of the European Monetary Union has highlighted, the absence, or the nonobservance, of good rules can create difficulties for the role that the government plays in a market economy (see Tanzi, 2013b).

The government failures that (especially) critics from the School of Public Choice and the Austrian School (and to some extent those of the Chicago School) believe to be natural are, in part, of a different nature than the failures caused by an absence of competent administrators. They attribute the failures not so much to the low quality of the employees in the public administration, but to more fundamental issues that could not be corrected by simply hiring more and better-trained administrative staff.

Weak institutions and unclear or poor rules within the public sector; specific attitudes and biases on the part of policymakers and high-level bureaucrats; pressures coming from powerful vested interests; rent-seeking in different parts of the public sector; increasing corruption and governance problems in general, at both the administrative and the political level; and, in more recent years, new problems that have become intrinsically more difficult to solve, due to the fact that markets have become more complex, public sectors have become larger and more difficult to control, and some problems have become global – all of these concerns are making government failures more likely, even with much improved national, public administrations. The failures may also have become more damaging in their consequences.

Rules, especially those related to fiscal and monetary policies, had not been given great importance by Keynesian economists, at a time when governments were seen by many as benevolent and knowledgeable. Rules that would limit the discretion of policymakers to act in these areas – for example, a balanced-budget rule, a limit on public debt or public spending, or a rule to keep the discount rate at a constant real level, or one that instructed the central bank to increase the money supply at a constant rate – discretion that Keynesians had considered desirable for promoting good stabilization policies, started to be considered appealing by some economists (including Buchanan and Friedman) and by some political scientists. The reason for this change was that discretion makes it easier for politicians to increase public spending by more than they should; to give tax incentives to enterprises and individuals; to promote easier monetary and fiscal policies to win elections; or to favor particular groups, including themselves, rather than to promote the public interest, however defined.

When good rules are absent, or when precise and transparent rules are not observed, some version of what, today, is called "crony capitalism" can make its appearance, as had been recognized by Max Weber a long time ago. Without good rules, we can have a modern version of the mercantilism that Adam Smith had criticized three centuries ago and that exists today in more subtle ways. That version essentially assigns some but at times non transparent monopolistic power to some privileged groups or individuals. In later chapters we shall provide various examples. Naturally, not all rules are good rules, and bad rules can in some cases create more difficulties than the absence of rules would create.

Keynesian policies can lend themselves easily to abuse by governments that are not fully responsible or are not fully benevolent. The pursuit of, and the importance given to, short run objectives, another approach that characterizes Keynesian stabilization policies, often contributes to creating, or to aggravating, long run problems. As Milton Friedman commented at one time, a bit sarcastically, on Keynesianism, "What a wonderful prescription: for consumers, spend more out of your income, and your income will rise; for governments, spend more, and aggregate income will rise by a multiple of your additional spending; tax less, and consumers will spend more with the same result" (cited in Wapshott, 2011, p. 249).

A world like that would indeed be a nice one to live in. It is a world that some highly vocal economists continue to believe exists today. On the short run objective of Keynesian stabilization policies, and on the often-cited statement by Keynes that we should focus on the short run, because "in the long run we are all dead," it may be worthwhile to cite von Mises's reaction. He wrote that the trouble with that Keynesian view is that "nearly all of us outlive the short run and ... spend decades paying for the easy money orgy of a few years" (Von Mises, 2005, p.130). Over the years, several governments have discovered the truth behind von Mises's observation.

Some discussions, promoted especially by James Buchanan and his collaborators, and, to some extent, independently by Mancur Olson (1965), were initiated in the 1960s on the role of fiscal institutions in determining policy outcomes, and on the need for rules that would reduce the policy discretion that policymakers have when they make policy decisions. This, to some extent, is the problem of dealing with "soft budgets." As mentioned earlier, the need to have some rules had been recognized for a long time by writers including David Hume, Max Weber., and others.

Keynesian economists, including, prominently, Paul Samuelson, had considered *discretion* an important *asset* for policymakers to have in the pursuit of countercyclical policy, because it allowed them to react quickly, easily, and sufficiently to economic crises. The proposal mentioned earlier, made in the 1962 *Economic Report of the President*, to give the president of the United States the discretion to change, at his own initiative, the tax rates, or the public spending on capital projects, was a manifestation of the merit attributed to discretion by Keynesian economists. It should be recalled that prominent Keynesian economists, including Paul Samuelson, had contributed to the writing of that *Report*.

However, as time passed, an increasing number of economists started to see discretion not as an *asset* but as a significant *liability*, because it allowed nonbenevolent or less-benevolent governments, headed by policymakers who did not have the interest of *all* the citizens (the public interest) as the main goal of their policies, to take policy actions that were nonoptimal and that could be potentially damaging. It allowed governments to give more weight to short run policies, with the objective of winning elections, rather than to policies more likely to promote the public welfare over the longer run.

Starting especially in the 1970s, there were increasing calls for fiscal rules, rules that would limit the actions of policymakers, thus preventing lax fiscal policies from being introduced. A few countries, such as Switzerland, already had rules in their constitutions that constrained fiscal actions. Some of the new rules called for "fiscal responsibility laws," and some countries started introducing them. James Buchanan, in particular, had been critical of the fiscal deficits that had characterized the Reagan years, which had contributed to increasing the debt level significantly in just a few years in the first half of the 1980s. The increase in the cost of servicing the public debt had also been caused by the sharp rise in the real interest rates that had occurred during the early 1980s, when the Federal Reserve had tried to reduce the high rate of inflation.

On the aforementioned issue Buchanan's views had diverged significantly from those of Friedman, who seemed to be less worried by the fiscal deficits and more by the growth of *primary* public spending. Some conservative politicians in the United States have continued over the years to be less concerned by fiscal deficits when they were caused by tax reductions. They believed that the deficits would finance themselves over the longer run, because the tax reductions would promote faster growth. Some still believe in this outcome.

If rules were needed, the choice could be to create new ones, or to make existing constitutional rules more constraining. The economic implications of constitutional rules attracted attention. Buchanan and Tullock (1962), as well as Francesco Forte (1998) and other members of the School of Public Choice, argued that government failure was to be expected when rules were flexible; when there were no rules; or when institutional arrangements made it possible for politicians to promote their personal interests or the interests of their clienteles. They believed that only clear and strict rules, for example, a balanced-budget rule, or specific limits on public spending levels or public debt, could constrain the degrees of freedom that politicians enjoyed and that often led to bad policies.

For members of the School of Public Choice, the main problem is less the honesty of the policymakers or the technical competence of the public employees, and more the fact that policymakers often face little or less-effective constraints on what they do. Without constraints, policymakers and public administrators are likely to follow their biases and their self–interest. Buchanan stressed that politicians essentially operate in a political market, and, like consumers in the economic market, they try to maximize their welfare in that market. This literature justified fiscal rules and contributed to their introduction in several countries. It probably influenced the rules that were created for the European Monetary Union when it was established.

In recent decades many countries have created *fiscal councils*, public institutions that are expected to promote more discipline and better-informed fiscal policies aimed at preventing the rise of potentially damaging or unsustainable public debts. Other countries have passed "fiscal responsibility laws." In the United States the nonpartisan Congressional Budget Office was created to provide guidance to policymakers and objective warnings on fiscal policy (see the papers in Kopits, 2013).

Balanced-budget rules had been introduced at the state level in the United States in the middle of the nineteenth century, after some bad fiscal performances by various states. These rules have been credited with having helped limit the public debts of the American states. However, the balanced-budget rules have not been adopted at the federal level, which has been accumulating a growing and increasingly worrisome and potentially unsustainable public debt. They also have not prevented the rise of growing implicit liabilities associated especially with unfunded defined-benefit pensions.

Some countries have introduced rules that have stressed the need to balance the budget, but that often do not require the countries to actually balance the budget every year (see, inter alia, Kopits, 2013; Poterba and von Hagen, 1999). There is also the important problem that a balanced budget can have different meanings, because there are technical difficulties in determining when an annual budget is truly balanced (see Irwin, 2012). A public budget can also be balanced at a tax level that is so high that over the longer run it is likely to be damaging to the economy. For this reason some countries have preferred to put limits on the level of public spending as a share of GDP.

Government mistakes become more frequent and possibly more damaging when: (a) the involvement of politicians in the economy becomes more pronounced and more frequent; (b) policymakers are not constrained by precise rules or by limiting institutions, such as political constitutions or powerful fiscal councils; (c) the bureaucracies do not act in the proper, efficient, and *ideal* ways, theorized by Max Weber; (d) the growth of government has significantly reduced the role of the market; (e) there are many areas of contact between public-sector and private-sector activities, so that joint decisions are required for some actions; and (f) policies become so complex that it is difficult for the policymakers to fully comprehend and control the policies they must decide upon.

The conclusion from this discussion is that there may be both political and administrative government failures, in addition to those due to adherence to misguided ideologies and, occasionally, due to honest mistakes. These failures are likely to grow when public sectors become larger and especially when policies and institutions become more complex.

The socialist ideology that, for a long time, directly or indirectly influenced the thinking and the actions of many politicians, especially in

European countries, contributed to some of the economic problems. With time, and also with the disappointing economic performance of the Soviet Union, especially in later years, and its final collapse at the end of the 1980s, the influence of socialist thinking and of forms of central planning diminished significantly, although it never completely disappeared. The termites created by socialist thinking took refuge in the woodwork, waiting for a better time to reemerge, when the new generations had forgotten or had not been aware of the past experiences with that thinking. For example, the push to nationalize important sectors of the economy (sectors that had been called the "commanding heights" of an economy) that had characterized the period during or immediately after World War II has largely disappeared in recent decades, but it may return. In the United Kingdom the leader of a major party has recently resuscitated the idea.

Some aspects of that thinking have continued to influence the governments of some countries to this day, especially in the use of regulations and in the support given to some sectors and enterprises, especially enterprises that, at times, are considered "national champions." That support is not always provided in transparent, explicit ways, as it was in the past. In recent years some countries have seen the resurgence of socialist parties in reaction to what are seen as failures of the market. In other countries, including the United States, populism and protectionism have attracted a significant following. If this trend continues, future years may bring some unpleasant surprises.

In the 1970s, problems associated with the fast growth of public spending in many countries and with the accompanying growth in tax levels started to worry an increasing number of economists and made them look more carefully than they had in the past for possible disincentive effects of some of the policies that the countries had been pursuing. This occurred at a time when a process of globalization had started to affect the economies of several countries, making efficiency a more important objective for economic policy. These worries contributed to the progressive change in the intellectual climate that had dominated the previous, postwar decades. They contributed to making more respectable and more worthy of attention a different perspective than the one that had prevailed until then. It was a new perspective that favored a reduced government role in the economy, lower tax rates, and fewer regulations. In some sense it was a return to some of the policies associated with laissez-faire, but in the presence of a larger government role.

As mentioned, in earlier years most economists had paid little attention to the disincentive effects of high tax rates and of some government programs. They had assumed that, if they existed, these disincentive were not significant. The discovery of what were believed to be significant disincentives connected with high tax rates led to an almost revolutionary change in thinking that brought the *supply-side revolution*. A politically significant part of that revolution was the *Laffer curve*, a presumably important economic relationship that was assumed to exist between tax rates and effort and output. That curve would be used by conservative economists and politicians to press for major future reductions in tax rates and in tax levels.

CHAPTER 8

Giving Markets More Freedom

The so-called supply-side revolution, which had rediscovered and reintroduced the role of the supply side of the economy in economic performance, and its implications for economic policies directed at long run growth, arrived in full force toward the end of the 1970s. It was a "revolution" that would influence, or even dominate, economic thinking and economic policy in some important countries, especially the United States and the United Kingdom, for the following three decades, until the arrival of the financial crisis and the Great Recession of 2007–2008. The latter would again shift, for a while the attention of many economists and policymakers back toward policies directed mainly at stimulating aggregate demand.

As mentioned, a popular aspect of the supply-side revolution that would attract a lot of popular and political attention was the "Laffer curve" (see Tanzi, 2014a, for a recent evaluation). The Laffer curve became an article of faith for conservative politicians in the United States, and created strong pressures on governments to reduce tax rates and to institute what came to be called "dynamic scoring" of policies, a process that would contribute to complicating the analysis of tax policies and that at times would make fiscal deficits seem almost virtuous when they were associated with tax cuts. Thus, the world went from the *virtuous* spending increases of Keynesian economics to the *virtuous* tax reductions of supply-side economics. Especially in the United States, some conservative politicians became convinced that tax cuts *always* financed themselves. Some went from the extreme Keynesian view, that higher spending would solve many economic problems, to one that supposed tax cuts would be the solution to many problems. The combination of the assumed impact of the Laffer curve on economic incentives and the concerns about the impact of globalization on taxes on capital incomes set the stage for a frontal attack on the existing tax structures, as I shall describe in a later chapter.

In some important countries, and especially in the United States and the United Kingdom, the change in the intellectual landscape created opportunities for articulate and conservative politicians to acquire a large following, among ordinary citizens who had become disenchanted with, and critical of, ongoing pro-government policies. A combination of high tax rates, politically questionable spending programs, the power of labor unions, and the increasing number of new regulations contributed to this disenchantment, as did well-publicized stories about abuses of programs on the part of some of those who received government benefits. In the mind of many observers, the government had become a problem. That combination made it possible for conservative politicians to win elections. In the years that followed, this happened in the United Kingdom and the United States, as well as in Australia, New Zealand, Ireland, Canada, and, perhaps, even Italy in 1994.

New Zealand became an early example, or a pilot project, of daring and radical changes in economic policies. In 1993, the policies of that country led the British magazine *The Economist* to comment that, "During the past decade New Zealand has implemented free-market reforms more radical than any other industrial country's." In several areas, that country had become a pilot project for conservative economic policies. Unfortunately, those policies did not seem to have the expected and hoped-for impact on the country's rate of growth. For a highly critical evaluation of that experiment see Jane Kelsey (1995).

New pro-market, conservative, and articulate leaders, especially Margaret Thatcher in the United Kingdom and Ronald Reagan in the United States, helped promote the view that, when governments increase excessively their involvement in the economy, they become problems, rather than solutions to problems. As Reagan put it, in an expression that became memorable, "the most terrifying words in the English language are 'I am from the government, and I am here to help.'" These political leaders managed to reduce (or, at least, to slow down) the growth of regulations and public spending. They also significantly and importantly reduced marginal tax rates. With the "fundamental tax reform" of 1986, President Reagan reduced the marginal tax rate for the US federal income tax from 70 percent, when he came into office, to 28 percent, after the reform. This reduction in the tax rates influenced other countries and set the stage for global rate reductions (see Tanzi, 1987a). Thatcher eliminated many of the tax incentives for enterprises in the United Kingdom.

These political leaders were less successful in reducing the levels of public spending, or the fiscal deficits, while they succeeded in promoting the return to a greater faith in the role of private markets. For information on the failure to reduce public spending in the United States, see Tanner

(2007). It was a faith in a market in which governments: (a) had more indirect controls than they had had in the second half of the nineteenth century, the period when the laissez-faire ideology had reigned; (b) had more efficient public administrations; and (c) taxed and spent a significantly higher share of GDPs than they had in the nineteenth century. The governments were thus able to still significantly influence the lives of citizens and the operations of the market, through manipulation of the level and the composition of public spending, as well as the level and the structure of taxes; through regulations and authorizations; and through monetary policies that in time (with Quantitative Easing policies of later years) would come to resemble and even to some extent replace fiscal policies.

The return of faith in the free operations of the market economy contributed to creating, in conservative circles and among an increasing number of economists, an almost ethical or religious belief that the market could not be wrong, that its results were always legitimate, and that it did not need to be (much) regulated, because it was able to regulate itself. The affinity of this view with religious beliefs merited the term that came to describe it: "market fundamentalism." Fundamentalism can come in many colors and shapes!

An implication of this view was that, if the government would just stay out of the way and let the market do its work, it would promote efficiency and would not make mistakes. The higher economic growth that it would generate would help solve many social problems, thus making it possible to reduce the social and redistributive role of the state. Everybody would benefit, and those who did not were probably for the most part individuals who suffered from personal shortcomings, including lack of ambition and incentives. Some attributed the status of those who failed to basic laziness, encouraged by the existence of public programs that made failure more easily tolerable.

This attitude was in some sense different from the view, described in an earlier chapter, that had prevailed in the nineteenth century, that the government would simply not be able, for administrative or institutional reasons, to promote good policies, so it was better if it did not intervene and *let it be, laissez-faire*. Rather, it was based on an almost religious faith in the intrinsic virtue of free markets to solve problems. It was as if a benevolent God had created the free market to do His work on earth. Thus, to some extent, the religion that Keynes had found in 1925 in Russia, socialism, or that dedicated Keynesians had found in the Keynesian policies of the 1950s came to be replaced by a different but similar kind of religion, *faith in the free market*.

This new orthodoxy emanated especially from the University of Chicago and from some other intellectual, libertarian, or conservative centers, including some leading "think tanks," both in the United States and abroad, especially starting in the 1970s, although, as mentioned earlier, institutions such as the American Enterprise Institute in Washington, the Institute of Economic Affairs in London, and some other centers in Switzerland, Austria, Canada and other places had been operating and promoting faith in the market well before that time.

For some economists, including a few who would win Nobel Prizes in economics, the religion of market fundamentalism was based on highly theoretical and abstract economic analyses, at times undertaken by individuals who were able to use advanced mathematical tools. See Romer (2015) for a criticism of what he has called "mathism," or the excessive dependency on the part of some economists on the economic results from essentially mathematical analyses. In spite of their rigor and their elegance, these analyses inevitably ignored the fact that market operators do not always behave according to precise mathematical assumptions, or according to rational and honest behavior. These analyses tended to ignore the role that human nature plays, in often complex ways, in the operations of markets. They also ignored the role that random events play, as some writers have stressed (see Taleb, 2007). The question remains whether these events are truly random, or whether they were simply ignored but could have been anticipated, as some economists have argued to have been the case for the recent financial crisis. An anticipation, or a prediction, of the financial crisis, attributed to the increasing complexity of the financial market, can be found in Tanzi (2007a).

Whether one likes it or not, some humans are *not honest*, as the world has always known, and as Adam Smith was well aware three centuries ago. If they were honest, there would not have been a need for God to issue the guidelines of the Ten Commandments. Some humans are *not rational*, as some psychologists – especially Daniel Kahneman, who received the Nobel Prize in economics for his economically relevant psychological work – and as some economists have shown in recent years (see Kahneman, 1994; Kahneman and Thaler, 2006; Ariely, 2008; Thaler and Sunstein, 2008; Lewis, 2017). Also, unexpected "black swans," statistically improbable events that tend to be ignored because they are rare, make occasional, unexpected, and unwelcome visits (see Taleb, 2007).

Furthermore, in increasingly common, real-life settings, some market operators may acquire so much space in the economy, and implicit monopoly power, that they may come to believe that, if things go badly in some of their market operations, the government will be forced to come to their rescue. This belief may encourage them to take more risks than they would or should have taken otherwise. This is now believed to happen when some financial institutions, and especially some banks, become "too big to fail" (see Shiller, 2000; Lowenstein, 2000). Some operators may simply not be as well informed as they believe they are when they make investments, and these errors may not be completely random. Some may underestimate the risks they are taking, or believe that they are nimble enough to outrun potential bad events. This may happen when there is a secondary market for bonds that allows some, who believe they are better informed than others, to download bonds before future increases in interest rates. Some may take actions that come close to being illegal, but without formally and explicitly crossing the forbidden lines.

The combination of the aforementioned factors is not likely to lead to a world in which there is no need for an authority to act as an impartial and occasionally compassionate referee, or to establish rules aimed at encouraging good behavior. Whether the authority will always be impartial, whether the rules that it will establish are good rules, and whether there will be too many rules are, of course, different and more difficult questions to answer than the question of whether the market needs some rules.

Belief in market fundamentalism and the new, pro-market thinking of the 1980s and 1990s, until the financial crisis of 2007, became widely shared by economists and by market operators. They contributed to promoting the view, endorsed by some policymakers, that governments should minimize their interference in the market and should reduce their economic role to an absolute minimum. This led to the reduction in the number of regulations on some parts of the market, and especially on the financial market; to the reduction of tax rates; to the privatization of some public enterprises and the outsourcing of many government activities; and to a greater acceptance of the results of the market in terms of income outcomes. Many came to believe that this libertarian route would lead to a better and more prosperous future world.

Michael Sandel, the previously cited, influential political scientist and philosopher who teaches at Harvard, in his 2012 book argued that, because of the ideological push that it received from market fundamentalists, the market stopped being just a highly useful and efficient instrument for facilitating economic exchanges among individuals and for coordinating *economic* activities, which it undoubtedly is. Rather, it came to be seen as being also an *ethical* framework for guiding general behavior in society. This was a fundamental change.

Society moved in the direction of becoming a *market-ruled society*, rather than a *community of individuals* who would give importance to various nonmarket exchanges among its members, and in which money should not play a dominant role in *some* relations. A society in which *all* relations are characterized by and valued by exchanges of money ends up giving more power and more leverage to those who have more money, even in areas in which they should not have more power, including, for example, politics or access to human organs. Such a society ceases to have the characteristics of a community but becomes an aggregation of disconnected individuals. As a result, it ceases to be a society of equals.

Sandel argued that an increasing number of what had been relations and exchanges among individuals, exchanges that had taken place *outside* the market and that had been guided by implicit, traditional rules and values that had developed in true communities over many years, have been progressively pushed into the market. For example, one may no longer send Christmas wishes to friends and relatives but may send a list of addresses to a private company that, for a fee, sends cards or messages to one's friends and relatives. This behavior implies that the market has replaced personal relations and has acquired an ethical value or a role that it had not had previously and that it should not have.

In another example, also mentioned by Sandel, one may no longer give flowers or specific gifts for anniversaries, but instead give money or a gift card. This behavior follows the conclusion reached by economic theory, that $100 in cash is always more valuable (or is at least equally valuable in the market) than a specific gift worth $100. In terms of purchasing power this conclusion is clearly correct, but one feels that something is amiss. For example, one does not donate blood or kidneys; one sells them. Sandel's point bears some relationship to comments made by Pope Francis, elaborated in his 2015 encyclical letter, *Laudato Si'*. On the other hand, see Nordhaus (2015) for an economically based criticism of some of the pope's views on how to deal with global warming.

Influenced by the new economic thinking, several governments moved in the previously reported, more pro-market direction, especially in the 1990s, when a related movement, called "Washington Consensus," mainly directed at developing countries, acquired some influence. Perhaps stretching a little, the Washington Consensus could be considered a stepchild of the supply-side revolution because it also stressed the importance of the supply side of the economy and of the market. That thinking influenced also developments then underway in the economies of countries that were moving from central planning to markets, especially in Eastern Europe (see Tanzi, 2010a).

The main refrain at that time became "the market will do it." In the financial market, some of the regulations were removed that had been introduced in the United States by the Roosevelt administration in the 1930s, during the years of the Great Depression, to reduce risks and abuses in the banking sector. Some questionable activities that had not been tolerated in the past were allowed. Some exchanges that had not been market exchanges became market exchanges, and money came to play a larger role than it had had in political elections and also in the market of ideas, as the activities of many think tanks came to be influenced by those who financed them.

Astronomical salaries and bonuses started to be paid to some of those who operated in the financial market, managed enterprises, or operated in particular market sectors. The prevailing view became that economic success is always associated with greater effort and greater talent, and that luck or other factors play no or marginal roles. Higher money compensation attracts to particular activities the more talented and the hardest working individuals. Therefore, it was no longer embarrassing for an individual to receive million- (or even billion-) dollar incomes and large bonuses, as it might have been in the 1950s and 1960s, even when the enterprises in which they operated performed badly (see Tanzi, 2012, for some specific examples).

Million-dollar bonuses and salaries came to be seen as normal and ethically justified compensations for the presumed superior contributions that some people were making to economic "value." If a free and presumably well-working market allowed these salaries and these bonuses to be paid, they must have been legitimately earned, and thus justified. This behavior spread to other roles (such as college administrators, presidents of museums, managers of large charities, coaches of sport teams in colleges, and so on). Large compensation for managers became common, and the payment of this compensation was often financed by reducing the compensation of dependent workers whose bargaining power had been reduced by globalization and by the weakening of labor unions.

The ratio between the compensation of the managers of corporations and the average compensation of workers, a ratio that the first Nobel Prize winner in economics, Tinbergen, had considered normal when it was about 5:1, and that the famed management expert Peter Drucker had advised should not exceed 20:1, rose to more than 300:1 in the United States These ratios of compensation were not questioned, because they were implicitly justified by the ethic of the market. If the market allowed them, the assumption was that they must have been earned, because they presumably reflected the value that those who received them had contributed or would contribute to the market. The market was the ultimate judge, and it was a judge that could not be wrong.

Interestingly, a sector that seemed to escape this trend was the public sector, where salaries remained relatively modest for those in the top positions, at least while the individuals remained in their public jobs. When they left their jobs, some became millionaires many times over within a few years. Obviously, the move to the private sector magically increased their productivity.

As I shall discuss in a later chapter, the incomes received were no longer subjected to the high marginal tax rates that they would have been subjected to until the early 1980s, because the view was that high tax rates rob individuals of their deserved compensation, in addition to creating negative incentives. An ethical argument had been combined with an efficiency argument to justify large reductions in marginal tax rates. That view came to be widely accepted, and high taxes came to be seen by some as thefts. Many economists had come to believe that the incentives of highly talented people would be significantly and negatively affected by high marginal tax rates and that, as a consequence, the operations of the market would suffer.

The growing disengagement of governments from some market activities in the 1990s and until the financial crisis, regardless of the merits of the specific policies followed, inevitably created more space for questionable or, at times, clearly dishonest behavior, and also for irrational acts by some market operators. Many of these questionable behaviors would be uncovered after the financial crisis, and they have continued to be uncovered on an almost daily basis since then. These acts played their nefarious roles in connection with the financial crisis that hit in 2007–2008; in the growth of corruption in recent years; in increasingly frequent reports of manipulation of financial and other markets; and in other manifestations. A recent development that has attracted a lot of media attention is the abuse of monopoly power by managers of some pharmaceutical enterprises in sharply increasing the prices of drugs that are essential for patients with particular illnesses. These price increases have been accompanied by large increases in the compensation of the managers of these enterprises.

In some cases, the government's disengagement from regulating the market created situations in which excessive risks were taken by some banks and other large financial institutions, with the implicit expectation that the gains from those risks would be privatized, while the losses, if they occurred, would be, in some ways, socialized, because of the impact that they might have on the economy if they were not.

The socialization of the losses incurred by some very large financial enterprises has, in fact, been justified (by those who made the decisions to help them) on the grounds that, without the government rescue, the economy would risk falling into a depression similar to or worse than the one in the 1930s. As the justifiers might put it, when a house is on fire, firefighters cannot worry about the moral hazard consequences of putting out the fire! Of course, these interpretations of what might have happened might be right or wrong, and we shall never know. The same argument will be offered in probable future crises, as long as the banks and the other financial institutions remain "too big to fail." See Bernanke (2015) and Geithner (2014) for a defense of the rescue operations in 2008–2009. See King (2016) for a more skeptical view.

Market capitalism was replaced, at least in some areas, by what some have called "casino capitalism" (see Sinn, 2010). In casino capitalism the government would allow gamblers to bet any amount, but it would assist them in case of losses, to prevent potentially bad social outcomes. Many recent books have dealt with this topic. Among them see Shiller (2008); Sinn (2010); Rajan (2010); Admati and Hellwig (2013); Miam and Sufi (2014); Lewis (2010); and Posner (2010).

While the 1970s witnessed some changes in intellectual winds that were less favorable to the larger economic roles of government, by the 1990s the pendulum had swung all the way toward a pro-market and more anti-government paradigm, at least in some countries and among an increasing number of economists. The pro-market thinking attracted not only academic economists but also influential policymakers, including, prominently, Alan Greenspan, who, at that time, was the powerful head of the Federal Reserve system, as well as some members of the Clinton administration, including to some extent Robert Rubin and Larry Summers (see Greenspan, 2004; Rubin and Weisberg, 2003).

During the second Bush administration, that thinking would influence the heads of regulatory commissions, such as the Securities and Exchange Commission (SEC) and others. It had generated the pro-market policies associated with the Washington Consensus. After twelve years of Republican administrations, the new Democratic president, Clinton, could declare that the "time of big government was over" and could get set to reform some welfare programs, reduce regulations, especially in the financial sector, and reduce some taxes by enacting more tax expenditures. Also, the number of federal employees in relation to the US population would shrink considerably, in part because there were fewer individuals in the military. Many members of the military personnel were replaced by private contractors, so the fighting of wars was in part privatized.

The economic thinking behind those policies influenced the policymakers of various developing and emerging markets and affected their policies on trade, financial liberalization, taxes, privatization of enterprises, and other areas (see Krueger, 2000). The rush to privatize enterprises in developing countries was accompanied by reports of corruption taking place in the process. Nobel Prizes were earned by economists who advocated policies that, in some ways, reflected modern versions of laissez-faire. It was another proof that the assignment of Nobel Prizes is inevitably influenced by the prevailing intellectual winds.

The "normative" role of the state – that government involvement in the economy is essentially one of correcting the market for "failures," including, for some economists and politicians, the "failure" of generating excessively uneven income distributions, high unemployment, and very high incomes for some individuals – was replaced, in the mind of a growing number of economists (among whom the most prominent and influential had been Milton Friedman, George Stigler, Robert Lucas, F. Hayek, James Buchanan, Gary Becker, and a few other winners of the Nobel Prize in economics), by a view that advocated a limited governmental role.

As we have seen earlier, it also gave a legitimate or almost ethical role to market outcomes, thus reducing the moral rationale for governmental intervention, as well as the rationale that had existed in the past for interpersonal, nonmoney exchanges based on traditional norms and community spirit. Interestingly, as mentioned, even heads of large charitable institutions, presidents of universities, and directors of museums started demanding and getting very high salaries. Clearly, at the top of the salary scale, a demonstration effect had started to operate. It would contribute to making the income distribution less even and, in the view of an increasing number of people, less equitable.

It came to be believed that only the market established the value of and the rewards for economic performances, and that those values and rewards should not be challenged. If an edge fund manager earned a billion dollars by placing a successful, or a lucky, bet, often with other peoples' money, he or she clearly deserved the gain. Furthermore, that income should not be taxed with high marginal rates, otherwise the manager's incentives (or luck) would be hurt and the market would suffer. If a CEO received an annual compensation that was 500 times that of the average worker in his/her enterprise, he or she deserved it. If the market was the judge, as it was argued, the earnings that it generated should not be challenged, and their levels could not justify governmental intervention with high marginal tax rates.

The results of the market, in terms of both the allocation of resources and the distribution of income, came to be seen as fully legitimate. They had acquired ethical values, and knowledgeable individuals should accept them, otherwise they might be accused of promoting "class warfare" and of wanting to limit the personal freedom of individuals, thus damaging the efficiency of the market.

The new ethic created by "market fundamentalism" reinforced the view that had prevailed during laissez-faire periods in the past, that *governments fail and make mistakes*, a view that was undoubtedly true. It also reinforced skepticism about the ability of governments to improve the welfare of the citizens with policies that might interfere with market decisions, as it could be argued many policies did to some extent. In this newly prevailing view, economic incentives were seen to play much more important roles than they had been thought to play in the past.

The view that the economic freedom of individuals should be given a lot more weight in economic policies also became more prevalent. There were frequent complaints about the extent to which governmental actions, especially regulations and taxes, were excessively and unnecessarily restraining the economic space and the freedom of individuals and enterprises. Some even dreamed of a world without government, without taxes, without regulations, and without official money. The "deconstruction of the administrative state" became a dream or a goal for some.

Until the financial crisis of 2007 and the Great Recession that followed, Keynesian, countercyclical fiscal policies had lost the academic appeal that they had acquired in the 1950s and the 1960s, especially during the long period of expansion that lasted until the financial crisis. On the other hand, monetary policy, which had been considered of marginal importance by Keynes and by the early Keynesians in pulling countries out of crises, became important. In the hand of "maestros," monetary policy could smooth out economic fluctuations and bring a "great moderation" in economic performances. It was given credit for having done that through the 1990s and the following decade, until the financial crisis.

Theoretical concepts, such as "rational expectations," "Ricardian Equivalence hypothesis," "efficient market hypothesis," and others, had been advanced by influential economists, especially in the 1970s and the 1980s, to challenge the Keynesian orthodoxy and the market interventions by governments. While psychologists (and a new, growing group of "experimental economists") were discovering irrationality in many of the actions of individuals, general, academic economists were giving more weight to rationality.

In academia, but less so in international institutions and in government circles, the pro-market thinking acquired many followers. It would lead to some reductions in the role that the state had been playing in the economy. These reductions would be especially important in some areas, such as the financial market, foreign trade, state ownership of enterprises, reliance on the private sector for building infrastructures (through "public-private partnerships"), and the increased support for outsourcing many public activities (including some related to security and the fighting of wars).

At the same time, there were increasing pressures on governments, and especially on the US government, to expand their protection of intellectual property in various forms that would lead to a growing number of time-limited monopolies. This protection of intellectual property became central in negotiating international trade agreements, where the role of the government was enthusiastically welcomed by some of the same individuals who complained about that role in other areas.

As mentioned earlier, one area where the new thinking was less successful was in reducing the level of public spending in some important countries. Inertia, the political difficulty of undoing past policies, as in pensions, the political support that some programs continued to receive from voting citizens, and what we have called "the law of expanding public spending" made it difficult, even for influential leaders such as Thatcher and Reagan, to cut spending significantly. However, the *rate of growth* in public spending was reduced, and, as mentioned earlier, some countries (Canada, Sweden, Norway, Ireland, the Netherlands, and some others) did reduce spending by significant amounts, but they often did it for macroeconomic reasons.

At times, the new thinking went too far, as, for example, when it asserted that the market required little monitoring and that market participants were essentially rational and law-abiding operators. Therefore, if left alone, the market would be able to deliver optimal results, not just in terms of efficiency but also in terms of social justice. This view reflected the one that had prevailed in the United States before the Great Depression. As a student of that earlier period had put it in describing it:

> Enlightened businessmen, they insisted, were developing a social conscience, a growing awareness of social problems and the need for remedial action; and since these people knew more about the business system than anyone else, business groups should be allowed to govern and discipline themselves with a minimum of government supervision" (Hawley, 1966, p. 8).

Similar claims have continued to be heard in recent years and have influenced recent election results.

Regulators were instructed to be less vigilant, more flexible and more accommodating, and, based on various media reports in several sectors, they seem to have followed those instructions, especially during the period that led to the financial crisis. Characteristics of human nature, such as greed and the desire to acquire wealth and other benefits, which could have been expected to make some individuals take advantage of opportunities that complex systems and economies offered (by skirting social norms and government rules), were ignored or minimized. In some cases, greed came to be advertised as a positive force for society, a force that presumably helped create market value. This leads to the question of what a minimum economic role for a state would look like in a modern economy. This more theoretical question is addressed briefly in the following chapter and is related to the dream of "deconstructing the administrative state."

CHAPTER 9

A Minimum Economic Role for the State?

Human beings are social animals. They socialize and aggregate in groups for the obvious reason that aggregation provides important benefits to the individuals in the groups. A human being in isolation, like Robinson Crusoe, would be like a fish out of water. He or she would not survive for long. Aggregation, which normally starts as extended families and which, in Rousseau's words (1983, p. 18), is "the prototype of political societies," leads progressively to the creation of larger communities. Communities facilitate social interactions and encourage economic exchanges with other members of the communities. They also require some exchanges between the individuals and the community as a whole.

Many readers of this book may be surprised to learn that, according to *Webster's Encyclopedic Unabridged Dictionary of the English Language*, the concept of "individualism," that is, "the doctrine or belief that all actions are determined by, or at least take place, for the benefit of the individual, not of society as a whole," did not appear until 1825–1835. The word originated in France and not in the writings of Adam Smith as some may believe. It was probably a result of the French Revolution. As Alexis de Tocqueville wrote in *Democracy in America*, "individualism is a recent term originating from a new idea. Our fathers had recognized that as egotism" (cited in Desiderio, 2003, p. 61; translation by author).

The idea that there exists an implicit social contract, a covenant, between the members of a community and the community as a whole (a kind of implicit contractual agreement between individuals, as individuals, and the community to which they belong) is an old idea that has influenced much political thinking on the role of governments and on the writing of constitutions (see Hobbes [1651] 1958, p. 139, and later Rousseau, 1983). It should be noted in this connection that, for a very long time in history, most individuals have, generally, been born into already existing and established communities. Therefore, they have not had the option of choosing the community in which they were born. As a consequence, some have been luckier than others, in being born in freer, better-organized, and richer communities. And some have been even luckier than others in being born not only in freer, better-organized, and richer communities, but also in wealthier and more influential families within those communities. The family and the country where a person is born remain the most important determinants or predictors of the economic and social life and status that a human being is likely to have. In both of these events, individuals, qua individuals, have no input. Those choices are made for them by fate, and they determine different starting points among individuals that are difficult or impossible for governments to equalize with their policies.

The community provides protection and some other kinds of benefits to its individual members, while the individual members have in turn some obligations toward the community, including that of providing financial support for communal activities, such as the provision of public goods, and that of behaving according to rules that the community has established. Those rules may not always be to the liking of particular individuals but must be respected.

The obligations that the individuals have toward the community and that are specified by the community rules, rules that may have existed even before the persons that make up the community were born, inevitably reduce some of their liberty as individuals. However, the obligations created by the community must be enforced, because, as Hobbes puts it, "covenants without the sword are but words, and of no strength to secure a man at all" ([1651] 1958, p. 139).

Whether the payments that the individuals make to the community (which can be in money or in other ways, including direct services) should be considered prices for the assistance and services that they receive from the communities is an important question. Whether those payments can be considered truly *voluntary* has been a controversial issue in the relevant public finance and political economy literature. In part the question depends on what the community does with the money and whether the individual has any say (and any influence) in the exchange and in the decisions on what to do with the money. In any case, even in democracies, the person's power is, or should be, limited to his or her vote. Some rather advanced societies (including the vast empire of the Incas in pre-Colombian America, an empire connected by a road network that was at least 25,000 miles long) did not have money or democratic institutions but had still developed advanced social institutions and, in some ways, could be included among advanced societies.

This issue becomes more controversial when the payments (the taxes paid) become high, and especially when a large part of the revenue is used by the community not to provide public services or public goods that all the members can enjoy, such as essential infrastructures and protection, but for redistributive purposes and for payments that benefit mainly only parts of the community. It is even more controversial when the receiving part of the community is ethnically different from the rest and when it is considered to be less hard working; or when part of the money is wasted or is pocketed by corrupt politicians, as happens in not too few cases.

The closer, *physically*, the members of the community are to one another, the more likely it will be that some of their actions will have the potential to create positive or negative effects on others, effects that economists call *externalities*. Density in living conditions tends to create more negative externalities. Insignificant or positive externalities can be ignored. However, when they become significant and are negative and damaging, they may require the community to step in and to establish community rules to deal with them. These rules are intended to benefit the community *as a whole*, and to avoid potential conflicts between community members. The rules that are created may be seen as *restricting the freedom* of some members of the community. Just consider speed limits for drivers! They restrict the freedom of those individuals who like to drive fast; and even more the freedom of rich individuals who drive BMWs or Ferraris.

Economic exchanges among the individuals of the community create markets. In turn the markets create additional needs for rules and for infrastructures. At some point, they also create the need for the establishment of particular institutions to monitor the application of the rules and to punish individuals who do not respect them. The economic activities of the individuals and the existence of markets encourage specialization on the part of individual members; and specialization makes individuals more productive in what they do, as Adam Smith pointed out a long time ago, with his example of the making of pins. Specialization also promotes more exchanges. If the exchanges are free and are accompanied by full information on both sides of the exchanging parties, on the value of what is being exchanged, they can be assumed to *always* increase welfare for those who participate in them. In these circumstances a good index of *development* might be the number of exchanges that take place in a community.

Initially, the exchanges are likely to take place within the community and among members of the community. They may involve barter and also exchanges of favors without money being used. Then, increasingly, they will involve more individuals and progressively individuals from other communities. They will also be facilitated by the use of money. With the passing of time, the exchanges are likely to become more formalized, requiring "trading posts" and "contracts" between the parties. The more distant (physically or socially) the individuals in a transaction are from each other, the greater will become the need for contracts. The contracts might initially follow implicit and informal rules, established by the participants over time. As the economies become more developed, and as the communities become larger, the contracts will tend to become more explicit, more detailed, more precise, and more formal, and they will require rules that may need to be supervised by independent private or public institutions.

Implicit, informal contracts prevail in primitive and less developed societies. These informal contracts continue to characterize many of the markets that one can observe in developing countries and, on weekends, in some areas of advanced countries. In these informal markets, when individuals engage in transactions, the buyers are more likely to know the sellers, or at least to be able to assess directly and to value correctly what they buy; or at least they can assess the risks associated with the exchange. In these circumstances exchanges can be assumed to be almost always welfare enhancing, because participants would not engage in them if they did not see a benefit in the exchange.

Explicit and more formal contracts become common and more necessary in developed and modern societies, especially when the communities become larger, the participants are more distant physically or socially from one another, and the items in the transactions become less standardized, more numerous, more complex, and more difficult to value a priori, *before* they are actually bought and used.

Increasingly, the exchanges take place between individuals who do not live in the same area and do not know each other, and the goods or the services exchanged are difficult to evaluate fully and correctly *until some time after* the transaction has taken place. In an increasing number of cases the exchanges take place between individuals who have not met and may never meet, and between real people and enterprises on one side and what seem to be virtual entities on the other.

In the exchanges in which the participants have full information on the products and services that are exchanged and on the parties in the exchanges, the contracts (or the exchanges) could generally be assumed not to require more than informal moral and social codes, or rules that develop spontaneously within the communities. In these circumstances the prices at which the exchanges take place tend to convey all or much of the needed information to the buyers. This is the world that Hayek described in his writings on the value and the role of markets. In these circumstances the prices also help coordinate the actions of producers (as sellers) and of consumers (as buyers). As Hayek pointed out, in these circumstances, the market will maximize the use of the knowledge that is available to all participants and that is dispersed among the many participants, to determine what is produced and consumed. Nobody needs to plan the production of the goods sold or to monitor the consumption of the goods bought. And nobody needs to regulate the market. There is no, or very little, need for the government to play a role.

As societies become more developed; as the exchanges concern more and more products and services that are not standard, that are new, and that are increasingly complex; when the exchanges are not frequent or repetitive (as was, for example, the buying of bread at the corner bakery) but concern the buying of tour packages from distant tour operators or complex medical procedures, the choosing of a college for a child or an insurance policy or a mortgage, or the purchase of home or car repair; and especially when the exchanges take place between individuals, on one side, and large distant enterprises, on the other, the exchanges begin to carry risks that are increasingly connected with potential asymmetry of information. Just think of the exchanges that took place in the housing market during the subprime period, when many buyers did not read or did not understand the fine print in their mortgage contracts, and those who provided mortgages could sell the mortgages to other financial institutions.

Some exchanges create a need for explicit and formal contracts, for example, the purchase of houses or cars, and, consequently, for institutions that regulate, register, and, when necessary, enforce the contracts. A world without such institutions is less likely to be a desirable world. The institutions can be private ones, but increasingly individuals and communities have preferred public ones. The argument that has been made by some economists, that the market is self-correcting, becomes less convincing in these cases. That argument contrasts with many real-life experiences and with daily reports of abuses in several areas, even in the presence of rules.

It could be maintained that the market is more likely to be self-correcting ex post, *after* some individuals have suffered losses or have been damaged by some exchanges, if those who have created the damage are somehow penalized and, as a category, they adjust their *future* behavior, because of the penalties or the economic costs incurred in terms of reputation. We all have occasionally bought "lemons," using Akerlof's terminology of a bad deal, or been cheated in some exchanges (see Akerlof, 1970).

In some cases the formal contracts themselves may become so complex and so difficult to read and understand that they create other forms of asymmetries in spite of the information that they contain. It is at times claimed that much of the needed information is in fact in the contracts, if one would just take the time to read the fine print carefully in an effort to understand it. The truth is that asymmetry in information can come in many different ways and can reflect varying degrees of transparency, or occasionally even differences in the timing of when the information is received by the two parties. The use of insider information often creates asymmetries in time that create advantage for one side of the exchange in the market.

As a basic right in market economies, individuals accumulate various kinds of personal assets. In the distant past the assets, or the properties, were exclusively *tangible* (land, tools, cattle, horses, houses, barns, ships, shops, gold). Strong doors, good locks, or occasionally private vigilance could help protect those assets. As the communities became more developed, assets or properties of an *intangible* or *intellectual* nature became increasingly more important. In many cases they came to constitute an increasing share of the total wealth of many individuals. This accumulation of personal assets (both tangible and intangible) created the need for their protection. In principle and for *tangible* property, this need could still be satisfied privately, by hiring private guards, by building protective walls, by having stronger doors and better locks, and so on. This is how this need was satisfied in the distant past, and how it is still satisfied to some extent today.

In the modern world, and especially for intellectual property and for wealth that is not *directly* and *physically* held by the owners (as is the case with shares in corporations, savings held in banks, government and corporate bonds, and/or wealth in *intangible capital* such as patents, copyrights, trademarks, and similar items), the protection is increasingly provided by the government, as an important service to the property owners. For the latter the government has become more important than it was in the past. In this connection it is useful to note that, while in centuries past much of the role of governments was directed toward the protection of *real* property, to the point that some had argued that this was the fundamental role of the state, in modern times the role of the state or government has been importantly directed to the protection of property not held directly and physically, including *intellectual* property. For example, trade agreements among countries are now often more connected with questions about the protection of intellectual capital by trading partners than with import duties. As I shall argue later, this fundamental change is likely to have had important consequences for the creation and distribution of income.

Individuals need to be protected against criminal elements within their groups, or against dangers that may come from outside the community. Economic development and especially globalization have made some criminal activities less local and more global. They have increased dangers that come from outside the community (see Tanzi, 2002). Therefore, any significant aggregation of individuals and any accumulation of property (whether tangible or intangible) require the existence of at least some rudimentary institutions (military, police, justice, patent system, etc.) that will perform the aforementioned functions. Therefore, the need to provide safety increases with greater development. Law and order are essential requirements of a minimal role of the state.

This kind of protection may be considered more important for individuals who have more to lose from criminal elements and who require more protection from the government. It is also more important for rich countries that require protection against invasion from poorer countries, or protection against illegal and unwanted immigrants. Both of these protections are likely to have higher values for individuals with higher incomes and more property.

Even though the laws or the constitutions of countries, such as the US Constitution, may state that all individuals are created equal, and that statement is often repeated ad nauseam, the reality is that the lives of high-income individuals have often been given higher economic values by economists, in economic analysis, and by the courts, in legal proceedings, than the lives of poor individuals. Nevertheless, protection against (local) crime is very important also for poorer individuals, because the places where they live tend to be more exposed to local criminal elements, and criminal activities can significantly restrict the liberty of movement for individuals who live in poorer communities. Therefore, the pursuit of individual liberty *for everyone* in democratic societies requires that governments pay attention to this problem. To do so, governments need financial resources and efficient rules and institutions.

Communities require some basic infrastructures, such as roads, canals, ports, airports, schools, waterworks, sewer systems, parks, and so on, to sustain economic activities and to increase the freedom of movement of individuals and their well-being. For various reasons, these infrastructures can in many cases be best provided collectively. In the past the provision of some of these infrastructures, together with defense spending, absorbed much of the public budget of countries. Today this spending accounts for a small share of total public spending, because governments have assumed obligations that they had not had in the past, and also because some have reduced spending for public infrastructures. These other obligations now absorb a large part of total public spending, especially in programs related to sustaining income and consumption, leaving little for more traditional spending.

The institutions and the social rules mentioned earlier could be considered the ones most needed by communities and the ones that would justify the existence of a "minimal state." The need for and the existence of such a state requires "public" resources to be spent collectively. This in turn raises the questions of both the *level* of public resources that the community will need and *from whom* it will get these resources. Much of the literature on taxation has been concerned with these two questions.

A related question is whether the way in which the public money will be spent should have some implication for the way the money is collected. Can it be assumed that the two sides of the budget (spending and taxing) are not related to each other, except at the total, national level, as much of the academic public finance literature seems to imply? There is also the question of whether the public needs, even in a minimal state, can be determined objectively and precisely, let alone optimally, and whether the countries' income distributions must play a role in that determination.

The social needs described previously constitute broadly an essential role for a government, a role that a government would need to play even in primitive societies. They constitute a *minimal* role of the state in *any* society. No organized society could exist without a government playing that role. As societies become larger, more developed, and more complex, and as the interactions and the exchanges among their members become more frequent, the minimal role outlined earlier is likely to become inadequate. The state will be pushed to assume additional functions, and some of these functions will require more public resources, more rules, and additional institutions.

This will also happen because, as already mentioned, due to greater population density in some societies, think of the megalopolis, some actions by individual members or by enterprises are more likely to create negative externalities for other members that cannot be easily ignored, especially in increasingly urbanized communities. Urbanization and population density are important elements of this process. For London in the nineteenth century, these problems created the need for social action in this area, an action that had not been necessary in rural societies (see Walvin, 1987).

Econometric studies have shown that the more urbanized societies become, the larger governments they tend to have, as measured by the societies' levels of public spending and taxing (see Tanzi, 1987b) or by the number of specific regulations, or, even, using a term that has become fashionable, by "nudges." Individuals living in isolation, such as hermits, or in rural and not densely populated areas are less likely than those living in urbanized societies to create negative externalities for others. However, enterprises operating in rural areas, especially some engaged in mining and energy activities, can still create significant environmental problems if they are not controlled. There are many examples of such problems from around the world. In the United States there are thousands of mines, abandoned decades ago when government controls were absent, that are potential environmental hazards. In any case, rural populations create less demands for governmental intervention except potentially in terms of income maintenance. Urbanized societies create more needs and, especially, needs that can be best addressed by governments, if not exclusively by them. Therefore, urbanized societies tend to have larger social or collective spending and more regulations. It is not surprising that in the United States complaints over excessive regulations come mainly from less urbanized states.

Over the years some economic literature has argued that even gangs or criminal associations require, within them, some *social* organization and some *rules*, in order to operate more efficiently in the pursuit of their (criminal) objectives. The Mafia has been reported to be a highly regulated criminal association. These rules can be considered as constituting a rudimentary form of government (see Skarbek, 2014; Skaperdas and Syropoulos, 1995).

In a book that five decades ago attracted much attention from conservative economists and politicians, at a time when attitudes vis-à-vis large government roles were changing and becoming less positive, Robert Nozick (1974), a philosopher, described in detail his view of the responsibilities and the role of a minimal state in democratic communities. His view was based on the controversial premise that only individuals and not communities have rights, a relatively recent view that was endorsed by Margaret Thatcher and that has continued to be shared in some of the more conservative literature on the role of the state, especially in the United Kingdom and the United States. That view is less popular in continental Europe.

A minimal state would have no role in *forcing* income redistribution, although it would endorse or even encourage *voluntary* assistance to poor individuals, especially to individuals who were clearly unable, because of serious physical or mental handicaps, to take care of themselves. Nozick was also highly skeptical about a Keynesian stabilization role in the economy. In the related literature on a minimal state, the concept of the economic liberty of individuals is given a large weight, and also the view that the larger the role of the state becomes, the greater is the reduction in individual liberty, a reduction considered damaging to both individuals and society.

The concept of a minimal role of the state has continued to attract conservative economists and political scientists in the United States who consider the expansion of that role in new directions in recent decades, and especially during the Obama administration in the area of health, as an unnecessary and dangerous encroachment on personal liberty and on the vitality of the country's economy. They are convinced that the United States has been moving in the wrong direction. Similar arguments have been made in other countries and especially in the United Kingdom, where the Cameron government had set the goal of reducing the role of the state in the economy over the years. Such a reduction would come by reducing budgetary allocations and designing new ways of achieving societal objectives, in part by encouraging experimentation at local government levels.

Because of President Woodrow Wilson's historical importance and his cultural sophistication, it may be worthwhile to mention briefly the views that were held by him in the late part of the nineteenth century on the topic of the economic role of the state (see Wilson, 1889). His views are especially interesting because his name appeared in the list of members of the first council of the American Economic Association. "Wilson divided state functions into 'constituent' and 'ministrant'" (see Fine, 1964, p. 277). The former comprised functions that every government must perform, such as the protection of persons and property from violence and robbery, the determination of contractual rights between individuals, the definition and punishment of crime, the administration of justice, and the conduct of foreign relations. These are the functions of a minimalist role of the state, functions that even a government that followed a strict laissez-faire ideology would have to perform.

The "ministrant" functions were considered nonessential but optional functions, although they could be desirable and could increase the general welfare. These functions were "the regulation of commerce, industry and labor, the maintenance of means of transportation and communication, the ownership of public utilities, the care of the poor, and the establishment of a system of public education" (ibid.). In spite of his rather conservative views, Wilson considered the government not evil but the indispensible organ of society. In this his views were similar to those of Adam Smith and of philosophers such as Hegel.

In the United States, conservative or libertarian individuals often make appeal to, and continue to be guided by, the needs of society at the time when the Declaration of Independence and the US Constitution were written. At that time the United States was still a largely rural society, as a visit to Mount Vernon or Monticello makes clear. The country was still settling in a new, immense territory, and few individuals lived in cities or especially in large cities. Therefore, many of the modern needs for the government's role had not manifested themselves at that time, and those who wrote the Constitution could not have anticipated them. For example, the need to defend the borders from illegal immigrants, even at the cost of building a wall thousands of miles long, could not have been anticipated; neither could that of protecting the country against terrorists.

Some conservatives continue to believe that rules that had spontaneously developed in communities in past centuries, for example, the "lex mercatoria," the set of implicit rules that guided commercial exchanges in centuries past, could play important roles in, or even guide, today's world in social and economic interactions among individuals. Spontaneous rules, developed by participants in a free market, would in their view make it less necessary for governments to get involved in issuing regulations for various activities, and would reduce the need to create new regulatory institutions.

Conservatives argue, with some merit, that, by issuing government rules, the modern state has made it more difficult for spontaneous rules to be developed, in both markets and human relations. It must also be stressed that there are many rules in today's world that are not created by *national* governments, but are created or pushed by pseudo-public groups within communities, or by subnational governments. These rules may be more numerous and at times more restraining than those set by national governments.

Attempts to transfer some modern US rules to foreign traditional societies in countries in which the United States has been active have often led to disappointment. Press reports have commented on the failure of using rules based on the US justice system in Afghanistan. It has been reported that, in spite of more than a billion dollars spent in training that countries' lawyers, the population of Afghanistan continues to rely on more and to trust more the informal decisions made by Taliban elders, even though they are primitive and often cruel (see *New York Times International*, 2015, p. 7). An article reported that "[a] common refrain is that to settle a dispute over your farm in [a public] court you must first sell your chickens, your cows and your wife" (ibid.).

In modern societies, conflicts continue to exist, but justice has become costly, slow, often corrupted, and increasingly manipulated by clever lawyers. So the choice may, in some cases, come down to the use of either traditional justice, with its biases (against women and against some ethnic groups) and its harsh punishments, or modern justice, with its different problems, such as, in the US case, the large number of (lower-income) individuals who end up in jail for committing minor crimes, while some stay out of jail in spite of having committed major white-collar crimes, and the high costs of justice procedures that make justice unequal for rich and poor individuals.

In some cases, clever lawyers may extract huge compensations for some injustices or for past sacrifices experienced by some individuals. For example, in December 2015, it was reported that the American diplomats who had been held in captivity in Iran in 1979 would get compensation for their sacrifices at the rate of $10,000 per each day that they were held. Each of them, or each family of those who had died, would get $4 million from the US government. It is difficult to identify the role of the state in this public spending, but it is easy to identify the role of clever lawyers who will get large shares of the total money paid.

In the second part of this book I shall focus on developments that have complicated the economic role of the state. I shall also discuss developments that have cast doubts on the claims, made by some economists and politicians, that a market that is little controlled always delivers good outcomes.

The more corrupt the state, the more it legislates.

Tacitus (55 AD?–120 AD?), Roman historian

The laws must be brief so that even the non expert can understand them.

Seneca (4 BC–65 AD), Roman philosopher

PART II

Complexity and the Rise of Termites

Implications of Excessive Government Withdrawal

The market fundamentalism that had been promoted by economists and, to some extent, implemented by some governments, starting from the 1980s, contributed to the growing acceptance of wide differences in incomes, and to the justification of what were at times extraordinary or, even, absurdly large compensations for some individuals. The view that came to prevail was that, if these incomes were paid within a presumably well-working and free market, they must have been "deserved" and "justified." Therefore, they should be considered legitimate and should not be challenged.

Managers of private enterprises started receiving compensations that, with the passing of time, became hundreds of times larger than those of the workers that they supervised. Because of competition among enterprises (based on some form of benchmarking criteria used by those who decided on the compensations or by those who advised on the determination of the compensation packages), even positions held by some individuals in poorly performing enterprises ended up being compensated at levels that, in some cases, were clearly unjustified or even absurd. There have been many examples of enterprises that performed abysmally while their managers continued receiving salaries and bonuses in the tens of millions of dollars (see examples in Tanzi, 2012). Enterprises did not want to face the embarrassment of compensating their top managers less than competing enterprises did.

These high compensations in the business sector inevitably had a demonstration effect on compensations in other sectors and in other areas of activity. For example, directors of museums, presidents of universities, and even managers of large charitable institutions or of think tanks started commanding annual compensations that at times were in the millions of dollars. One US college president received a salary of more than $7 million in 2012. Two others received more than $3 million. Several coaches of college sport teams received incomes of several million dollars. At one college, a weight-lifting couch received an annual income of $600,000.

In the financial market, a market that had been growing quickly in size and was becoming more complex and more global (and for which doubts had started to be expressed about what value it truly contributed to society), the new thinking and the growing complexity of the financial instruments and transactions that the financial sector was generating created a true revolution. The revolution was aided by new computer technologies that had become available in that period, and especially by the Internet, which had increased connectivity.

Some individuals came to believe that newly developed financial instruments and particular arrangements could solve many economic and even social problems. For example, it was believed that they could make it possible for individuals with low incomes and highly unstable jobs to become home owners, a goal that was considered socially important. Or governments with very limited finances could build expensive infrastructures, with the financial and technical help of private investors, through what came to be called public-private partnership (PPP) contracts.

That revolution made it also possible, once past policies were changed, for enormous sums of money (trillions of dollars a day) to cross national frontiers, increasing enormously the number of transactions in the market. Access to credit became much easier for governments facing large fiscal deficits, such as Greece and others. Standard and Poor estimated that global sovereign debt would reach $44 trillion by 2017! The presumed miraculous impact on the economies of the financial revolution helped justify the enormous compensations that some of those who operated in the financial market were receiving. This was the case for hedge fund managers, for those who sold mortgages, for traders, for bank managers, and for some other operators, even though the genuine contributions to the real economy of the activities of these institutions and their managers remained, or would become, increasingly questionable.

The revolution also made it easier for rich individuals and for profitable enterprises to operate globally and to use their global operations to reduce their tax payments, through various tax-avoiding maneuvers suggested by a growing industry of clever lawyers and accountants. These maneuvers included shifting profits or tax bases to places where they were not taxed, or where they were taxed lightly. Old-fashioned and explicit tax evasion was also facilitated. We shall come back to this issue in a later chapter.

The difference, which had been sharp in the past, between *real* investment and *financial* investment has largely disappeared in recent years. In the financial market, the identification of creditors (savers in the past) and debtors (investors in the past) became vague, because of increasingly complex financial engineering maneuvers that at times made it difficult to distinguish creditors from debtors. In some cases the same individuals or the same enterprise was on both sides of a financial transaction.

Because of the growing use of "rocket scientists" and other individuals with sharp quantitative skills, the financial instruments became progressively more complex and more difficult to understand, even for some of the managers of the financial enterprises in which the new instruments were created. The new instruments changed hands continually, shifting the risks away from those who had originally created them. The transactions increasingly crossed national frontiers. It has been reported that the average share of an enterprise now changes hands every few seconds. Increasingly, only a small part of the total money borrowed is used by the borrowers to make real investments, especially outside the housing sector. Much of it is used for placing bets, in a modern form of gambling, in the "casino capitalism" market.

In recent years some of the credit that was made easily and cheaply available to banks, governments, and some individuals, by novel policies of central banks, has been used by the managers of many enterprises to buy shares in their own companies, rather than to make real investments. These maneuvers contribute to raising the value of the shares and to reducing taxable profits, which, in turn, contribute to increasing the short run compensations of the managers, which are often linked to the short run values of the shares. This is one of many examples of how some of the very high incomes (those of the top 1 percent) have become increasingly disconnected from true, genuine market forces, and how compensation arrangements for managers have contributed to making markets more risky, by encouraging enterprises to follow short run maneuvers. In these maneuvers social objectives have often taken a backseat.

After the onset of the financial crisis in 2007, when the value of many new houses that had been bought with cheap, short run credit fell sharply, the interest rates on the mortgages of many who had bought these houses went up (after some grace period that had been used to attract unwary or naïve borrowers had expired), and when some of the house buyers lost their jobs, many became unable to keep servicing the debt. Some of them had difficulties contacting the institutions that were holding the claims to the mortgages. The mortgages had been packaged, securitized, and sold by the original creditors to distant and, often, misinformed investors, including foreign pension funds. This maneuver had removed the original lenders from later risks of insolvency by the borrowers. It had also made them less careful about ascertaining the ability of the borrowers to service the loans. Some mortgages had been given to individuals without incomes and without jobs who had bought the houses anticipating that they would soon sell them at higher prices.

Casino capitalism, a term taken from the title of a book by Hans-Werner Sinn, a German economist, had come on a large scale to the housing market, and the distinction between genuine investing and gambling had largely disappeared. This was not the way in which a market economy was supposed to work. It also made it more difficult to accept the view that the high incomes, often in many millions of dollars, received by those who had originally approved the mortgages and had lent the original money were "earned" and, thus, "deserved," and that they should be taxed lightly.

Asymmetry in information became and has continued to be common in many transactions. Shadow banking activities became progressively more important within the financial market, and the shadows became progressively more difficult to penetrate by normal citizens, by those who were responsible for guaranteeing the sustainability of the market, or by those who invested funds in it, such as pension funds. These activities often hid asymmetry in information between two sides. Even "stress tests" for banks became highly questionable and less valuable. Accounting standards were increasingly questioned and were often clearly inadequate, as were the ratings assigned to some bonds by rating agencies.

The conditions for potential future crises had been created, raising valid questions, on the part of many experts, about the merits of market fundamentalism and of the deregulation policies that it had promoted and that had reduced the role and the responsibility of governments. Questions as to what should be the role of government in modern economies became more pertinent, more urgent, and more difficult to answer.

In the past couple decades, many able individuals have used the quantitative skills that they acquired in their academic training not in producing genuine value in the economy but in placing bets on particular outcomes. Whether those bets produce genuine economic value has remained a controversial issue. Many able individuals, including "rocket scientists" or even biologists, chose to work in the financial market because of the high incomes that they could earn in that market, rather than performing the directly productive activities they would have done in the past, given the formal training that they had acquired.

As already mentioned, the world that had been created allowed huge sums of money to cross national frontiers to sustain the excessive spending on the part of some governments (Argentina in the 1990s; Greece, Portugal, and several others in the new century); to finance private investments in, at times, questionable activities (such as excessive house building in the United States, Ireland, Spain, and other places); or, in one particular case, to finance a billion-dollar airport in an area of Spain where it did not seem to have much economic justification and would never open. Clearly, easy and cheap credit can lead to inefficient or irresponsible spending.

Without the deregulation that had led to the creation of the largely unregulated global financial market, some crises would not have happened, or would have been less damaging. Also, some governments would have been more restrained in their public spending. "Irrational exuberance" in the private sector and excessive government spending (a form of irrational exuberance by governments), both fed by the availability of large amounts of foreign borrowing, would have been more contained. The new paradigm had already been a major factor in the financial crises that had hit several Southeast Asian countries in 1997–1998 (see Tanzi, 2008a, pp. 85–92 and 139–141). It surely was a factor in the crisis that hit the United States in 2007 and led to the Great Recession there and in several European countries.

The major unanswered question at the time this book was written (2016) is what impact policies of Quantitative Easing promoted by central banks, which have been feeding exceptionally cheap credit to a financial market that has continued to have the characteristics described earlier, will have over the longer run. Only time will tell. One thing is sure – that the total debt of many countries (public plus private debt) has reached and has remained at exceptionally high levels (see Tanzi, 2016b). The IMF *Fiscal Monitor* of October 2016 reported that total (public and private) debt of the nonfinancial sector in the world economy was 225 percent of world GDP at the time, a historic record.

Another major question is what impact the intention by the Donald Trump administration to get rid of the Dodd-Frank law will have. The American Action Forum, a conservative think tank, has estimated that this law has imposed costs equivalent to $36 billion.

CHAPTER II

The Growth of Termites

In the coming chapters I shall discuss ways in which governmental interventions occasionally, or even often, failed to deliver the expected results; some of the reasons why this has happened; and how developments in the private sectors might be contributing to these outcomes. I shall not repeat the arguments described in detail by scholars of the School of Public Choice or the Chicago School. Those arguments are known to economists and are easily available in several good books (see Mueller, 1989; Ebenstein, 2001). Rather, I shall focus on arguments, some connected with recent developments, that have attracted less attention or less analysis. The description shall be based largely on direct observations, minimizing reliance on armchair theorizing, which tends to be more easily influenced by personal biases and preconceived views (see Lewis, 2017).

An underlying thesis of this book is that, as economies and markets become more developed, they tend to become more complex and more interconnected, thus creating greater reasons and new justifications for monitoring and, presumably, for governments to intervene. Such governmental interventions would be consistent with, and would be justified by, the *normative approach* of the government role, the approach that became popular in the 1940–1950s, especially in the United States. In those decades, important contributions to the relevant public finance and public economics literature were made by leading economists, including famous articles by Paul Samuelson and others, and by the seminal synthesis in the 1959 book by Richard Musgrave.

Those contributions generally called for, or implied, the need for governmental intervention when market failures were identified. The normative view held by many economists was that, when the market failed, the government must intervene. The government was seen in the same light as people see fire brigades – they are called and intervene when there is a fire – or the way they see doctors, who are called when a person comes down with an illness. The more fires or illnesses there are, the greater must be the interventions. There were few if any doubts expressed in the 1950s by the authors of many of those papers about the need for the calls and perhaps also about the ability of the firefighters or the doctors to perform satisfactorily the functions they were called for.

However, as Gunnar Myrdal, the Swedish Nobel Prize winner in economics, had pointed out in a brilliant article, originally published in Swedish, as early as 1929, "all normative economic doctrines are largely rationalization of political attitudes" (Myrdal, 1954, p. 137), and political attitudes are likely to change over long periods of time. Thus, what some may see as market failures, others may see as normal developments that may not justify governmental intervention.

This is clearly the case with income distributions when they become more uneven, and with the incomes that some individuals receive today, which some consider to be too high and perhaps unjustified. Not all economists and observers would consider these as market failures in the classic sense, even though many citizens now see them as political, social, or, even, market failures. This attitude also extends to other areas, and increasingly to the growing use of regulations by governments, or, perhaps, even to the pursuit of stabilization policies. For example, a recession that followed the bursting of a bubble could be seen as an occasion to eliminate elements that had increased the probability of future bubbles, and to get rid of unproductive or excessively risky activities, as Schumpeter and some members of the Austrian School would have argued. If stabilization policies and the interventions by central banks reduced the incentives to make the corrections, history would be more likely to repeat itself.

As economies become more developed, and as governmental activities and interventions increase, complexity is likely to become an issue; principal agents' problems, which are always present in the real world, become more common and potentially more damaging within the public sector; the identification of what is the public interest, always a difficult enterprise, as Kenneth Arrow pointed out seven decades ago, becomes more difficult; failure or policy mistakes of various kinds become more likely; various forms of asymmetry in information in market transactions become common; corruption, either of the clearly illegal and thus punishable kind or, in its more modern versions, of a "legal" kind (the one that hides itself behind the interpretation of existing norms, or even in the drafting of norms that are created specifically to help some vested interests), becomes more common; and so on.

The increasing complexity of the market and the growth of governmental intervention have contributed to the development of less transparent, or seemingly less legitimate, relationships among individuals in the private sector, or between individuals in the private sector and some in the public sector. These relationships have been leading to, or contributing to, what some observers now call "crony capitalism."

In this kind of "capitalism" personal connections, especially connections with strategically placed individuals in both the private and the public sector, can acquire great economic values for some individuals, while the grey, and growing, areas between the two sectors become larger and more important. Outsourcing some activities, including the increasing use of private contractors in many public-sector operations, the execution of public investments by private enterprises, the growth of public-private partnerships, the assumption by the government of implicit or explicit responsibility for some private-sector failures, and so on have increased these "crony capitalism" possibilities. Today, to some extent, even military operations and security operations have been partly privatized and are thus exposed to these problems.

As some have been arguing, the market economy, within a democratic society, is running the risk of becoming a system that allows some individuals, enterprises, and groups to use their political and financial influence to buy, or to influence, political decisions; to receive government protection on some activities, government contracts, tax incentives, favorable interpretation of some tax rules or regulations, questionable authorizations for some activities or for some uses as with zoning laws, or cheap credit; or to extract various kinds of rents by restricting entry into some activities, or making entry into those activities more expensive or more difficult for others and easier for themselves.

Because of nontransparent actions taken by some public officials in favor of some groups or of some individuals, the market and the government have been running the risk of becoming instruments for, or complicit in, the extraction of rents by some groups, rather than instruments for generating social welfare for all citizens. Even receiving access to social assistance by various groups may acquire competitive characteristics, when various groups compete, and when one group manages to get benefits denied to other groups, using nontransparent political pressures or contacts. This is likely to happen in public housing, or in access to good schools, for example.

In the modern globalized market, many transactions take place not so much because of the information transmitted by market prices to buyers and sellers (and with full information, on both sides, about the quality of what is being exchanged), as Hayek had argued, but because of the role that some individuals play in initiating these exchanges, which leads to the not always legitimate benefits that some participants derive. The view that market exchanges are always beneficial to both parties in an exchange is an illusion in an increasing number of cases.

An attractive activity for individuals who have held significant government jobs has increasingly become lobbying in various forms or, alternatively, going to work on behalf of activities that they had regulated in their former employment roles. This is now common in the energy sector, the pharmaceutical and health sector, the financial sector, the defense industry, and some other sectors. In these activities some individuals can capitalize on the insider knowledge, the contacts, and, especially, the close connections that they had previously acquired. At times and perhaps increasingly financial contributions to the political campaigns of particular politicians can help individuals achieve specific objectives.

There is also the related experience of powerful financial enterprises sending their personnel to high-level positions in important public institutions, or hiring individuals from public-sector activities who have held high positions and have thus developed important contacts. For example, it is remarkable how many high-level US public officials (or even officials in foreign institutions, such as the European Central Bank) have come from institutions such as Goldman Sacks, Citibank, or similar financial institutions. And it is even more remarkable how many have recently gone from high-level, public positions to financial or other private institutions.

Recent examples have included former prime ministers of Germany and the United Kingdom, the former president of the European Commission, former chairpersons of the Federal Reserve System, governors of the Bank of England, and various high-level officials from the IMF and other international institutions. These individuals naturally bring some useful knowledge. However, they especially bring connections, which are useful to the new institutions that they join and for this they get paid handsomely. Some of these individuals had been critical of the financial sector in their official activities, but the temptation of large financial compensations is a strong incentive and is capable of making them ignore their previous feelings or views. In one example, a compensation of $2.5 million a year for a few days of work must have been considered a strong enough incentive for Tony Blair to ignore some of his previous feelings or views.

President Francois Holland of France defined the move to Goldman Sachs of Jose Manuel Barroso as "morally unacceptable," and articles in the

Financial Times sharply criticized the move of Melvyn King, the former governor (2003–2013) of the Bank of England, to Citibank Tim Geithner was also criticized for going to work for a financial institution and an earlier move by Stanley Fischer, from a high IMF position to one at Citibank, that had paid many times his earlier salary, also attracted strong negative comments. Some of these moves can be considered important aspects of crony capitalism. They make the particular individuals very rich within a few years. In these moves connections developed in public positions can bring large financial benefits to some individuals.

It is now more likely than it was in the past that some private-sector transactions are characterized by significant asymmetry in the information available to the two parties in the exchange. It is very rare that two parties in a transaction share fully the knowledge of the characteristics of what is exchanged. Modern markets, especially in the financial sector, the health sector, the insurance sector, and increasingly even sectors such as the automotive industry and those providing various services (including, for example, those connected with touristic activities or home repairs), are becoming increasingly different from those imagined by F. Hayek or Milton Friedman, for whom the market was the legitimate instrument that, through the price system, and only through the price system, distributed needed and available knowledge to those who engaged in the transactions, from both sides.

As was mentioned earlier, the importance of sectors in which it is difficult to get full, ex ante, and timely information on the value of what is being exchanged, *before* a transaction actually takes place, has grown over the years, while the economic importance of sectors that remain close, in their characteristics, to those described by Hayek and Friedman has been much reduced. The transactions in sectors that match Hayek's view of the role of prices in market exchanges now account for a much smaller share of most households' spending than they did a century ago.

Even food products, which now account for a far smaller share of families' expenses in rich countries, are often produced industrially, using chemicals or ingredients (hormones, pesticides, damaging fats, too much sugar) that were not contained in the foods that people bought many years ago. Or the food products may come from faraway places, so there is less warranty that they have been grown or produced in a pollution-free and safe environment. For example, the fish that one now buys is often farmed, or it may have been caught in polluted waters; and the chicken meat that one buys is often produced in a very unhealthy environment, rather than in free ranges. In the past, before refrigeration became common, the asymmetry in information was often related to the freshness of the food products.

It should be stressed that the market economy still generates results that are broadly satisfactory, and, for sure, the health of most individuals in advanced countries has improved, as life expectancy statistics indicate. Also, in some areas, the Internet now allows users to register some spontaneous rating of particular services and products that is useful to new buyers, as long as the rating is honest and truly spontaneous and it has an impact. The question is not whether a different economic system would generate better results than a market economy. Rather, it is whether the changes described here have created easier circumstances for abuses, and whether these circumstances are likely to become more frequent in the future and to promote naïve and dangerous populist policies that would lead to a worse world than we have experienced. This concern might seem to justify a more significant and more efficient government role than we have seen in recent years.

Recent and increasingly frequent media reports seem to indicate that some problems may have become more frequent than they were in the past, for example, car recalls; drugs with serious side effects; abuses in the financial market; and other issues. These reports challenge the assumption that all the operators in the market are guided by socially responsible and honest behavior, and make that assumption appear naïve. The nature of some individuals predisposes them to take advantage of circumstances for their own benefits when they can do so at low or no costs. This seems to be the key conclusion of a recent book by two winners of the Nobel Prize in economics, Akerlof and Shiller (2015). The key question, which is difficult to address, is how the government should respond to these developments.

In recent decades some forms of crony capitalism have accompanied casino capitalism and what could be called "piñata capitalism" (because some of the participants to many market transactions are largely blindfolded, or not fully informed). As mentioned earlier, the importance of transactions that justify the "piñata" denomination has been growing in recent decades, creating difficulties for market economies led by democratic governments, and also increasing the *theoretical* justification for the government to intervene. To believe that the private market, without regulations and controls, will naturally and always promote the public interest and the general welfare in today's world, as some economists continue to argue, amounts to closing one's eyes to much reality and to much daily evidence.

Consider the rise of the financial sector, of the private health sector, and of several other sectors that share broadly similar characteristics. Taken together, these sectors now account for a large and growing share of the total market transactions and of the total spending of most individuals. Therefore, the problem is now no longer limited to occasional "lemons" bought from used-car dealers, in the example made famous by George Akerlof in his classic 1970 article on asymmetry in transactions. The problem has become more general. Ironically, in the automobile industry, it has moved from the sale of used cars, with defects unknown to buyers, to the sale of new cars, with defects also hidden from unwary buyers or even from car dealers, but probably known to the car producers.

In principle, for the reasons mentioned earlier, these problems in market transactions might lead to demands for, and might justify, a larger government role, one aimed at better protecting less sophisticated individuals from potential abuses, for example, the unsophisticated individuals who bought new houses with mortgages obtained from unscrupulous agents during the period that led to the financial crisis; individuals who are charged astronomical fees for simple surgical procedures; or those who buy new cars with serious or even dangerous defects. Not surprisingly, calls for consumer protection agencies and for some regulations have grown in recent years.

Perhaps not by coincidence, the subprime financial crises exploded in the least-regulated financial market, that of the United States, and after that market had been significantly deregulated. In their 2015 book, Akerlof and Shiller provided several examples of areas in which consumers can be and are being manipulated and deceived. It is interesting to observe that prescription drugs are now advertised at dinnertime in television ads directly to the potential patients and not to their doctors, as they should be. Doctors are often compensated in various ways for prescribing new drugs or for praising them. In many countries this is forbidden by government regulations.

Advertising on television has moved, over the years, from selling soap and cars to selling prescription drugs or the services of lawyers for consumens who have been damaged by the bad drugs. However, while creating *theoretical* reasons for governments to intervene and to play an increasing role in regulating the market, these developments are, slowly but inexorably, transforming that role into one that at times creates increasing complexities and inefficiencies; or alternatively it creates advantages and opportunities for some groups or persons, by allowing them to receive rents or unjustifiably high incomes.

Complexity also increases the difficulties that the government encounters in promoting good policies and in monitoring past policies to ensure that they continue to promote the objectives for which they were created. When a policy requires complex laws and institutions, as many policies now tend to do, it becomes more difficult for a government to forecast correctly the outcome of the policy, and easier for some individuals or some vested interests to try to benefit from it, or to become free riders. An analogy would be a drug that is needed to fight an illness but that is accompanied by side effects that, with time, may become damaging to the patient.

These issues raise also the legitimate question of whether the high incomes that some individuals now receive from their market activities are always truly deserved, as some economists continue to claim. If they are not, there may be more justification to reduce them, say by the use of progressive taxes on high incomes or by taxes on wealth, if the work of the market cannot be improved, to make incomes more deserved. Especially for conservative individuals and economists, these issues also raise the equally important question of whether (apart from the *theoretical* justification) growing government involvement would in fact be beneficial, in the sense of contributing to the citizens' welfare. The intervention by the government might be theoretically justified, but it could also be practically damaging if it were accompanied by problems. Another analogy may be useful. If the intervention of the fire brigade causes more damage than would the fire, a justified question would be whether calling the fire brigade more frequently would be expected to be a good policy. This is indeed a difficult question to which there is no easy answer.

Developments in more recent years seem to be allowing a new kind of economic aristocracy to come into existence and to acquire a privileged position in society. This position is not inherited, as it was in some countries in the past. However, in some ways, the position is acquiring characteristics that are becoming similar to those that existed in the past, and some of the individuals involved may be isolating themselves (physically or socially) from the rest of the citizens and slowly developing attitudes similar to those of the aristocrats of the past.

These individuals tend to live in exclusive and increasingly secluded areas, to frequent exclusive clubs, to send their children to exclusive private schools, to increasingly marry individuals with similar backgrounds, to attend vacation places frequented by individuals with similar incomes and backgrounds, and so on. It is a modern aristocracy founded partly on acquired wealth, partly on exclusive education, and partly on access to valuable connections, including access to useful and clever experts, such as lawyers, accountants, etc., that wealth, the best education, and valuable connections facilitate. These developments again raise the difficult question of what governments should, or better, *could* do about them. Ignoring these developments is not likely to be or to remain a valid government option, as recent electoral results indicate. Governments cannot simply continue to *laissez-faire*.

There seem to be largely two alternatives, and the choice between the two may reflect the political attitudes that Gunnar Myrdal wrote about ninety years ago. Or it may reflect the practical question of which alternative is politically and administratively easier to adopt. It should be added that the choices are not, necessarily or completely, mutually exclusive.

The first alternative is to accept the market developments as they are and to try to correct the redistributive results by relying on *ex post redistributive policies*, as many peoples have been asking, and as countries such as Denmark, Sweden, France, and some others have tried to do over the years. In other words, taxes and public spending programs can be used intensively to try to correct or mitigate, ex post, market results, in terms of income distribution, to make them more acceptable to the majority of the citizens and to try to create and maintain good opportunities for everyone. This alternative would make the market results more equitable, but would still leave them uncorrected in terms of the allocation of resources, because distortions would continue to exist, or might even be intensified by the higher tax rates.

In principle, some abuses could be reduced by using regulations and/or the courts more actively to punish those who violate clear rules. In some countries, and especially in the United States, there would be obstacles to the raising of higher taxes and spending, and it might be costly for individuals to use the courts to redress some torts. Those difficulties have been increasing in a globalized, modern world in which the justice system seems to favor those who have more money. In some countries the justice system might be too slow to respond to specific abuses. Institutional asymmetry is often a significant obstacle.

The second alternative would be to make much greater and genuine efforts to try to remove through legislation and effective governmental action some of the elements and the conditions that have contributed to making the income distribution less socially acceptable and more inequitable, and the market less efficient in terms of the allocation of resources. This second alternative would require the removal, or at least the reduction, of illegitimate or undesirable market power from some individuals and enterprises, or from some economic activities, especially, but not only, when that power comes, directly or indirectly, from governmental actions or often inactions. It also requires better rules and more efficient institutions, which may not be easy to provide.

For example, financial institutions that are "too big to fail" or are too much in the shadow would need to be reduced in size and made more transparent; enterprises that have acquired too much power would need to be made truly competitive; positions that, because of difficulties to enter provide too much market power and generate rents to some individuals, would need to lose their monopoly power; and some protection now justified on grounds of "intellectual property" for some individuals and enterprises would need to be reduced. Norms and regulations would need to pass a clear test of transparency, to reduce the possibility of alternative interpretations.

This second alternative would put strict limitations on individuals who want to become lobbyists and on government officials who have contacts with lobbyists. It would also put limits on some individuals who want to work for sectors that they have been regulating in their past employment roles, reducing the effect of revolving door policies. The difficulties of introducing changes in these areas are all too evident. In practice this alternative may not be easy to implement.

In conclusion, neither of the aforementioned alternatives would be easy or without costs, and neither would be optimal, in the sense of necessarily solving the problems mentioned. Governments would necessarily be choosing between second-best alternatives, although the second alternative would make the market more efficient and more legitimate if it could be implemented. However, the first alternative may be easier to implement, provided that, politically, a government were allowed and were capable of implementing it without too much political opposition and too many loopholes, and provided that the government would want to apply it without the use of "fiscal illusions."

The choice of the first alternative would be, to some extent, a return to the use of the tax systems with higher marginal tax rates and spending programs for significant redistributive purposes, as they had existed or had been attempted a few decades ago, before they started to be reformed in the 1980s to respond to various efficiency concerns expressed by influential economists and reflected in changing attitudes. On the tax side it would be a return to the tax system that Henry C. Simons, a Chicago professor, recommended in 1938.

Termites of the state, various elements that enter into the political system and that corrupt, or distort, the legitimate economic role that governments try to play, and *termites of the market*, which distort the legitimate function of the market, have been entering into the formulation and implementation of economic policy. The termites enter in the passing and in the application of the laws, and in the functioning of the public administrations after policies have been enacted, creating governance problems and contributing to administrative abuses including corruption.

It should be no surprise that, as indicated by annual surveys provided by Transparency International, an institution based in Germany that keeps track of corruption developments around the world, and by other sources, and as witnessed by the number of academic articles and newspaper reports dealing with corrupt practices, corruption seems to have been growing in recent years in many parts of the world. In some, for example, in Russia, India, Brazil, Italy, and other countries, it has reached worrisome levels, in spite of the increasing attention paid to it. There must be some reasons why corruption had been less prevalent, or at least had attracted less attention, until the 1990s. Until that time few academics and few articles by economists and by political scientists had dedicated much thought to it. One plausible reason is that corruption has increased in recent decades because of the increasing complexity that now characterizes many economic and political systems (see Tanzi, 1998a).

In recent decades, the problems mentioned earlier seem to have become more common. They have also become more difficult to deal with. Slowly, they have been changing the relationship that should exist, in democratic societies, between the state and the citizens, while also changing the legitimacy, in the eyes of many, of the market economy, and increasing the danger that populism may become an irresistible force. Worrisome signs have been coming from several countries. Increasing shares of countries' populations seem to have less trust in the ability of governments to alleviate social problems than they had a few decades ago, while they also trust less the role of the free market. The view that the systems are "rigged" now seems to be accepted by a significant share of the countries' populations.

Those problem sectors are inevitably changing the benefit-cost calculation between the official justifications provided for some public-sector interventions and the official estimates of the benefits from them, on one hand, and the genuine benefits that the citizens get, or think they get, from the interventions. This may be particularly the case for some spending programs and for some regulations. Some see only the negative sides of regulations.

Other developments that are also creating different and difficult-to-solve problems for *national* governments are connected with cross-country spillovers or externalities. One is the already-mentioned increase in global tax avoidance and tax evasion. Another is the growth of *global public goods* (or, more often, of their opposite, *global public "bads"*). Dealing with these developments would, in principle, require the interventions of a *global* government, if such a government existed (see Tanzi, 2008a). Such a government does not exist, and the solution suggested by the Coase theorem (arbitration between or among the parties) is also not likely to be of much help in some of these cases, when the externalities are negative ones and especially when they involve many actors (see Coase, 1960).

A global government is not likely to come into existence in the foreseeable future, if ever. The many international organizations that have been created over the years, perhaps as implicit proxies for ministries that such a government would have if it existed, do not have the power to impose and the resources to monitor needed solutions. The existence of global public *goods* and public *bads* makes the role of *national* governments and the possibility of promoting policies that can deal with them very difficult. Just think of the topical problems of terrorism, illegal migration, international crime, or climate change. Uncoordinated national initiatives are not likely to lead to efficient solutions for these global goods, and there is no global invisible hand to lead to good solutions.

Returning to the economic role of *national* states, it seems logical to think that there must be some desirable, if not necessarily optimal, levels of public spending, taxes, and regulations that would make it possible for governments, given present circumstances, to play the role that they are expected to play in correcting market failures and in promoting the welfare of citizens. Those desirable levels are likely to differ significantly across countries, because they depend, inter alia, on the community spirit that exists within countries, which may determine, for example, how much redistribution of income the citizens are willing to support through governmental policies; on the ability and honesty of the policymakers, which would keep low the inefficiency costs and corruption; on the quality of the public employees; and on other characteristics of the population and of the economy, such as the degree of urbanization or even the geographical size and the population of the country.

My observations, over many years of professional work in different countries, have led me to believe that a *very rough* but plausible, realistic *range* for the level of public spending and taxes, for advanced countries, might be somewhere *around* 30–35 percent of GDP. That level can be financed with tax systems and tax rates that should not create excessive difficulties for a country's economy and for its tax administration. It is a level that has allowed countries such as Switzerland, Ireland, Australia, New Zealand, and several others to operate well. Some economically successful countries or economies, such as South Korea, Singapore, Taiwan, and Hong Kong, spend even less.

When the spending level of a government exceeds that range, questions should be asked as to what that government is buying, or is trying to buy, with the excess spending, and why it is doing it. The higher level of spending will require higher tax rates, which might create difficulties in the longer run. It is also likely to lead to some questionable spending that may be associated with inefficiencies or with citizens' dependencies on some public programs. When the spending is much lower than the rough range suggested earlier, one must ask what the government could do with some extra public money and what difficulties would be encountered to raise and use the money efficiently. This lower level is more likely to be found in poorer and less developed countries, not because of less need for public spending in those countries but because of less administrative capacity to raise taxes and to spend the money raised efficiently.

A country with a homogenous population – as well as a good tax system and a government that is seen to spend well the public money, without creating economic difficulties, and where the citizens are collectively willing to pay higher taxes without excessive complaints or strong negative reactions, for example, Denmark – might justify a higher spending level than the upper part of the range indicated previously. However, the justification for the high spending should be the actual results obtained from it. It should not be justified simply on the basis of a government's promises or the hope that the higher spending will inevitably bring more welfare to the citizens and solve more social or economic problems.

There are several advanced countries that do quite well in generating good benefits for their populations with the suggested spending levels, and a few with even lower levels. It should be stressed and repeated that the aforementioned range is not based on any theoretical consideration, but only on intuition and on direct observations. It should thus not be seen as indicating optimality. As I shall argue in the following chapter, it is more difficult to even suggest a guess about the desirable number of regulations. That number is more likely to be influenced by factors such as urbanization, technological development, and others.

CHAPTER 12

Termites in Regulatory Activities

While one may venture a guess about limits to how much governments should spend, it is difficult, or impossible, to set limits to the number, or the use, of regulations in today's economies, in part because those limits would need to be adjusted frequently to accommodate technological and other changes. For example, the introduction of cars required many new regulations and so did that of planes. Regulations significantly reduced the number of car accidents over the years. Self-driving cars will require new, different regulations.

There are growing complaints about the number of regulations in today's world that some, and especially representatives of enterprises, libertarian economists, and conservative politicians, see as excessive. At the same time there are complaints from other groups that various activities are not regulated enough, and abuses, presumably due to the absence of regulations, are reported with increasing frequency. It is obvious that whatever limit one might think appropriate for the number of regulations at a moment in time, it may have to be adjusted later, because of changing needs and circumstances. Some regulations may no longer be needed, while others might become necessary. It is also likely that whatever limit is established, it will not be the one that some individuals or enterprises will consider appropriate.

Regulations have been and remain important in the role that governments play or should play in an economy. When Adam Smith complained about "mercantilism," he was complaining about some regulations that he considered damaging. Centrally planned economies were essentially "regulatory states." In a modern economy the number of regulations needed is clearly well more than zero. However, some regulations may be seen by some as more essential than others. Essential regulations, for example, are those connected with the traffic, with the disposal of garbage and toxic material, with the safety of buildings and drugs, and similar ones.

The need for and the number of regulations cannot be stable over time in dynamic economies and in changing societies, because circumstances, needs, and perceptions keep changing. Some regulations are the direct consequence of lack of full information and of limited rationality on the part of some individuals, as some exponents of behavioral economics would argue. Asymmetry in information, on the part of individuals engaged in exchanges, may justify the use of particular regulations by governments. If individuals had full knowledge of risks, and if they always acted rationally, a libertarian argument could be made that there would be less need, or no need, for regulations.

Regulations can easily become damaging when they become excessive and when they extend to areas where the government has no business getting involved, because the regulated activities are not creating "significant" actual or potential risks, or negative externalities, for other individuals or for the community. Just think of rules that in the past prevented individuals from marrying individuals of different races; prevented purchasing beer on Sunday morning; or prevented renting or selling houses, or apartments in particular buildings or areas, to blacks or to individuals of Jewish or Islamic background. The adjective "significant" is key, however, because someone must determine when an externality is significant enough to justify a regulation. In fact, this is the reason for many current controversies on the use of regulations, especially those related to the environment.

Abusive uses of regulations, often described as "red tape," are a form of corruption. They have become common in many countries. Some of these may initially have been introduced to increase controls over some particular actions, perhaps to reduce corruption or abuses. However, in some cases they may exist or persist mainly to give power to some governments or to some bureaucracies, over particular groups of citizens, or, perhaps, to make it easier for some public officials to extract bribes, as much literature on corruption has argued. Examples are controls by public officials on the hygiene and the safety of restaurants, or other similar activities. In these controls, which may be justified, it is always easy for an inspector to claim to have found some irregularity. In some countries visits by tax inspectors to taxpayers' premises can lead to similar results and can create requests for, or offers of, bribes.

Although many regulations presumably exist to protect individuals in particular areas, for example, the visits to restaurants by health inspectors, some may exist to create rents for some categories of individuals by restricting entry for outsiders in particular activities, thus creating some monopoly power and some rents for those who are already operating in those activities. Categories that have attracted attention, especially in European countries, are those of pharmacists, notaries, and taxi drivers. For these activities it is difficult, or costly, for outsiders to acquire licenses to operate, and the licenses may be largely inherited, or sold, by those who own them, at high prices. In some activities, for example, for the medical profession, the rents are created by restricting the number of individuals who can enter the medical schools. Restrictions that create rents can be imposed by central governments, by subnational government, or by private groups that have been given the power to impose them.

A 2015 report on the United States issued by the White House showed that regulations connected with the need to acquire licenses to practice various activities in American states are a significant problem, as they are in other countries. In the United States these regulations are generally issued by the individual states and not by the federal government. "Occupational licensing requirements" are now required by the governments of most US states for individuals such as barbers, florists, travel guides, tourist guides, real estate agents, plumbers, and auctioneers. These licenses may require months of training in special centers and are in addition to the requirements by states to practice law, dentistry, medicine, and other professional activities, which are often limited to practice in the specific state that issues the license.

Ironically, some of the states where public officials complain most loudly about excessive *federal* regulations do not refrain from imposing these often-unnecessary requirements. It is difficult to understand why, for example, an individual needs to obtain a state license to work as a barber or to sell flowers, while it is easy to understand why being an airline pilot or a medical doctor should require a license. In the United States most licensing requirements are imposed by states. They make it more difficult and more costly for individuals in these categories to move from one state to another and to exercise the same activities that they have been practicing, without having to spend additional time and money to obtain a license in the state of destination.

A few years before the publication of this book there was a lot of commotion and media attention when France requested that Polish plumbers obtain French licenses before working as plumbers in France. This was interpreted as defying the European Union's single-market rule, which was supposed to allow labor mobility within the EU single market. That rule has so far worked better for the movement of goods than for the provision of services. The same problem seems to exist in the United States, where the share of workers needing state licenses to practice their activities varies from a low of 12 percent in South Carolina to a high of 33 percent in Iowa. The bottom line is that the United States is less of a single-market area than many American economists seem to believe (see Tanzi, 2013b, on this topic).

Not too many years ago, US banks could operate only in one state, and they could be either commercial banks or investment banks. It should be repeated that in the United States many regulations are not federal, but are imposed by states or by counties or municipalities. In other countries, they may be imposed by regional or municipal governments. These kinds of regulations have been growing over the years, thus progressively reducing labor mobility and imposing constraints on the economic liberty of individuals. Available information suggests that labor mobility may now be as high or higher in Europe than in the United States (ibid.).

In the United States many regulations on enterprises and on individuals continue to be imposed by both the federal government and local governments. Some aim at reducing abuses. As a recent source put it, "every week, the White House approves dozens of paperwork and reporting requirements." That source also reported that "a routine adjustment" to the reporting requirement for the Supplemental Nutrition Adjustment Program, connected with the large rise in recent years in the number of recipients of food stamps caused by the Great Recession, will require that "14.6 million Americans will provide 658 million responses to the Department of Agriculture annually." The cost to the households and the enterprises to comply with states and local governments will be $958 million, and to comply with the federal government it will be $356 million (see AAF, 2016). The American Action Forum (AAF) has reported that the "paperwork burden" has increased in all cabinet-level agencies in the United States, but especially in the Agriculture and Justice Departments since 2008. The AAF has also reported that the Dodd-Frank Wall Street Reform and Consumer Protection Act (Dodd-Frank) has required more than 400 new, costly rules.

Each year the federal government imposes about 3,000 "final rules," as reported in the *Federal Register*, and the total federal regulations now cover 168,000 pages in the *Code of Federal Regulations* (see Crews, 2014). The number of government programs now exceeds 2,300 (see Edwards, 2015). It is difficult to verify the accuracy of this information, but, if it is correct, it clearly points to a potential and growing problem. Other evidence indicates that regulations related to the tax system and to the payment of taxes have increased dramatically over the years, making the tax liability increasingly more difficult to determine and increasing the cost of compliance for American taxpayers. Similar complaints have been reported in several other countries (see Tanzi, 2013a).

Many regulations take the form of "mandated disclosures" connected with various activities (doctors' visits, credit card statements, etc.). They are directed at reducing the asymmetry of information that characterize those activities and at ensuring that existing rules are being followed. The usefulness of these disclosures (often intended to make consumers better informed on what they are buying and paying for), which inevitably add costs to the related activities, has been questioned. In most cases few read these disclosures. For example, in hospitals nurses now seem to spend more time filling out forms than taking care of patients, and many police officers spend more time doing the same than dealing with criminal activities. This reporting is required in various activities supervised or controlled by the government.

The threat of law suites and the perceived need to monitor some activities have contributed to this trend (see Ben-Shahar and Schneider, 2015). If these disclosures are as useless as these authors have indicated that they are, they must be classified as important termites of the state, termites that add to the costs of many activities but little to benefits. A major problem and one that reduces the disclosures' usefulness is that the information that they provide is often contained in fine print that few ever read or understand. Therefore, while the disclosures increase the costs of activities, they probably do little good for those who are supposed to benefit from them.

An interesting aspect of this development is the number of forms that the government now uses. There are some data available for the US federal government. According to a report by the AAF, that number is now 23,000. The Department of Health and Human Development and the Treasury Department combined account for more than 6,600. The Department of Agriculture imposes more than 3,700 forms. Interestingly, the latter department is also responsible for implementing important housing and welfare laws, such as the Rural Rental Housing Program and the Rural Energy Program. It is estimated that these forms generate more than 11 billion hours of paperwork per year. The AAF has suggested that there should be a "paperwork budget" within the government to limit the use of forms and papers. It would be difficult to establish the size of that budget.

Regulators defend these "mandated disclosures" as tools that help prevent abuses and that make information more available and, thus, more symmetric to the parties in particular exchanges. Many of these "mandated disclosures" were added after major abuses were revealed in past activities and after people were damaged, as happened after the Enron and the subprime disasters. Within a few weeks, Enron went from being one of the most admired enterprises in America to declaring bankruptcy. Lack of transparency in its operations, assisted by highly creative accounting that had been validated by a major accounting firm, had played a major role in creating the perception of a highly successful enterprise. After that disaster, which cost billions of dollars for many citizens, laws were passed for enterprises to provide much more information, increasing the costs to the enterprises and their complaints.

As John Campbell, a Harvard professor, put it in his 2016 American Economic Association (AEA) Ely Lecture:

> Within the last ten years, the reach of regulation has been extended by the most important US consumer financial legislation since the New Deal of the 1930s, notably the Pension Protection Act of 2006, the Credit Card Accountability Responsibility and Disclosure Act (CARD Act) of 2009, and the Dodd-Frank Act that created the Consumer Financial Protection Bureau. Similar trends are visible around the world.

Once again, it is difficult to determine whether the benefits from these regulations and especially the disclosures, in the forms in which they are provided, exceed the costs that they impose. It must be repeated that these developments generally *followed* major disasters or problems, as had the regulations introduced in the 1930s, and were designed to prevent future disasters.

When governments impose many regulations to protect some groups or some individuals from abuses, they are likely to create some obstacles that did not exist before to the functioning of the economy, and to impose some potentially high costs for the activities of some individuals and some enterprises. They might also create some rents for others. For example, regulations on the production or the use of coal implicitly imply subsidies to other forms of energy. The new regulations may also encourage some forms of corruption by giving discretion and monopoly powers to particular public officials charged with enforcing the regulations. Therefore, there are inevitably both some costs that attract more attention and some benefits that are associated with the use of regulations.

An aspect that has not attracted much attention from economists is that bad or unnecessary regulations not only restrict the supply side of the economy by increasing costs and reducing potential output; they may also restrict aggregate demand by reducing some investments and preventing some economic actions that would have taken place and would have created jobs and increased demand (see Tanzi, 2015b). However, without *essential* regulations, governments might also encourage abuses created by lack of disclosure and excessive risk taking, or the creation of negative externalities for others or for the environment. Again, there are costs and benefits. The benefits are rarely quantified while the costs often are.

Problems often develop when: (a) existing regulations are applied arbitrarily and selectively; (b) they are not clear and give rise to different interpretations; or (c) the regulators end up being captured by the regulated, as often happens. Regulatory capture has been recognized for a long time to be a serious problem for the economic role of the state. It has been an important termite of the state for a long time. In the United States it was a problem in the past that had attracted the attention of George Stigler, Richard Posner, and others. The problem has not disappeared today, especially at the subnational level.

Unfortunately, these problems seem to have become more frequent in today's world, especially in sectors where relaxing (or ignoring) some regulations that enterprises are required to adhere to, for safety or environmental reasons, may bring large financial gains to the enterprises and potential costs or occasional dangers to the citizens. For example, relaxing regulations would allow some enterprises to put more carbon in the atmosphere or more pollution in rivers, without paying the price for it. Or it would allow some enterprises to reduce costs, leading to reduced safety of workers.

Enterprises, or organizations that represent them, spend a lot of money to fight the introduction of new regulations, or to repeal or relax existing ones. In the United States, the pharmaceutical industry, the energy industry, and the financial sector have been particularly active in fighting regulations that increase their costs and reduce their profits. It has been reported that they have spent billions of dollars in attempts to stop the introductions of new rules, or relax existing ones. The Trump administration has promised and has started to act to do away with many regulations and to reduce the budget of regulatory agencies.

Salary disparities between government jobs and jobs involving particular private activities have become larger in recent decades, making the latter jobs more attractive, especially for the "best and the brightest". Additionally, many government jobs no longer bring the prestige and the social status that they used to bring in the past. Therefore, they may no longer be attracting the same quality of individuals as they did in the past. At the same time, some of these government jobs create opportunities of future gains for particular individuals if they can use the acquired skills and the connections to assist some regulated sectors after they leave their government jobs. Therefore, some government jobs may be attracting people more motivated by money gains than by the desire to contribute to the public good.

In today's world, many new regulations do not originate from the governments' own realization of particular needs. Rather, they are pushed by civic associations or by groups of citizens who share particular interests. Groups of citizens often criticize the government for not intervening in the face of what they consider obvious needs for intervention. This is especially true at subnational or local levels, but also at the national level. In some sense the push for these regulations may be seen as an expression of the democratic process at work. But, as the late Mancur Olson argued a long time ago, the creation of too many private interests inevitably introduces obstacles that end up reducing economic growth (see Olson 1965, 1982).

Regulations aimed at restricting some activities by individuals, because they are damaging or are simply annoying to other individuals, have become more common, because of the growing urbanization that is inevitably accompanied by greater population density. Also, regulations that promote the particular interests of specific groups have increased in democratic societies. Examples of these regulations are those that aim to preserve historical or architectural features, to preserve biological diversity, to restrict noise in public places, to limit overbuilding in some areas, to restrict the size of houses built on particular lots, to restrict parking to specific areas, to require minimum amounts of land (at times ridiculously large amounts) to build houses in some areas, to prevent the removal of old trees, to prevent the ownership of pets in some communities, to cook outside, and so on. In New York City there has even been discussion of introducing a regulation that would prevent "leg spreading" in crowded subway cars! And in San Francisco one can have chickens in the houses but not roosters because of the externalities that they generate for sleeping individuals in early morning.

These regulations often bring tension between the perceived freedom of some individuals and the perceived needs of communities or groups of individuals. The new regulations often cannot be prevented by "covenants" made hundreds of years ago, because those covenants could not have anticipated some aspects of modern living; and some would no longer be tolerated in modern societies, as those against particular ethnic or religious groups used to be in the past. Some of the existing restrictions have at times made it difficult to bring major economic developments to underdeveloped areas close to urban centers, because the changes need to have the endorsement of a myriad of civic organizations, some with conflicting interests and views. The above explains why regulations are more familiar in cities than in rural areas.

What economists call the promotion of the "public interest" in today's societies is not a goal only interpreted and promoted by the government. Furthermore, the definition of "public interest" tends to change, and has changed, over the years with the increasing share of the population that can vote, compared to the case a century ago. It has become progressively more debatable and more difficult to define what the public interest is, especially in a society that has lost the sense of being a community and of having common, shared goals, a society that is made up of increasingly heterogeneous aggregations of individuals with fewer common interests and with many separate and conflicting ones (see Putnam, 2000). Even the increase in life expectancy, clearly a desirable development, has increased the heterogeneity of the population in terms of the distribution by age, and has made the public interest more difficult to define or to identify.

CHAPTER 13

A Brief Inventory of Government Tools

Together with the more common instruments of policy that attract much of the attention of economists (public spending and taxation), regulations play an important and growing role in the promotion of governments' goals in the modern world. As happened with other policy tools, and as we saw in the previous chapter, termites have been active in the field of regulations. At times they have distorted the function of regulations from what it would have been in an ideal world, assuming that such a world could be defined. In this chapter I shall discuss in more detail some areas where problems have developed. These problems contribute to the difficulties that governments have been facing in recent years in pursuing an optimal or desirable role in their economic operations.

Over the centuries, the development of communities and societies had often been mirrored by the rules that they had developed to govern personal behavior. Rules were seen as necessary for organized communities to guide the behavior of their members, to prevent antisocial behavior on the part of some, and to promote certain agreed and desirable conducts of citizens. Economic exchanges and other interactions in those communities were assumed to be guided by "codes of behavior" considered appropriate by the communities. This is still true today within clubs, professional associations, and other groups, which members have the option of not joining if they do not like the rules or the less formal norms. But once they are club members, they must observe the rules and respect the norms. It is also especially important for countries in which, because of size and diversity, some citizens may be less predisposed to follow rules considered desirable by the community. Immigration clearly contributes to the need for clear rules for everyone. As societies become more advanced, more heterogeneous, and more complex, they are likely to require *more* and more-*precise* rules for their members because traditional norms may guide their behaviourless.

One relevant question is whether the rules need to be imposed by the state, or whether they could arise spontaneously from the free actions of the relevant members, as they often did, and still do, in traditional communities. Who should be the regulator? And do societies necessarily need regulators? A related question, which will not receive attention until later in the book, is, if a regulator is needed, who will regulate the regulator? These questions lie at the heart of the ongoing debate about economic actions and their regulation. A further question, in federations, is the relative role of the central government vis-à-vis that of the subnational, regional governments, and that of municipalities in unitary governments.

Some economists, political scientists, and historians who have studied past societies have concluded that, in some important instances, for example, in commercial activities, in the pursuit of justice, in urban planning, and in some other areas, various rules developed spontaneously from the interactions among individuals, without the active intervention of a government (see, inter alia, Beito et al., 2002). These experts have argued that the spontaneous rules had contributed to relatively smooth and efficient economic and social relations and exchanges. The rules had been enforced by those who took direct part in the activities and not by governments, which in any case might not have been able to do much, given their limited administrative capability at that time. The penalty for not following the rules was exclusion from certain spheres of economic or social activity. Some have argued that the intervention of the state, when it came, resulted in the crowding out of the traditional rules, and that the government rules were often less flexible and more costly in implementation and produced less effective outcomes.

Advocates of this position, which include conservative politicians and "market fundamentalists," believe and argue that markets or, more broadly, the economic behavior of free individuals in free markets tends to be largely self-regulating, and that formal, government-imposed rules are often not necessary. When they are applied, they lead to less desirable outcomes. Some advocates of rule-free markets have blamed the government – which had pushed or encouraged private banks to lend money to low-income individuals, to induce them to buy houses that they could hardly afford – for the subprime problems that led to the financial crisis of 2007–2008. They have argued that government-imposed rules are, in many situations, damaging to the economy, because they eliminate the self-correcting action of markets or of groups, making transactions more costly. By doing so, they may reduce the innovative spirit that drives and should drive market economies. In the long run, they may reduce economic growth and individual liberty.

The aforementioned important argument, which in the decades after the 1970s acquired many followers and which in more recent years has been subjected to criticisms (because of the financial crisis and other episodes), will be considered further a little later. However, there are also examples that indicate that in premodern societies some rules and regulations had been motivated by attempts to exclude, or to discriminate against, particular groups or, in some cases, to favor some groups. It must also be kept in mind that traditional societies were generally more homogeneous than are most modern societies. Therefore, some forms of community spirit were more likely to be present than in today's societies. When that spirit was particularly strong, it tended to transform these communities into extended families and to facilitate the use of the traditional rules.

Regulations are among the tools that governments use to promote various goals. Organized societies need governments, and governments need tools to promote the communities' goals and to guide the actions, by individuals and enterprises, that the governments wish to promote. Behind the use of the government tools there is today the expectation that democratic governments will promote goals assigned to them by the *majority* of the voters in fair elections, and that politicians and policymakers will follow the instructions that they receive from the voters. Therefore, no principal-agent problems should develop between voters and policymakers. At the same time, groups of citizens who share common interests, or who represent particular sectors of the societies or the economies, are free to organize themselves in political parties or in other groups to lobby the policymakers to promote policies favorable to them.

Not only do governments have a number of tools at their disposal to promote their objectives, but, to an extent greater than realized, the tools available can be substituted among themselves, and, for various reasons, some of them become more important than others, and are preferred by governments at various times. For example, over the past half-century US governments have favored "tax expenditures" to encourage some forms of private spending, while many European governments have given preference to public spending. Some economists have argued that these two tools can be used to promote the same objective and, therefore, can be considered as interchangeable. Particular kinds of administrative or political incentives influence the governments to make more use of some tools compared with others. The main tools, or instruments, of economic policy include:

(1) **Public spending**. Both the *level* and the *structure* of government spending are important. In recent decades, in advanced countries, both became more important than they had been in the past or than they are in poorer countries. Both were affected by the changing role of the state in the economy, which took place in the past hundred years and generally pushed for more public spending (see Tanzi and Schuknecht, 2000; Tanzi, 2011). To some extent, public spending can be replaced (in the pursuit of some objectives) by regulations or by "tax expenditures."

(2) **Tax levels and tax structures**. Once again, both the *level* of taxation and the *structure* of the tax systems are important tools of policy. Both have been affected by: (a) the changing role of the state; (b) changing tax technology (the invention of new taxes, such as the value-added tax); (c) the changing structures of economies (see Tanzi, 2014c); and (d) the changing capacity and sophistication of the tax administrations. In today's rich countries tax levels are much higher than they were a century ago, and governments have greater administrative, if not always political, discretion to raise higher tax levels.

(3) **Tax expenditures and tax incentives** have played major but different roles in recent decades in most countries. The concept of tax expenditure was promoted in the United States by Stanley Surrey, a lawyer, in the 1960s. Tax expenditures are tax credits for taxpayers; they can mimic and, thus, replace to some extent public spending. For example, when mortgage payments, or health or educational spending, are allowed to be deducted from taxable income (before the rates for taxable income are applied), the effect of the tax expenditures is to reduce the cost of that spending to the taxpayers and presumably to increase the spending on those goods. Both tax expenditures and tax incentives represent challenges by policymakers to consumer choices and to market decisions. Thus, they are challenges to the free market and individual freedom.

(4) **Public ownership** of enterprises or of other assets. In various countries, and during particular periods, governments have either nationalized or privatized some enterprises to promote particular social objectives. Socialist ideology has always promoted more public ownership. Most governments own public assets that they use to promote particular goals. For example, it has been estimated that, for historical reasons, the Italian public sector owns about three times as many public assets, as a share of GDP, as the British government. The US government owns enormous extensions of public lands. Some of these lands have become national parks.

Some countries, such as New Zealand, have developed statistics that keep track of the "net worth" of the public sector, that is, the difference between the value of all the assets that it owns and all its liabilities. Some economists have maintained that the net worth of a public sector is an important fiscal statistic, because it provides information on the fiscal health of a country at a given time. Information available for some countries has indicated that the rate of return on the assets held by the governments is generally low. In any case public ownership allows governments to pursue particularly important noneconomic or nonfinancial goals. In the United States some complain that public lands are not available for free and unrestricted private economic use, including mining or grazing.

(5) **Expropriation and rezoning** power. Governments (national and especially local governments) occasionally use their legal power to expropriate privately held properties, or to rezone land use, to promote particular economic or social goals. Depending on the countries' constitutions, these actions are easier to accomplish in some countries than in others. Rezoning can dramatically change the market value of some properties and especially the value of land close to cities. Zoning classification is used to promote particular community objectives, such as city planning, to create industrial parks, to build airports or roads, and so on. The fact that the value of a property can be significantly changed by the decision of a few bureaucrats makes this a very sensitive policy instrument and one that can easily lead to governance problems.

(6) **Conscription**. Governments have used the instrument of conscription, for example, compulsory military service, for a long time. This instrument has become less important in the modern, democratic world, in which governments prefer to buy the services of the citizens using public money. In the distant past conscription was often the major instrument used to fight wars, to build roads and canals, or to help with other major projects. As a result, heavy burdens were occasionally imposed on the populations but were not reported in statistics that measured the tax burdens. Many of the great public works of the past, such as the Great Wall of China or the pyramids of Egypt, Mexico, and Central America, were probably built using the tool of conscription. The walls around many old European cities were often built in this way. In past centuries, in some countries, the "nobles" had the power to impose some of these burdens on the "serfs" who lived on their lands. This led to occasional revolutions.

(7) **Certifications and authorization.** An increasingly important instrument over the last century has been "certifications" or "authorizations" that can be obtained from the national or local governments to perform particular activities. These permits are given by public institutions or, at times, by private institutions authorized by the government to grant them. In today's world and in some countries more than in other countries, many activities require these permits. The certification documents are often obtained (at times after some training) through the payment of fees. In less democratic governments, or in governments with poor governance, they may be used to grant favors, and monopoly powers, to some individuals. They form an integral part of crony capitalism. These certifications are important in activities related to specialized services, and especially in the provision of medical, legal, and personal services. In sixteenth-century France, even beggars needed a city authorization, or license, to be allowed to beg in a city. At times the authorization specified the street corner where the beggar could beg (see Solomon, 1972, p. 30).

(8) **Contingent liabilities.** This is a modern instrument of great and growing importance for governments. It is the assumption (by the government) of a possible future, contingent liability related to some possible events. Because of its relative novelty and its growing importance in the modern world, this instrument deserves more space than the others. Contingent liabilities are guarantees given (implicitly or explicitly) by governments for some private activities, including deposits in commercial banks. By so doing the government may be able to influence some economic activity at a given time, without directly, immediately, and often explicitly spending money. However, the contingent liability exposes the government to potentially large future financial risks.

The importance of this instrument has been growing in recent decades, and, at times, it has been behind some recent crises. It grew when governments started to guarantee some of the deposits that savers held in commercial banks, or when, especially in the 1990s, governments pushed toward the privatization of infrastructure that had previously been publicly built, through the use of PPP contracts. In PPPs the building of infrastructures (roads, airports, metros, etc.) is assigned to private enterprises, which build at their expense and operate them with some government guarantee (at times an implicit one) on the rate of return on the investment. Also, activities that in the past had been fully private (such as deposits of savers held in private banks) acquired government guarantees and exposed governments to the risks that were taken by the financial institutions. Activities that in the past had often been public (the building and management of some infrastructures) became private, but with government guarantees. In some cases governments provide insurance for properties located in disaster-prone areas (those subject to hurricanes, earthquakes, etc.).

When the instrument of contingent liability is used, the government, or at times some publicly financed or publicly guaranteed institution, assumes the financial risk in the event of the private activity's failing, or, in some cases, when it does not meet agreed earnings expectations. This also happened on a massive scale when banks or insurance companies failed during the financial crisis, and various governments were forced to spend huge sums to protect and preserve the financial system, even though in some of these cases the governments had formally no legal obligation to do so. These guarantees have removed the firewalls that had existed in the past between the public and the private sectors.

Contingent liabilities may be associated with private activities or with the activities of subnational governments or quasi-public institutions. They tend to transform hard budgets into "soft budgets" for some institutions. As mentioned, some of the guarantees provided by the government may be implicit, rather than explicit, which makes it more difficult to assess the financial status of and the risks assumed by governments. The guarantees may not be based on formal agreements but on the strong expectation that the government will intervene if certain events occur. This is more likely to happen when the government has encouraged some lending or some actions on the part of private banking institutions or public enterprises. This was the case with Fannie Mae and Freddie Mac in the United States during the financial crisis. Also, banks in other countries were often encouraged by governments both national and sub-national to lend to some politically privileged sectors. This probably happened in Ireland Spain, and Italy which left those governments exposed to large fiscal risks.

The expectation that the government will intervene in the future may be influenced by its past behavior and may create what economists call "moral hazard," which may make some institutions take greater risks than they would have otherwise. The danger created by "too big to fail" financial institutions is based on these expectations. Some institutions, and especially some banks, may become so big that the expectation that the government would not allow them to fail, because it would put a country's economy at high risk, comes to be widely shared. This also allows some banks to get credit more cheaply, thus distorting competition.

Contingent liabilities and moral hazards may become particularly important in catastrophic events. By (implicitly or explicitly) assuming the potential risks, the government, intentionally or unintentionally, encourages private concerns to enter some activities, or to continue operating in some riskier circumstances or places. This is widely believed to have happened in the financial sector in the last decade. It is also likely to happen in areas subject to hurricanes, floods, or earthquakes when investments in those areas are (expected to be) protected by government insurance. Contingent liabilities have become a major termite.

As mentioned, contingent guarantees or liabilities are at times explicit and at times implicit. The explicit ones are given and are known in advance by those who engage in particular activities. The implicit ones remain uncertain until the problems arise. Whether the government will intervene or not in a crisis may depend on the political power of those exposed to the losses, and on their relationships with the policymakers who will make the decisions. In either case, the expected assumption of these risks by the government is likely to promote more risk taking by some individuals or institutions. See Polackova Brixi and Schick (2002) in connection with risks in public–private partnerships.

The potential but uncertain costs to the governments associated with these guarantees are not included in the countries' budgets. Thus, these guarantees do not change the official "look" of the fiscal policy stance of a country, while they may change substantially the "substance" of it; in some cases, they may put governments at risk of large potential expenses, as happened in Ireland, Iceland and other countries during the financial crisis. The financial crisis, which forced many governments to come to the rescue of banks, left various governments with much worsened fiscal (and economic) situations, because of these contingent liabilities. It proved that there were no firewalls between the public and the private sectors and that some private debt can easily become public debt so that the rise of private debt should be a government concern.

Governments have been encouraged to give details, in budget documents, of the explicit commitments that they undertake. Of course, they cannot do it for the implicit ones, without formally committing themselves to expenses that are still unknown. When some information is provided, which often it is not, it is contained in footnotes or in memoranda added to budgets, which may receive little attention. However, many contingent liabilities are not visible or explicit ex ante and might reflect private and nontransparent understandings.

The more complex the financial system becomes, and the greater the chance of failure, the greater becomes the reason to keep the official fiscal accounts of countries in good shape in normal times, so that the countries can more easily assume the extra costs of financial failures. Ireland could cope better than Greece with the fiscal consequences of the financial crisis, because its fiscal accounts had been kept in better shape. Greece's already overburdened and unhealthy fiscal situation made it more difficult for the country to deal with the financial crisis.

Contingent liabilities represent one way in which governments promote some of their goals without immediately revealing problems for the future and without the immediate use of money. Thus, they help give the impression, to unsophisticated or unwary observers, that the role of the state is more limited than it actually is. This can create dangerous fiscal illusions and promote bad policies. The growth of contingent liabilities in many countries in recent years should be cause for concerns.

Contingent liabilities are related to but must be distinguished from the future government liabilities associated with defined-benefit pensions or with public health care systems, in which the costs of these programs are expected to grow over time and to significantly exceed the assets allocated to them, as is now the case in the United States and in many European and other countries (see Tanzi, 2016b). These liabilities are also not reported in the fiscal deficits and thus also lead to statistics that do not correctly measure the true fiscal situation of a country. However, these liabilities, which arise from demographic changes or from the rising cost of health protection, are not the result of unlikely and catastrophic events but, within some ranges, are known and anticipated costs, deferred in time and not shown in the current budgets.

A comprehensive system of accrual budgeting that better measures the impact of public activity would show these future costs. However, their estimation should be subjected to careful analysis to take into account potential alternative developments in future years that might increase or decrease the size of the liability. Changes in growth rates, in interest rates, and in life expectancy are examples of these developments.

As mentioned, some of the contingent liabilities are implicit rather than explicit, making current accounting more difficult. For example, many observers had believed that the liabilities assumed by Fannie Mae and Freddie Mac, the large US financial institutions that buy the mortgages of many home buyers, had had the formal backing of the US government. This had allowed these institutions to get cheaper credit from the market and to promote more house ownership, further pushing upward the prices of houses, which created the bubble. Thus, before any crisis had developed, these commitments may have already distorted economic activities in various ways. The enormous expansion of this activity in the United States put the US government at risk of huge liabilities when the institutions failed and forced it to assume a trillion dollars of additional gross liabilities. Global warming might create similar situations for some governments and so could a return to historical interest rates on the part of central banks.

(9) **Economic Regulations.** The use of regulations is another important instrument of governmental economic policy through which behavior and economic activities can be influenced. At various times and in particular situations, this instrument has been extensively used and abused by governments, at both the national and the subnational levels. Economic regulations are among the most powerful tools of government policy. In many ways they are no different from budgetary tools and should receive the same amount of attention by public finance economists as taxes and public spending receive. We shall return to this important instrument more fully in the next chapter.

(10) **Nudging or cajolement** is another instrument that governments occasionally use to influence the behavior of citizens. This instrument has been attracting much more attention in recent years on the part of experimental and behavioral economists. Traditionally, it had been used by mothers and grandmothers to promote good behavior on the part of children, and it had been used occasionally in the past by governments, especially in war periods, to induce citizens to do certain things, such as buy government bonds, donate gold for financing wars, or enlist in the army.

Recent behavioral economics research has been suggesting new ways of influencing individual behavior in desirable directions, e.g., inducing people to save more, to smoke less, to eat less bad food and more vegetables, or to sign up to insurance schemes. Nudging or cajolement represents a *tutorial* approach through which governments now can try, more systematically than in the past, to influence the decisions of citizens about health, happiness, wealth accumulation, moral codes, and other areas, without seeming to force them. Talks about irrational behavior by individuals and the market have become more frequent. They have challenged the traditional view, often stressed in the past by Milton Friedman, that most individuals act rationally. Some books have provided interesting discussions of the potential use of this instrument. Like all the instruments available to the state, nudging can be used to promote legitimate and, when used by a bad government, possibly less legitimate objectives. Therefore, termites may also easily enter in its use.

When he was mayor of New York, Michael Bloomberg used this instrument to change some bad habits of New Yorkers, and some foreign governments have also been using it. When it influences the use of taxes, as was the case recently when Philadelphia started to tax soft drinks to reduce the consumption of sugar, this instrument may cease to be "libertarian."

(11) **Fees and fines**. Governments can raise public resources and achieve particular social objectives by imposing and changing fees on access to some publicly provided activities. For example, the cost of getting a passport or a driver's license, of studying in a public university, or of getting access to a national park or to public transportation can be adjusted, as can the cost, or the co-pay, for getting drugs or some health procedures in a public health system. Some of these payments are increased to cover costs to governments, to restrict access to over-crowded facilities, or to achieve some other objectives. Also, fines for various violations of rules, such as traffic regulations, may be used to reduce the frequency of the violations, or simply to raise additional public revenues.

There is evidence from several sources that, in recent decades, some governments have been making more use of fees and fines to raise revenue to increase public spending or to reduce taxes. In the United States, some towns now raise more revenue from these sources than from traditional tax sources, and local governments collect about one-fourth of their total revenue from these sources. Some cities have installed machines that control presumed traffic violations (exceeding speed limits or going through red lights). These machines have become major revenue sources. There have even been reports that in some cities they have been "doctored" to catch more presumed traffic violators to raise more public revenue.

The aforementioned developments have reflected the intellectual winds of recent decades on the economic role of the state. The revenues collected from these sources are often collected regressively. They tend to reduce the redistributive role of the state, while they make more use of the presumed effectiveness of financial incentives (in these cases, penalties) in promoting particular behaviors.

The list of instruments that governments use to promote their objectives gives a better idea of how wide and how complex governmental intervention in the economy has become, and how naïve are statements that the government should stay out of the way and let the economy and the private operators do their thing, in an economy and a market free from governmental intervention. The list also provides an idea of the many ways in which "termites" can enter and have entered the economic system and the actions of governments. The most exposed areas are the ones in which private and public activities intersect or are supposed to cooperate.

To keep the length of this book within reasonable limits, its focus will remain on the main instruments that governments use in the pursuit of their objectives.

CHAPTER 14

A Closer Look at Regulations

Let us return to the policy instrument of regulations, an instrument that has become increasingly more important and more controversial in the modern world and especially in the United States. Regulations are now used in various areas to achieve collective purposes. As was indicated earlier, it is not possible to determine in any empirical sense what would be an optimal number of regulations in an economy. Presumably, it is *only* when the benefits expected from a regulation exceed the costs that it should be used. This valuation is obviously difficult to make. There is likely to be an increasing need for regulations in changing social and economic activities for individuals and enterprises that can create significant negative externalities, and it is possible for governments to overuse regulations. Alternatively, governments may not respond sufficiently to the citizens' requests for some regulations.

An attempt follows to provide a brief taxonomy of the regulations observed in modern societies.

(1) **Nuisance regulations.** These are regulations that seem to have little other purpose than that of empowering public bureaucrats charged with their enforcement. These nuisance regulations can be seen as "stealth taxes" to achieve particular nondesirable objectives. These regulations may benefit some group by imposing costs on other groups, and they may extract taxes by imposing fees, fines, or constraints for particular activities. In essence they may be considered taxes for some and subsidies for others. For example, restaurant managers or workers may be required to take training courses for safety or for other reasons *from specified providers* to be allowed to do their work. This happens in several countries.

This is also often the case with the myriad of authorizations imposed by local governments on legitimate activities, such as opening new shops and factories and continuing to operate these activities, owning cars, renewing driver's licenses, and performing other activities. In some cases, there may be legitimate reasons for requiring authorizations, but they may be easily abused. The International Finance Corporation (IFC) at the World Bank has reported that the time, the cost, and the number of steps required to start a new economic activity, or to set up an enterprise, vary from a few hours or days in some countries (Ireland) to years in others (Greece). It is often difficult to understand the reasons for this range.

In some European cities, the authorization of city mayors is required for shops to sell at discounted prices during sales. Other rules establish the opening and the closing hours of shops, or the hours of the day when particular taxi drivers can operate their vehicles. Items such as newspapers, aspirins, etc. can only be sold in specified places (e.g., newsstands or pharmacies), and the sale of a used car may require the use of a specialized lawyer who charges a significant fee (including some transfer tax) for the service.

At times it is difficult to understand the rationale for certain rules or regulations, some of which may have historical antecedents. For example, during the reign of Louis XVI in France, the government issued a rule that handkerchiefs could only be produced in the form of squares and that they had to be of a specified size! Also in France, as reported earlier, beggars needed to have a license from the municipality to be allowed to beg in the streets, and the license specified the street corner where the beggar could exercise the begging right or activity. In California at one time, only bread of a specified weight (one pound) could be sold! In several US cities, alcoholic beverages cannot be purchased on Sunday morning!

By installing administrative obstacles for various activities and by requiring authorizations, regulations might increase the safety of citizens, but they also increase costs and encourage corruption, because public employees acquire some discretion over their application. Not surprisingly, in recent decades when regulations have become more common, corruption has become an important termite in the activities of many governments. Especially when regulations are accompanied by opacity in wording and discretion in their use, they create fertile grounds for acts of corruption.

(2) **Second-best regulations**. At times regulations aim to achieve social objectives that, in principle, could have been promoted by other means. However, for political, administrative, or financial reasons, regulations may be preferred. Examples include rent controls, minimum wages, controls on the prices of some essential goods, rationing,

requirements for enterprises to ensure that a proportion of the workers they hire have some physical handicaps or ethnic characteristics, or requirements for universities to admit some proportion of students from minority groups. Better results might be achieved by taxing some groups while subsidizing others. However, the alternatives might not be considered politically or administratively feasible or desirable.

Rent controls and similar programs may contribute to the creation of poverty traps if those who benefit from them lose the subsidy when they get a higher-paying job that disqualifies them from the benefit. A country that adopts a policy of rent controls loses national income, while the government loses tax revenue, because of the lower rental income and lower property values. Similar arguments could be made for regulations that establish minimum wages. They help some workers but are likely to hurt others who remain unemployed by restricting the demand for labor. Regulations that establish price controls for some products often lead to black markets and to scarcity of the goods whose prices are controlled.

(3) **Purely social regulations** establish official working hours for shops, obligations for them to be closed on holidays, vacation times for workers, limits to overtime, age limits for workers, limits on when alcoholic beverages can be sold, quotas for some categories of workers, etc. They may lower the demand for labor and the percentage of the population that works, while at the same time providing protection to some categories of workers. Some economists have attributed certain economic problems that have been faced by European countries in recent decades (slow growth and high unemployment) to the excessive use of social regulations.

(4) **Safety-related regulations** aim at reducing accidents or damages from accidents or from the use or consumption of some products. They are necessary to allow particular activities to operate smoothly and safely, such as traffic regulations, regulations that impose good standards in operations of mines and similar risky activities, or regulations that aim at reducing environmental problems or risks connected to the use of some drugs, chemicals, or even some food products. There continues to be criticism about some of the regulations that relate to the environment and to the use of some drugs, because of their relatively high impact on costs and the (presumably or questionably) low impact on safety. The problem is that the safety of new chemicals is often known only much later, rather than when a chemical has been first used. For example, in the United States drinking water often has been tested for

a specific list of chemicals, but not for new chemicals that have been in use in agriculture and in other activities only more recently. Normally, the effected industries or enterprises exaggerate the costs that the regulations impose on them and minimize or ignore the benefits to the consumers.

Among the safety-related regulations we could include those that require the wearing of seat belts in cars or helmets when bicycles or motorcycles are ridden. Some libertarians object to these regulations because they do not create externalities that affect others, and thus do not satisfy one of the essential elements set by John Stuart Mill's essay "On Liberty." However, in a society that has introduced a system of public health, a system of compulsory health insurance, or a system of liability insurance for driving cars or motorcycles, greater health expenses by some individuals, caused by lack of safe behavior, always generate *some* forms of externalities, such as higher health or insurance spending for other members of society. In a modern society, no person is truly an island, and Mill's argument has more limited relevance.

(5) **Externality-correcting or -reducing regulations** are closely related to the regulations in the previous category. They aim at reducing some negative externalities, when more flexible and more efficient tools are not (or are not easily) available. This is also the case for the environmental policies that use regulations, instead of taxes on the polluters, to reduce pollution. Regulations are generally less costly and easier to impose, administer, or, perhaps, enforce, although, as we saw earlier, they may impose costly reporting requirements and may promote corruption. Environmental regulations have become increasingly more numerous and more controversial within the regulated industries, especially the energy industry, which complains about the costs imposed on it and challenges the scientific justification of some of the rules, as well as the financial market.

(6) **Regulations for natural monopolies** have attracted the attention of economists for a long time. Natural monopolies, or public utilities, run by private interests need controls over tariffs to limit excessive monopoly profits. Because of the monopoly power that the enterprises have, or are assumed to have, some regulation seems justified. However, the regulations may continue when the monopoly power begins to be eroded because of new competition. The protection given to intellectual property has created many new types of time-limited and unregulated monopolies in recent years. A later chapter will address directly issues connected with intellectual property rights.

(7) **Regulations to protect consumers**. The aim of these regulations is to protect the public in economic exchanges where full, honest, and transparent information is not available to everyone, especially when that information may be necessary, for example, in food, drug, transportation, and banking safety. These regulations concern the growing number of activities in which information tends to be asymmetric between the two sides of an exchange. For example, passengers need to have some confidence that a plane, train, or bus meets reasonable safety standards when they board it. Bank depositors need to have some warranty that the bank does not take excessive risks with its money. Patients need a guarantee that the medicine they take does not have serious or lethal side effects. Patrons of restaurants need to have some guarantee that the restaurant respects a minimum standard of hygiene, so that they will not be exposed to food poisoning. In essence consumers need to have some guarantees that the claims made by the sellers for what the consumers buy reflect reality, because they cannot always trust those on the other side of exchanges.

While in a market economy an ideal course would be to trust the honesty, the judgment, and the incentives of the providers or sellers (so as to make supervision and regulation by the government unnecessary), daily evidence suggests that such a course would not always be consistent with the people's welfare. Thus, it may seem reasonable for the government, or for a proxy of it, to have some responsibility in regulating the activities of these sectors, in making the necessary information available to the public, and in forcing the providers to give full, reliable, and easily understood information or to respect some useful codes of conduct.

By and large, especially in advanced countries, it can be maintained that the market still works reasonably well and better than any feasible alternatives. However, in the view of many observers, and as indicated by various experiences reported by the free media, the market does not work well enough, especially in some sectors. Furthermore, in some areas, problems appear to be growing.

In free, competitive markets, those who operate in them seek to make profits, and profits can often be made more easily by reducing costs and exploiting asymmetries in information, of which there are many kinds, including some created by false, or biased, advertising, and occasionally by the irrationality of consumers. Psychological weaknesses of buyers, or of some categories of buyers, can be exploited by clever, less scrupulous sellers. In free markets, buyers are free to choose, but as a recent book by two

Nobel Prize winners has argued, sellers are free to fish ("phish") for fools ("phools"). Today, at times using big data, sellers have increasing amounts of information on some (irrational?) attitudes of consumers, so they can more easily identify and exploit buyers' weaknesses. With their publicity, the sellers can create stories that aim at pushing buyers to purchase particular products. "Marlboro men" will be made to look attractive for smoking men and "Virginia Slims women" to look sophisticated and liberated for smoking women. See Akerlof and Shiller (2015) for a discussion of these characteristics of free markets.

Some of these problems have been aggravated by globalization, and some are increasingly connected with the complexity of arrangements in various areas. The more complex exchanges become, the more they lend themselves to potential abuses. In some sectors, these problems seem to be becoming increasingly frequent and more serious with the passing of time, making it more necessary for governments to intervene, but more difficult for governments to do it efficiently and successfully.

To give intuitive and concrete sense to the aforementioned problem, we shall refer to some recent reports. One, issued in April 2016 by the Organization for Economic Co-operation and Development (OECD) and the European Union's Intellectual Property Office, has estimated that in 2013 the global trade in *fake goods* was worth $ 461 billion, or about 2.5 percent of world trade. About 5 percent of all goods imported in the European Union were estimated to be "fakes." Some of the fake products (auto parts that fail, pharmaceuticals that make people sick, etc.) can put lives in danger. Many of these products infringe on trademarks, design rights, or patents. The countries most affected by these fakes were, in decreasing order, the United States, Italy, France, Switzerland, Germany, and Japan. Many of the fake products originated in China.

While this report focused on fakes in trade among countries, another report focused on fakes within the domestic food market, specifically in the United States. It showed that much of what is sold as food *produced in the local market* has little relation with the local market. Most of the claims made are false (see Reiley, 2016). Another report, by a nongovernmental organization (NGO) called Oceana, found that one in five fish sold had been mislabeled and that fish rich in mercury had been used in sushi and other restaurants (It was reported in an article of the *Economist*, December 23, 2016).

The aforementioned reports make a case for some regulation of the goods market, which, if effective, can improve safety and reduce abuses. In fact, the report by Oceana indicates that regulations introduced by the

European Union had reduced the mislabeling of fish in Europe from 23 percent of instances in 2000 to 8 percent in 2015. Information coming from China and India could be added; serious cases of food poisoning have been reported in these countries in recent years. In October 2015 these events led the Chinese government to issue a revised Food Safety Law aimed at improving food safety. It remains to be seen how effective that law will prove to be. Obviously, to get a better impression of the full problem of the fakes, or the dangerous *products* traded in the goods market, one has to add all the false claims and the dangers in the *service* market, including the medical areas, the financial sector, and others.

Some regulations are likely to be considered necessary by most objective observers – for example, most of the regulations that regulate road or air traffic. However, even in these instances, there may be disagreement on the level of, or the need for, particular aspects of the regulations. For example, there may be speed limits for automobiles that may be considered too high by older people and too low by younger ones, or limits to the number of hours that truck drivers should be allowed to drive per day that may be considered too low by enterprises. Disagreements may also exist on the qualifying age for getting a driver's license or for losing it, on the freedom to drive in the center of cities at any hour of the day, on the use of car horns in particular areas, on the need to enforce fuel efficiency of cars or even of lightbulbs for environmental reasons, on the need to have liability insurance, on the amount of alcohol in the blood that should prevent a person from driving, and so on.

Clearly, views on these aspects are likely to differ, but decisions must be made, and the decisions inevitably will leave some individuals dissatisfied. A visit to Delhi or Dhaka and then to Seoul or Singapore will quickly indicate how different traffic regulations, including the use of horns, can be.

(8) **Market-enhancing regulations**. In recent decades regulations have played an important role in various sectors of the economy. Industrial policy often depends on them, and countries have used regulations in import substitution and employment-promoting policies. For example, the Trump administration, which wants to reduce regulations, wants to force American enterprises to buy pipes made from American steel. Modern regulations are expected to reflect some specific, genuine needs of citizens and even of countries' economies.

The sectors where economic regulations have been especially important in market economies are: (a) financial markets; (b) labor markets; (c) foreign trade; (d) markets for some goods and especially services; (e) housing markets; and, increasingly, (f) the energy market, the drug market, and some others.

Economic regulations have a number of declared objectives, some less legitimate than others. They are: (a) to protect the public; (b) to protect domestic producers from (unfair) foreign competition; (c) to protect the economic positions or the incomes of particular groups or sectors; (d) to replace some taxing and spending policies by regulations, because the latter are often administratively and politically easier to use; and (e) to provide some "internal subsidy" to particular activities in order to subsidize other activities, as discussed by Posner (1971) in an early and classic article on regulations.

Regulations that are largely, or more obviously, substitutes for fiscal action can be called *quasi-fiscal regulations*. When used, they implicitly tax (penalize) some groups while subsidizing others. In this way they can broadly replace taxes and public spending. One classic example is "financial repression," in which interest rates and the use of financial resources are regulated by the government. The regulations tax the lenders and subsidize the borrowers. Of course, not all regulations are quasi-fiscal, although, on close analysis, most regulations have some element of taxing and subsidizing. For this reason, they should be treated in the same way, and should receive the same attention, as explicitly budgetary measures. Examples of quasi-fiscal regulations abound around the world (see Tanzi, 1998b).

While the *theoretical* case for regulation has become easier to make, on account of urbanization and recent crises and other difficulties, the possibility of falling into the "nirvana error," an error identified many years ago by the economist Harold Demsetz, should not be ignored. The nirvana error occurs when reality is compared against some idealized alternative, e.g., comparing what happens in the real market with what would happen in a world regulated and supervised by individuals who have the wisdom attributed to Solomon, the knowledge stored by Google, and the honesty of saints. Many problems arise when real-life regulators are given the regulatory responsibility over particular sectors or products. The real-life regulators will not have the aforementioned qualities. Some of the problems that are likely to arise have been mentioned earlier. They suggest that regulations should be used wisely, and there should not be unrealistic expectations on what can be achieved with their use.

There is no worse outcome for the market and for society than one in which some market operators observe, or are made to observe, strict rules, while others do not. This is likely to happen when the regulators have too much discretion in the enforcement of the rules, or when they are not doing their job fairly and efficiently. It may also happen when the resources available to the regulators to do their jobs are too limited, creating problems of selective enforcement. Regulation is a powerful tool to which governments are attracted and, like taxing and spending, is one of the most important policy tools. But, it is one of the least understood, except, at times, by the regulated and by their lawyers.

Some regulations can play an important role in protecting citizens from potential abuses on the part of unscrupulous participants in the market; some can help maintain competitiveness of markets and can prevent the establishment of monopolistic practices. These considerations have become more important in the modern, complex world. Governments can regulate airlines to keep them safe; pharmaceutical companies to prevent them from selling drugs that may turn out to have dangerous side effects; railways and mines to limit the number of accidents; public utilities to prevent them from overcharging customers; the financial market and especially banks to protect those who entrust them with their savings; and enterprises that have significant impact on the environment to lessen that impact. To do this well governments need financial and especially human resources. It is also obvious that governments may, and at times do, go too far in their use, or not far enough.

In a later chapter we shall come back to some issues regarding the use of regulations by governments.

CHAPTER 15

Modernity and Growing Termites in Market Activities

In addition to the growing number of perceived and actual externalities in modern societies, changes in social and economic relations, brought about by modern arrangements, by new products, and by new technologies, have made it easier for less scrupulous, less honest, and greedier individuals to act in ways that, at times, are or may be damaging to other individuals, currently or in the future, as, for example, when the environment is damaged. In traditional communities it might have been more difficult and more costly for these individuals to put into practice less socially inclined actions, because the monitoring of the community and the importance of reputation within close-knit communities would have acted as restraints, or simply because there were fewer exchanges with strangers and thus fewer opportunities for abuses. A self-sustained community is less likely to generate major externalities that knowingly damage individuals in their communities.

In modern societies, dishonesty, lack of community controls, growing exchanges between total strangers, the search for profits by at times greedy market operators, and the greater number of circumstances in which asymmetry in information in economic exchanges exists have been creating more situations than in the past that lend themselves to potential abuses. In some of these situations the damaged citizens expect and push governments to intervene and to play a protective role. Whether governmental intervention always, or often, makes things better is a different and more-debatable issue. The answer to that question depends in part on the quality and the effectiveness of the governmental intervention, in part on cultural characteristics, and in part on personal perceptions. However, a constant is that the intervention of the government is often accompanied by *potential* benefits, in addition to some obvious costs, and by increasing complexity.

Some individuals, and especially many of those who represent the interests of enterprises or particular economic sectors and that judge the governmental intervention from their specific, narrow perspective (that is, the impact that it has on their costs and their profits), are more likely to believe that fewer regulations and lower taxes are needed by the modern world, *especially in the areas in which they operate.* This is also a constant belief on the part of libertarian politicians and economists. They believe that the private market would be able to operate more efficiently and to monitor itself more satisfactorily with less government intervention, or that the costs of the interventions almost always exceed the benefits. At the same time they may expect the government to protect *their* interests, for example, when they call for protecting their intellectual property from "piracy," for protecting their investments in other countries, and for keeping in good shape the public infrastructures on which their operations depend. It must be recognized that in these complaints specific costs (on some sectors or enterprises) are compared with diffused or more general benefits.

Modern societies are characterized by frequent debates between government representatives, on one side, and representatives of enterprises (banks, pharmaceutical enterprises, mining and energy enterprises, and other industrial groups) that would like to operate with fewer rules and with lower taxes *on them*, giving them more liberty of action and allowing them to earn higher profits, on the other side. The representatives of enterprises complain that government regulations and taxes increase their costs, as they often do, and reduce their productivity, without, in their view, necessarily bringing particular advantages to society at large. They can often find examples of regulations that justify their complaints. However, having fewer regulations would also give them more liberty to, occasionally, generate damaging externalities and/or to impose significant costs and dangers on others or on the environment.

Associations of citizens and consumers often ask for new regulations or for new public spending, and (national and local) governments occasionally respond to these requests by creating new rules and by increasing some spending. Different groups of citizens, inevitably, have different perceptions about the importance of some new citizens' interests or goals, so while some push for particular interventions, others oppose them.

The creation of new regulations can be seen as a response by democratic governments to legitimate requests by groups of citizens in a free society, unless one believes that the regulators always act arbitrarily or stupidly. Whether the regulations that are created increase or decrease the welfare *for the whole community* is more difficult, and may even be impossible, to determine. The reason is the classic one: it would require a lot of not-often-available knowledge, and would require comparisons between different individuals and different groups. At times it is also difficult to make, *ex ante*, a benefit-cost evaluation of new rules, as some groups request should be made for all regulations. Often, the costs are immediate and more certain, while the benefits are spread through time and may be more uncertain.

Enterprises tend to emphasize the negative effects of some regulations *on their operations*, and some think tanks that represent them often produce estimates of large costs as a result of regulations and ignore the benefits. The government and some citizens' groups emphasize the positive effects of regulations on the quality of life or on the quality of the environment such as air and water. Often, it would require too much time to conduct a complete evaluation of the impact of each new rule on the economy, while the impact of the negative externalities that the rule attempted to reduce might have a cumulative and not easily reversible effect. This clearly happened when regulations that aimed at reducing smoking were being debated. Millions of people have died and many will continue to die prematurely because of the delays in introducing those regulations. The same may happen with air pollution, which is estimated to be killing many people annually worldwide. Therefore, the tendency on the part of some governments might be: *when in doubt, regulate*, which inevitably, occasionally, leads to the adoption of some unnecessary regulations. A debate similar to that about smoking in public places is now ongoing about some environmental rules, and especially about what to do about global warming and the contamination of drinking water.

The US government and the governments of other countries, as well as the Federal Reserve and other central banks, have needed to intervene at great financial costs to taxpayers and citizens in the case of failures by financial institutions, as had happened earlier with Long-Term Financial Management, Enron, and more recently of some other large financial institutions, during the subprime financial crisis. This kind of intervention had not been contemplated by past theories about the economic role of the state, discussed in most economic textbooks. Over the years, *systemic* risk in the financial sector has introduced a new, important economic role for the state and a danger for public finances. It is a role often requiring potentially costly regulations, ex ante or large public spending after the crises.

In each of the crises mentioned previously, there were observers who argued that the government should have intervened earlier, with regulations, to prevent them, and other observers who argued that it should not have intervened at all, before or during the crisis. Some observers have argued that, in a market economy, individuals and enterprises should be held financially responsible for the consequences of their actions, especially when they take excessive risks, as clearly did some banks that had lent money and some individuals who had bought houses that they could not afford, with credit that seemed very cheap. In these positions the implicit assumptions are those of rationality and symmetry of information.

In their respective writings on the 2007–2009 financial crisis, and on the Federal Reserve's and the US Treasury's responses to deal with it, both T. Geithner, then the US Treasury secretary, and B. Bernanke, then the Federal Reserve chairman, argued that a decision not to intervene might have led to another Great Depression. Therefore, in their view, the government had an obligation and no choice but to intervene, as it did. The intervention "saved the world" from more serious consequences. For a good review of Geithner's memoir, see Gorton (2015). Some people, including Mervyn King, the past governor of the Bank of England, have taken a more skeptical and more critical view about those claims.

Financial crises often involve and damage citizens who had trusted the institutions in which they had invested their money, and who had believed that the government was effectively monitoring those institutions. Many of these citizens were not sophisticated enough to realize that they had been taking risks with the money they had entrusted to those institutions. As Campbell (2016, p. 25) put it, "The *complexity* of twenty-first century financial arrangements poses a daunting challenge to households managing their financial affairs, to regulators attempting to assist them, and to the economic profession," and "Household financial mistakes create a new rationale for intervention [by governments] in the economy" (italics added). Thus, *more complexity justifies more governmental intervention.*

Nonintervention by the government during a financial crisis *might* in fact lead to disastrous consequences, as Bernanke and Geithner argued in their writings, but we will never know for sure. The problem is that, while governmental interventions may prevent potential, but not certain, current disasters from occurring, they also create expectations of interventions in future crises. The previous interventions, tend to create problems for future governments and for society, putting future governments at greater risk, and creating more reasons to keep the fiscal accounts in good order (see Tanzi, 2013b).

The expectation of governmental intervention creates a "moral hazard" and tends to distort the operation of the free market, creating (unfair) advantages for institutions that have become "too big to be allowed to fail" and that, because of their size, have come to expect being rescued in future crises. These institutions' lower risks allow them to borrow more cheaply than smaller enterprises can, thus distorting the market and increasing the likelihood of future crises and of future government interventions during crises.

To preserve the efficiency of the market and to reduce the chance of future governmental interventions, some have argued for *effective* regulations of the financial institutions, including the forced shrinking of the size of those banks and other financial institutions, including insurance companies, that have become "too big to fail." Former Federal Reserve Chairman Volcker and others have been arguing along these lines. However, the political power that the large financial institutions exert on the legislators and on the executive branch of government has been significant enough to prevent reforms from being introduced or to dilute reforms that have been introduced.

When financial institutions break existing norms, thus creating or contributing to crises, those responsible for the actions that damage others should be punished. While enterprises cannot be jailed and, because of their size, often cannot be shut down, those within them who have been responsible for breaking the norms should be punished. In recent years there has been a lot of evidence that, while some important rules were clearly broken during the financial crisis and later by several of these financial institutions (using cartels, fixing Libor rates, issuing false information on cartelized mortgages, using insider trading, and in several other ways), there have been no punishments for those responsible. Several recent books have provided evidence on the scope of the violations, the costs that they imposed on others or on society, and how the violators escaped punishments.

To try to prevent some of these problems from recurring in the future, in the United States, an alternative has been at times to try to create more rules, or to re-impose some of the rules that had been introduced during the Great Depression, especially in 1933–1938 by President Roosevelt's administration. Some of these rules had been removed, mainly in the late 1990s, as the result of the lobbying by bankers and the growing popularity of market fundamentalism. Another alternative could have been to reduce the number of rules but to increase the number of more concrete and more explicit ex post penalties, in an effort to punish those who created or would create problems by breaking the existing rules. This possibility has been under consideration in some countries, including the United Kingdom, and has been suggested in some recent books (see, for example, Hill and Painter, 2015). This alternative was generally not followed. In the recent arrangements, those who really got hurt were, often, normal and less sophisticated citizens, not the bankers who made the wrong, or the illegitimate, decisions.

In recent years, banks and, occasionally, energy and pharmaceutical companies or car manufacturers have agreed to pay at times large financial penalties for problems that they had created when they had broken, or had ignored, existing rules. They have paid these penalties without an admission of guilt, which would have exposed the companies to lawsuits by some of those who had been damaged. The financial penalties have been paid by the shareholders of the banks and other companies and not by the individuals who made, or had allowed to be made, the decisions that led to the problems. In most cases the managers of these institutions have continued to receive huge annual compensations and large bonuses for allegedly good performance, compensations in the millions of dollars. The penalties are indirectly paid by the taxpayers, because they reduce the taxable income of the enterprises.

The literature associated with "market fundamentalism" has continued to insist that a world with fewer or almost no rules would operate better than one with government rules that guide, and at times interfere with, the work of the free market. Some have gone as far as to blame the government for the problems associated with the recent financial crisis (see, for example, Taylor, 2009). It must be stressed that the aforementioned conclusions are often based either on abstract, theoretical models or on the experience gained in a world that no longer exists.

Unfortunately, almost daily evidence and many recent examples – from the financial market, the energy sector, the health sector, the transportation sector, and other areas – of the difficulties that the absence, or the nonobservance, of existing rules can create raise questions about the real-life relevance for the modern world of some of the arguments based on the distant past, or on highly theoretical analyses. We shall return to some of these issues in a later chapter of this book.

Naturally, there are arguments and examples from the other side that may lead to the conclusion that *some* of the existing regulations *may* reduce productivity and growth, or *may* not achieve what they had intended to achieve. Therefore, even when some of the existing rules may reduce risks and negative externalities, it must be recognized that there *may* be genuine costs, in terms of lower productivity and lower growth, associated with them. Some would argue that these costs, including the reduction of economic liberty for some individuals, might be high, or even too high to accept or justify. The rules may reduce risks but at too high a cost.

Whether or not those costs are considered high for society may also depend on who would benefit the most from higher rates of growth, and who would be hurt the most by the problems caused by lack of, or by fewer, regulations. Here, the issue of the distribution of costs and benefits becomes important. If the higher economic growth that would be obtained with fewer rules but with greater risks benefits only a small share of the population, say the top 1 percent, while the costs associated with negative externalities and with occasional disasters fall mostly on the remaining 99 percent, the arguments for having more regulations become stronger, regardless of their impact on growth. Therefore, what has been happening to the income distribution is relevant in this discussion of rules. In the third part of this book we shall return to the issue of the widening income disparity of recent decades.

A *minimal role* for the government would be a necessary ingredient even for a market that functioned in the ways in which "market fundamentalists" believe that it could function, with little governmental interference and greater trust in the market. The individuals who share these views tend to see the state as at best a necessary medicine for the health of societies, but a medicine that must be taken in very small doses. They are convinced that the medicine becomes damaging when taken in larger doses. At some point, it may even become dangerous, because, they believe, it would inevitably limit personal liberty and reduce incentives, economic efficiency, and the assumption of personal responsibilities by citizens. It would create a "nanny state" by fatally damaging the vitality and the economic growth of countries.

Hayek had been especially concerned with the impact of *economic planning*, i.e., with the direct interference in market decisions by governments. In some sense it could be argued that regulations *are* a form of planning. However, Hayek had accepted some of the essential *social* functions of the state (see Hayek [1944] 2007, [1960] 2011; also see Tanzi, 2015c, for a review of Hayek's views on this issue). Modern conservatives and economists are less concerned with the kind of economic planning that worried Hayek, because it is no longer a major problem in most market economies. They are more concerned with high taxes, high public spending, and the increasing number of regulations related to particular behaviors of individuals and enterprises, even when they aim at reducing particular actions that create, or can create, potential risks for others or for the environment. For these conservatives, economic liberty has a higher value, and it promotes personal effort and faster growth in the longer run.

Not surprisingly, economic and political liberty seems to be far more important for individuals who have high incomes than for many of those who find themselves permanently at the bottom of the income distribution. Conservative economists do not accept Amartya Sen's argument that social public spending can increase the *economic* liberty *of low-income individuals* who benefit from that spending. This argument is especially valid when the spending is efficient and is directed at individuals who truly do not have choices and thus are not just temporarily at the bottom of the income distribution.

Conservative economists would strongly debate Jean-Paul Marat, the French revolutionary, who asked, "what is the point of political liberty for someone who does not have bread?" For a starving man, the right to vote and to engage in other such "liberties" is clearly less important than the right to have bread. That man may also not have the freedom to borrow money even when central banks are making credit available at zero interest rates. The aforementioned question contrasts with the classic situation of the college student who, temporarily, has a low income, because she is away from home and is waiting to obtain her first job. For her, political and economic liberty remains clearly important, in spite of a low *temporary* income. In a society with great social mobility, economic and political freedom is important for larger shares of the population. When social mobility is reduced, Marat's question becomes more relevant.

Market fundamentalists and conservative economists and politicians believe that the medicine now taken by many countries – including the United States, which in contrast to European countries does not have particularly high taxes – has become excessive, a belief that seems to be shared by many others. And, of course, the managers and operators in many business enterprises complain about the many rules that *they* must respect in *their* activities, which may include the obligation of providing health insurance to their employees and other benefits. These benefits may not be called taxes, but are still costs to the enterprises'. These costs may not be balanced by lower cash wages paid to workers'.

On the other side liberal economists and large sections of the public continue to complain about abuses, occasional disasters, and other difficulties created by some economic operations, or about actions by enterprises and individuals that create negative externalities. They also complain that the costs from these disasters and from abusing the environment are often socialized, or pushed into the future, while the benefits from taking excessive risks and abusing the environment are often privatized by present operators and end up as large incomes for few. It is important to keep in mind Edmund Burke's ([1790] 1987) view that "society is [or should be] a partnership of the dead, the living and the unborn."

In conclusion, and with all due respect to Robert Lucas and to other conservative economists who share his viewpoint, the economic role of the state cannot be discussed in isolation from the impact that it has on the distribution of the income that economic performance and economic growth generate in a country, at present and in the future. When social mobility is lacking, or is significantly reduced, the distribution of income becomes more important. An increasing number of observers have concluded that in recent decades this has been happening in several countries, and especially in the United States.

Citizens' groups push for a larger role of the state, a role to be played with more regulations and higher spending in the particular areas in which they are mostly interested and worried about. These may be the rights of women, of the aged, of African-Americans, of immigrants, of children, of the physically challenged, of gays and lesbians, and so on. All of these are classified as "*civil* rights." Clearly the concept of "civil right" changes with time. Many citizens push for shifting more of the tax burden toward higher-income groups, which have more taxable capacity, and toward private enterprises. Many complain about *corporate welfare* policies, which, through the manipulation of the tax system, reduce the tax payments of many enterprises, at times to levels well below the (in the United States) relatively high statutory, corporate tax rates. See Farnsworth, 2012.

In the United States and in other countries, if the statutory rate on corporate income were applied to all corporate profits and the enterprises paid taxes on the profits held abroad, the tax payment by corporations would be significantly higher, thus allowing reductions in the statutory tax rate. The elimination of preferential tax treatments, which would simplify the tax system, should be a priority for policy. Loopholes reduce the tax payment that American enterprises make. An article by Gordon Cramb, in the *Financial Times* of April 28, 1999, showed that tax incentives for EU corporations reduced the tax rate at that time from an average statutory rate of 36.45 to an effective rate of 26.86, or by almost ten percentage points. The difference between statutory and effective rate was highest in Portugal, Austria, and Belgium, almost 20 percentage points, and lowest in Sweden and France, less than two percentage points. Estimates for the USA have shown also very wide differences.

Many citizens point to the continuing high poverty rates, to the stagnation of real wages for many workers, to the growing unevenness in the distribution of income and wealth, to occasional financial or environmental disasters, and to other social and economic problems as clear indications that more government intervention may be needed in the United States. The implicit assumption for these individuals is that more governmental intervention would alleviate some of those problems and would increase social welfare, without creating other kinds of problems. On the other side some citizens complain about what they consider excessive and unwarranted state intervention that, in their view, reduces liberty, increases costs, and leads to reduced growth.

The question that is difficult to answer is whether *more* or *less* government is needed, or whether a *different* government role is needed. Some countries (Singapore, the Republic of Korea, Switzerland) do remarkably well with public spending levels that are significantly lower than those of other countries, and some countries (Sweden, Canada, Norway, Ireland, New Zealand, and others), at some point in time, reduced significantly their public spending, as a share of GDP, without paying a noticeable price for that reduction. The reductions in public spending in some of these countries were indeed very large (see Tanzi, 2011, p. 235).

In the following chapters I shall take a closer look at the economic role that the state has played in recent years, focusing especially on the United States, because of its importance and because more information is readily available for it. I shall continue to make frequent references to other advanced countries. I shall use the normative framework that Richard Musgrave made popular in his 1959 book, utilizing the main government instruments of public spending, taxes, and regulations. I shall continue to focus on the regulatory role of governments, because it has become much more important in recent years, but continues to receive less attention than taxing and spending from traditional public finance scholars. I shall also refer occasionally to the *tutorial role* of the government, a role that has acquired more importance in recent years with the work of behavioral economists and psychologists, but that was not included in Musgrave's seminal book.

CHAPTER 16

The Allocation Role of Modern Governments

As societies become more urbanized and complex, and as the groups that constitute them become larger and less homogeneous – because of longer life expectancy, immigration, varying educational backgrounds, marriages between individuals from different religions or ethnic groups, racial background, occupations, or less even income distributions – governments are pressured by some of the citizens to assume additional responsibilities in the economic and social spheres. For example, the increasing age differentiation in the population, due to longer life expectancy, and the varying occupations create different demands for government action by different age cohorts, even when the per capita income of a country may not have changed much. Also, formal rules progressively replace past, informal norms.

As mentioned in an earlier chapter, in more urbanized communities, in which a growing share of the population lives closer together in larger and more densely populated cities, various kinds of negative externalities appear or become more common. Urbanization and the higher population density that it brings among individuals are frequent generators of externalities. Just think of the many *non*government rules that those who live in condominiums or in privately managed communities must abide by. Increasingly, the externalities include some that may be of a psychological or even of a *sensory* kind, caused by the closer contacts and shorter distance between individuals. Economists may be reluctant to call some of these outcomes externalities, but they do affect the welfare of individuals other than those who generate them.

High population density increases the impact and the importance of externalities of a visible, odoriferous, or audible kind. These externalities are not tolerated, or are less tolerated, by at least some members of the community, inviting or pushing them to ask for rules and for public intervention. In these situations, the appeal to *individual* rights of "Life, Liberty and the Pursuit of Happiness," as in the American Declaration of Independence, becomes increasingly constrained by the *respect for the rights*

163

of others. Thus, the right that an individual has to liberty, for example, to play one's radio at high volume, to produce smells with one's cooking that are unpleasant to others, or to throw garbage out of one's window, must be balanced by what that right implies for the liberty and welfare of other members of the community. My right to make noise, or to move at great speed in an urban area or on a highway, must be balanced by the right that others have for silence and safety. The rights of hermits inevitably tend to require different and fewer rules compared with those of dwellers in crowded and large cities.

When the government deals with these externalities (excessive noise or smells, ugly or dirty sights, excessive speed, cars parked illegally or in spots reserved for others, passengers disturbing others by talking loudly on a cellular phone on a train or bus, and other externalities), it improves the welfare of some individuals in the community, while it inevitably reduces the perceived freedom of others. This is clearly the case with "reasonable" regulations, as distinguished from "arbitrary" or "unreasonable" regulations. It inevitably raises the question of the optimal balance between comfort, safety, and freedom for some individuals, and reduced actual or perceived comfort, safety, and freedom for others.

Some decades ago, the search for this balance led to an acrimonious public debate when banning smoking in public places was being considered. The rights of smokers (many at that time) were being clearly violated, while those of nonsmokers (waiters in restaurants, flight attendants on planes, teachers in classrooms, nonsmoking patrons in public places, and so on) were being protected. It was not an issue of government against citizens but of some groups of citizens against other groups. Because of the impact of smoking on health costs, public spending and spending for medical insurance were also impacted. Activities by individuals – such as playing loud music in houses, in apartments in the middle of cities, or in cars parked in urban settings, or parking in spots that belong to others – have created annoyance (an externality) that has occasionally led to reactions by others, at times with even tragic consequences.

These externalities do not exist, are less common, or have fewer serious consequences when individuals live in less crowded, rural spaces, or, perhaps, they tend to be ignored when individuals have more pressing problems, such as lack of bread. They become serious and less tolerated in modern, crowded cities, and perhaps even less so in crowded cities inhabited by higher-income individuals. It can be argued that many negative externalities tend to become more important, more felt, and less tolerated when incomes rise; they tend to be income-elastic.

Just think of the growing dangers that drones have been creating for planes and the security and privacy concerns they have been creating for individuals. It seems logical that at some point the governments will need to intervene with strict regulations and with serious penalties imposed on those who violate them. This is just one of many in a range of problems connected with technological and other developments that call for governmental intervention. It would seem disingenuous to argue that the free market will deal with them, or that *personal* liberty must always prevail. So far, aided by an amendment to the US Constitution, this argument has allowed individuals in the United States to own guns with few regulations for them, in spite of the huge and increasing number of individuals who accidentally or otherwise get killed by their use every year.

While economic development and new technologies create new products and new market activities that are capable of better serving some individuals' needs, some of these can also develop undesirable characteristics and, at times, generate serious difficulties. The reasons may in part be due to ignorance (for example, those who operate drones may not be aware of instructions for their use or of the dangers that they may create), or to the fact that some of those who participate in the new markets feel less constrained by social norms than they would have in the past, because of the closer monitoring and enforcing by other members of the communities that may have been more common in earlier times. Consequently, the participants in new markets do not behave in the ways those who theorize about perfect markets and harmoniously working communities and economies assume they will, in the absence of government rules.

Some of the participants in new markets (the stock market or markets for various products and services) have incentives to provide information that may not be fully accurate on the goods and services that they sell, or have incentives to hide or bury less favorable information on new products in the fine print of complex documents or descriptions, thus creating some asymmetry in the information available to the two parties in the exchanges. Misleading publicity may at times contribute to this objective. Think of drugs that may have serious but less reported side effects, or new cars that may have particular, serious defects. The combination of potentially *unscrupulous or at least nontransparent behavior* by some and *asymmetry in information* or even in understanding of the information can create problems that are ignored by those who have great faith in perfect markets. This lack of symmetry makes it easier for some participants to take advantage of other participants. The market does not operate with a uniform denominator of honesty and information. This leads to calls for governments to intervene and to try to play a monitoring or controlling role.

Asymmetry in information also affects relations between private individuals and government agencies, or between individuals and insurance companies or credit providers. Take the example of fake invalids who manage to get invalidity pensions by providing false information to the government on their physical or, increasingly in recent years, on their psychological conditions. Another current example that is growing in importance is the false information provided to the government by those who supply medical services to the public. Recent US estimates have shown that fraud created by false information in the medical area now runs in the tens of billions of dollars. Some forms of corruption at times hide themselves in asymmetry of information, and the difference between the two may be difficult to recognize. Some forms of tax evasion or tax avoidance also reflect asymmetry of information or interpretation of rules between taxpayers and tax administrations.

Clearly, the greater the role of the state in public spending and in taxation becomes, the greater are the opportunities for fraud against the state, partly based on the asymmetry of the information available to the two parties. In 2016 there was a reported backlog of more than a million applicants for disability pensions in the United States, and there were obvious difficulties on the part of the US government to screen the applicants in an effort to avoid fraud. It is one of many examples of termites of the state. And there are reports about billions of dollars of fraudulent claims against the government associated with the Medicare and Medicaid programs in the US public health system, or even fraudulent tax refunds obtained by some using stolen information from other taxpayers.

Greater population density, more heterogeneous populations, increasing disparity in incomes and in ages, and more complex products and market activities all combine to create an increasing number of physical, financial, or psychological externalities and asymmetries. These factors create opportunities for some individuals and for some enterprises to take advantage of other individuals, other enterprises, or even the government, in various ways. The damages created may not always be intentional, because as countries become more developed, some of the goods and services traded in the market become more complex, or their characteristics become less ascertainable to both parties, than when the exchanges were among closer parties and involved traditional and simpler products that were for the most part locally produced.

This, for example, is increasingly a problem with food products. It is now impossible for buyers to know the circumstances under which products bought in supermarkets were produced, and even where they were produced. Occasional reports about the conditions under which some products are produced or grown (for example, chicken or chicken nuggets, sausages, or farmed salmon) make one hope that *effective* government controls have been put in place. In this context certain products, such as industrially produced food and medicines, require some (government?) guarantee of safety.

At times the safety of some questionable products has been made to depend on studies by academic researchers who have been financed by the same companies that make the products. For other products, such as energy products, the production side of the market may require controls to prevent oil spills, mining or other accidents, or excessive damage to the environment, as has been reported to happen with "fracking." To argue that these activities do not require any controls and that the companies that produce them will always control themselves amounts to closing one's eyes to the reality and the dangers of the real world.

The market may also be distorted by growing monopolistic practices, some increasingly connected with intellectual property or other obstacles to entry. Monopolies tend to be less obvious to identify when arising from intellectual property than they were in the past, when one could monopolize the steel, the petroleum, the railroad, or the car industry. Today's monopolies may be associated with the use of particular technologies or products by enterprises that have obtained (temporary but at times easily extendable) monopoly protection from the government, a protection provided to those that have acquired intellectual property rights. However, in some sense, and regardless of the justification used for protecting intellectual property, that protection inevitably restricts markets. Furthermore, many patents are never used by those who apply for and obtain them. They serve to restrict potential competitors from getting related patents that would reduce the value of the existing monopoly power. This happens in the pharmaceutical industry, when companies buy the patents of other companies to prevent them from introducing drugs that would compete with their own drugs.

In some of the markets described here, the prices at which the exchanges take place convey much less information about the real value of what is bought than was the case in the past. In some cases the enterprises impose costs on societies that are not reflected in the cost of production of the enterprises; that is, the social costs exceed the private costs. This implies that, in some sense, the enterprises (and/or those who use the products or the services) are getting implicit subsidies on their productions or consumptions from society. Using the terminology of economists, the full social costs are not internalized by the enterprises, so more is produced (and consumed) than should be. Someone inevitably ends up having to pay the subsidies in various ways. Increasingly, the costs are shifted to future generations.

In other cases, as I mentioned earlier, some enterprises, and especially some banks, may become so large or so important for the national economies that their size encourages them to take excessive risks in an effort to increase their profits. The protection of these "too big to fail" banks or enterprises creates a controversial role of the state that was not contemplated in the literature on the normative role, It is a role, connected with *systemic risk*, that is often not contemplated ex ante and that can easily be criticized, but that becomes difficult to resist or to avoid ex post, when the need arises (see Gorton, 2015, on this issue). When a house is on fire, the firefighters cannot base their action on whether the owners should have been more careful, or whether the rescue will encourage less prudent behavior in the future. It is more rational to require fire detectors in the houses.

The way in which the compensation contracts of some of those who manage the banks or other large enterprises are now written often encourages them to pursue short run, profit-maximizing strategies that may add to the risks and may make their operations socially less efficient. If the strategies succeed as intended, they will be advantageous to the managers, who will get higher compensation, and also to the shareholders, whose shares or dividends will increase. If the strategies fail, the costs will in part be borne by the workers, who will lose jobs, by the citizens, who may have to pay the tab, and by the banks' shareholders. These strategies may also encourage the writing of contracts for managers in ways that are less transparent than they should be, thus contributing to the growing asymmetry in information that exists in the modern market among relevant actors. In this connection the role that top managers have in choosing members of the boards of the enterprises is important. That role, indirectly, has important implications for the income distribution that comes to be determined.

There have been attempts to keep the full compensation information in managers' contracts from becoming publicly available or available in more easily understandable ways. This has created an increasingly serious problem of asymmetry of information between the wages received by workers and the compensations received by CEOs and other managers. This asymmetry may affect popular views of the working of the market and, indirectly, voting decisions and government policies. It is one example of the many complex ways in which the income distribution gets determined in modern societies.

The relation between managers' full compensation and that of workers has been attracting increasing attention in recent years. A proposal in the United States for enterprises to publish this information in a clearly understandable form was strongly opposed by those who represent the enterprises. Asset managers have also fought the requirement to disclose the fees paid by pension funds to them. Thus, in many areas of the market, the transparency that a market system should have has been compromised by developments over the years.

As previously mentioned, being "too big to fail" reduces the risk of lending to these banks and allows them to obtain cheaper credit than smaller banks can, thus creating imperfections in the market. This creates additional reasons for better regulating these banks and, perhaps, for forcing them to reduce their sizes, as many observers have been unsuccessfully demanding in recent years. Instead of being reduced, the sizes of the big banks have actually grown since the beginning of the financial crisis, and they now account for a larger share of the financial market. In conclusion, modern markets are suffering from increasing and new imperfections that are somewhat different and more difficult to identify than those that existed in the past. They may also be more difficult to deal with.

The fact that corporations cannot be jailed, or cannot be shut down except in extreme circumstances, may have helped create a culture within them that implicitly encourages some of their employees to take more actions that are not consistent with established market and government rules. Often, it becomes difficult for governments to identify and punish the specific individuals within large enterprises who have been directly responsible for violating or abusing some rules. The top managers generally declare themselves not responsible for specific acts, claiming that they were not aware of them. The result is that, in modern societies, managers are assumed to deserve to be handsomely compensated for the good performances of their enterprises, but they are rarely held responsible or penalized for their bad behavior.

As mentioned earlier, in recent years the US government has asked some of the enterprises that have violated or abused rules to pay financial penalties while allowing them to avoid admitting guilt. The justification has been that there were not enough lawyers or resources within the Justice

Department to take the enterprise to court. While the penalties may appear large, they are generally small compared to the profits of big enterprises, and their payment ends up penalizing the shareholders, rather than the specific individuals who broke the rules or the managers who, perhaps indirectly, encouraged them to break the rules. Given these circumstances, the financial penalties are not likely to change the future behavior of the enterprises.

Inevitably, these developments are corrupting the market and are raising questions about its fairness and its efficiency, and also about the rules under which the enterprises operate (see Rakoff, 2015). Clearly, this is not the efficient and ethical market that market fundamentalists and libertarian economists rave about.

It is not surprising that the aforementioned developments have inevitably led to pressures from some quarters to create more and better rules and to monitor more closely the behavior of individuals and enterprises. They have also created more demands for enterprises to provide essential information to the government and to the citizens on the products and the services that they sell. These requirements inevitably lead the enterprises and some individuals to object that they are being overregulated, and that these demands are unreasonable and costly. However, as the anthropologist David Graeber put it in a recent book, perhaps with some exaggeration, public and private bureaucracies have become largely indistinguishable, and it is an illusion to believe that the rules that are created apply, or apply equally, to everyone (see Graeber, 2015). The rules often end up benefiting some (often those with more money) over others.

The degree to which the governments should apply regulations, and whether they can do it in an efficient, objective, and equitable way, has become a progressively more contentious issue in the modern world. As Campbell (2016, p. 25) put it, "financial regulators face a difficult trade-off between the benefits of regulation ... and the [total] costs of regulation." This is also true for other forms of regulation.

Increasingly, the laws that governments create to deal with these problems are contained in legislative bills that are often thousands of pages long and that often lend themselves to conflicting interpretations by clever lawyers. After the new regulations have been approved by the legislative branch and become laws, they often require interpretations and elaborations by relevant offices, such as the tax administrations, the regulatory agencies, and others. This process, which at times requires years to be completed, lends itself to lobbying by the regulated to soften the rules and to make them more flexible and less demanding on those who have to observe them. Often, a change in a few words, buried in a bill that may be thousands of pages long, is sufficient to achieve this objective.

Enterprises that have more money (for example, banks, pharmaceutical and energy companies, and others) and that are able to pay for the best-connected lobbyists or for the best lawyers or accountants acquire real-life advantages, compared to other enterprises, which do not have that money, or with respect to the general public. This leads to additional market imperfections and to valid questions about the functioning of the democratic process and the impartiality of the market economy.

Lobbying by *professional* lobbyists has become one of the fastest-growing activities in modern economies. This activity or profession has attracted some of the most-able and better-connected individuals and many former, high-level members of Congress or administrations. For example, it was reported that the trade group Pharmaceutical Research and Manufacturers of America (PhRMA), since 1998, had spent a quarter of a billion dollars on lobbying and that a former congressman, who had dealt with these issues in the past while he was in Congress, had been its president for some of those years (see Brill, 2014).

The value of lawyers and of lobbyists is enhanced by the connections that they have with relevant public officials. The better connected they are, the more valuable they become to those who hire them, and the more they can charge for their lawyering and lobbying services. Money often ends up replacing votes in determining legislation or rules or at least in determining some interpretations of them. Those who have more money end up getting the most votes, where it counts. This inevitably raises questions about the connection that now exists between democratic processes and the equity of the market, and increasingly about the efficiency and equity of the market and of the government itself. Some of the lobbying is done through contributions to the political campaigns of candidates. Like an entry ticket, these contributions create easier access to the candidates, if or when they are elected, and access can at times perform miracles.

Because governments can fail in their activities, there is the danger that they will introduce too many, or the wrong kinds of, regulations, while they may not introduce some needed ones. It should be realized that regulations do not drop from the sky, like manna. There is normally someone pushing for them, and at times someone attempting to stop them from being introduced. That someone is a person, a group, or an enterprise with an interest in wanting a regulation to be passed, or one with an interest in stopping the introduction of a new regulation. The view that bad or unnecessary regulations are due to the stupidity of some bureaucrats, which, for example, is one of the arguments made to criticize the European Union, in most cases is not a realistic, or a correct, view.

The increasing complexity of the market is undoubtedly contributing to the regulatory debate. Governments end up being criticized for what statisticians call type one and type two errors. Often, the need for new regulations is recognized only *after* major problems have developed or disasters have occurred that might have been avoided by the timely existence and enforcement of some regulations. However, once introduced, regulations tend to remain in place long after the need for them may have disappeared. The consequence is that, for regulations, government failure can come either by introducing and keeping too many of them or introducing the wrong ones, or by not having introduced or enforced some essential ones. It is difficult to achieve the optimal balance in this important government role. There is no formal and efficient mechanism capable of determining and ensuring it, and much uncertainty about the impact of some regulations.

Perhaps, there ought to be some formal process by which the regulations introduced in past years and, as in the United States, codified in the Code of Federal Regulations, which records all the regulations created by the federal government, would be reviewed at regular intervals by a competent, responsible, and independent institution (a kind of supreme court for regulations) and would be adjusted or deleted to reflect changing needs. Technical and political difficulties, inertia, pressures by the regulated, lack of resources, the power that some bureaucracies acquire from existing regulations, or other difficulties, inevitably, would make this review process difficult. The outcome of the existing situation is that some unneeded regulations (both federal *and* local) remain in force for years, after the need for them has long passed, while new, important, and necessary ones are not introduced. This is an area in which government failure is common, and it is failure as a result of doing too much or too little, or acting too soon or too late.

Occasionally, a recent, major market failure, for example, the bankruptcy of an enterprise such as Enron, some major physical disaster such as the BP oil spill in the Gulf of Mexico, or the failures that accompanied the 2007–2008 financial crisis, brings a rash of new regulations that, because of the hurry to respond to the problem, may end up being the wrong ones. There is also always the danger that some of the regulations will not be as clearly written as they ought to be, or that they will leave too much discretion to government bureaucrats or to the lawyers of the regulated in their interpretation. This will open the door to potential abuses or acts of corruption, or to *regulatory capture*, an outcome in which the regulators end up being "captured" by the regulated.

In federal countries, such as the United States, Brazil, Canada, Argentina, and others, regulations issued by subnational governments tend to give the enterprises operating in those jurisdictions more incentives and more possibilities to capture the regulators. Because of the proximity of the regulators to the regulated, and the economic importance of the enterprises that are regulated, this capture may be easier than it is at the national level. This may also happen when the regulations are issued by the national government, but must be enforced by officials at the local government level, where the regulated enterprises have more political power, because they create local jobs and, often, finance the political campaigns of some local politicians. The regulations often end up being interpreted in ways that allow the enterprises to largely ignore the restrictions that they impose. According to various newspaper reports, this has happened with energy-related activities in some US states, including West Virginia (for coal production) and Oklahoma and Louisiana (for petroleum production). The results have been occasional accidents, caused by the little respect that some enterprises had paid to safety or environmental rules. Not surprisingly, the conservative Frazer Institute in Canada has classified Oklahoma's government as the most favorable government for enterprises engaged in oil and natural gas investments.

Constraints on government salaries, large potential financial gains on the part of the regulated industries if they can avoid the costs imposed by regulations, and coziness between regulators and regulated, especially at the subnational levels, have encouraged some industries to hire individuals directly from the regulating agencies in order to benefit from the latter's inside knowledge and, especially, from their connections. Close relations between regulated industries and local politicians, in the areas in which the enterprises operate, contribute to rendering some regulations ineffective. A recent academic article by authors who have studied the lobbying process in the United States at the federal level concluded that lobbyists are often hired not so much for their technical expertise but for their contacts and connections. It is these contacts and connections that make some lobbyists particularly valuable to those who hire them (see Bertrand et al., 2014).

Some institutions must be created to deal with the needs and the operations of governments, in the hope that they will be able to perform their tasks efficiently. The absence of principal–agent problems in behavior and the assurance of efficiency in performance are necessary elements for these institutions. However, the more complex the issues become, the more difficult it is for governments' institutions to perform well the tasks assigned to them, and the more likely it is that governance problems of various natures will develop and become serious.

Institutions are in some ways similar to cardiovascular systems. With time they almost inevitably tend to develop bureaucratic and legislative cholesterol. The growing reports and evidence of corruption and inefficiency in several countries (both advanced and emerging or poor countries) in recent years may be a barometer of the increasing complexity of the operations that must be conducted by public institutions. Furthermore, various forms of corruption now hide themselves behind particular rules that have made some forms of corruption appear legitimate. It is not likely that this process can be stopped, but it ought to be possible to slow it down with adequate reforms, as a few countries, including Scandinavian countries, New Zealand, Singapore, and some others, have attempted to do in recent years.

CHAPTER 17

Public Goods, Quasi-Public Goods, and Intellectual Property

The theoretical literature on public economics, especially as it developed in the 1940s and the 1950s, a time when the role of the state was changing rapidly, both in theory and in practice, and was becoming more important, had focused a great deal on "public goods" – such as defense, security, justice, basic or fundamental research, city streets, essential infrastructure, and so on. It was assumed that only the state could provide these goods. The reasons for this conclusion were largely technical, as Paul Samuelson had explained in two fundamental and much-cited articles published in the mid-1950s.

These public goods may be essential to a country, and the government should provide them. The theory on pure public goods argued that, in a market economy, private individuals would have no interest in providing them, because free riders (those unwilling to contribute to the costs of their provision) could not be forced to contribute to their costs in proportion to the benefits that they derived from the use of the goods. Furthermore, and a separate issue, once these goods were produced and had become available to the citizens of a country, it would be inefficient to restrict their use to only those who had contributed to their costs. The reason is that if they are *pure* public goods, additional users can consume them at no extra cost. Therefore, it would make no sense to exclude them from consuming these goods. For less-pure public goods such as highways, schools, and similar facilities, the users could be excluded, but at possibly high costs.

The problem of *free riding* was one of the important technical reasons why the government had to provide public goods. Defense spending was, perhaps, the best and the most classic example of a pure public good. Once the protection that defense gave to a country's citizens was provided, extending that protection to additional citizens would cost nothing. It would thus be inefficient for a society to exclude from that benefit individuals who had not contributed to the cost of providing the goods. The characteristic that additional consumers can utilize the public goods at zero cost is shared with various kinds of intellectual properties. However, governments have allowed (and *supported*) the owners of these intellectual properties to exclude from their use (when that is technically possible) users who do not pay for them.

The US Constitution, in Section 8, specifically mentions the role of the government in protecting some kinds of intellectual property: "To promote the Progress of Science and useful Arts, by securing for limited Times to *Authors and Inventors* the exclusive Right to their respective Writings and Discoveries" (italics added). Therefore, the *promotion* of "Science" and "useful Arts" by "Authors" and "Inventors" was given, by those who drafted the US Constitution, as the justification for the government to protect the intellectual property of some individuals "for limited Times."

The incentive effect of the "Progress of Science and useful Arts" was assumed to overwhelm the inefficiency cost of (temporary) exclusion of users, who in principle could be added at zero cost. It must be recognized that the protection that the government provides to intellectual property can be financially very important to the owners of that property, because it creates for them temporary monopolies and allows some individuals to earn large incomes when they can get the "exclusive Right to their respective Writings and Discoveries." Therefore, the incentive may play an important role.

The conclusion that public finance experts reached with respect to pure public goods was that if some of these goods are essential to society, they must be financed and provided (though not necessarily produced) by the government. Once produced, they can be consumed freely by every citizen. As mentioned, in 1954 and 1955, Paul Samuelson, in two short, brilliant, and much-cited articles, outlined the theoretical justification for the reasons why pure public goods must be provided by the state (although the concept of public goods had been known long before). The conclusion that he reached was that a government that has the characteristics of being omnipotent, benevolent, and all-knowing will know what and how many of these goods to produce, because individuals would not and could not be forced to reveal their preferences for them. The government would finance the production of these public goods with general revenue including public debt.

The provision of public goods (at least of *pure* public goods) attracted a lot of attention by economists in the years after the publication of Samuelson's articles and after the publication, in 1959, of Musgrave's *The Theory of Public Finance*. That book provided an articulate and, at that time, the most complete framework for assessing the role of the state in the pursuit of several objectives in a market economy. Neither Samuelson nor Musgrave explained how a real-life government, one that did not have the characteristics of being omnipotent, benevolent, and all-knowing, would decide how much of each public good to produce and how the cost of the production would be allocated among the citizens. These important questions remained unanswered. Perhaps the belief was that, through their votes, the voters would choose the right policymakers, and the latter would know how to answer these fundamental questions.

While the concept of public good is useful for understanding an important part of the essential *allocation* role of the state, it does not go very far in explaining the current level of total public spending in market economies or the reasons for its growth over past decades. In most countries, the focus on public goods would not explain why governments spend what they now spend. Pure public goods do not absorb, for their provision, more than a few percentage points of countries' GDPs, and they account for only a small share of that spending in many of today's advanced countries. Furthermore, the spending on pure public goods seems to have gone down, as a share of GDP, over the years. We need to look elsewhere to understand why public spending has grown and why it has reached the levels of recent years.

A few additional comments on the practical significance of the concept of public goods may, nonetheless, be appropriate because there has been less discussion of the practical, as opposed to the theoretical, significance of the concept. Most public finance textbooks have continued to essentially repeat what Samuelson wrote sixty years ago.

The theory of pure public goods refers to a concept that, although clear and important in its theoretical formulations, is much more difficult to recognize and to relate to what happens in the real world. Take defense, the most classic and most used example of a pure public good. The theory tells us why defense must be provided by the government and also why, once produced, its benefits can be enjoyed by every citizen, whether or not they have contributed to its financing. However, it tells us nothing about how much defense spending would be appropriate for a country at a given time; how that spending ought to be carried out; and who should pay for it. Most importantly, it does not tell us whether the optimal level ought to be 1 percent, 5 percent, 10 percent, or some other share of GDP. The assumption is that a benevolent and all-knowing government would know how much to spend on defense, in what form to do it, and who should pay for it.

Fortunately, democracies are not run by benevolent, all-knowing *dictators*. Therefore, in the real world it is easy to see how the concept can be abused. Furthermore, while the abstract *benefits* derived from having a country protected by defense spending exist, and while those benefits should make everyone in the country feel safer, it is not likely that everyone will assign the same value to those benefits, and the weight assigned may only indirectly be related to the citizens' incomes (see Tanzi, 1972). If these values could be determined, they could be used to decide who should pay the taxes to produce the public good, using a benefit-received principle of taxation. The Italian Scienza delle Finanze had solved this difficult problem by simply assuming that the benefits from public goods to the citizens are broadly proportional to their incomes, so public goods should be financed with taxes that are broadly proportional to income. Still, it had nothing to say about the level of that spending.

In the real world, not all the money spent for defense produces a *pure* public good. The reason is that defense spending has another face and, often, other destinations for the money than the generation of the pure public good. Some industries, some enterprises, some regions, and some individuals benefit not just from the protection offered by the defense of the country (which in principle should benefit every citizen) but especially from the spending itself, because that spending provides jobs to some individuals, incomes to some enterprises, and political benefits to some politicians.

Six decades before the publication of this book, President Eisenhower had warned about the existence of a military-industrial complex that in his view was pushing for more military spending and was, as a consequence, transforming a pure public good, at least in part, into a private good. Since the 1950s, a frequent problem in the United States has been how to stop the production of some useless weapons systems, or how to close useless military bases that serve no defense function at all but provide good jobs and incomes to individuals and to enterprises located in certain geographical areas, areas that are of interest to particular members of the US Congress. The latter members fight to keep the particular spending going, regardless of its real value in terms of the protection of the country and the delivery of a genuine public good. Cuts in particular aspects of defense spending that the military wants to make at times cannot be made because of political opposition by powerful politicians.

High-level military personnel often take early retirement to go to work for enterprises that produce weapons. In their new positions they use their connections to lobby for military contracts for the enterprises that now employ them. At times this creates inefficient spending that limits the real value (in terms of genuine defense of the country) of the money budgeted for defense. The diversion of resources and of public money to potentially unproductive spending does not contribute to the public good that defense spending is assumed to generate. Rather, it provides concrete benefits to some individuals, some enterprises, and some politicians. In the process it transforms a *public good*, at least partly, into a *private good* and, perhaps worse, into a *useless* private good.

As another example, take NASA. In the years after the creation of that public agency, following Russia's success in putting Sputnik into space, NASA had been given the clear and important political goal of sending an American to the moon (a pure public good in military terms and in terms of the prestige for the United States, at a time when competition with Russia, for the hearts and minds of the world's people, was important). After having achieved that important goal and, in the process and as an important positive externality, having generated some important fundamental research that would prove useful for later developments in private-sector activities, for many years NASA seemed to lose sight of what its objective, or main raison d'être, was.

After the goal of going to the moon had been achieved, for some years, it became difficult to identify clearly the specific public good that NASA's spending was producing, and to determine whether the resources that it was using could have been used more productively in other public areas. Perhaps, it would have been easier to find out who was benefiting directly and privately from that spending, which generated incomes and profits for some individuals and enterprises, and political benefits for the politicians from the geographical areas where the spending was taking place. Informed media articles reported that some politicians had, at times, been instrumental in pushing NASA to make expensive, but seemingly unproductive, investments.

Similar issues arise in connection with other kinds of public goods, and not just in the United States. For example, government expenditure for research in some European countries seems to be more beneficial in creating jobs for those who find employment in those activities than for the pure public good (in terms of new scientific discoveries) that they might generate. In the rare cases when research does generate some valuable scientific results, results that can be considered a potential, pure public good, it may lead to spillovers that will help particular areas of the private sector, in both the country that has financed the research and in other countries, because ideas from basic research cannot be patented.

Spillovers from pure research can generate knowledge that can lead to patent applications by some private individuals or enterprises, and patents can produce large incomes for some lucky individuals. Spending money for fundamental research is one of several examples where society pays the costs and *particular* individuals, rather than the *whole* of society, end up receiving many of the benefits. The spending, or at least part of it, justified by the generation of pure public goods ends up creating private incomes for a few individuals.

Many public goods are of a less-*pure* kind (education, health, highways, etc.), and it would be possible, but at times costly, to exclude nonpaying individuals from using them. There is debate on whether the spending on some of these goods should be the responsibility of governments, and if so, how much to spend on them. Equity considerations inevitably enter these debates. For these goods, the allocation and the redistribution objectives often combine and influence the decisions. Individuals could be excluded from using the goods (many roads, schools, health services, and others) if they were not willing or able to contribute to their financing through fees or in other ways. However, that exclusion could be seen as inequitable, and might even be damaging, in other ways, for society. For example, excluding nonpaying individuals from vaccination against some contagious diseases could be a danger to other members of societies; and individuals who are illiterate may not be able to read traffic signs, causing more accidents.

These dangers tend to increase in urban settings, creating stronger justifications for the public financing of these semipublic goods. But, once again, it must be recognized that this spending may also generate private benefits for those who deliver the services, especially when the delivery is made inefficiently, or when corruption plays a role (see Tanzi, 1974). Apart from the externality considerations, there is the ethical question of whether individuals who do not have the means to contribute to the financing of some of these goods should be excluded from them, and whether the state should in some ways be involved in the provision, or at least in some financing, of them. Margaret Thatcher got into political difficulties when she insisted on instituting poll taxes in the United Kingdom to produce public goods, taxes that would be paid equally by everyone, rich and poor.

These issues arise especially in the cases of schools, access to health services, and, to some extent, access to public housing. They also arise in less-known programs, of which there are many in most governments, programs that receive less attention. For example, in the United States there are about eighty means-tested programs. For some of these, participation has increased significantly over the years. According to a 2013 report by the US Congressional Budget Office, the participation in the Medicaid program increased from 16.5 million in 1972 to 53.2 million in 2011; the use of food stamps increased from 11 million in 1972 to 44.7 million in 2011. Later information released by the USDA Supplemental Nutrition Assistance Program indicated that in some states as much as 20 percent of the population was receiving food stamps.

What if there were no government assistance, and individuals with low incomes did not have the means to pay for these goods? Would private charities step in to fill the gap? Would the poor work harder to get the means to pay for them? Would families stay together to help members in difficulties? Some have argued that welfare programs have to some extent been an attack on families. In some cases they have destroyed the small communities that comprised the extended families. As mentioned, the exclusion of some individuals from access to these services might, or would likely, generate significant negative consequences for the less fortunate members of society and some negative externalities for the rest of society. These externalities might include higher crime rates, higher incidences of some diseases, or even some externalities of an aesthetic or psychological kind. Some of those with higher incomes might also experience guilt feelings, which could be considered a form of psychologically based externality.

Should the free provision of these goods by the state be considered an attempt to equalize *opportunities* for all citizens, as many insist that the government should do? If the answer is yes, the next question is, again, at what level and quality should the government provide these goods to achieve that objective? Should it make the quality of the public provision equivalent to the average, or even to the best, private quality? This second question is often more important than the first. Can it be assumed that the right to access these goods is a civil right, and that everyone should have access to them *at the same level of quality*? In this case the state would largely lose control of the spending if, for example, private pharmaceutical companies kept producing new drugs, which might have only marginal benefits over existing and cheaper ones, or if hospitals kept introducing new costly procedures, while the law required their free provision to all individuals who needed them. The state would also reduce the liberty of some individuals if all individuals were forced to rely on the same *public* health services.

The production or the consumption of some goods or some activities by the private sector may generate positive (i.e., desirable) or negative (i.e., undesirable) externalities, which are not captured or internalized by those who produce or consume them. Many of these externalities may be minor and can be ignored. Some externalities may still be uncertain in their long run effects and subject to controversies among experts. This, for example, is the case with genetically modified goods or chemicals that some individuals believe to be potentially damaging, while others insist that they are safe.

This raises the question of who decides when an externality is too minor or too uncertain to address? What if some are convinced that the damaging externalities exist, even when there may not be a definitive scientific proof? At times scientific uncertainty about the effects of an externality creates arguments and justifications, for some, to ignore its potentially significant, long run negative effects. This was the case for a long time with the effect of smoking, and later with the effect of secondhand smoking. It may now be the case with the consumption of too much sugar, some fats, and genetically modified goods, or with the effect of some environmental pollution on life expectancy. The long run effects of many chemicals in drinking water are also not known, because they have not been tested.

Many environmental regulations are challenged on the ground that the scientific issues are not definitively settled. Unfortunately, at times, waiting for definitive scientific certainty can expose a society, or the world, to potentially serious dangers and costs in the longer run, especially when the externalities have cumulative and long-lasting effects. For example, as mentioned earlier, many people have died, and will continue to die, prematurely because they kept smoking while the issue of the danger of smoking was being debated.

In the case of genetically modified food, American food exporters have pressured European countries to remove any obstacles to the importation of this food, and American and other governments have been pressured to even prevent labeling that indicates whether particular foods contain genetically modified elements or pesticides. It is difficult to understand, or justify, a role of the state aimed at *depriving* consumers of this information, regardless of what one may think of the scientific basis for the consumers' concerns.

Lobbyists, including willing and, at times, financially well-compensated academics, have been engaged by large producers of these foods to argue and to push the view that genetically modified foods (or some drugs) are not dangerous to consume, and also to push the regulatory agencies not to tighten regulations of pesticides used on insect-resistant seeds that increase agricultural productivity. These issues have increasingly affected trade negotiations. Apart from the scientific questions of whether these foods are damaging and whether they increase agricultural productivity, as long as some individuals believe that they are damaging, the goods may generate (at least psychological) negative externalities. Therefore, the citizens should be allowed to be informed and to decide whether or not to consume them.

When the externalities become significant, and the scientific consequences are largely settled, it becomes more difficult for governments to ignore them. However, some individuals may claim that dealing with them may be too expensive in terms of reduced economic growth or loss of employment opportunities. These concerns merit attention. What if genetic modifications significantly increase the productivity of a crop but generate a few cases of cancer? This benefit-cost criterion is in part at the base of the argument, promoted by Ronald Coase, about how to deal with externalities. It has been increasingly used in the fields of law and economics.

Coase pointed out that just because an externality exists, it may not be, by itself, a sufficient argument to stop the activity that generates it, if that activity has great social value, such as a large increase in productivity. One would not stop planes from flying because their noise disturbs some individuals. This argument is now used by some against policies that would reduce the consumption of coal and oil in an effort to reduce the impact on global warming. These concerns deserve to be evaluated, because they tend to be ignored by environmental fundamentalists. Careful evaluation of costs and benefits should influence government decisions but should not become an excuse to delay action when the delay may prove costly.

Often, the costs of the externalities are spread over large areas, while the benefits from ignoring them are more concentrated, so, for reasons already known to Machiavelli and stressed by Mancur Olson in his 1965 book, it is easier for opposition to proposed regulations to be organized in the latter case. Some externalities tend to be of this kind. In these cases the government must play a well-informed role. In some cases two government regulatory agencies, such as the Environmental Protection Agency and the agency in charge of protecting wildlife, may have different standards and reach conflicting conclusions. The standards used to protect wildlife from the impact of some chemicals may be much more strict than those used to protect humans. These conflicts may open some governmental actions to easy criticism of excessive regulatory zeal.

If externalities occur *within* the national borders of a country, and if the national government does not intervene, the (national) private market is likely to underproduce or overproduce the goods or the activities that generate the externalities. It may, therefore, be seen as necessary and more justified for the government to intervene. In the United States some conservative politicians would like to limit this kind of intervention only to the states' governments, thus removing that power from the federal government. This might reduce actions for externalities that cross state limits. The traditional solution of economists had been to require governmental intervention in dealing with negative externalities that indicate market failure. The traditional solution, largely attributed to the British economist A. C. Pigou (1920), had been that the government should tax those who generate significant negative externalities and subsidize those who are damaged by these externalities. Alternatively, the government could impose regulations to eliminate or to reduce the negative externalities.

In 1960, the British economist Ronald Coase, who later earned a Nobel Prize in economics, challenged the Pigouvian view with what came to be called the Coase theorem, which has already been referred to in this book. Coase pointed out that the activity that generates an externality might be important to society, so it might be socially inefficient to stop that activity because of the negative externality. Additionally, the activity that generates the externality might have existed before the activity that was damaged by it was created. The approach suggested by Coase, and later promoted by his followers (especially economists associated with the University of Chicago, where he was teaching), would be for the involved parties to deal directly with the problem to find the solution that would be least costly for society as a whole. Depending on the existing legal rights, the least-costly solution would be borne either by the generator of the externality or by the recipient of it.

In some situations, the Coase solution indicated that there was no need for the government to intervene, although the solutions might have required some arbitration. George Stigler, another Nobel Prize winner and a colleague of Ronald Coase at the University of Chicago, would refer to Coase's intuition as an important "Eureka moment" in economics (see Stigler, 1975; Coase, 1994; Mueller, 1989, chapter 1; Polinsky, 2003).

Coase had theorized that the relevant parties (the producers and the consumers of an externality) should negotiate directly (with the help of arbitration if necessary) and agree on the least costly solution to society. Essentially, the generator of the negative externality would buy the acquiescence of the damaged party, or the damaged party would buy the least costly corrective action on the part of the generator, depending on their respective legal rights. This solution might be achievable without direct state intervention. The Coase theorem has greatly influenced the development of the fields of law and economics, fields that have grown in importance over the years, among both economists and legal scholars.

R. A. Posner, an influential US judge, has been an important contributor over the years to the field of regulations and a promoter of Coase's solution to externality issues.

Complications and difficulties naturally arise when the negative externalities do not involve just two parties but many parties, as is the case for activities that pollute the environment, or when the externalities cross national frontiers and become multinational or even global. This is often the case with some environmental problems, including the contamination of rivers, the diversion of the water of rivers, the acidification of oceans, the excessive exploitation of fishing in the oceans, global warming, or even the exploitation of loopholes in international aspects of taxation (see Castellucci, 2014; Sandmo, 2003; Tanzi, 2016a). Often, the transaction costs are high, especially when lawyers need to get involved.

Because of growing economic activity and population density, and also because of the globalization of economic activities, multinational or global externalities have become common in recent decades, although they have always existed. The "discovery" of America by Columbus generated enormous global externalities (both positive and negative) in the years that followed (see Mann, 2011). Some of these global problems arise spontaneously. Others may be created when jurisdictions take advantage of particular situations to shift the cost of their actions on others. This may be happening today in the area of water use and taxation (see Tanzi, 2016a). In the tax area, some jurisdictions attempt to attract to them part of the world tax base, or, alternatively, they try to export to other countries part of their tax burden. It is also happening in various environmental areas.

In these global cases the solution proposed by Coase, while still theoretically possible and desirable, becomes a lot more difficult, or at times close to impossible, to apply. The Pigou solution also becomes difficult when the externalities cross national frontiers and, especially, when they involve several countries with conflicting objectives, as is the case with global warming.

There is no global government, and no single government with the power to enforce solutions and agreements among countries with conflicting interests. The solutions would require difficult and often unproductive negotiations among many of the world's governments. Some of the governments in the negotiations about global warming, such as India, have argued, with some justification, that the reduction of poverty through economic growth in their countries is, for them, more important, at least in the short run, than a cleaner environment. Furthermore, past policies and actions of the now-developed countries are partly to blame for the

amount of carbon that is in the atmosphere and that is presumably causing global warming. Thus, these newly developed countries claim, the
advanced countries should bear a greater financial cost of dealing with
global warming.

Cross-country externalities have proved difficult to deal with, in spite
of continuing efforts by the United Nations and by other international
organizations. In some cases, such as utilizing the water of rivers that cross
several countries or fishing in parts of the sea claimed by specific countries,
if agreements are not reached, the externalities might lead to future wars.
In other cases, such as the pollution of the atmosphere, which many scientists believe is leading to global warming, they might lead to global or
existential disasters if scientists' forecasts prove to be correct. The problem
of allocating water rights in the Western part of the United States is also
proving difficult to solve, even within a single country.

All the aforementioned cases are examples of situations that require, or
might require, some government role that, in the public economics literature, goes under the name of resource *allocation*. By and large the literature
has been more specific in suggesting what to do about these situations
when they are internal to a country and when a national government has
the power to act. It has been less specific, or it has been silent, on what to
do when the situations concern several countries, or even the whole globe,
as in the cases of global warming, the growing resistance of viruses to anti-
biotics, or illegal immigration. Although some problems of allocation can
be dealt with by the use of regulations and taxes, or by free negotiations
among market participants, others require public spending. Furthermore,
problems connected with the working of public sectors make some of the
theoretical solutions now available not always practical to implement.

CHAPTER 18

The State's Economic Objectives and Its Institutions

After the publication of Musgrave's *The Theory of Public Finance* in 1959, a book that provided a useful and often-used framework for addressing issues related to governmental intervention in a market economy, it became natural and usual for public finance scholars to classify the actions of governments into three virtually distinct, or compartmentalized, parts of a theoretical public budget: allocation of resources, redistribution of income, and stabilization of the economy. These parts were assumed to identify the main reasons why and the main areas in which governments intervene in market economies, as well as the main justifications for the intervention. Musgrave had theorized that three separate, virtual "branches" of the budget office of a country would be responsible for each part, respectively, and each branch would specialize in the pursuit of its assigned objectives, assuming that the other two branches were doing their parts.

This approach was helpful in organizing discussions, but it was a bit naïve because the pursuit of each objective almost inevitably would affect the desirable outcomes of the other two. Therefore, it might not be realistic to think of the objectives separately, and the interactions among them are likely to be complex. Each time a branch acted, it would force the other two also to act. This, in turn, would create a need to reassess and perhaps change the original action. Establishing a final, desirable outcome may be more difficult than Musgrave realized. Nonetheless, this complication will be ignored in the discussion that follows.

If the state must perform the role of allocating resources or other roles that require public spending, it will need public resources. In principle, a powerful state could appropriate directly the needed resources by forcing individuals to contribute their time or their wealth to the provision of the required output – as many governments did to some extent in the past, and as some continue to do today, with compulsory military service or with some forms of expropriation of property. In ancient times, roads, city walls, canals, pyramids, and other public works were often financed in this way. However, a more efficient, more modern, and potentially more democratic and more equitable alternative is to use financial resources obtained through taxation or through public borrowing, or, occasionally, obtained from the printing of money by central banks or the sale of publicly owned assets. For example, in recent years, in China, regional governments have obtained considerable financial resources by selling the use of publicly owned land, for extended periods of time, to private enterprises, and at some point Italy and other countries obtained large numbers of resources from privatizing public enterprises.

In a modern economy, there is an obvious need for a tax system and for institutions that collect taxes; and there is a need to make decisions on what kind of taxes would be desirable to have, or what kinds of loans to obtain. There is also a need for the establishment of institutions responsible for spending the public money and for keeping track of the money spent, of the *output* produced with that money, and, ideally, of the *outcome* of that spending. See Schiavo-Campo, 2017.

These taxing and spending activities should, in theory, be considered jointly, although, in practice, they tend to be looked at separately. The huge amount of literature on taxation now available tends to ignore, for the most part, the uses to which the tax revenues are put. It considers the collection of taxes and their uses as independent and unrelated decisions, except at the total level, when macroeconomic considerations become important. The same is the case with the printing of money, although it is less clear than it is for taxes who ultimately pays for that action and who benefits from it. In any case a central bank seems to be less essential for the actions of governments than a tax office. The United States did not even have a central bank until a century ago.

In all these activities, especially in a market economy with democratic institutions, an efficient state would be expected to want to minimize the costs that its activities and its actions impose on the society at large and on particular individuals. It would be desirable for both the economic and the social costs to be kept at a minimum. As a consequence, a public sector *of high quality* should promote and require an efficient tax system and tax administration and a public expenditure management system that minimizes inefficient and unproductive spending, while it promotes equitable and welfare-creating spending. It should also require a budget large enough to allow the state to perform its essential functions and to achieve its objectives in a satisfactory way, without the need for accumulating, over the years, large public debts and without causing inflation by creating an excessive amount of money. Random events can, occasionally, create the need for public borrowing, but significant accumulation of public debt over time ought to be avoided. See Tanzi, 2016b.

The costs that must be minimized are not just the financial and economic costs that the state imposes directly on the citizens, including compliance costs in the payment of taxes or in observing regulations, but also costs in terms of (actual or perceived) loss of economic freedom, or the costs that arise as a result of disincentive effects by those who pay the taxes or those who receive the spending. Social costs, such as those imposed on the environment, and costs imposed on future generations also ought to be taken into account as Edmund Burke's had assumed. In this book I shall ignore the issue of what to do, if anything, about externalities and about public goods that have cross-country or global dimensions. These externalities cannot be dealt with satisfactorily by *national* governments acting independently, because their powers are limited by the countries' borders. On global goods and global challenges see Kaul et al. editors, 2003 and Kaul and Conceição, editor, 2006. I shall continue to focus here on the activities of *national* governments.

In addition to the essential, original, and most fundamental role of the state described earlier, namely the *allocation* of resources, a role that had been recognized and described by economists at least since the time when Adam Smith published *The Wealth of Nations*, two or, perhaps, more additional economic roles have been assigned to the state in the twentieth century by economists who write about market economies in democratic countries. These roles had not existed in the past, at least not in the modern versions.

As already mentioned, these main new roles are: (a) the *redistribution* of income (and wealth) and (b) the *stabilization* of economic activity. With more confusion and less precision to these two roles could be added (c) the promotion of *growth* and *employment* as well as what could be called (d) a *tutorial* role. The promotion of growth and employment has been considered, by economists, part of the allocation of resources and not a separate objective. However, given its importance in the economic policies of many countries in today's world, and given its synergy with the other roles, it might perhaps have its own distinct place as a separate policy objective. These later tasks, or roles, are less firmly grounded in economic *theory* than the allocation of resources, although Keynesian economists might dispute this assertion, at least with respect to the stabilization role. See the fascinating debate between Hayek and Keynes on this issue in Wapshott (2011). The tutorial role is definitely a new one and is growing in importance, in part as a result of experiments conducted by experimental or behavioral economists and the contribution of psychologists to economic thinking.

Regardless of the theoretical justifications offered by economists, in today's real world, the new roles have become, and many governments consider them to be, important. Their *empirical* importance grew especially in the second haft of the twentieth century, when welfare states were created and the countries' economies became more globalized and more competitive. That importance has continued to grow in the twenty-first century due to high levels of unemployment and concerns about job creation. The tutorial role has been growing in importance especially in the last two decades. The role connected with income distribution, broadly interpreted, has become so important that it now accounts for, or explains, much of the total public spending of many countries. In other words, it explains how or why the share of public spending and of taxes into GDP grew from, say, around 10 percent in the nineteenth century to exceed 40 percent or even 50 percent in several countries at the present time.

Until the Great Depression, the levels of public spending and taxes had been much lower. For example, until that time, the share of the general government's taxes and public spending in the United States (i.e., federal plus state and local governments) had been only around 10 percent of GDP. In Sweden, one of today's best examples of a mature welfare state, the tax level had been only around 15 percent of GDP until 1940. Until that time, the allocation of resources by governments and their focus on the production of public goods (defense, justice, personal protection, some educational spending, and some infrastructures) had played the dominant role and had absorbed most of the then-available public revenue.

After the Great Depression and World War II much of the growth in public spending that took place could be attributed to the new, nonallocation roles of the state, and especially to the redistribution role. There was, thus, a dramatic change in what governments did and in the roles that they were expected to play between the nineteenth and the twentieth centuries, and especially between the first and the second half of the twentieth century. This change not only was apparent in the level of public spending but also is now apparent in the official reasons that governments give for spending public money.

In the third part of this book, we shall focus on the growing importance of the redistribution of income over recent decades and, in later chapters, on the growing concerns about developments that seem to be making the income distribution less equitable than many would like it to be, in spite of the high levels of government spending. We shall explore some reasons why this may be happening and the role that government policies and market developments may be playing.

CHAPTER 19

The State and the Distribution of Income

Markets produce goods and services for citizens, as consumers, and for enterprises, as investors and producers, and they provide incomes to them, either as workers or as owners of productive assets. The incomes received by the workers and by the owners of productive assets depend on their human capital and talent, their personal effort, the assets that they own, their luck and risk taking, and, significantly, on *government policy*. Those incomes greatly affect the workers' and owners' welfare (see Jones and Klenow, 2016).

Given the general, legal, and institutional framework of a country's public sector (a framework that includes *all* the policies, *all* the institutions, and *all* the laws, rules, and regulations that governments have created over the years), a given distribution of income and of wealth comes to be determined by the working of the free market, *before* the government intervenes with its *taxing and spending actions* to change the market-determined outcome and the impact on welfare. Therefore, the government influences the distribution of income, wealth, and also welfare, *first*, with its *general* policies and rules and, *second*, with specific, ex post redistributive policies, mainly of a fiscal nature (taxes and public spending) but also including some regulations and monetary policy.

The government's *total* action can bring a minor or a significant change in the distribution of income and wealth compared with what the market would have generated *if the government had not existed*. It can also bring significant changes to factors such as life expectancy, literacy, and others. It is a mistake to assume that the role the government plays *in redistributing income* is limited to its *fiscal* actions, that is, to its fiscal actions *after* the market has generated and has distributed the incomes.

The distribution of income determined by the working of the market is inevitably influenced by the institutions, the laws, and the general formal and informal rules that govern the operations of the market at the given time, as well as by those that have been governing the country's economy for some time. The income distribution that results from the work of the market may or may not match the prevailing societal perception of the degree of inequality that would be considered fair and desirables at a given time, assuming that such perception could be determined with quantitative precision, which may not be easy or possible.

The divergence between the results from the operations of the market and the desired income distribution leads, or should lead, to the explicit redistributive fiscal policies that the governments introduce or are expected to introduce. These policies are often associated with *taxing and spending* but also occasionally with regulations and monetary policy. They are aimed at changing the market-generated income distribution in order to make it more socially acceptable. It must be repeated that this redistribution takes place *after* the market has done its work in generating the total income and in allocating it among the owners of the factors of production.

The *explicit* redistributive role attracts most of the attention. It is the role that, in the view of conservative observers, changes the income distribution away from the presumed "legitimate" allocation that the "free" market has generated. The reality is that, before the government intervenes with its explicit redistributive taxing and spending policies, it has already played an important role in the market's generation and distribution of income, as a result of its past and present *general* (i.e., nonfiscal) policies. The norms, the regulations, and the formal and informal institutions that the government has created over many years for the operation of the market and even for the promotion of social relations have played an important role in the distribution of income, before the explicit intervention by the government with *taxes and spending programs.*

So it is not correct to assume, as many do, that the government role in distributing income is solely connected with spending and taxing. This assumption ignores the many other, but less direct, ways in which the government, with its rules and institutions – both formal and informal – over the years has played a major role in how the market operates and allocates income to the owners of the factors of production. With different general rules and policies, the market would have generated a different income distribution.

Let us review briefly some of the ways in which governments affect the income distribution, *before* they use *current* taxes and spending. Obviously, a full listing of these ways is beyond the scope of this book.

First, there has been the government role in providing part or most of the physical infrastructure that exists at a given time in a country. That infrastructure has allowed private economic agents (both individuals and, increasingly, enterprises) to operate more efficiently and to produce at lower costs. Without the roads, the ports, the railroads, the airports, the canals, and many other infrastructures that the government has created, or has contributed to creating over the years, many economic activities would not take place, and many private incomes would not have been generated.

Second, there is the role that the government has played in contributing to the education and the human capital of the workers that employers hire. Without that human capital, the workers would be less productive, and the enterprises would be less efficient, thus generating lower incomes for them. It is no mystery why workers are less productive in poor, developing countries, where less human capital has been created by their governments.

Third, there is the government role in:

(a) *Certifying* whether some individuals are able and are allowed to perform particular activities, while stipulating that others are not, which in several cases may also contribute to the creation of *positional rents* for some individuals or groups of individuals and, at the same time, and hopefully, to the reduction of some risks for the citizens. These rules have created large incomes for individuals who perform certain activities (medical doctors, dentists, lawyers, and some others).

(b) *Protecting* the rights of property owners and, increasingly, property rights that are connected with broadly defined *intellectual* property (rights owned through patents, trademarks, copyrights, brand names, image rights, and various other rules on what constitutes *intellectual property* and on who can make use of that *property*). The concept of intellectual property has become much more elastic and more encompassing with the passing of the years. It has moved well beyond the rights that existed or were contemplated centuries ago that were mentioned in the US Constitution. Over the years, intellectual property rights have been extended to cover areas not originally covered, while new technologies have assisted and made possible that extension and the appropriation of the economic benefits from it, which go to the owners of the property rights. We shall return to this important issue in a later chapter.

Intellectual property protected by the government creates (temporary and largely unregulated) monopolies for those who have claims to it. Occasionally, it can contribute to the creation of very large incomes for individuals who are exploiting the temporary monopolies without government regulations, as happened in the past with traditional monopolies. Furthermore, the related incomes may be more due to luck and chance than to ability and sustained efforts. The intellectual property has been made more valuable by the existing technology. In any case it is the government's protection that contributes to the existence and often to the size of those incomes. Remove that protection and many of these large incomes would vanish.

(c) *Establishing many market rules* in labor markets, such as those that limit the role and the power of unions, as well as rules on the hiring and firing of workers, on minimum wages, on working hours, and on requirements to use unionized workers for public works, national ships for some operations, or national firms for government procurement operations.

(d) Perhaps more importantly, *establishing rules about the formation and the market power of corporations*; about the consequences of bankruptcy; about the limited responsibilities and liabilities of shareholders and managers of corporations; about inheritance of property; about the power of managers to choose members of the executive boards of enterprises; about the operations of corporations; and about the power that banks have acquired in remaining "too big to fail," power that is allowed by the government and that, in some ways, distorts the operation of the market and creates high incomes for some banks.

Fourth, there is the *investment activity* of the government in creating new infrastructure that may not only reduce the costs for private enterprises but may also contribute directly to capital gains for some of the owners of real properties (land and buildings) that are located near where the public infrastructures are built or that benefit more directly from the investments. Consider, for example, the value of land located near new highways or metropolitan routes or in the vicinity of new airports, or land used to produce an output that can more easily be sent to places where it is in high demand or land from where the output can be exported to where it is needed. Some countries have considered imposing "betterment taxes" to claw back some of this value, but these taxes have rarely been used.

Fifth, and of particular importance in the United States and in some other advanced countries, there are the benefits to private operators that come from present and past *fundamental research and development* activities financed by the government. These activities may have involved research on new crops that has benefited the owners of agricultural land, as conducted over many years by institutions such as the Agricultural Department in the United States; fundamental research, such as the development of atomic power, of the Internet, and of computer technology conducted in government institutions including various laboratories, for example, the Pentagon's Defense Advanced Research Project Agency (DARPA); research by the huge National Institute of Health that generates results that allow pharmaceutical companies to develop new drugs; research by NASA that allows private enterprises to develop activities related to space; research on fusion and on new sources of energy; fundamental research in biology; and so on.

The private sector has generally little or no interest in generating and advancing truly *fundamental* or *basic* knowledge, because that knowledge does not lend itself to being patented and does not have direct, immediate commercial uses. However, the knowledge generated by that research in time opens new lines of investigation by private concerns, lines that, through *applied research and development*, lead to new discoveries and practical applications that generate usable intellectual property, the kind of knowledge that can be patented and that can lead to large earnings for some individuals or enterprises. Governments finance *fundamental research* that generates the new basic knowledge and the new ideas that at first may not have a direct, immediate, and obvious economic value. However, that knowledge leads to *future* developments and to outcomes and discoveries that *can* be patented and that *can* generate high incomes.

The value of *recent and some older* fundamental research can only be known and appreciated at a *later* time, when someone perceives practical implications for the new ideas and, through applied research and further developments and is able to develop practical applications. These applications can lead to new products, and the new products can lead to high incomes for some individuals and enterprises, especially during the time when a patent has given them a monopoly. Without the new fundamental knowledge financed by the government, a financing that can be costly to society and, as mentioned, is not accompanied by any direct and practical uses initially, there would be less creation of intellectual property and fewer millionaires today.

The modern world is full of examples where new theoretical ideas that seemed useless at the time when they were generated led to extraordinary applications and to the birth of new economic and technological giants. Some of today's largest enterprises have originated in this way. They have replaced the industrial giants of the past, which had been the products of the Industrial Revolution. In most cases the fundamental research that led to these developments was financed by public money. Some literature has argued that without the *scientific* revolution of the eighteenth century there could not have been an *Industrial Revolution* (see Jacob, 2014).

Other literature has challenged that view. In any case, the governments had played a more limited role in the Industrial Revolution than they did and do in the computer and digital revolution.

Today, governments, and especially the US and a few other governments, *support* much of the fundamental research, including research that takes place in major universities and in various research institutions. For example, billions of dollars of public money have been supporting basic research related to *fusion*, a process that one day could lead to the generation of unlimited energy and to enormous financial gains for some private enterprises. Several private enterprises are now trying to develop specific commercial uses of the available basic research. The same has happened with space travel. To repeat, basic research, financed by public money, leads to occasional and later discoveries that favor some sectors of the economy and that make some individuals very rich. Just think of the Internet and the creation of the commercial activities that today are connected with it.

In an interesting book, *The Entrepreneurial State* (2013), Mariana Mazzucato, a professor at the University of Essex, has shown, with many examples, the importance that this government role has played in generating large economic value and private incomes. A recent article by Bill Gates has made similar points. Calling attention to "America's unparalleled capacity for innovation," Gates has suggested that the formula "is not complicated" (electronic article by Reuters News Agency, 2016). It is simply the government funding world-class research institutions, which produce the new discoveries that lead to the new technologies that private entrepreneurs take to the market. See also Campanile (2016) on the birth of the information society. For a contrarian view, see Mingardi (2015). The countries whose governments invest more in innovation (Korea, China, Japan, Finland, etc.) generally do better economically. As Gates (2016) put it, "the Microsoft revolution was made possible by US Government research," and "early advances in wind and solar technologies were developed with federal money."

A recent example of this potential government role was the signing, in the summer of 2015, by President Obama of an executive order to establish the National Strategic Computing Initiative, which would have the goal of building a supercomputer capable of processing a much larger quantity of data than current computers are now capable of processing. Such a computer would give scientists in various areas the capacity to solve important problems that cannot be solved with the current capacity of computers. Once such a computer became available, it would open the way for many commercial applications and would earn large incomes for the individuals and the enterprises able to first use the new knowledge. Building such a supercomputer is going to be difficult and costly to the public budget, as it was costly going to the moon. In passing, it could be mentioned that the system that makes it possible for people to know their precise location while they are driving and that directs them to where they want to go is made possible by "a network of twenty-four geosynchronous GPS satellites built and maintained by the U.S. government" (see Brynjolfsson and McAfee, 2014, p. 59). The value of the GPS to many current private activities is obvious. It is often a free service, and its benefits are not measured by GDP.

Not all the money that the government allocates to these economically risky activities leads to benefits to society. Some countries allocate research money to institutions that are not *world class and efficient* in generating new ideas or discoveries. However, the important point is that failures are government failures and are shared by society, while the gains eventually become private gains, first for a few lucky individuals who become very rich, and later more broadly for society.

Sixth, there is also the impact of monetary policy, especially the one pursued by the central banks' increasingly unorthodox policies, such as Quantitative Easing, which, in some cases, has resembled fiscal policy by a different name. That policy has helped some private enterprises and some individuals to access large financial resources at very low cost and to use those resources to earn large incomes. For example, some private enterprises have used the cheap loans obtained from the central banks to buy shares in their own enterprises, rather than to make real investments. This policy may be creating large incomes for some individuals and potential bubbles in some sectors of the economy. It may also be exposing the central banks to potentially high future risks.

Seventh, some policies, such as the deregulation of the financial market, have led to the generation of large incomes for some strategically located sectors. They may also have created the potential risk for the government to have to come, again, to the rescue of large financial institutions that are still "too large to fail," should they get into trouble. While it has been difficult to identify the genuine value to society of the large incomes generated in the financial market, the past financial crisis led to high unemployment and great losses for many citizens, and was unquestionably very costly to society (see Zingales, 2015).

The aforementioned selected examples indicate some of the many ways in which the intervention of the government has changed, or can change, the incomes of many individuals, increasing them for particular individuals. In other words, the examples indicate ways in which the role of the government can change the distribution of income *before* it intervenes with its explicit, ex post *redistributive* role, the role that is more visible and that is carried out mainly with taxes and with spending programs. It is the latter role that attracts much criticism from conservative economists and politicians, and also from left-leaning economists and individuals, for being too modest.

Finally, the increasing complexity of government laws and operations has created a category of insiders with superior knowledge of those laws and the ability to exploit existing government programs and rules, and even to push for the creation of new government programs and actions to their advantage. These possibilities contribute to *the termites of the state*. For various reasons these termites have become more important in recent years, and their importance has continued, and is likely to continue, to grow. I have mentioned some of them. I shall mention others later in this book.

Because of the aforementioned factors, it is not correct to maintain, as some do, that in the modern world the "market" determines a *natural* and *legitimate* income distribution and that, after that determination, taxes and public spending change it in an illegitimate way, and, by so doing, limit the economic liberty of (especially) higher-income individuals. According to this view, held by some economists and politicians, if the government did not exist, the distribution of income, before the fiscal action has taken place, would be the same as the one that the market would have generated. Therefore, it is argued, society should respect that distribution, and government policies should change it as little as possible. According to this view, high marginal tax rates amount to an expropriation of legitimate and deserved incomes. Some go so far as to consider them an expression of class warfare, and taxes some kind of theft.

I have argued that this interpretation is not correct because the alignment of political power – which has existed in various countries over many years, and which has given to some groups, and especially to many of those in the higher percentiles of the income distribution, more market and political power – has contributed to the creation of rules, institutions, and situations that, often unintentionally and at times intentionally, have favored higher-income individuals and have created rents for some of them.

To repeat, the various government rules, created over many years, play a significant role in determining the market's distribution of income, *before taxes and public spending enter the scene*. More often than not, they increase the incomes of those in the higher-income groups who are better able to exploit them. Whether the explicit redistributive policies of the government are sufficient or are appropriate to generate an income distribution closer to the one that society would consider desirable is, of course, a different and more difficult question to answer.

What could be called the *invisible hand of the government*, in all its manifestations, plays a much larger role in the distribution of income than most people realize. This means that the income distribution that the majority of the population might consider desirable might not require only the explicit, visible, and redistributive ex post policies of the government, played with taxes and public spending, that lead to strong negative reactions by some. It may also require other actions, including especially reforms aimed at making the working of the economy different, and more neutral, than it is, and it may require that governments become less exposed to manipulations and cronyism.

The state may not only have to rely on redistributive taxes and public programs if it wants to make the distribution of income more legitimate and change it in desirable and more-sustainable directions. It may also need to make the market operate in a way closer to how a free and well-working market, one not affected by government intervention, if that were possible, would operate. If it were possible to reduce, or to eliminate, the ex ante, *invisible hand of the government*, a less-explicit ex post redistributive role might be necessary. Obviously, that might be difficult and in some sense even impossible to achieve, because some governmental intervention would be inevitable. Later, I shall mention some areas where policies could be changed.

The government must look at the whole apparatus of rules, regulations, laws, and existing institutional arrangements, both formal and informal, that determine the environment or the social ecology in which the private market operates. As I have argued, it is likely that some of those laws and arrangements have played important, but not always transparent, roles in creating and in allocating incomes. This argument is similar to that used by feminists who insist that there are many hidden rules that have created discriminations based on gender. A different and perhaps more neutral apparatus might have generated an income distribution that would have required less-explicit ex post redistributive policies, and that would have been closer to what a truly neutral market would have generated, in terms of income distribution. *Termites of the state and of the market* often play major but not visible roles in these processes.

As already mentioned, the explicit, redistributive role of the state is criticized by some for challenging the result of the market, while it is criticized by others for not challenging enough that result. The less-explicit, ex ante role generally receives little attention or is ignored, except in particular areas such as inheritance, which traditionally has attracted some attention by Piketty and others before him, and justice (see Rakoff, 2016).

Most conservative economists and politicians consider the results of the market and the incomes of those who receive them as fully earned and deserved. Therefore, they argue that the incomes that they provide to those who are engaged in market activities, especially those at the upper end of the income distribution, should not be challenged by redistributive fiscal policies. This argument is defended by conservative think tanks. The argument loses some of its merit when it is realized that, by the time the government redistributes income *using its fiscal tools*, it may have already played a major but less-visible role in generating the *pre-redistribution* results of the market.

The truth is that we have no idea about what income distribution the market of a country would have generated if the state had not existed, or, perhaps more realistically, if the general government rules under which the market has operated had been different and more neutral. It is not difficult to make a case that, having been created by the high-income groups of years past, the rules that were introduced in many countries favored these high-income groups. As a historian put it, writing about the US experience:

> On the whole, the views of the legal fraternity during the decades after the Civil War were pronouncedly conservative. Training and social positions combined to make lawyers and judges supporters of the *status quo*.... In the ideological conflict between *laissez faire* and the general welfare state, bench and bar were almost invariably to be found among the champions of *laissez faire* (Fine, 1964, p. 127).

Laissez-faire policies had not been popular only in the United States. In later years and especially after World War II the situation changed, but many of the old rules and institutions were not changed.

Strangely, the rather obvious point that was just made seems to have attracted little if any attention in the extensive literature on equity, except for the role of inherited wealth and its treatment, which over the years did attract attention and which, in the book by Piketty (2014), was given particular importance. The *explicit, visible* redistributive role of the state in recent decades, which is promoted with progressive taxes and with redistributive social spending, and which attracts much of the attention of commentators, has led conservatives to challenge it on the ground that, in a market economy, the results of the market have ethical justification and should not be changed by the government.

In recent years the globalization of economic activities, and the growing mobility of financial capital and of high-net-worth individuals (HNWIs), has given these economists other arguments in favor of calls for reducing marginal tax rates, especially on incomes from capital sources, the incomes that are of greater importance to high-income individuals. As a consequence of these arguments, the marginal tax rates were significantly reduced in recent decades, contributing to widening income disparity (see Tanzi, 2014c). We shall return to this issue in more detail in a later chapter.

CHAPTER 20

Market Operations and Income Distribution

Apart from the obvious observation that markets rarely function perfectly and that, as a consequence, many individuals are likely to end up getting higher or lower incomes than they would have gotten in a well-functioning market, there are various considerations that may justify a significant, *ex post* redistributive role by the state.

The first consideration, already mentioned, is that the state in all its activities, combined with some important technological developments to which it may have directly or indirectly contributed in the past, is likely to have played an important role in establishing the rules under which the market generates and redistributes incomes. Some of those rules were established over long periods and were promoted by the social classes that had more power. Those rules influence the way economic activities are conducted and incomes are generated and distributed among the market participants. They change slowly over the longer run, often in imperceptible ways. In the past they tended to favor the propertied classes who held much of the political power and the influence on policies. Some authors have gone so far as to argue that a "shadow government" exists and largely determines what rules the market follows. The shadow government is presumably maneuvered with strings pulled by powerful individuals who use their wealth to influence policies and to get results that they want (see Lofgren, 2015).

As a consequence of the aforementioned considerations, the protection of property has been and has continued to be a major goal of governments in market economies and especially of the American government. James Madison, who was very rich, had recognized this a long time ago when he wrote that "government is instituted ... for protection of the property ..." (Federalist Papers (No. 54) p. 334). In spite of some changes in policies, especially in more recent decades, that protection has continued to create a strong correlation in market economies between past and present family incomes, as Piketty stressed in his best-selling 2014 book.

As an important example of government rules that have helped richer individuals or have allowed some individuals to become rich, think of the income that some individuals would have received if there had been no government protection, or less government protection, of intellectual property. Compare the situation in the past with that of recent years, when individuals have earned huge incomes and have accumulated enormous wealth within a short time span, wealth that they can easily pass on to their children, because of the protection that they have received and continue to receive *from the government* on their intellectual and their real *property*.

Recall that some of the world's greatest composers of the past died poor (Mozart was buried in an unmarked grave), in spite of the enormous and extraordinary musical output that they had created. Beethoven and Vivaldi had to rely on giving music lessons to earn a living. In today's world, with the benefit of the government's protection of their intellectual output, they would have become very rich. Their artistic output would have been protected by different government rules and would also have benefited from being distributed more widely to users with the help of modern government provided technology. The effort of the composers would have been the same, but their earnings would have been very different. To get a feel for how the modern world is different, consider *Forbes's* estimates of the earnings of 2016 for thirty of the best-paid musicians. They ranged from $38.5 million (for Drake) to $170 million (for Taylor Swift).

Let's change the focus from composers and musicians to inventors. An article published in the *Economist* of August 8, 2015, pointed out that those who made the Industrial Revolution in England in the eighteenth century did not benefit from government-protected rights on their discoveries. They could not patent their inventions and could not establish patent-protected monopolies, as they would be able to do today. Therefore, the gains to them from their discoveries were often modest.

The government's expansion of the protection of intellectual property, assisted by new technological developments (largely financed by public money), has dramatically changed the economic landscape in the past century. Today, some of the largest incomes received by individuals are, directly or indirectly, connected with the government's protection of intellectual property. Especially when new intellectual property can be used in combination with new communication technology – which allows the owners of the intellectual property to sell their services to wide audiences around the world, while limiting the access of nonpaying users, even though new users could technically be added at practically zero costs – the owners of the intellectual property can earn huge incomes.

Some of the highest incomes received today by individuals or by enterprises are directly connected with the *expansion*, over the years, of the concept of property right to new forms of intellectual property. The US government has been very active in this expansion. By having contributed to the development of the new technologies, which made possible the distribution of particular intellectual outputs to very large numbers of people around the world, it has, in addition, played a fundamental role in the creation of the large incomes for some of the individuals and enterprises that have created new intellectual capital. By so doing, it has also, most likely, contributed to making the income distribution less even.

These factors have made it possible not only for important inventors and for great composers and successful writers but also for athletes and other performers to benefit, far more than in the past, from their output and their performances. Furthermore, these factors have also made it possible (especially for athletes and some other performers) to dramatically raise their incomes by selling the access to their performances to a much larger number of radio listeners and television viewers, or through other means such as videos and DVDs. In the official tax declarations of many countries, some of which are publicly available, some of the taxpayers who now declare the highest taxable incomes are athletes and other successful performers.

It should be noted and emphasized that these athletes and performers earn large shares of their total incomes *without making any extra effort* compared to efforts made in the past. They simply earn large additional sums because of the larger audiences and because of the endorsements by private enterprises, which allow enterprises that buy the rights to place the names or the images of the athletes on products (such as cereal boxes) or to place the enterprises' names on the shirts of the athletes. The athletes become vehicles to be used for publicity purposes. For example, an expensive watch attracts more buyers after it has been worn by a famous athlete. Intellectual property rights give high financial value to these endorsements. It would be difficult to make a case that these incomes are tied to extra effort on the part of the athletes or the performers and that taxing them at higher rates would reduce that effort. They are essentially rents.

The earnings of many successful individuals have increased sharply in recent decades: (a) because the individuals' performances can now be broadcast to large audiences using new technologies; (b) because their faces can be used to publicize products; (c) because their performances can attract far more viewers than in the past, while access to the broadcasts or the performances can be legally restricted; and (d) because the unpaid use of the faces or the names of the athletes for publicity can be prevented by government policies. By creating these rights the government has allowed the creation of *rents* for top athletes, top performers, and some other individuals. These rents could not have existed in the past.

The liberalization and the globalization of the financial market have also made it possible for some individuals who operate in that market (a market that has become much wider in the areas in which it operates, and narrower in the number of banks and institutions that control large shares of the market) to earn large incomes from activities and transactions that, in the judgment of many economists, seem to be largely disconnected from the real economy. As a consequence, the real contribution that the financial market now makes to the real economy has become more questionable than, perhaps, it ever has been (see, inter alia, Kay, 2015). Some economists have attributed the slowdown in productivity growth in recent decades to the growth of the financial market, which has been absorbing increasing shares of talented individuals and total profits. That market is no longer seen as one contributing to productivity growth, as some had seen it in the 1970s–1980s, but as increasingly contributing to high and questionable incomes for some. See McKinnon, 1973 and Fry, 1988.

The financial market produces nothing directly. Its role was and has remained that of transferring funds from some hands (savers) to other hands (investors). This, in principle, should allow some individuals to make productive investments. However, the way in which this has been done in recent years has become increasingly complex and at times highly questionable, and the money borrowed has been increasingly used to make bets that have made some economists think of a casino economy (see Sinn, 2010). The total earnings of this market and of some individuals operating in it have increased sharply over the decades, once again not necessarily because of higher efforts on the part of the individuals involved or because of higher genuine value contributed to the economy by them, but because of particular market situations and also because of increasingly creative accounting, which has increased the levels of total (private plus public) debt of many countries and the connected risks that, occasionally, have led to financial crises. See Mian and Sufi, 2014; Tanzi, 2016b.

While some lucky individuals have seen their incomes grow and become very high, other individuals have not done so well. Because of inadequate physical and mental characteristics of some individuals and because of characteristics such as advanced age, illnesses, difficulties in getting jobs, lack of opportunities, bad luck, and, at times, even laziness or lack of ambition, some individuals have not been able to earn incomes high enough to sustain themselves and their dependents at a level that society considers desirable and that modern conditions require.

This problem has always existed, but it became more acute and more difficult to ignore in urban and richer environments, in which individuals, whether rich or poor, live in the same metropolitan areas, and in which large differences in income and consumption are more easily noticeable and increasingly less tolerable. Additionally, the informal safety nets that the large families of the past had offered to individuals within them who were not able to take care of themselves have largely disappeared in today's urban settings, where households' sizes have shrunk, and where large and extended families, living in close spaces, no longer exist.

When ignored, the problems created by deep poverty can lead to undesirable social, environmental, or even aesthetic consequences for communities, as cities such as Baltimore and Ferguson have found out recently in the United States, and Paris and London had found out in earlier years. For example, ignoring these problems might promote more criminal acts by individuals who have not been able to earn an income, or it might make streets less attractive because of the presence of homeless peoples.

The evidence that some people have too much while others have little, inevitably creates undesirable and antisocial attitudes and problems on the part of some. These problems tend to become more acute in urban settings. They have in part been addressed by the creation of welfare states and of programs aimed at assisting the poor, such as food stamps in the United States. Some have considered these welfare programs wasteful and expensive. Others have considered them insufficient. In any case those who find themselves in the lower percentiles of the income distribution in modern, advanced societies have benefited from programs of assistance that have helped them to some extent and that have increased their consumption (beyond the means of their cash incomes), reducing the poverty levels.

However, increasingly, the *working middle class* especially in the USA has found itself in a situation in which some of the costs that it faces (health costs, college tuition costs for children, and others) have increased significantly while their wages have stagnated. Many of those in these percentiles of the income distribution benefit less or little from government redistributive programs when these programs are not universal but are means-tested. This has happened while the incomes of those at the very top of the distribution have been increasing sharply. This development, in recent decades, has created a social climate different from the one in the decades immediately after World War II, which was characterized by higher optimism about the future and when workers expected rising future incomes for them and their children.

As the modern economy and the activities of the state grew and became more complex, they created increasing ways for higher-income and better-connected and -educated individuals to extract more benefits from the government and from the market. Often, they were benefits that escaped easy observations. Lower-income individuals have far fewer of these opportunities, except through criminal actions or, occasionally, through their voting power, which can help create government programs that support them, especially those who can be officially classified as "poor." The more complex the world becomes, the easier it is for some higher-income and better-informed and -connected individuals to exploit that complexity and to extract hidden rents through governmental activities or rules.

After World War II various programs were created in advanced countries to provide assistance to the poor and, in several countries, safety nets for the whole populations. In many European countries some of the safety nets tended to be universal, rather than directed specifically to the poor or the lower income workers, although there were also programs that specifically focused on the poor, such as public housing and assistance for large families. The newly invented *value-added tax* came to play an important role in financing the programs, while the income taxes, at that time, were less distorted by the use of *tax expenditures* that would become more common, especially in the United States, starting in the 1960s. As a consequence, the welfare programs created in the European welfare states were generally more popular and had broader support than those in the United States.

The US social programs were different. Apart from the important social security program directed at retired workers (which included several related programs such as medicare) and the Aid to Dependent Children, created in the years of the New Deal to assist families in which the women had lost their husbands, most recent welfare programs have been *means-tested*. They have been aimed at individuals who could prove to have incomes below established poverty limits, giving some people the incentive to keep their incomes below those limits, either through tax evasion or by remaining unemployed or continuing to work in low-paying jobs. The consequence has been that individuals at higher but still modest income levels, for example, those with incomes above the thirtieth or higher percentile of the income distribution, have paid significant taxes but have benefited much less from the means-tested government programs, of which there are now reportedly some eighty in the United States, many of them not well known.

The previous discussion may explain why surveys in the United States have found little support for redistributive policies and, perhaps more surprisingly, no support for those policies among those who are now the major beneficiaries of existing social programs, the aged and African-Americans (see Ashok et al., 2015). Because of the absence of the value-added tax in the United States (the only OECD country without such a tax), and because of the relatively high personal exemptions and deductions from income before the income tax is applied to taxable income, a large share of the US population pays no income taxes. Among this share, there are some with pretax incomes as high as $200,000 according to Internal Revenue Service statistics. African-Americans and the aged are likely to be concerned that, given the US social and political environment and the strong resistance to higher taxes, redistribution would come at their expense. Many Americans may be surprised to learn that among the OECD countries, the United States is where the share of taxes into GDP has grown the least in the past fifty years, and it has remained at a relatively low level.

In the United States those in the income categories above the poverty line are generally responsible for their health care costs, either directly or, for some of them through insurance cofinanced by their employers. And they are directly and fully responsible for the educational spending for their children, which can be very high, at the university level or for private schools (popular where public schools are of low quality). To some extent, they are helped in these expenses by the "tax expenditures," the value of which depends on the tax rates. The payments (for health care costs and educational expenses) are not classified as taxes. However, they increase the expenses for the individuals themselves, and, with regard to the enterprise-financed insurance costs for health care, they increase the costs especially for small enterprises. The latter has been a complaint about the Obama health reform law, the Affordable Care Act, called Obamacare, which has increased these costs for many small enterprises.

The consequence of these policies has been that in the United States many workers have come to not see the government as a friend, one ready to come to their aid. When, over the years, health care costs and educational costs increased faster than the rate of inflation, and real wages stopped growing, while taxes on many households in the middle income classes remained unchanged, complaints and resentments about some programs rose. It should not be a surprise that resentment has been heightened in recent years by what has been happening to the income distribution and by the astronomical earnings of some of those at the top. The financial crisis and the recession that cost the jobs of many workers increased that resentment and promoted populist reactions.

Historically, at least since the time of Elizabeth I in England, and longer in some other countries, the state has been expected to assist some of the less fortunate and more "deserving" individuals (especially orphans, widowed women, insane individuals, or totally disabled people) with some transfers (often in free goods and services). This kind of assistance has often existed in organized communities. That redistribution was not influenced by statistics, such as Gini coefficients, but by the poor conditions of *some* individuals. However, historically, much of the formal redistribution that had actually taken place in countries had been upward, toward the nobles or the aristocrats in control. In European countries this kind of upward redistribution becomes obvious when one visits the residences, the castles and mansions, and the hunting lodges of nobles and aristocrats.

The fundamental debate cannot be whether some collective obligations toward individuals truly in need exist. They obviously exist. Rather, the debate is about what kind of assistance should be provided, for whom, and *at what level.* The reason is that the cost of the assistance and the risk that some individuals may become dependent on it depend on the level of the assistance and on who receives it. If the assistance is unconditional and is given especially in cash at a relatively high level, and if those who receive it come to feel that they have a right to it, the assistance is likely to become costly to the budget and to a country's economy, unless strong community norms limit that kind of dependency, as some have argued to have been the case in Scandinavian countries in the past, before the recipients of the assistance started to include many immigrants. That view is now being questioned even in those countries, and political opposition to it has been growing.

Economists who are strong believers in the power of incentives generally assume that *unconditional* and *generous* assistance generates dependency by some of those who receive it and leads to an increase in the numbers of those who come to depend on it. It may also create "poverty traps" that weaken the recipients' incentives to look for work, cause them not to accept some kinds of less attractive jobs, and weaken their incentives to improve their situations with their own efforts. These poverty traps may be created by potentially large *implicit* tax rates on the additional incomes of those who have been benefiting from means-tested subsidies when they lose them upon acquiring jobs. These dangers exist especially in what some call "nanny states."

Two centuries ago some economists, especially French ones (Bastiat, Say, LeRoy-Beaulieu, de Tocqueville) were already warning about the possibility that nanny states could lead to dependency. At a time when the role of the state in terms of public spending was still very small, Frederic Bastiat (1864) could worry that "everyone want[ed] to live at the expense of the state." His countryman Alexis de Tocqueville, in his "Memoire sur le paupérisme," an essay published in 1835, had pointed out that in England at that time, one-sixth of the English population was benefiting from some kind of public assistance.

The possibility of dependency has remained a major and increasing concern for economists, given the higher levels of public assistance that some individuals and families receive in modern states. The combination of means-tested programs and high levels of assistance has given more substance to the worries about dependency in the countries with those programs. Lower tax burdens on those who benefit from these programs and try to exit them by getting jobs may reduce the poverty traps. Higher minimum wages for those who can get jobs might also reduce the implicit taxes associated with the loss of means-tested governmental assistance, thus encouraging them to look for work. They might, thus, alleviate the potential effects of poverty traps. However, a growing concern that deserves increasing attention is that high minimum wages might also reduce the demand for labor by employers, especially if robots or other forms of automation can replace routine manual workers, as some economists increasingly fear. It should be stressed that poverty traps exist mainly when the benefits are means-tested, not when they are universal and are financed by general taxes, as, for example, they are in Denmark.

A Specific, Radical Proposal

In principle, if the government's objective were mainly that of improving the income distribution of a country, while leaving to the market much of the function of creating incomes and allocating resources, that objective could be promoted, most simply and most efficiently, by taxing all the citizens with broad-based taxes that could be either proportional or reasonably progressive with respect to income. Part of the revenue could be distributed to all citizens, rich and poor, in equal, absolute amounts, leaving to them the freedom to spend the money received as best as they wished.

This approach could lead to a great deal of simplification and lower administrative costs, because many government programs could be eliminated, many government employees could be dismissed, and thousands of pages of tax and spending program regulations would be eliminated. However, there would continue to be a need to provide assistance to some seriously disabled, deserving individuals who would continue to need special assistance. These individuals should be relatively few in number, unless the definition of what is a serious disability were stretched to accommodate questionable cases. Existing charities might be encouraged and redirected to assist those in these circumstances. There would not be social programs.

To follow the policy outlined here the government would need mainly an accurate census of the living in order to make the payments to them, as well as the information required to tax individuals and enterprises. The value-added tax could play a role in tax collection. The amount of redistribution that would be achieved would depend on the share of national income collected in taxes to be distributed in this way, and on the income distribution that existed in the country before the redistribution took place. That income distribution would determine the taxable capacity. The higher the share of total income collected in taxes for this specific purpose, and the more uneven the initial income distribution, the greater would be the improvement in the distribution of income as measured, for example, by the Gini coefficient.

A broad-based and flat-rate value-added tax would be an especially efficient instrument for pursuing this objective in addition to a broad-based income tax. It should be stressed that this redistributive instrument *should replace many or most of the public programs* that now exist. Therefore, it should not be used as an *additional* redistributive mechanism, as some have proposed, and as Switzerland recently put in a referendum that was defeated. With the extra income received, all the citizens' basic income would be sufficient enough that they could use it at their discretion. If this income were high enough, they would be able to use it to buy from the market many of the goods and services that they needed, including basic education and health care services. As mentioned earlier, charities would continue to play a role by concentrating on those who, because of serious disabilities or other difficulties, needed special assistance. This was the main role of charities in the past.

The main role of the government, beside the one of collecting the taxes to be transferred as indicated previously, would be restricted to the allocation and stabilization functions, i.e., to the generation of pure public goods and to making sure that the market operated efficiently. The stabilization role could be played by the government by simply changing, on a temporary basis, the amount allocated per capita to each citizen. In this simple and transparent system, there would be many fewer incentives for cronyism, lobbying, and other activities by individuals, by groups of individuals, and by those representing enterprises, except in relation to the regulations connected with environmental, health, and safety issues discussed in an earlier chapter.

The idea of a basic minimum income for every citizen is not a particularly new idea. Some past thinkers, including economists such as John Stuart Mill, occasionally proposed it, but generally they limited it to transfers to poor individuals. Milton Friedman's negative income tax might also be considered part of this general approach. The past proposals were directed at providing a minimum income for the poor and not a basic income for the whole population. There were always questions as to how this income would be financed. A truly broad-based value-added tax imposed with a flat rate applied in a country with highly uneven income distribution, and thus with highly uneven distribution of consumption, would make the aforementioned proposal very simple to implement and highly effective because the rich would pay a large part of the money received and would get back little. A more ambitious version would have to rely also on income taxes levied with broad bases.

When governments started to promote the objective of income redistribution, mainly at the beginning of the twentieth century, and when welfare states were created, mainly after World War II, they could have chosen this simple approach, but did not. Perhaps, one reason was that the value-added tax was not yet invented and the income tax was still little used. Governments also thought that they could do better. They decided to play a specific, paternalistic role in deciding the form of income distribution with programs often directed at particular groups of individuals who appeared to be more deserving or who had more political power, and often delivering services produced by the public sector itself, as with public health care and public education, and with many means-tested programs.

As was mentioned in an earlier chapter, using examples from Brazil and from the United States, the social programs soon became numerous, and the situation became progressively more complex. And complexity created increasing numbers of problems. Each potential group saw the public budget as a "common" and tried to have its own specific program financed by general public revenue, including public debt. Each group tried to attract the government's attention and to get its assistance. With the passing of time the programs became not only more numerous but also more generous in practice, if not always in terms of legislation. The complexity led to abuses and to corruption, and corruption grew in many countries.

The example of the United States can be useful to validate this point, even though that example is far from being an extreme one among countries. I shall cite from a recent (March 2016) report on poverty in the United States published by the US Department of Health and Human Services. After the signing of the Economic Opportunity Act of 1964 (President Johnson's War on Poverty), which can be considered the cornerstone of the modern-day social safety net for the United States, food stamps, community health centers, and Head Start were established in that same year. These programs were followed, in 1965, by "the additional blocks of Medicaid, Medicare and expanded anti-poverty programs" (US Department of Health and Human Services, p. 1). In the following fifty years, "to better alleviate poverty and better meet the needs of low-income individuals and families," the following "major" programs were added to the safety net: the Supplementary Security Income (SSI) program of 1972, the Women, Infants, and Children (WIC) program of 1975, the Child Support Program of 1975, the Low Income Home Energy Assistance Program (LIHEAP) of 1981, the Children's Health Insurance Program (CHIP) of 1997, Medicare Part D (Low Income Subsidy) of 2003, and the Affordable Care Act (ACA) of 2010.

In addition to these major programs, there were dozens of smaller ones. In the decades after the fall of the Soviet Union, a large part of the cost of these programs was financed by the resources that came from the reduction in military spending, and from reductions in spending for infrastructures and for government-financed R&D. Many now complain that these reductions have become damaging to the growth of the economy. It is one of many examples in which short run benefits may have come at long run costs.

In the United States and in other countries, in recent decades, governmental assistance has been directed at increasing the living standards for *some* low-income individuals and households by providing them with income to buy basic necessities, and by protecting some citizens against particular risks with economic consequences (disability, unemployment, illness, old age, having young children, etc.). Some of this assistance was provided in kind. Indirectly, governmental assistance has also been directed at protecting the incomes of less poor individuals through various, not always transparent, governmental rules and through "tax expenditure." Think of rules that impose the use of domestic suppliers for government contracts; the requirement to use unionized workers in public investments; or rules that restrict access to some activities. These lead to higher costs for public projects and to higher incomes for some workers and enterprises.

Or, think of laws that in various countries prevent the firing of (even unproductive) workers.

In some sectors, abuses in certain public programs have attracted media attention. They may not represent common experiences, but they do receive media attention and influence the attitudes of individuals who do not benefit from the programs and of those who pay for them. In other cases, in some countries, relatively young individuals have been able to leave work with good pensions. Or, some individuals earning high incomes have continued to live in highly subsidized public housing projects.

Some countries, for example, the Scandinavian countries, France, the United Kingdom, Italy, Belgium, and some others, had created universal welfare programs that provide some services to *all* citizens (and not just to those with low incomes) to protect them against particular risks, such as health risks, illiteracy, low human capital, and old age. In other countries, such as the United States, the programs have not been universal and have been focused toward categories of low-income groups. The government does not have the information that would allow it to make informed and corruption-free, or abuse-free, decisions related to the needs of different, specific individuals. Thus, though the programs are means-tested, they are directed to groups with individuals who have certain traits that fall within certain ranges, rather than to specific individuals. It is almost impossible to identify a truly homogeneous group of individuals, all *deserving identical* government assistance. This implies that serious horizontal inequity problems are likely to abound in some programs, because, within the groups, some individuals are likely to be far more deserving than others. As a priest (Don Milani) was once reported to have put it, "To give equal response to unequal needs can generate great injustice." This problem characterizes many government programs. It is clearly the case with disability pensions, public housing, food stamps, and many other programs.

In centuries past, religious or other mutual assistance groups had helped those in need, especially the truly *disabled* and the *orphans*. Often, these groups had done it with greater focus on the truly needy individuals, because of the greater information that the charities had. A century ago there had been no universal programs that protected *all the citizens* of countries against particular risks, as exist today in several countries in areas such as public health, public education, and public pensions, and the assistance had been provided locally, by parishes or local charitable institutions.

This new role of the state, a role that has created entitlements or rights of individuals against the community at large, has represented a radical and fiscally costly revolution. It was part of the redistributive role that led or would lead to the large increase in public spending and in taxes in many countries in the second half of the twentieth century. It changed the debate parameters from who should get assistance to the level at which the (universal) assistance is provided.

In the past, charitable (often religious) groups and other associations of mutual assistance, at times financed by paternalistic aristocrats who owned much of the wealth, played some of the roles that governments now play. In fact, the assistance that Elizabeth I introduced in England came because the previous monarch (Henry VIII) had confiscated the assets of the religious charities when he split with the Roman Church, leaving the truly poor without any assistance. As mentioned, that assistance was channeled toward the *truly deserving needy*, and was provided at very low levels. It was clearly *charity*. It was not a claim, or a right, on the part of those who received it, against society. As Edmund Burke once wrote, "What is the use of discussing a man's abstract right to food or medicine? The question is upon the method of procuring and administering them."

CHAPTER 21

Poverty, Inequality, and Government Policies

The concept of poverty inevitably changes when a country's per capita income grows. It changes from being a biologically determined and absolute concept into an increasingly relative concept, one that is influenced by the goods and the services that have become available to the population, by the perceived needs for them, and by the spending of those in the upper percentiles of the income distribution. In some cases it also changes because some goods that the poor of the past used to buy from vendors close to where they lived may no longer be available, or may no longer be closely available. At the same time some old goods have become more expensive, while some new goods are now considered necessary. The inflation rate is a poor indicator of how the real income of the poor is affected by price changes. Goods such as cellular phones, whose ownership by the poor is now subsidized by the US government, because the poor need them in their search for jobs or in contacts related to jobs, have acquired the status of necessities. Even car ownership may become a necessity when available jobs are far away and public transportation is expensive and not accessible or reliable.

Some of today's poor in rich countries have, undoubtedly, incomes that would have placed them among the middle classes of the past, or would still place them among the middle classes in many of today's poor countries. However, psychologically and in terms of factors such as life expectancy or the probability of children dying at birth or of moving up in the social scale, *relative* poverty can be as damaging as *absolute* poverty.

Given the importance played by the media, in all its expressions, in today's world, the spending habits of some of today's rich and super rich are much better known by the whole population than they were in the past. These habits are likely to create externalities of a psychological nature, especially in democratic societies, where politicians and the laws state that "all citizens are created equal" or "are equal before the law." The spending habits of the better-to-do have become more visible to all, not only because of the impact of television but also because of the greater mobility and education of the population. Often, the poor have access to and visit some of the same shopping centers visited by the rich, and some of them work as maids or in other capacities for the rich and the super rich.

The spending habits of the rich make many of those at the lower end of the income distribution, and not just the truly poor, feel poorer than they would have felt in the past, especially in societies that are no longer assumed to accept or to justify the (almost divine) privileges that traditional aristocracies used to enjoy in the past. Just think of the psychological impact on low-income citizens of what *The Financial Times* calls "monster homes," houses that may cost hundreds of millions of dollars, or of cars that cost hundreds of thousands of dollars. Whether we like it or not, and whether we continue to consider it a "vice," envy exists and is accentuated by very large variances in income and spending, differences that have become much larger and better known today than they were in the past.

Envy is likely to create resentment and psychologically based negative feelings that in a more unequal society are likely to lower the sense of self-worth and the welfare of those who are subject to them, even when their absolute income may not have fallen but it has fallen in relative terms. These are individuals who in modern societies have acquired the power to vote and have been told that they count politically. Envy may also create or intensify perceptions that the political and economic systems are not as fair as they could be and that, for many of the poor or even for some from the lower middle class, working hard will not make much difference. In democratic countries, these feelings are likely to create pressures by some groups for populist policies such as those against free trade that, when introduced, are likely to damage the working and the growth of market economies.

The Pareto Optimum, a concept that has played an important role in welfare economics in evaluating policies, is likely to be influenced by envy, and, when it is used to compare policies, it ought to pay attention to psychologically based externalities. When envy is taken into account, and the income distribution changes significantly, the traditional Pareto Optimum is likely to reach different conclusions on the impact of policies and growth. The negative externalities created by envy are likely to grow in importance when economic growth is accompanied by increasing and highly visible inequality, as statistics indicate to have been the case in recent years, especially when all or most of the growth that takes place in a country increases the incomes of a small minority, while the majority, including many workers with full-time, demanding jobs, benefit little from it. From much statistical evidence now available, this seems to have happened in recent decades in the United States and in many other countries. For changes in the Gini coefficients in recent decades for a large number of countries, see IMF (2012b, appendix, table 1).

As mentioned earlier, in the distant past there were no *entitlements* or *rights* on the part of citizens to governmental assistance, in most countries. When assistance was provided, it was clearly an act of charity, and, as such, it was seen as temporary and not something that one could count on for a long time. At that time it would have been less likely that such assistance could have generated dependency, although, as mentioned, some observers were already concerned about such a possibility in the nineteenth century. Also, in the absence of democratic governments, which allow most citizens to vote, and of media outlets, and given the more rural settings that were common at that time for most people, inequality did not have the impact that it can have today. However, even in the distant past it occasionally contributed to strong reactions that in some cases led to revolutions. It had been repeatedly criticized by philosophers such as Aristotle, Plutarch, Montesquieu, Rousseau, and many others over the centuries.

In a well-known and sad historical episode, some English policymakers opposed the provision of public assistance to the starving Irish population during the potato famine of the 1840s in Ireland. The fear was that the starving people of Ireland might develop dependency on the assistance. Ireland was allowed to continue to export grain at a time when many Irish families were dying of starvation. Many Irish were saved by mass emigration to the United States. However, a large share (up to an estimated fifth) of those who tried to emigrate during the famine died during the cross-Atlantic trip, because of their poor health, the hardship of the trip, and the atrocious sanitary conditions in the ships (see Woodward, [1938] 1962, pp. 353–355).

The assignment of an explicit and formal *redistribution role* to the government of a market economy, by *mainstream economists*, is a relatively modern development, even though, as mentioned earlier, it had been around, not as redistribution but as assistance to the poor, at least since Elizabethan days in England in the early seventeenth century, and earlier in some other countries. It had always been and has remained a guiding principle for the Catholic Church and for Islam. That explicit role for the government in a market economy had been strongly endorsed, in the latter part of the nineteenth century in Germany, especially in the writings of Adolph Wagner, a very influential economist at that time (see Wagner, 1883). This government role in a market economy should be distinguished from that pushed by socialists, including Karl Marx, Pierre-Joseph Proudhon, and others who wanted to abolish private property and the free market and make income equality the guiding goal of economic policies. For some of the participants in the 1848 Revolution in Europe this had been the goal.

The welfare reforms introduced by Bismarck in Germany at the end of the nineteenth century, though very modest by modern standards, and though they were focused on workers and not on citizens in general, were to some extent consistent with that new role. They assigned to the German state, for the first time, a specific responsibility for the welfare of German workers. As a consequence, they required a state bureaucracy to supervise that function (see Tanzi, 2011). That policy, though initially very modest in terms of public spending, represented a truly revolutionary policy change that, in future years, would have a great influence on the welfare policies of many countries.

In the twentieth century, other countries started following the example set by Bismarck's reforms, making policies of redistribution and income maintenance progressively more ambitious and more fiscally expensive. With time, those policies would become very costly after World War II, especially in some countries, for example, when the United Kingdom introduced the far more ambitious "Beveridge reforms" that created the British welfare state, and when other countries followed suit with similar reforms.

The formal acceptance of a redistribution role by the state changed, permanently and deeply, the character of the state's intervention in the economy, making it progressively more expensive and *more political.* It introduced, in an *explicit way*, politically based considerations in the actions of governments, considerations that were influenced by ongoing political developments and electoral results. It also opened the government to the pressures and the lobbying of many specific groups.

Society and the public budget became a kind of "common" that different groups would try to exploit at their advantage. From that time on, the issue would no longer be whether governments should engage in policies of redistribution, but whether *how much* redistribution and *what kind* of redistribution would be desirable. Because poverty and human needs have many dimensions, in principle, there could be an infinite number of programs aimed at, and justified by, the objective of assisting some group in need. And redistribution would not always be from individuals with higher incomes to those with lower incomes. It would often be from those who worked to those who did not, or from the young to the old. There would not be a clear reference point, such as a given level of, or change of the Gini coefficient, that would guide redistribution policy. No level of the Gini coefficient could receive *universal* endorsement as being the optimal level. And no clear economic variable, such as annual income, permanent income, family income, average income within families, wealth, etc., would form the basis on which the policies would be applied.

At least in principle, the government's role in the *allocation* of resources in a market economy could be determined from technical and objective criteria that economists had developed, such as efficiency and neutrality, based on arguments about market failures. Intervention in the *allocation* of resources could be justified by economic analysis. Therefore, the role of the state *in the allocation of resources* could be considered independent from value judgments and from politics, although in practice this was often an illusion. On the other hand, the optimal role of the state in *redistribution* could not be established objectively by relying, solely or mainly, on economic principles. Income level, occupation, age, health status, gender, race, ethnic background, wealth, family size, degrees of handicaps, and other criteria could and would be used for justifying some programs presumably aimed at making the income distribution more acceptable. Redistribution was and has remained dependent on political, and only to some extent on economic, considerations. But the income distribution has become, more than in the past, a central statistic.

Because of the aforementioned reasons, the optimal level of public spending justified by the *redistribution* role of the state could not be determined objectively by economic analysis. As Musgrave had already recognized in his seminal 1959 book, redistribution would inevitably remain a political issue. There is no objective way to determine what an *ideal Gini coefficient*, or another ideal measure of distribution of income or wealth, should be for a country. Nor, for example, is there an objective way to determine what should be the share of income going to the top quintile compared to that going to the bottom quintile, or the share of total income that should be received by the top 0.1, 1, or 5 percent of the income distribution.

Unavoidably, the ideal and the decisions undertaken to promote whatever might be considered ideal are influenced by the personal interests and the biases of the policymakers, by the political support that they receive from their supporters or clienteles, and by the ability of specific groups to organize themselves and to get more from the common pools that are the national economy and the public budget.

Countries that were becoming progressively more democratic by giving the right to vote to larger shares of the population, and in which government spending was going up, would have been expected to promote less uneven income distributions and a larger share of total income going to those at the lower end of the income distribution. This in fact happened in the first few decades after the welfare states were created following World War II. However, after the initial improvement in the income distributions, broadly from the 1940s to the 1970s, and the creation of several programs that were more favorable to those at the lower end of the income distribution and that were financed by highly progressive taxes, the Gini coefficients stopped falling and started rising in several countries, even though the share of public spending into GDP and the welfare programs had not been significantly changed in the later decades.

In recent years the Gini coefficients and other measures of unevenness have reached politically worrisome levels in several countries, especially in Anglo-Saxon countries, but also in countries such as China, India, Brazil, and Argentina. Individuals at the very top of the income distribution (at the top 1 or even 0.1 percent of the income distribution) seem to have appropriated much of the economic growth of recent decades, while the wages of dependent workers and the incomes of the middle classes have largely stagnated. In the United States some of those who may have been part of the middle class, largely individuals with lower education but with well-paying jobs in traditional industrial enterprises, saw their jobs migrating to China and other poorer countries, and their health care costs and the college tuitions for their children growing. For these groups recent decades have not been good ones.

There is more controversy about what has happened to those in the lowest percentiles of income distribution, especially in the United States, because they may have continued to benefit from programs specifically directed to them, such as, in the United States, food stamps, Medicaid, public housing, and other means-tested programs, and from the fact that they pay little in taxes (see US Department of Health and Human Services, 2016).

The aforementioned developments have raised questions about one of the axioms that concerns the implicit exchange, assumed to exist in democratic countries, between the policy decisions made by governments and the political support that they get from the electorate for those decisions. This exchange does not seem to have remained constant over the decades. Factors such as globalization, demographic changes, and political and intellectual changes are likely to have been influential in determining what actually happened. I shall argue in the third part of this book that, for a variety of reasons, in the last four decades the economic role of the state has become more favorable toward high-income groups and less favorable especially toward the middle classes, with more uncertainty about what has happened to those in the low percentiles of income distribution.

In support of this conclusion, I shall focus on three aspects that contributed to these developments: (a) *cronyism and other termites of the state* that were made possible by increasing complexity in government and market operations; (b) *the increasing protection* and importance of *intellectual property*, made more valuable because of *recent technological developments*; and (c) the changes that occurred in recent decades in the *tax systems*. These factors will receive closer attention in the following chapters.

A complicating factor is that, increasingly, policies that influence and determine the distribution of income and the role that governments can play in it have, at any moment in time, been made by previous governments, for example, those policies related to public pensions or public health. They had been made on the assumptions that the cost of these policies, as shares of GDP, would not increase over time and that the growth rates of countries would continue to be robust. Some of these past policies created vested interests for relatively large and politically influential groups of citizens, including retirees, that make it difficult to change these policies for all governments.

Once in place, these policies are difficult to change (even when they become more expensive because of the aging of the population or the introduction of more-expensive drugs and medical procedures), because those who benefit from them have in many countries acquired strong political power capable of opposing changes. Once these policies are in place, they reduce the scope for other redistributive policies that would require more public spending and higher tax levels. The political backing of these groups becomes important for policymakers. Therefore, the past policies end up tying, to a considerable extent, the hands of future governments and preventing the introduction of additional redistributive policies. If taxes and especially progressive taxes or taxes on capital incomes cannot be raised further, the government's ability to improve the income distribution, with taxing and spending policy, is much reduced.

In several countries, including the United States, the long run sustainability of pension and health systems, at currently legislated levels, has become increasingly questionable, but reforms in these sectors are difficult to make. In today's world the discretionary share of a year's public budget, the part that can be changed with lesser difficulties by the current governments, has become relatively small, creating great budgetary rigidity and often forcing reductions in spending for infrastructure. This implies that more attention should have been paid, and should be paid, to the rules that contribute to the allocation of income among income recipients, *before* taxing and spending policies are introduced. Generally, the short run effects receive more attention than the long run consequences.

The growing attention paid to income distribution came in a period when several countries had become more democratic than in the past and were allowing and encouraging larger shares of their adult populations to vote. In the more distant past, many citizens had been excluded from voting and from influencing policy decisions. This had created biases in favor of richer individuals and property owners, who had had the right to vote and the power to influence the policies. At that time much of the wealth (which then, more than income, was the relevant variable in equity) had been concentrated in a few hands; wages had been low; social legislation had been absent; monopolies had been common; and the use of progressive income taxes had been still in its infancy.

The situation started changing in the early decades of the twentieth century, which in the United States were called by some the "Progressive Era." The changes accelerated after World War II. In an empirical or statistical sense, until the Great Depression the situation had changed little, although thinking and attitudes were changing rapidly. Until the late 1920s, public spending in various industrial countries had remained as low as 10 to 20 percent of GDP. Inevitably, many of the rules and the institutional arrangements that had been created until that time, on inheritance rights, on property rights, on market organizations, on the treatment of intellectual property, on the rights and responsibilities of corporations, and so on, had had a bias in favor of higher-income classes. When having a better income distribution became an important objective for governments, the pressure was to introduce programs that would distribute income *after* the market had generated the incomes, using fiscal instruments. The existing institutional arrangements were little changed, or changed much less than they could have been.

Government programs that aim at redistributing significant income shares toward lower-income groups, or that create universal social programs for the whole population, rather than programs that only assist specific individuals or specific groups, require a lot of public resources. These resources can be obtained from higher tax rates imposed on much of the population and, at least in the shorter run, from borrowing. If the income distribution is significantly uneven, the tax system must be progressive in order to make the higher-income groups, who have higher taxable capacity, pay higher average tax rates and contribute more to total tax revenue.

Proportional taxes would require higher tax rates on lower-income groups to generate the same total revenue.

Redistributive programs require also the presence of efficient public institutions responsible for administering them. These programs inevitably need large levels of public spending and taxation, and able and honest administrators. They are often associated with high and rising public debts. This has been the general experience of the *welfare states* and to some extent also of countries, such as the United States and some others, that are not generally considered to be welfare states.

A 1997 development report by the World Bank had argued that the process of taking over new, significant redistributive functions by the governments was likely to distract the policymakers of the countries from the pursuit of the more fundamental role of the state, the allocation role, especially in relation to the generation of pure public goods. The redistribution objective and the large resources needed to promote this equity objective tend to crowd out the resources available to pursue other less-pressing objectives. This situation especially distracts the attention of the policymakers away from building essential infrastructures, from maintaining the existing infrastructures in good conditions, and from spending the required sums for other essential but less urgent public goods, such as research and development.

Current evidence indicates that this is what has happened over the years in several countries, including the United States, even though that country has not been as generous with its welfare programs, especially toward the middle classes, as some European countries have been, with free education and universal public health. Public infrastructures, such as roads, bridges, airports, and schools, have suffered from lack of attention and lack of public resources and major infrastructure gaps have developed.

In recent years, growing numbers of observers have lamented the large share of total income that has been going to, or the wealth that has been accumulated by, the top 1 percent, or even the top 0.1 percent, in the income distribution. They have lamented the increases in the estimated Gini coefficients observed in the United States and in several other countries, in spite of the still high level of social spending. Some have used the statistical information about the worsening of the income distribution to recommend that governments should spend even more than they have been spending for social programs in an effort to redistribute more income from the richer groups toward the rest of the populations. More public spending would require higher tax rates or more progressive tax systems, or higher public debts.

The implication of this recommendation is that the market is working more or less as it should be, that the general rules that the state has adopted for the work of the economy are adequate, but that the government is not doing enough, in terms of both spending and taxing, to redistribute income *after* the market has performed its presumably legitimate function. Thus, in some sense, it is a case of government, rather than market, failure. It is a failure in not redistributing more income through spending and taxing, or even in not using more borrowed resources made cheap by the current monetary policies, as some vocal observers have been urging the governments to do, especially after the economic crisis that followed the Great Recession. A possible alternative interpretation of the developments of recent decades is suggested in the following chapter.

CHAPTER 22

Market Manipulations and Economic Outcomes

A possible interpretation of recent developments and of the impact that they are having on the income distribution is based on the view that in recent decades, and especially since the 1980s, the market has become progressively more amenable to various kinds of not always transparent manipulations. The market, which has become more globalized, is being taken advantage of, with greater frequency, in various and at times in less-legitimate ways, by operators who are capable of using it to their greater advantage. Looking at the issue from another angle, the market is also being influenced by those who are able to use and to take advantage of government rules. Some of those rules, with their complexity, have created opportunities for some individuals and enterprises to increase, at times less legitimately or less fairly, their incomes and profits from market exchanges and actions.

If this alternative angle has some validity, the desired future action of the government should be not only to redistribute income *after* the market has determined the income distribution, but also to make efforts at correcting and redirecting the way the market works. This does not imply or require a return to the direct government interventions that had become more common in some decades of the past, the ones that had been criticized by Hayek and, before him, by Adam Smith, but involves removing preferences and reducing complexities that have given advantages to particular individuals. It is thus not a question of replacing the market with governmental decisions, but to make the market work closer to the way it is intended to work, to the extent possible.

Over the years several observers have argued that public policies are often poorly designed and poorly carried out and, therefore, that they reduce economic growth and may also harm the poor, while others have argued that governments should focus on economic growth and should ignore redistribution. The latter observers believe that growth would make *everyone* better off by creating more jobs and by raising real incomes. Faster growth would act like a friendly tide that would lift all boats. These individuals tend to focus largely on absolute income levels and on absolute poverty and pay little or less attention to *relative* poverty. See also Deaton (2013), who has argued that inequality can act as a stimulant for future progress, because it challenges those who are left behind to make greater future efforts, a view also held by Hayek in some of his writing. In other words inequality can become an incentive or a stimulus for some of those who are left behind.

These views are today more challenged than they were a few years back, because of the statistical results that have become available on what has happened to the income distributions in various countries in recent decades, and because of the disappointing growth rates in recent decades for most advanced countries, in spite of the reduction in the progressivity of tax systems and of the interest rates, and in spite of the reliance on presumably more growth-friendly policies since the 1980s by several countries.

While globalization and growth in some countries, especially in China and India, have made the distribution of income *for the world as a whole* more even by lifting hundreds of millions of Chinese and Indians from absolute poverty (see Milanovic, 2005, 2016), they have not improved the income distributions within countries such as China and India, nor within many advanced countries, especially within the United States. Data from Milanovic (2016) have shown that the lowest three deciles in the income distribution of the population of the whole world have suffered a decline in their *relative* incomes in the past two decades. That reduction was especially significant in the bottom, poorest two deciles. As I argued earlier, it is the *relative* position in the income distribution that is probably the more important variable.

The connection between *redistribution* of market income and *economic growth* continues to be a hotly debated issue. Conservative economists and political groups continue to believe that the connection between growth and less poverty is obvious. In their view, more income redistribution inevitably reduces incentives and economic growth, while it also reduces economic freedom. More-liberal economists, on the other hand, continue to express strong doubts about the existence of this connection, or at least about its empirical importance.

The sharp reduction in marginal tax rates in industrial countries in recent decades, and the liberalization of economies and of financial markets, did not lead to higher economic growth, as many had argued that they would. Rather, they led to a less even income distribution and to slower growth. Some economists have even argued that the greater concentration of income that has taken place in recent years, by reducing aggregate demand for various industrial products of mass consumption, may have been a factor that has contributed to slower economic growth (see, inter alia, the empirical work by Ostry et al., 2014). Those authors concluded that "there is surprisingly little evidence for the growth-destroying effects of fiscal redistribution at a macroeconomic level" (ibid., p. 26). Furthermore, whatever growth there has been in recent years, it certainly has not lifted the boats of many workers and many middle class families, as had been expected, or claimed, that it would.

In market economies, in the decades immediately after World War II, the redistribution objective had been pursued mainly through progressive taxation, and through many and often complex social spending and subsidy programs, directed toward income groups in the lower-income brackets. These policies had given rise to concerns, on the part of conservative economists and politicians, that they would reduce the incentives of workers to work, or to work hard, and would create dependency on government programs for those who received the subsidies and the transfers, creating the feared "poverty traps."

When governments require high spending for programs broadly aimed at sustaining and redistributing income, they need not only higher tax revenues and, often, more public debt, but also larger bureaucracies. Therefore, conservative economists claimed, with some justification, that the reduction in economic growth in recent decades might have resulted from the redistributive policies, from the still high taxes, even though much less progressive (in more recent years), and from the impact of the large bureaucracies and the "red tape" that they had created for those who operate in the markets. In the most recent years, some have also called attention to the growing number of regulations that governments have been introducing especially on enterprises.

Statistical results from advanced countries indicate that, normally, the higher is the level of public spending, regardless of whether it is financed with more or less progressive taxes, the lower are the countries' poverty rates, and the lower are the Gini coefficients. Denmark has one of the highest ratios of public spending to GDP in the world and the lowest poverty rate. Generally, countries that have high public spending (and the high tax levels to pay for the spending) show better income distributions and lower poverty rates than those that spend and tax less (see Tanzi, 2011, p. 27, table 1–5). What price these higher-spending countries have paid, in terms of lower economic growth for these results, remains, as I have indicated, still a largely open and hotly debated question. The empirical evidence that has been provided by some economists has not been as powerful and as conclusive as one would have wanted it to be (see, for example, Aslund and Djankov, 2017).

In the United States, not a high-spending or a high-taxing country by the standards of advanced countries, President Johnson's War on Poverty, which, as he put it in his address to the US Congress on January 8, 1964, was supposed to "relieve the symptom of poverty, [and] to cure ... and ... to prevent it," received more than $19 trillion in spending over the years to fight poverty, but poverty is still there for everyone to see, is high compared with the level in many other advanced countries, and, in some ways, is and has become more visible. There are today far more homeless people and beggars on the streets of American cities than there were in 1964. One could argue, as some do, that without Johnson's program, poverty would have been higher, or that, over the years since the program started, many poor peoples did enjoy a higher standard of living (at least as measured by consumption rather than by income) than they would have had without the War on Poverty programs. Some statistics suggest that the Gini coefficients may understate the redistributive impact of American social policies, because they understate the value of real transfers that increase the consumption by (but not the measured incomes of) the poor, and because of other factors.

Once again, this debate largely assumes that the market is working as well as it can be expected to work, and accepts the view that the income distribution and the poverty rates can be improved mainly by the *fiscal* actions of the government, actions undertaken *after the market has done its work*. Less attention has been paid to the possibility that, through its *many* actions, some not always transparent, the government might be playing an important role, not only in reducing the incentives of the poor and possibly of some economic operators, but also in determining the income distribution that the market generates. If this is a realistic and significant possibility, changes in that role, if they were possible, could help reduce the inequality that the market generates, *before* the government intervenes with its fiscal and social programs. It might reduce the need for or the scope of that *ex post* redistribution.

Putting it differently, the market might require more governmental intervention *not to replace it* in some aspects, as some economists and policymakers with leftist bents would like the government to do. Rather, the government would intervene *to make the market function more closely* to the way that an efficient market ought to function. The objective would be to remove, or at least to reduce, rent-seeking, abuses, cronyism, tax avoidance, tax evasion, and other factors that have been playing a growing and, often, invisible role in today's presumably "free" (but complex) market. In some sense it might be argued that this was the real call of the so-called Washington Consensus, the thinking that became popular in the 1990s but that was only partly and superficially followed by the actions then undertaken by some governments. That call may have been misinterpreted in the assumption that it reflected mainly conservative or rightist thinking, while it may have reflected a different view of how the economy should operate and about the role that the government should play (see papers in Krueger, 2000).

In various countries, and especially in Europe in the first half of the twentieth century, governments had often interfered in the work of the market not so much through high taxes and public spending, which at that time were still low, but through direct interferences in various economic decisions and, occasionally, through the nationalization of enterprises or the regulation of the prices and the profits of some enterprises. In some cases and in these ways, at that time the governmental intervention had been more visible.

In those years, price and income policies had been more common, as had been the ownership of large enterprises (the "commanding heights") by governments, especially when, around the time of World War II, various countries (including the United Kingdom, France, Italy, East Germany after the war, and others) nationalized several large enterprises. Governments also occasionally intervened in the allocation of credit and the control of exchange rates and interest rates and of foreign exchange to determine the investments that could be made, the imports that could enter a country, what could be exported, and so on. They had also played an important role in allowing labor unions (some significantly controlled by governments) to acquire economic power and to influence real wages and employment decisions, while they subsidized and assisted, in various ways, some enterprises. All these interventions, inevitably, had an impact on the distribution of income; however, it was an impact not easy to quantify.

In some cases and countries, the labor unions had acquired so much power that, in 1926, Keynes could write that "the Trade-Unionists, once the oppressed, [are] now the tyrants, whose selfish and sectional pretensions need to be bravely opposed" (Keynes, 1926, p. 341). He added, "The political problem of mankind is to combine three things: Economic Efficiency, Social Justice, and Individual Liberty" (ibid., p. 344). He warned, "The transition from economic anarchy to a regime which deliberately aims at controlling and directing economic forces in the interest of social justice and social stability, will present enormous difficulties both technical and political" (ibid., p. 335).

On the other side of the spectrum, F. A. Hayek pointed out that economic planning had been facilitated by the existence of strong unions and monopolies. In his view the existence of strong unions had encouraged governments to tolerate monopolies, as they had done in totalitarian governments in Italy and later in Germany, where the unions were largely controlled by the regimes. For details on the Italian experience during fascism in the coordination and control of organized labor, see Steiner (1938).

The direct or indirect control by the state of *some* economic activities had been common in the first half of the twentieth century, even while laissez-faire thinking continued to prevail, and had often been justified on grounds of promoting social justice and social peace. In Italy, a basic objective of the corporative state was to create a self-sufficient Italian economy (Steiner, 1938). However, as both Keynes and Hayek, from different perspectives, had recognized, that control often interfered with economic efficiency and limited the liberty of individuals. The individual workers, within the unions, as individuals had no genuine power.

In the second half of the twentieth century, governments (except those that chose the socialist way) generally made less use of those controls and preferred to use different and presumably less intrusive policies. They reduced the reliance on *direct* controls on economic activities and attempted to promote social justice and other objectives through the creation of policies associated with what came to be called welfare states *within market economies*. These policies required much higher levels of tax and public spending than in the earlier years, but less *direct* interference in the economic decisions of citizens and enterprises, except for regulations related to various kinds of actual or perceived externalities, which tended to increase with the years and except for the impact of taxes which were not neutral.

A difficult question to answer is whether, with the passing of time, the work of the market became significantly more efficient, approaching the efficiency of the classic efficient market of economic textbooks, or whether the assumed impartial ethic of the economic system, in the senses of being impersonal and efficient and of delivering economic results to the participants who generate more economic value, became truly impartial and not subject to less transparent manipulations. Putting it differently, one must ask whether individuals who are insiders to the system and have more information and more contacts with those who make, enforce, and interpret the laws and the regulations can more easily exploit political connections and the growing complexities of economic policy and of the working of the economy. In other words could they gain nonlegitimate, though not necessarily illegal, advantages that are not available to average citizens?

A lot of mostly anecdotal evidence has become available, almost daily, from major newspapers and from other sources that suggests that in today's world some individuals have learned, better than others, how to manipulate the market (and also the justice system) and how to take advantage of existing government rules and programs to promote their advantage. The evidence also suggests that, with possibly increasing frequency, some government rules are being created, are being amended, or are being reinterpreted to favor certain categories of individuals or certain activities.

The financial market in particular seems to have been a major beneficiary of some of these manipulations in recent decades, but not the only beneficiary. Doubts have been raised with increasing frequency about the genuine value that this market contributes to the real economy, value that would justify the large incomes of the individuals who operate in it (see, inter alia, Kay, 2015; Zingales, 2015).

The complexity of many laws and regulations has created situations in which, because of personal ability or because of the positions they have currently or had in the past, some individuals are better able than others to know and to interpret the complex rules and to use that knowledge and those interpretations to benefit themselves, their institutions, and/or their clients. Or, they are even able to promote the introduction of new rules by the government, rules that would be beneficial to them or to their clients. Some individuals have higher financial means to buy the more qualified assistance.

Some authors have argued that there is a kind of "shadow control" of certain market forces that some individuals have acquired (see Lofgren, 2015). It is a control that often escapes the attention of casual observers, leaving the impression that the market is still operating freely and that its outcome should be respected to preserve the economic and political freedom of those who operate in it. Some elements of this shadow control by a "shadow government" of the apparatus and of the operations of the market and of the government itself will be discussed more fully later. They are part of what I have called the *termites of the states*.

A large proportion of the *public* employees of many countries is now engaged in providing public education, public health, administrative services, and many other social services to citizens, in addition to dealing with bureaucratic rules, rules that are supposed to guide the behavior of citizens and enterprises. Some regulatory agencies have thousands of public employees. A large share of the total public spending of industrial countries goes toward the financing of social programs, which include the major ones that attract much of the public attention, such as public pensions, health care, and education. The spending also includes many smaller programs (which in the United States include the subsidization of cellular phones, rents, school lunches, and many others). These smaller programs attract less attention even though, when taken together, they can use considerable resources and can add to the complexity of the public action. Furthermore, in the United States "tax expenditures," just like direct spending programs, play major roles in allocating resources, even though they do not appear in the public spending budget. The tax expenditures seem to be more important in the US tax system than in the tax systems of various other major countries, and contribute to reducing the ratio of tax revenue into GDP for the United States.

While it is the total level of spending and taxes that attracts much of the attention of economists and economic commentators, the complexity of the public apparatus (of both spending and taxes) ought to attract more attention than it does. It is that apparatus that often creates the opportunities, for some individuals and enterprises, for gaming both the government programs and the market economy. That apparatus imposes additional costs. For earlier discussions of complexity and its impact on the economy, see Tanzi, 2007a, 2011, 2013a). In recent years the complexity of the tax system and the opportunities that it offers to enterprises and individuals to game the system have been attracting more attention than in the past, at both the official and the popular level, especially in connection with the opportunities that they offer to corporations and to high-income individuals to reduce, legally or illegally, their tax payments. See Reid, 2017.

It was reported earlier that there are an estimated 2,300 government programs in the United States. The US Tax Foundation has reported that the US federal tax code and regulations now require more than ten million words. As the blog that reported that information put it, "the more there is to know about federal tax law, the harder it is for Americans to file their taxes quickly or correctly" (see Greenberg, 2015). Some newspaper articles have called attention to the fact that the tax code had become mind-numbingly complex; and that there were now 11 different kinds of IRAs, 3 different kinds of child care incentives, and 14 different education incentives. All of these had complex rules and differing and conflicting definitions of terms."

To take another example from another country, the latest Brazilian Multiyear Plan (2016–2019) for the public budget listed 54 "thematic programs," 562 "indicators," 303 "objectives," 1,118 "destinations," and 2,860 "initiatives" (see Dweck, 2015). To these one must add the operations of the Brazilian subnational governments. To believe that this complexity is equally distributed in its positive or negative impact on the operation of the market and on individuals at different income levels would be equivalent to believing that donkeys can fly. For Italy it has been reported that a commission in 2007 had counted 21,691 national laws. To these one should add 30,000 regional laws plus thousands of those of autonomous provinces and about 70,000 regulations (see Amis, 2013). A recent report by the Italian Corte dei Conti counted 799 tax incentives (see also Cassese, 1998).

As mentioned earlier, the share of public spending that now goes toward the building and the maintenance of public infrastructure and other public goods has fallen significantly in most countries, in some countries quite dramatically, raising concerns and generating frequent difficulties or accidents. Various reports for particular countries have pointed to the great need to maintain and modernize infrastructures, which in some cases were built a century or more ago. For example a 2014 report to the US Congress by the American Road and Transportation Builders Association estimated that there were 63,000 deficient bridges in the United States. These bridges occasionally fall and can affect the efficiency of the economy and the safety of the citizens. Old gas pipes create frequent accidents. In the Washington area, the breaking of water pipes in winter months, some of them installed a century ago, has become a common occurrence. The aging of these infrastructures (bridges, sewers, roads, water pipes, dams, airports, etc.) creates growing risks and inefficiencies, in addition to those that climatic changes are creating. These risks are not distributed uniformly. The accommodation of the climatic changes that have been forecast will require enormous public expenses that will compete with already-high public spending and with other growing needs.

Governmental intervention has shifted income across distributional percentiles, across age cohorts, across generations, across regions, across industrial sectors, and across various individuals, often not intentionally. In recent years the health and pension sectors have been major beneficiaries of governmental spending. Their demands on the public budget, already high, are expected to continue to grow because of the aging of the population, the continued generation of new, expensive drugs and new medical procedures or instruments, the "discovery" of new diseases, the occasional visits of new epidemics, and the absence of a real limiting budget or clear criteria to decide how much a country should spend for these sectors.

Some inefficient public enterprises have been kept alive in certain countries mainly because of the employment that they provide to individuals and because of the reluctance of governments to let the employees lose their public jobs, especially when markets are not creating many new ones. In other words, in these public enterprises the government at times produces government jobs, more than government goods and services. To keep them alive the government has to provide subsidies and other kinds of protection including tax incentives, protection from competitive imports, and various kinds of regulatory protection.

CHAPTER 23

Termites in the Stabilization Role

For a variety of reasons, countries' economies do not operate smoothly and do not grow at a steady pace while maintaining full employment. They experience fluctuations and periodic booms and slowdowns. Some of these may be generated by wrong policies. The slowdown may occasionally become a full-fledged recession and, less frequently, may even acquire characteristics of a depression. Slowdowns and recessions lead to high unemployment and to losses of potential output. Some of the workers who lose their jobs during the slowdowns may never get them back and must settle for less attractive ones. Some may exit the labor force permanently, because there may not be good retraining programs to prepare them for the new jobs that become available when the recessions end, or because they are too old and close to retirement, may have accumulated assets to sustain them in retirement, or may have family members who can support them. The lack of investment during the recessions may lead to permanent income losses. However, it is rarely recognized that booms may have the opposite effects.

Controversies continue to exist among economists as to the real causes of recessions. Some believe that they may be caused by an unexplained weakening of "animal spirits." Therefore, they assume that these events are mostly random and unanticipated, not connected with the problems or the policies of a country. This seems to have been the prevalent view of many Keynesians. Some believe that recessions are due to the bursting of unsustainable economic bubbles that may have developed because of easy monetary policy, sustained for too long, combined with "irrational exuberance," which makes some individuals behave in irrational ways in the investments that they make (see Shiller, 2000). At other times, the recessions may be imported when weakening economic conditions in other countries reduce a country's exports, or they may be generated by sudden increases in key prices, such as petroleum prices, or interest rates.

Recessions or slowdowns may also be due to reductions in investment opportunities when there are no new major technologies to attract new investments, or due to major structural problems and obstacles within a country that have become major impediments to new investments or have reduced the productivity of the economy and the propensity to invest. The reduction in investment and the slowdown in economic activity may also be due to the cumulative effect of concerns about the sustainability of current fiscal policies and the level reached by the public debt, which may have reduced the enthusiasm of investors to invest.

In a globalized world in which economies are closely linked, problems developing in one country, especially an important country, are more likely to spill over into other countries, as happened with the subprime crises that started in the United States in 2007 and spread to European and other countries, generating an almost global recession. Countries that already have some of the structural problems mentioned earlier, or some of the concerns about the sustainability of their fiscal policies, may be more-easily exposed to these spillovers.

From the late 1930s on, and largely because of the tragic experience during the Great Depression in the 1930s and the seminal work of John Maynard Keynes, economic fluctuations have led to the creation of another major justification for state intervention in the economy: the promotion by the government of full, or at least high, employment and the stabilization of economic output. Because of this new responsibility, after World War II, the term "fiscal policy" changed meaning, from its earlier association with redistribution of income to indicate attempts by governments to use fiscal tools to influence aggregate demand and to stabilize economic activities. Even before the 1930s, some governments had occasionally attempted to promote employment in periods of crises, through public works, to help create jobs for some unemployed workers. However, in the past this had been done in an ad hoc fashion and had not been considered as a regular, expected role of the state. Keynes had provided a strong, theoretical justification for that role. Before Keynes's time, there had been no view that a government's additional spending could have a multiplier effect on an economy.

The economic fluctuations encouraged the creation of government programs that made it less painful for some individuals to remain unemployed for limited periods of time, benefiting from unemployment compensation and from other government-provided benefits, and, perhaps, also from the anticipation, for some of them, of the age of retirement. In the view of some economists, these programs may have reduced, for some individuals, the incentive and the effort to search harder for other jobs when the workers became unemployed, or reduced their willingness to accept lower-paying or more-demanding jobs or to get some job retraining to prepare for new jobs that became available. Furthermore, the growing importance of public and private pensions made it possible, at least for some individuals, to leave the labor force at an earlier age, when they lost their jobs and when other jobs became scarce. While the magnitude of these effects is subject to controversy among economists, their existence is less controversial.

The promotion of this so-called stabilization, or countercyclical, Keynesian objective (named after its originator) is decided by policymakers with the approval of legislatures and is carried out by officials in the public administrations. However, this is generally not the case for attempts at stabilizing the economy promoted with monetary policies, which do not require legislative approval. This may have shifted the emphasis of countercyclical policies toward monetary policy. The use of monetary policy for stabilization has become more common in recent decades, and, in the most recent years, the use of that policy may have been carried too far with still-unpredictable long run consequences.

This use had not been part of the original Keynesian framework, which had assumed that monetary easing would not be helpful. Also, "built-in stabilizers," which are automatic changes in the desired countercyclical direction, in tax revenue, and in some public spending, can play a stabilizing role, without the need for explicit (discretionary) government intervention. The desire to have these built-in stabilizers may have contributed, in earlier decades, to larger levels of public spending and to the greater use of fiscal tools, such as corporate income taxes and progressive personal income taxes. These taxes were assumed to be more sensitive to economic fluctuations, and to have more automatic, built-in stabilization power. In more recent years, built-in stabilizers have lost importance. Stabilization policy, promoted through fiscal tools, requires by definition the use of fiscal instruments and must rely on relevant and timely data, on institutions for the use of the fiscal instruments, and, of course, on financial resources to cover fiscal deficits. There continues to be a great debate about the claims of the effectiveness of monetary instruments and their equity implications (see, among much recent writing, Rogers et al., 2014; Tanzi, 2015a).

Although they were not part of the original Keynesian framework, *structural policies* can be part of stabilization packages (see Tanzi, 2015b). It can be argued that in several European countries such as Greece, structural obstacles had become so damaging to the performance of the economy that the elimination of some of them would have been equivalent to or, perhaps, even more important in impact than a fiscal injection. This would be a kind of supply-side approach to economic stimulus. It reflects the debate that has been going on in Europe and in Japan about whether economies already highly indebted can be helped more by further fiscal stimuli, largely based on public spending, or by serious and significant structural reforms. If the fiscal accounts are already in precarious conditions, especially when public debts have become very high, then Keynesian recipes are likely to lose some or much of their power, while structural reforms may still be highly effective (see Tanzi, 2015b).

The public officials responsible for the narrowly defined fiscal policy (the policy promoted through traditional fiscal tools) must decide on the changes in tax revenue and/or in public spending that are needed to influence, in the desirable direction and by the needed degree, the *aggregate demand*. Clearly, some changes in taxes and some kinds of public spending can be more effective than others.

The officials must have the power to obtain the necessary legislative changes within a reasonable time, changes that will be implemented by the public administration, without having the original proposals significantly modified by the legislative body or later by governance problems during the implementation of the policies. It should be recalled that, to shorten the time lag and to avoid the aforementioned problem, during the Kennedy administration in 1962, there had been a proposal to give this power to the US president, thus bypassing Congress. Not surprisingly, Congress had rejected this proposal, because it would have reduced its own political power on spending decisions.

In all of these actions there will be inevitable mistakes, time lags, departures from the optimal size and structure of the stimulus package, and the appearance of possible principal–agent problems within the policy actors (executive branch, legislature, and also the individuals in the public administration), as the early debates between supporters and skeptics about the Keynesian stabilization policies had stressed in the 1940s through the 1960s (see, for example, the informative book by Stein, 1969).

All the aforementioned problems were present and debated in the US fiscal expansion in 2009. The growing complexity of policies has increased the power that some individuals or groups have to change the proposed policies in directions that would help them or their clienteles. This became evident in 2009 when a large "stimulus package" was introduced in the United States to fight the recession. Some of the money in that package was used for objectives that some observers considered questionable and that were not directly related to stabilization, such as trying to subsidize the production of green energy.

In the promotion of Keynesian stabilization policies, lack of *aggregate* demand is generally assumed to be the primary cause of a slowdown or of a recession. Other possible causes are given less importance or are ignored. However, the true causes of slowdowns often remain mysterious, although particular causes often push themselves forward as proximate causes at particular times. The assumption that lack of aggregate demand is always the fundamental cause, and that injecting additional demand will always deal with the slowdown, has questionable credibility. Different causes are likely to require different cures. Therefore, if there is disagreement on the cause of a recession, there will not be agreement on the cure.

The *cumulative* impact over time of poor structural policies that are recognized to be damaging to the good economic performance of economies may, at some point, contribute in various ways to economic slowdowns and, at times, even to full-fledged crises. This possibility tends to be dismissed by those convinced Keynesians who continue to believe that with enough public spending, countries can be pulled out of any recession, regardless of structural impediments and regardless of initial conditions as to the level of public debts and fiscal deficits. Some even believe that more public spending may be a long run cure for low economic growth, because of "secular stagnation."

The public officials responsible for the stabilization objective must have the information, the technical knowledge, the power to act, and the wisdom to make the right and timely decisions on spending and taxing, decisions that are never easy to make in real-world situations and that always tend to be distorted by the pressures of vested interests and by honest disagreements among economists and policymakers. The use of different tax or spending actions is likely to require different time periods to be introduced, and is likely to have a different impact on the economy, even when the magnitude of the package is the same. For example, changing the rate of a value-added tax is much easier than changing the rates of an income tax and is likely to have a more immediate impact.

Various studies have tried to determine whether increases in spending or cuts in taxes are more effective in both the short and the long run. Some economists, such as Alberto Alesina at Harvard and some of his coauthors, have argued in various papers that tax reductions are more likely to be more beneficial than increases in spending, over the long run. Other economists, and especially Paul Krugman, have questioned this conclusion. There is, however, considerable evidence that some countries that cut public spending, at times by very large shares of GDP, performed well in the years after the cuts (see Tanzi, 2011).

Often, what the executive branch proposes to deal with a recession is different from what the legislative branch approves. And, for various reasons, what the legislature approves may be different from what the public administration actually implements. Therefore, different results, in terms of the impact of the fiscal policies on the economy, may be obtained, even when the ex ante, total magnitude of different "stimulus packages" proposed by the executive branch is similar in magnitude.

Keynes himself had stressed in his work the importance of spending on "grand" public work projects, such as the Hoover Dam. However, grand public work projects require unusually large amounts of technical preparation if they are not to lead to the promotion of bad and unproductive investments. Grand projects also require a long time to be completed. Therefore, they require budgetary expenditures distributed over several years. As a consequence, their impact on aggregate demand may be more delayed than, say, an immediate tax cut, especially one in a value-added tax.

Projects that could be initiated immediately must be ready to be employed ("must be on the shelves") when the time to use them arrives. They should be projects that do not require excessive time to be completed; otherwise, much of the impact of the spending may take place and be felt when it may no longer be needed, making it potentially procyclical, rather than countercyclical. However, if the projects are truly useful to increase the growth potential (the supply side) of the economy, this could be seen as a less important problem, because the projects should have been undertaken in any case, regardless of the business cycle, perhaps at a later time.

As already mentioned, the countercyclical fiscal actions must not contribute to already-existing concerns about the size of the public debt and the sustainability of the fiscal accounts. This implies that the effectiveness of countercyclical policy is likely to depend on what can be called the *initial conditions* of the public accounts. The better are the initial fiscal conditions and, thus, the fewer are the worries about the fiscal sustainability of the policies, the more effective is likely to be a stimulus program. A stimulus program introduced in a country that has already a public debt of 200 percent of its GDP, for example, Japan or Greece, or even one introduced in a country such as Italy, which in 2017 has a debt of 133 percent of GDP, is likely to have a different impact than would have the same program introduced in a country with a public debt of 50 percent of GDP, ceteris paribus (see Tanzi, 2013b, 2015b). This points to the need to keep the public debt below some prudent level. In a recent policy note issued by its Economics Department, the OECD (2015a), after pointing out that "at very high debt levels, countries can lose market confidence and see their borrowing rates increase steeply," concluded that "debt above 80% of GDP has detrimental consequences." Obviously, that level should be considered as indicative. For various reasons, different countries are likely to have different threshold levels.

In the aftermath of the 2008 financial crisis, the stimulus programs enacted in several countries were introduced when the fiscal situations of some of them were far from good. In some of them, especially *for the longer run*, the fiscal situation was considered unsustainable. In these conditions, a fiscal stimulus should have been expected to have less of a positive impact on the economy, while the removal of structural obstacles, which in some of those countries were major impediments to the efficient use of productive resources and to new investments, should have appeared to be more desirable. In many countries there have been far fewer genuine structural reforms than would have been desirable. At the same time the public debts have continued to grow (see Tanzi, 2016b).

As mentioned earlier, in the last three decades the attitude toward the role of monetary policy in promoting economic stabilization has changed. It has changed from the earlier view, that "you cannot push on a string" or "you can take a horse to the river but you cannot make it drink," to one that believes monetary policy can bring "great moderation" and that those who conduct monetary policy have become accomplished "maestros" who know how to use the right policy instruments. Central banks have come to be expected to play a growing role, with their monetary actions, in the stabilization of national economies. Until recent decades the role of monetary policy had been limited to the promotion of price and financial stability. It had been assumed that these objectives could be achieved mainly by the steady growth of the money supply, by the controls over the actions of private financial institutions, mainly banks, to reduce the risks that they assumed with the money deposited with them, and by insuring bank deposits up to some realistic limit. Now, major risks are taken by hedge funds, by insurance institutions, by equity funds, and by other institutions that are part of "shadow banking" and that largely escape official supervision. Also, the control of the growth of the money supply has come to be considered less meaningful in a world in which the meaning of "money" seems to have changed dramatically and the creation of virtual money (bitcoins) is frequently discussed. In the future monetary policy may become totally different than it is today. These changes are likely to have increased systemic risk.

The campaign some decades ago to make central banks politically inde-pendent had been based on the belief that the goals of central banks were the aforementioned ones. In the 1990s and in the first few years of the new millennium some economists concluded that central banks had in fact become so efficient and wise, and monetary policy so powerful, that they had been responsible for the "great moderation," a relatively long period of economic expansion without major fluctuations or inflation that had lasted until the middle of the first decade of the new century. Some econo-mists had gone so far as to believe that major fluctuations had become phenomena of the past. The policies pursued by the central banks had been assumed to have played a major role in the steady economic expan-sion of that period. While the central banks had supported the expansion with easy monetary policies, and the economies were becoming progres-sively more globalized, private financial institutions, and not just banks, had taken more risks than in the past. Often, the risks had been taken with their clients' money rather than with the institutions' own capital. These developments had put the whole system and not just specific institutions at significant risks.

A *shadow, global financial sector*, largely unsupervised and perhaps too complex to be effectively supervised, had grown over the years in size and in importance, competing with the traditional and better-supervised bank-ing activities, which had also become freer to take risks, because of dereg-ulation policies introduced in the 1990s. These monetary policies and the financial developments had increased systemic risks and made it easier for questionable debtors, including some governments, to get large loans, and had contributed to the distortion of asset prices, which eventually led to unsustainable bubbles. Access to credit became so easy that some countries could borrow sums that at times exceeded their GDPs.

When the financial crisis arrived in 2007–2008, the central banks (and especially the US Federal Reserve Bank) were accused of having contrib-uted to it, with their accommodating monetary policies, maintained for too long, which had generated excessive investments in assets (especially housing), the prices of which had been inflated and had been expected to keep going up forever, contributing to irrational investments and to the bubbles. These investments had been considered safe bets in which an investor who borrowed money to invest in them could not possibly lose.

The financial crisis of 2007–2008 had been to a large extent, with some obvious changes and a different set of countries, a repeat of the crisis that had hit Southeast Asia in 1997–1998. The lessons of the earlier crisis had not been learned, and the mistakes that had been made in that crisis had been repeated on a much larger scale (see Tanzi, 2008b, pp. 139–141; Tanzi, 2013b, pp. 109–110 and pp. 126–127, for comments on the earlier crisis).

The expectation that central banks should play a major role in fighting the recession that followed the financial crisis has not changed. To fight the consequences of the earlier *easy* monetary policies, the central banks were asked to pursue, and they did pursue, an even *easier* monetary policy. The central banks have been fighting that crisis ever since with extraordinarily loose monetary policies. Nine years later they are still fighting it. Huge liquid reserves have been created by policies of Quantitative Easing, interest rates have been lowered to levels not seen or even imagined possible in the past, and they have been kept at that level for many years. Central banks have been accumulating huge amounts of sovereign bonds and other questionable assets in their balance sheets. In some ways they have become again the governments' treasuries.

The Federal Reserve Bank now owns a large share of the US federal government's public debt, and the European Central Bank owns a large share of the debt of several European governments. This monetary policy has become, de facto and to a large extent, a fiscal policy camouflaged as monetary policy. However, it is also a fiscal policy not subjected to political controls. One can have the impression that the central banks do not know how to get out of their policies. As in the legend of the "sorcerer apprentice," they learned how to get the genie out of the bottle, but do not know how to get it back in the bottle. If this is the "new normal," time will tell what the longer run consequences of these policies and of this new normal will be. One can only hope that those who are making these decisions fully understand what they are doing.

Over the years, the repeated pursuit of the stabilization objective by governments has contributed to the increase of the level of public spending in the economies, as shares of GDP. The reason is the previously mentioned asymmetric nature of Keynesian fiscal policies. Simply put, it is often easier for governments to increase spending in times of recession than to reduce it when the good times arrive. Higher spending can easily find supporters among politicians or citizens that benefit from it, while attempts to decrease it find few supporters.

The repeated, active pursuit of economic stabilization policies (combined with redistributive policies) has been a factor in the growth of public debt in many countries in recent decades, because higher public spending has often been financed by borrowing. This increase in public debt has occurred even though, over several decades after World War II, the tax levels were increased considerably in almost all industrial countries, and there had been no major wars or major catastrophes to justify the debt. In some countries (Japan, Greece, Italy, Belgium, the United States, and others), the public debt reached high levels, increasing the likelihood of negative effects on current incentives and on investments, and on the future net wealth of those who held the debt. In the past, high public debts have been almost always accompanied by large *future* losses on the part of those who held the public securities, as Adam Smith had recognized three centuries ago (see Smith, 1937, p. 882). It remains to be seen if this time it will be different (see Tanzi, 2016b).

An interesting but not widely known anecdote worth recounting is that in the mid-1940s, Keynes had agreed, in a letter that he had sent to the economist Colin Clark, that 25 percent of GDP should be a *ceiling* for the *desirable* level of taxes in countries. The level in the United States has remained close to this level. However, in many other advanced countries, the tax level now exceeds 40 percent, and in some it has reached 50 percent! In spite of those levels, public debt has sharply increased. One must wonder how Keynes would have reacted to these levels if he were alive today.

The increase in public debt over the years created the need to service it and, consequently, contributed to the higher tax levels and also to direct or indirect pressures on central banks to keep interest rates low. It has made monetary policy dependent on fiscal policies, because of the need to keep low the servicing costs of the public debt in an effort to prevent crises created by increasing "spreads." In the most recent years, the assistance that monetary policy has given to fiscal policy by reducing the cost of financing public debts has been significant (see Tanzi, 2013b). It is an illusion to continue to believe that the central banks can be, in reality, truly independent from fiscal developments, and that they can ignore the impact of their policies on the borrowing costs of governments. Those costs have become important in the public spending of several countries, in spite of the low interest rates.

In recent decades, governments have been expected to promote policies that, at least in intention if not in results, are aimed at raising the rate of growth of economies and at creating employment. These policies have been often promoted with the use of public subsidies or tax incentives to private enterprises, and by providing other kinds of public support to *national champions*, including protection from foreign competitors. These *champions* are large enterprises that, like national sport teams sent by countries to compete in the Olympics or in the World Cup, are assumed or expected to give prestige and power to their countries. The problem is that these enterprises are often expensive to maintain and often not particularly competitive. In the past, national champions had included national airlines, public banks, telephone companies, steel mills, and other large enterprises. Populist policies may bring them back in some countries.

Various kinds of industrial policies, public investments in particular activities or regions, and subsidized credit and tax incentives given to enterprises are examples of the policies used by governments to create and support *national champions*, and to raise the countries' employment rates and, hopefully, their rates of growth. Regardless of the wisdom of and the results of these policies, which continue to be popular with the policymakers of many countries, particular public institutions have been responsible for executing them, and significant resources have been required to finance them. The management of these enterprises and the influence that politicians have on them often open opportunities for acts of corruption, including political corruption, on the part of those who administer them.

CHAPTER 24

Modern Government Role and Constitutional Guidelines

Having discussed the main roles of the state and some of the major problems encountered by governments in promoting those roles, I believe it may be worthwhile to review some related legal or institutional aspects. The theoretical or academic discussions of these roles often ignore problems that make it difficult for governments to achieve what they are expected to achieve with their interventions. In broad terms, the general objectives that governments must promote, regardless of the political coloring of the governments, are the following:

Governments must establish and enforce formal rules, including those that are related to contracts that protect property rights, that govern the collection and the use of public revenue, and that determine the legitimate economic behavior of enterprises and individuals. Governments must be clear about the limits to their own power and must respect those limits. The problem of how to establish those limits has preoccupied philosophers since antiquity and, more recently, economists and political scientists. Constitutions generally aim at setting limits to governmental powers, and governments must specify what actions by citizens are forbidden and what require government authorization, limiting as much as possible the number of both and especially of the latter.

The government rules ought to be clear, focused, limited in number, and known by the citizens. They must, thus, be easily available and understandable, so that ignorance or misunderstanding of the laws cannot become an excuse for not obeying them. The rules should form the basis for a society founded on so-called *rule of law* and not on arbitrary decisions or interpretations of the laws by the authority. Citizens, enterprises, bureaucrats, and policymakers should all be guided by, and should follow, the same rules. There cannot be different sets of rules for different groups of citizens, as there were in many countries in past centuries. Different interpretations, or different applications of the rules, should not distort the concept of equality before the law, a concept that is a relatively recent one and that should characterize modern democratic societies.

A controversial and important point to recognize is that the *rules*, as they apply concretely, ought to reflect the preferences of a *modern* society and not those of *distant* and possibly different societies. This last point raises the question of the economic role of political constitutions, the legal documents that are often the most important in guiding policies and behavior. A fundamental problem with the influence of and the dependence on constitutions is that these documents may have been created in periods when needs, perceptions, relations, and technologies were dramatically different, raising questions about their relevance for present economic activities. This is likely to be a very controversial issue on which views have differed and will inevitably continue to differ.

Let us take as a first example the Italian Constitution, which had been elegantly and competently written by prominent jurists. It was approved (shortly after World War II, when Italy became a Republic) by a large majority of the "Assemblea Costituente," the committee that had been created to write and approve the new constitution. It was a time when some forms of socialist thinking and *economic planning* were fashionable in Europe, and when organized labor and *labor unions* had acquired a lot of political power. Italy had emerged recently from more than two decades of the totalitarian Fascist regime, and from being a monarchy.

Not surprisingly, the new Italian Constitution stated, in its very first article, that "the Italian Republic is founded on labor." It then listed various *rights of workers*, while it referred to only the *social responsibilities of property and property owners*. The Fascist regime – with Mussolini as the head of government and the king as the nominal head of state – that had preceded the Republican and democratic regime had recognized the existence of property rights. However, while "the Labor Charter of 1927 admitted the right of private property in principle, [it] reserved to the State the power to intervene, manage, or operate property when its own interests required" (see Steiner, 1938, p. 91).

The new Italian constitution makes no reference to the role of the market and to the importance of protecting private property rights. Inevitably, the principles expressed in it have had an important impact on Italian policies and developments. They have guided the decisions of the Italian governments, of parliament, of the judiciary, and of the public administration toward giving strong rights to workers and questionable rights to property owners. As a consequence, the new constitution has allowed policies that have created difficulties for a market economy based on private property in a modern, globalized world, especially in the more competitive world of recent decades. For example, some of its articles have made it difficult to fire workers in enterprises that have more than fifteen employees, creating an incentive for enterprises to remain small. In a modern globalized economy, the market ought to be guided by principles that are more consistent with those of that economy.

In conclusion, the Italian Constitution has not been helpful in creating a labor market flexible enough for a modern economy and in protecting sufficiently legitimate property rights, rights that should not be reduced, at times, by what appears to be arbitrary governmental action, with inadequate compensation, when the government exercises its prerogative to use, presumably for its purposes, properties that have been in private hands. This has happened more often than it should have, especially in the actions of municipalities, but also occasionally at the national level. At times, private land has been expropriated, and buildings have been taken over, without, or with inadequate, compensation to their owners (see Tanzi, 2015a).

The US Constitution, on the other hand, was written and approved almost two centuries before the Italian Constitution, when few individuals had the right to vote or had political power. It was written by a small and privileged group of rich citizens of the original thirteen American colonies, after the War of Independence. Several of these individuals owned slaves, at a time when an important debate was whether inhabitants who were slaves should be counted as "individuals" or as "property." As James Madison, the successor to Thomas Jefferson as President of the United States in 1809–1817, had put it in *The Federalist Papers* (Hamilton et al. [1787–1788] 1982, No. 54, p. 332), "Slaves are considered as property, not as persons. They ought therefore to be comprehended in estimates of taxation which are founded on property, and to be excluded from representation which is regulated by a census of persons." Clearly, slaves were not considered to be persons and could not be citizens. As late as 1857, the US Supreme Court would decide that slaves could not be considered US citizens.

It should be noted that, in some states, slaves represented the majority of the population. Few members of the rest of the populations – including women, freed slaves, American Indians, and whites who did not own property – had the right to vote (see Taylor, 2016). James Madison, a very rich Virginia planter, owner of thousands of acres, had a net worth that has been estimated to have amounted to many millions of dollars. Other major contributors to the US Constitution, such as Thomas Jefferson and Alexander Hamilton, were also very rich, and some of them owned slaves, which constituted property. Those from the South were interested in the protection of their property. It is thus not surprising that James Madison would believe that "government is instituted … for protection of the property…" (Hamilton et al., p. 334).

At the time when the US Constitution was drafted, the young country was still largely rural and had a small population spread over a huge area, and its land area at that time was only a small portion of what it would become later and what it is today. At that time many American Indians were being killed. Given that origin, and the interests of those who drafted it, it was natural that the US Constitution would give a lot of weight to property rights, but it would be silent about the rights of "workers," who, except for those who were slaves and those who were not workers in the modern sense of dependent workers, largely did not exist. The creation of workers' rights would remain a lively and controversial issue for the American economy.

That origin inevitably determined the content of the US Constitution, just as the origin of the Italian Constitution determined its content. The content of the US Constitution, with the twenty-seven amendments that followed, has continued to influence the economic and social relations in that country in modern times. Indirectly, it has also influenced the income distribution that the American economy has been generating over the years.

In spite of their widely different constitutions, and regardless of the merits and the principles expressed by those two constitutions, the constitutions of the United States and of Italy must both operate today in the same modern, global, and competitive world, a world that is very different (especially in the US case) from the one that existed when each of those constitutions was written.

Of course, constitutions can be changed or amended and are occasionally amended to reflect changing conditions and important new developments. In some countries, for example, in many Latin American countries and to a lesser extent in Italy, the constitutions can be changed more easily than is the case in the United States. In the United States the rules that were also established a long time ago make it *very* difficult to change it. In more than 200 years the US Constitution has been amended twenty-seven times, and only sixteen times after 1800 and only eleven times after 1900 in spite of how the country has changed. Some rules, for example, those that allow the purchase and the carrying of weapons and those that elect presidents, have come under recent sharp criticisms from many citizens, but cannot be changed because of the rules established centuries ago.

Constitutions can cast long shadows on current and future policies, especially when it is difficult to change them. Countries have rules for amending them and appoint individuals to institutions (Supreme Courts) charged with interpreting them when they are asked, and when they agree, to do it. The Supreme Court judges are asked to make what are often very difficult choices between interpretations that give weight to "original principles," as, for example, was consistently argued should be done by the late US Supreme Court Justice Antonin Scalia, and interpretations that reflect modern and more flexible views (in customs, technologies, and attitudes), as has been argued, for example, by Ruth Ginsburg, another influential member of the US Supreme Court. See Wurman, 2017.

Antonin Scalia had consistently argued that the original principles of those who drafted the US Constitution should continue to guide the interpretations of it, unless those principles have been amended by constitutional changes, which are very difficult to make. On the other hand, Ruth Ginsburg has been arguing that the Constitution should reflect the prevalent views of the majority of today's citizens, and not those of white, property-owning *men* who lived in a world where few men (and *only men who owned property*) could vote, and where many of them owned slaves. That world no longer exists today, and in today's world "we the people" bear little relation to the "we the people" of that world. From various reports it would appear that Thomas Jefferson and James Madison had conflicting views on the above question. Jefferson view seems to have been closer to that of Ginsburg.

It is obvious that *personal* views and biases have inevitably continued to guide the interpretations of the US Constitution on the part of the two Supreme Court justices mentioned here, as they have continued to guide the interpretations of the other members of the US Supreme Court. It is also obvious that the biases of those who select these Supreme Court justices for their positions in the Supreme Court also guide them in the selection of justices. This became evident in the filling of the spot vacated by the death of Justice Scalia in 2017. Because most or some of the principles expressed by the US Constitution are rather vague, or are vaguely expressed, and can lend themselves to different interpretations, individual judges often have a lot of latitude in interpreting those principles and can have great power on legal developments, powers that are unmatched in other countries.

It would seem reasonable to maintain that new technologies and new social and economic developments over many years, including the fact that, today, most citizens can vote, must occasionally make some of the previsions in the constitutions appear less realistic or less desirable than they might have been at the time when the constitutions were enacted. However, because it is politically very difficult to change existing constitutional rules, even when clear *majorities* of citizens might support some changes, the written rules remain the same and prevent the changes. Some political decisions do not reflect the will of the majority of the people, and many believe that results can be manipulated in various ways by powerful interests (see Bartels, 2016). Some political scientists believe that the anti-government attitude that prevails in the US today is the result of the work of those powerful interests. See Hacker and Pierson, 2016.

It is also obvious that frequent and easy constitutional changes would reduce the value of constitutions and would create different kinds of problems. They would also make the constitutions potential tools of powerful governments to manipulate majorities, or of current majorities to reduce the rights of minorities, as the late James Buchanan stressed in some of his works, and as Mussolini undertook in Italy. Current developments in Poland and in Venezuela point to this danger.

The economic laws and the rules that exist in a country must aim at facilitating economic relations and at reducing the transaction costs that legitimate exchanges involve. They must keep low the cost of legitimately dealing with other individuals and also of dealing with the government, making these costs affordable to most. It can be argued that in some areas the costs of dealing with the government have increased considerably over the years, giving as a result more power to those who have higher means to cover those costs (see Rakoff, 2016). For example, today, a person who does not have the money to contest a lawsuit, or even to pay a fine, can more easily end up in jail than one who has the means to hire good lawyers or to pay fines. This has made the justice system more unequal than it ought to be. Not surprisingly, richer individuals who violate the same rules as poor individuals do go to jail far less frequently. The pre-jail incomes of those who are now in jail were likely to have been far lower than those of people out of jail, and not just because lower-income individuals are likely to commit more crimes or more serious crimes.

As a prominent US judge has put it, "Lawyers comprise a guild to which there are significant barriers to entry, not least the huge expense of a legal education. But in the past few decades, the price of hiring a lawyer to handle an everyday dispute has risen at a rate much greater than the average increase in income or wages. ... [B]etween 1985 and 2012 the average billing rate for law firm partners in the US increased from $112 per hour to $536 per hour, and for associate lawyers from $79 per hour to $370 per hour"; and "Individuals not represented by lawyers lose cases at a considerable higher rate than similar individuals who are represented by counsel" (Rakoff, 2016, p. 4). Rakoff added that "the belief of citizens … [is] … that the courts are … simply a remote and expensive luxury reserved for the rich and powerful" (ibid., p. 6). If he is right, that is a worrisome conclusion for a democracy.

The legal framework that exists in countries should promote both market efficiency and social cohesion through strategic but limited public intervention, especially when the market fails or when existing arrangements generate outcomes that many citizens find objectionable or damaging. An unemployment rate of 25 percent of the workforce, the rate reached during the Great Depression, was one of those outcomes. In the United States it led to frictions between the Roosevelt administration and the Supreme Court when the latter resisted some of the legislative changes that the Roosevelt administration wanted to introduce. An income distribution that gives the top 1 percent of the US population 25 percent of the income, and almost all of the income generated by economic growth over decades, may be considered another such outcome in today's world. And, the fact that 25 percent of all the individuals now in jail in the whole world are in US jails may be another of these undesirable outcomes. The low life expectancy in the United States is another outcome that ought to be considered clearly undesirable.

A situation in which a large share of the total income was going to those at the top had of course existed in the distant past, but the world of that time was a different world. It is not an outcome that the citizens of today's world seem willing to accept as passively, at least in democratic societies. See Thomas (1994) and Porter (1992) for descriptions of how societies have changed and how different modern societies are from older societies. The replacement of one aristocracy – the one that had owned much of the wealth and much of the political power in the past, power and wealth at times considered to be due to divine and other rights (as in France until the French Revolution and in Russia until the Bolshevik Revolution) – with another aristocracy that owns much of the wealth and receives a large share of the income (even though with less *explicit* political power), today, cannot be seen as a desirable or an acceptable outcome.

On a different ground, bureaucratic or pseudo-legal obstacles to legitimate and other transactions must be minimized. In some countries these obstacles have become excessive. Even signing simple rental contracts, opening or closing bank accounts, or getting permissions to open new commercial activities have become particularly burdensome in some countries. They require citizens to spend much time and effort. In some areas they have opened possibilities for "facilitators," or for intermediaries, who can find (not always legitimate) short cuts. "Red tape" and "bureaucratic cholesterol" have entered the economic systems of many countries, slowing down the efficiency of their economy and also contributing to inequities.

Bureaucratic obstacles must be seen as *termites* that can enter into many economic transactions, making them progressively more complex and more difficult to complete, especially for those who cannot rely on facilitators or on experts on those rules, or on valuable connections. Some of these obstacles have some justifications. Others have less or none.

At the same time, it must be repeated that societies in which many individuals live in crowded, large cities and engage in many transactions, often with strangers, are bound to need more rules than societies in which many live in rural areas, as most individuals did in the eighteenth century in a largely self-sufficient manner. Some of these differences influenced the content of constitutions. These differences cannot be ignored by modern governments or by economists and political scientists in judging what ought to be the economic role of the state. In spite of their good intentions, some libertarian aspirations suffer from lack of realism, because these libertarians would like to live with rules that are no longer appropriate for today's world. For a libertarian manifesto, see Boaz, 1997, 2015.

Connected with these issues, the government must ensure that operators who work in the free market as sellers of goods and services provide essential, accessible, and transparent information to the buyers to minimize abuses and problems. Asymmetry in information between transacting parties, a problem that has become increasingly common in particular sectors of the economy, can and often does generate difficulties. Reliable information has become far more essential in the modern world than it must have been in the distant rural world, when many families produced much of what they consumed and generally had more knowledge about the few products that they bought from others, who were mostly their neighbors.

Problems connected with lack of, or with misleading, information have become common and potentially more serious, because of the increasing number of transactions in the modern world, the increasing complexity of modern markets, and the fact that buyers and sellers no longer live in the same areas, nor do they often know one another. The issues are several. When is the provision of a piece of information "essential"? Who shall provide the information when the sellers and the producers of a product may be different individuals or enterprises? In what form should the information be provided?

Often, possibly misleading publicity has become a substitute for the provision of objective information and may have influenced the demand for some products. How transparently should objective information be provided? What happens if the information is not correct? What if the correct information is not available even to those who, as intermediaries, supply the goods and services to the final users, but do not produce them, as is the case with present-day supermarkets? These and similar questions make clear how much the world has changed, and how much the government's role needs to adjust to the new reality to remain relevant and optimal. However, it should adjust without becoming overly constraining.

Governments must provide *public goods* to the citizens at a desirable and affordable level, making sure that the provision of these goods does not create opportunities for some individuals and enterprises to appropriate the benefits derived from their *production*, thus transforming public goods into private benefits for some, as I described earlier in the case of some defense spending. This would change the relationship between the genuine benefits received by citizens from the public goods and the cost to them (as taxpayers) of financing the provision of the goods. Corruption, rent-seeking, and inefficiencies can easily distort that relationship.

Governments must pay attention to *major negative externalities* and especially to those that cannot and are not resolved by direct negotiations between the involved private parties. As I have stressed, externalities have become more frequent in modern societies, and some have acquired psychological characteristics. And, some may not be recognized immediately when new products are introduced.

The problem of globally generated externalities, of which there is an increasing number, is becoming one of the more difficult to address in a world in which (national) governments continue to have jurisdiction over only the limited territories in which they govern. Illegal immigration has become one of these important cross-country externalities, creating potentially existential problems for some countries. Cross-border crime is another.

Governments must promote *macroeconomic stability* with wise, time-limited, and symmetric interventions that, over the long run, should not lead to high and difficult-to-finance public spending or to difficult-to-service public debt, and that should not encourage "moral hazard" on the part of some individuals and institutions. There has been too much trust on the part of some economists in the view that more public spending almost *always* promotes what is defined as "growth" or "welfare," and that it will automatically alleviate the problem created by the burden of a high public debt by making countries grow faster.

As a normal policy, governments should always have a number of productive investment projects *ready to be started*, projects that have passed competent benefit-cost and evaluation analyses and that would merit being carried out in normal circumstances in some not-too-distant future time. Perhaps, legislatures might follow a two-step approach to some important investments. The first step would be to approve a project in principle. The second would be to decide when work on that project could start and the money for it could be appropriated. In most countries there are good and productive projects that the government should carry out in future years but that can wait for the best moment, in terms of economic conditions and perhaps also in terms of cheaper financing, to be started. A recession may be the right moment for macroeconomic reasons, but also because borrowing costs, and probably also building costs, tend to be lower during recessions.

The Hoover Dam, built in the United States during the Great Depression, was completed ahead of schedule and at a cost below the budget. It would be wise for governments to have always ready a list of such projects that could be quickly initiated in years when an economic stimulus was needed. However, as mentioned, what we have called the "initial conditions" in the fiscal accounts must not be such as to make additional public spending, financed by debt, risky. As much as possible, public debts and fiscal deficits must be kept under reasonable and prudent limits.

Productive investment projects could more easily justify higher fiscal deficits and *temporarily* higher public debts if they were likely to contribute to growth and to higher tax revenues. Governments should refrain from addressing stabilization objectives with policies that are costly over the long run, or with policies that are politically difficult to reverse when the need for fiscal stimulation comes to an end. By definition, spending for specific, productive public investment projects is always reversible when the projects are completed. If they raise the growth potential of the economy, they will finance themselves over the longer run (provided that taxes rise in line with the growth of the economy), as defenders of the *golden rule* have insisted to be the case for public investment. The problem with that rule is that not all, or even much, public investment is productive. For political reasons, or because of pressures by vested interests, there are often *roads to nowhere* that some politicians or some groups are interested in building.

Governments must do their best to promote market conditions that help prevent excessive income concentration, especially when that concentration is facilitated by the existing government rules or operations. They should adopt policies that help promote a distribution of income that is more consistent with the prevailing view of society, provided that that view can be broadly determined, and that the redistribution that it requires can be achieved without significantly damaging the economic incentives of individuals or the country's long run prospects for growth. Often, the direction of desirable changes is easier to determine than the final destination.

In a democratic setting, when all citizens have the right to vote, a highly uneven distribution of income will inevitably lead to unhappiness on the part of many, and, eventually and inevitably, it will lead to populist demands and policies. If existing (constitutional and other) rules make the needed changes in the income distribution difficult to effect, dissatisfaction will build up. In time it could lead to the use of policies with undesirable and potentially more serious economic consequences.

To achieve desirable results and to perform efficient functions, the state needs good laws and good rules, competent and honest policymakers, good institutions, good information, good policies, and an efficient, dedicated, and honest public administration chosen on the basis of merit. In addition it needs adequate resources, obtained, mainly, from efficient tax systems and not debt. Those who make the economic decisions should have some minimum understanding of how economies function, so that the decisions that they make do not follow unrealistic dreams and avoid major mistakes.

Unfortunately, in the field of economics there are always some economists who will suggest easy or even miraculous solutions to difficult problems. Furthermore, most individuals, and especially those who are in policymaking positions, often think that they understand economics and that they know what is best for the economy and for the citizens, even when their background is in other areas and when they may have little real understanding of how economies operate. At times they become slaves of "dead economists."

In recent years three miraculous solutions have been pushed by some economists: (a) for the government to completely disengage and let the market take over and do almost everything, largely ignoring distributional and other consequences; (b) for the government to abandon what is called "austerity" and to keep spending until, miraculously, growth will return and problems will disappear; and (c) for the state to return to an economic planning role.

A minimum level of economic literacy on the part of citizens (and on the part of those who seek high government positions, including presidential candidates and heads of governments) is a desirable public good. The votes that citizens cast determine to some extent the policies that the policymakers adopt. The latest miracle cures to economic problems should always be received with a good dose of skepticism, even when they come from economists with widely lauded academic reputations.

The list of essential requirements provided earlier, although long, is not exhaustive; it would be easy to add additional ones. Still, it indicates how difficult it must be for a government to operate well in today's world and how easily mistakes can be made. For most governments the period of honeymoon has become short. The previous discussion indicates the importance for governments of not being influenced too much by the short run and by what may appear to be easy solutions to difficult problems. Often, short run solutions, those that may appear almost as free lunches to the governments in charge, hide long run costs and consequences. This is especially true with short run fiscal stimuli when they lead to significant increases in public debts, and with other policies that increase future costs while they create vested interests that favor the new spending and that will make it difficult for future government to change the policies. Protectionism falls in this category.

As the Austrian economist Ludwig von Mises once put it – commenting on the often-quoted expression by Keynes that the focus of policies should be on the short run, because "in the long run we are all dead" – while he did "not question the truth of [that] statement," he added that "unfortunately nearly all of us outlive the short run. We are destined to spend decades paying for the easy money orgy of a few years" (see Mises, 2005, p. 130). If this is true for individuals, it is even truer for governments. Especially bad governments tend to push the difficult decisions and the costs of policies forward, expecting the governments of the future to deal with the costs of the bad decisions, expecting miracles to happen to solve the problems.

The role of the state has changed enormously over the past century. It has become much more ambitious, more demanding, and more complex (see Tanzi, 2011). During the second half of the twentieth century, public spending and tax levels grew rapidly. Many governments made promises to citizens, on pensions, public health programs, education, jobs, and other areas, that future governments would find difficult to honor, because of resource limitations. In making those promises, the governments traded and have continued to trade short run political benefits against long run costs. Changing technologies and global developments have influenced what national governments can and are expected to do in an increasingly global world.

It is also not realistic to argue, as some conservative or libertarian econo-mists and political scientists continue to argue, that the role of the state should remain unchanged over the years and that the role contemplated one or two centuries ago should largely continue to guide the countries in today's world. Whether we like it or not, we live in a different and fast-changing world, and that world has been made even more different by globalization. Hayek understood this when he categorically stated that he was not a conservative (see Hayek, [1960] 2011, pp. 519–553). He under-stood that one may favor a smaller and more efficient government, but one cannot favor a government that does not change and does not adjust its role to a changing world.

Economic and political developments, urbanization, technological progress, demographic growth, aging of the population, immigration flows, and globalization have been creating, and will continue to create, new demands on governments by creating new products and services, by changing perceptions, by stimulating contacts, by increasing the number and extending the range of negative externalities, and by increasing close-ness and connectivity *among* members of communities and *across* different communities and countries.

At the same time, by enlarging the size and the scope of the market, by creating new markets, and by reducing some market failures in particular areas, economic developments have also allowed individuals to better sat-isfy than in the past some of their needs directly from the market, without the direct assistance of the government (see Tanzi, 2005). For example, many new kinds of insurances are now available or can be made available from the market. Credit is now more easily available for most people and for different and longer time periods. The latter allows a better matching, for individuals, between income earnings and consumption needs over their lifetime. For many individuals, this facilitates the ability to deal with temporary income shortfalls for buying houses or cars, or even for acquir-ing education.

It is now also far easier for individuals to save in various forms, using private financial institutions. It is easier to get micro credit to start new economic activity. It is easier for families to control the number of chil-dren that they bring into the world, thus reducing the problems that families with numerous children had in the past to feed them. Medical assistance and educational services can be obtained abroad when they are not available domestically, as long as those who need them can afford the cost or can borrow the money needed, or they can have their private insurances pay for them. Many infrastructures can be built by private concerns. Venture capital is more easily available now than it was in the past for investors with promising ideas. Pensions can be obtained through private sources, and in principle even through foreign sources.

All the aforementioned examples imply that the quality and also the size of the public sector, in a market economy with democratic institutions, must be assessed in the light of current objectives, priorities, and needs of citizens, as well as the capacity of the domestic (and increasingly global) market *at a given point in time*, while not ignoring the capacity of governments to perform and to monitor the market. The objectives and the needs are likely to change, both across time and across space. Also, the preferences of the citizens and their contacts with the rest of the world, contacts that have increased significantly in recent decades, inevitably play a role in what citizens expect their governments to do. All these arguments clearly point to the need for a changing and adaptable government role, though not necessarily for a larger role in terms of public spending.

The countries and their governments continue to have *national* characters and to focus on *national* objectives, relying for guidance on constitutions, laws, rules, and institutions that are *national* in scope. Increasingly, international agreements and international institutions have been reducing somewhat the discretion and the area of operation of national states, and global needs have been changing, to a limited extent, the traditional government role. The higher is the quality of the countries' public sector, the better are the international agreements; and the more efficient are the international institutions, the easier it is to promote the public goods, *both domestically and globally*.

As the needs for global public goods and/or global regulations grow, there is inevitably the danger that the existing arrangements will become increasingly anachronistic. This has become a concern within the European Union, and especially within the European Monetary Union, where frictions between national rules and previously agreed European rules have created difficulties (see Sinn, 2014; Tanzi, 2013b; Fiorentini and Montani, 2012; Stiglitz, 2003). To some extent similar problems have appeared in federal countries, including the United States, where conflicts in various of these countries between the policies of the national governments and those of the states or regions seem to have become sharper in recent years.

Global public goods and cross-country externalities could in theory be dealt with more efficiently if there were an efficient and global government, one truly able to promote the interests of the world community. However, such a government does not exist, and, if it existed, and if it were democratically based, it would face enormous distributional problems, because inevitably the democratic weight of some large countries (such as China and India) would push the government to redistribute income. In such a global setting, the countries with the largest populations would have most of the votes. Alternatively, the issue could be faced by having billions of people try to move from the poorer to the richer countries, in a world without borders or restrictions in people's movements.

The growingly negative, national reactions to immigration flows in several countries provide a feel for the difficulties that such a global government would face. Immigration flows also provide a growing challenge to the globalization process that has been going on in the world in recent decades. Perhaps, the most important role of national governments is the protection of countries' national borders. Wars have often been fought to protect borders or to resolve border issues. The heterogeneity of the individuals taking part in a global community with a global government would create enormous and possibly insurmountable difficulties. To a large extent it would destroy the communities made up by nations. In this setting, the public interest and what the government could do to promote it would become extremely difficult, if not impossible, to define and even more to promote.

A question that we must ask without being able to answer is whether a world that is becoming increasingly globalized in many ways can continue to be a world of *independent* nations, with *national* borders that separate the citizens of individual countries from others. As recent experiences indicate, it is very difficult for democratic countries to keep out *large* numbers of migrants who do not come through official and controllable channels but risk their lives by moving across dangerous seas, or mountains and deserts, to get access to richer countries. Governments can more easily control official entrances at monitored frontiers, not at all frontiers. *National* rights have been coming in increasing conflict with the *civil* or human rights of individuals who try to escape wars, political persecution, or extreme poverty in their countries of provenence.

To a greater extent than is often realized, one of the main reasons why the role of the state is becoming more difficult to define and to implement is the fact that the communities governed by modern governments are becoming less and less homogeneous in large part because of globalization. The concept of community is disappearing, as Putnam and others have stressed in recent books. Immigration reinforces this process and tendency.

This implies that the *common interest, which is shared* by the citizens of a country, becomes more limited than it was when the communities were smaller and more homogeneous, or when some countries were still empty and in need of filling vacant and mostly rural areas. In many modern countries the need to put the individual and not the community at the center of policies has become more evident, whether we like it or not. This requires government rules and governments capable of enforcing them.

The view that the *individual*, and not the *community*, should be put at the center of policies in modern societies also requires rules and controls that are based on shared tradition to a lesser extent and that, as a consequence, require stronger formal enforcement. At the same time globalization and new technologies are making the world smaller and more open to the movement of goods, services, money, capital, intellectual property, cultural and criminal activities, pollution, and so on, but not to most individuals who would like to move and change their country of residence.

Another inevitable question to ask is the following: Is it reasonable to assume that in such a world the national borders of countries can remain closed for illegal immigrants, as some would like them to be? What will happen to the role of the state when or if immigration flows cannot be controlled, as has been happening to a large extent in European countries? As mentioned, to some extent, the control of national borders to protect a country from explicit foreign invasion or from uncontrolled illegal immigration was and remains the most fundamental role of the *national* state. Should we rethink that role?

CHAPTER 25

The Quality of the Public Sector and the Legal Framework

In recent years some literature has focused on the *quality of the public sector*, as distinguished from the *quantity* and *scope* of the state's economic actions. The quality of the public sector is obviously important in the promotion of the actions that governments want to take in the economic sphere. (See, for example, Deroose and Kastrop, 2008.) The quality of the public sector can be broadly defined as the characteristic that allows the state to pursue its objectives in an efficient way, given the size and the scope of its intervention. Therefore, the emphasis is on the public sector as an *instrument* that allows the state to promote its objectives, not on the quality of the objectives. The quality of the public sector is also not necessarily the same thing as the quality of economic policy. A high-quality public sector is simply the instrument that facilitates the formulation and the implementation of policies, whether those policies are good or bad, which makes it easier for the government to pursue the policies that it wishes to pursue and to achieve its goals.

Obviously, even a high-quality public sector as defined here cannot guarantee consistently good economic policies, because it cannot prevent policymakers from making mistakes or from choosing policies that are not in the public interest. However, one would hesitate to consider a public sector to be of high quality if poor policies were frequently pursued; and one would expect to find a high correlation between the quality of the public sector, as defined earlier, and the quality of economic policy. Over time, a high-quality public sector should and would be expected to be associated with better policies, while a low-quality public sector would be more likely to promote poorer policies.

The definition of a high-quality public sector, as formulated here, differs from the definition of "good government" that some experts have used, especially in the 1990s. For example, La Porta et al. (1998) defined good government as one that is good for capitalist development. They did not distinguish between the quality of the public sector and the quality of public policy. They also assumed that capitalist development was intrinsically and naturally superior to that of other forms of development. Although many would agree with them today, some might question this assumption, especially when capitalist development becomes associated with an increasingly uneven income distribution, and when capitalism develops characteristics of "crony capitalism." (See, for example, Reich, 2015.) After all, it is the welfare of the *majority* of the citizens that should be the goal of economic development, as utilitarian philosophers had stressed, not the growth of GDP.

The two objectives may not always coincide, although over the long run they have, as argued by Angus Deaton (2013). The problem is that many of those living today may not be around in the long run. When much of the growth goes to a small share of the population, making the majority feel increasingly poorer, at least in relative terms (even when they may not be poorer in absolute terms), it cannot be automatically assumed that capitalist development increases welfare. This, many argue, is what has been happening in recent decades in several advanced countries, and there is no evidence that things are changing for the better.

A poor-quality public sector renders the pursuit of good policy more difficult, because it does not provide the government with the needed information and the needed good institutions for promoting those policies. Furthermore, the policy decisions that the government makes, even when they are good decisions, might be distorted in the implementation stage by the public administration that controls the institutions or by other institutional defects. This is one of the important *termites of the state*. On the other hand, as mentioned earlier, even a public sector of high quality may not prevent occasional bad policy decisions from being made by policymakers.

In previous chapters the broad categories that have characterized the goals of state intervention in the economy were discussed. Each of these interventions requires specific programs, and each program requires a legal mandate and the institutions necessary to administer and monitor the program. As it was argued, the more numerous the programs become, the more complex things are likely to get for the public sector. In earlier chapters I gave some indications of how complex things have become in some countries, because of the large number of programs and the increasing number of objectives that governments want to promote. Next, I discuss some aspects of the legal framework that guides the action of governments.

The Role of Constitutions

In democratic countries with market economies the mandate to the state that allows it to intervene in the country's economy is often given, first, by a political *constitution* and then by various more specific laws. The latter must be consistent with the principles outlined by the constitution. Furthermore, as argued by an American scholar, to interpret correctly a constitution, it is not sufficient to look at its wording but is also necessary to consider its precedents (see Amar, 2012).

The constitutions and the laws establish the rules of the game, or the *rule of law*, which guide, or should guide, the actions of individuals and enterprises, on the one hand, and those of the public officials and public institutions, on the other. As North and Weingast (1994, p. 312) pointed out, "[a] critical political factor is the degree to which the regime or sovereign is committed to or bound by these rules." Another critical factor is the extent to which the employees in the public administration will follow and will apply, efficiently and honestly, not just the letter but also the spirit of the laws, when the laws are many, are complex, are not precisely and clearly written, and leave scope for different interpretations.

A still more controversial issue, mentioned in the previous chapter, is the extent to which constitutions reflect the prevalent views of the *current* electorate, and not just those of the individuals who wrote the constitutions. This is a particularly important issue, especially when it is politically difficult for later generations to change a constitution to make it reflect more closely the views of the *current* majority. Unlike the Bible or the Koran, which are supposed to reflect God's permanent (and obviously nondemocratic) instructions to guide and to regulate the behavior of the faithful *for all time*, the prescriptions of constitutions do not have and, it can be argued, should not have the same religious and faith-based content. Even the Vatican has recently seen it necessary to begin discussing the *interpretation* of time-honored, religious beliefs when they do not fully reflect the views of most current believers. Thus, the main issue should be how difficult it should be to change constitutions when a significant majority of the current population sees it as desirable to do so. This moves the question to what should be considered a *significant* majority.

When large gaps develop between the prescriptions of constitutions and the attitudes of the majority of the current electorate, difficulties are likely to develop and to grow with time. In the United States, it took a bloody civil war to change the prescriptions concerning the existence of slavery, and great difficulties and another century to prevent and change prescriptions that allowed discrimination against some racial groups with the 14th Amendment of July 8, 1968.

The important question is which side should adjust to which, recognizing that constitutions have also the important objective of protecting some *fundamental* rights of minorities. Without that protection, majorities could pass laws that, even though in some sense they might be considered "democratic," because they might be voted for by the majority, could be damaging to some groups or minorities. This simply moves the questions to: Which are the fundamental rights? And who is to decide? And are these rights permanent?

Majority rules, though they may be "democratic" rules, may not always be good rules, as James Buchanan and others have stressed. As Buchanan put it in a debate with Richard Musgrave (see Buchanan and Musgrave, 1999, p. 21), one of his books – *The Calculus of Consent* (1962, coauthored with Gordon Tullock) – had been essentially "an intellectual attack on … majority rule"; he added that "our inquiry offered support for constitutional limits in the exercise of political authority."

The problem is that many may see that attack as an attack on democracy itself. What if the minority rights are what have allowed discrimination against others? As argued in an earlier chapter, laws that are based on constitutions *written a long time ago* tend to reflect the points of view and the perceptions of the times when the constitutions were written. They may not always comprise the best laws *for the societies of a later time*. If the Incas had left a constitution for present-day Peru, they might have prescribed human sacrifices. This is especially a problem when the earlier constitutional rules make it difficult *for the majority* of later periods to introduce different laws or amendments to the constitutions that could modernize them and make them more relevant for later periods.

In authoritarian or totalitarian governments the problems tend to be different. Constitutions often exist, but they, play a more limited role, because the governments have the power to ignore them, to amend them, or simply to reinterpret them with greater facility. It has been reported that the constitution of the Soviet Union during Stalin's time was a good one. However, it did not prevent him from doing whatever he wanted, because he held the power, and there were no real checks on his actions or on those of the Communist Party that he controlled (see Getty and Naumov, 2010). Similar comments could be made about the Italian Constitution during Mussolini's Fascist times after 1923.

During the years of Fascism, from 1923 until the end of World War II, the Italian Constitution continued to be the same one that had existed in Italy since 1848, first in the Kingdom of Sardinia, before Italy was unified in 1861, and then after 1861, in the Kingdom of Italy. That constitution had been introduced in the Kingdom of Sardinia by the Savoy king during the turbulent time of 1848, thirteen years before he became the king of Italy in 1861, after the Italian unification.

As a very interesting and highly informed book, published in 1938 by an American scholar who had spent a couple of years in Italy to study the Fascist institutions, put it, it was remarkable that Mussolini could assume political power, and that the Fascist "revolution" could be "accomplished within the limits of the [1848] constitution" (see Steiner, 1938, p. 56). Citing from that book, "The basic fascist legislation [....] was enacted ... regard for the constitutional formalities" (ibid.). Chapter 5 of Steiner's book deals with the legal foundation of fascist government (ibid., pp. 56–68).

Neither Stalin nor Mussolini considered himself bound by the limitations imposed by his country's constitution, but while Stalin simply ignored his constitution, Mussolini found it convenient to pay formal respect to the constitution, because, formally, the king was still the head of state. In authoritarian regimes, those who have the real power have also the power to make the rules, or at least find it easier to reinterpret the rules. They are not limited by the interpretations of the rules as the rules had been legislated and had been interpreted by previous governments. If you cannot make new rules, or do not want to, you may be able to reinterpret the existing ones and still insist that you are respecting the "rule of law" to claim legitimacy for your behavior.

Though the aforementioned scenario might seem far-fetched, this could happen also in a country that is clearly democratic or republican, as in the United States, where the president is in the lucky position of being able to appoint a majority of the members of the Supreme Court. He or she could appoint justices that might interpret the often general, or even vague, principles of the US Constitution in particular ways.

In Italy in 1928, a "Constitutional Commission of Eighteen," headed by a prominent jurist and philosopher who was close to the Fascist party (Giovanni Gentile), was appointed by Mussolini to study ways in which the reforms that the party intended to introduce could be made to be in harmony with the existing (1848) constitution. The Commission concluded that the existing constitution should be retained, but it suggested integrating and adjusting the existing institutions to reflect the rather broad declaration of principles contained in the constitution. The constitution of 1848 (the "Statuto Albertino"), which was still the Italian Constitution in 1928, had the precise characteristics that Napoleon was reported to have desired in a constitution: "to be short and obscure." Such a constitution could be reinterpreted by the right Supreme Court and, thus, adapted to accommodate new situations. The main requirement was that those appointed to the Supreme Court should have the right political views or biases!

It is not just in authoritarian or totalitarian regimes that the rule of law, at times, in practice, means less than it should. Depending on the situation, the executive branch, the legislature, or the judiciary may *de facto*, if not *de jure*, assume greater power than it should, and the employees of the public administration may come to share some of that power when they cannot be properly controlled. For example, the relevant committee in the US Senate may decide not to send for a vote the name of a candidate selected by the president for a vacant Supreme Court position if in the not-too-distant future a new president is expected. That is more likely to happen when complexity is prevalent and, thus, allows different interpretations of laws, or when it makes it difficult for some individuals (such as whistle blowers) to challenge the behavior of parts of the government.

The US Constitution is a good and elegant example of a declaration of *general* principles. It is short (about 8,000 words) and beautifully written. However, it surprises modern, and especially non-US-born, readers by just how general its principles are. Some readers are likely to read into it what other readers find difficult to locate. Some may consider this a strength. As mentioned in the previous chapter, in two-and-a-half centuries it has been amended only twenty-seven times, and many of the amendments were introduced in the early years when the country and the number of states were much smaller and were changing. Given the existing rules, amendments are politically *very* difficult to make, which some may consider a virtue and others a defect. For sure this issue makes it difficult to bring the constitution more in line with today's prevalent thinking, especially in some areas, such as, for example, the right to bear arms or constraints on some actions by the president or by Congress.

The fundamental and often highly debated and criticized, but not challenged, role of the US Supreme Court, in interpreting the US Constitution, has allowed it to continue to play an active and decisive role in current American decisions. The nine members of the Court have a status unmatched in other countries. However, the splits among the justices of the Supreme Court, and the facts that the justices are nominated by the president and approved by the Senate when there are vacancies and that they are presumably chosen because of their known, a priori views on sensitive issues, have given rise to controversies and to sharp criticisms over some of the decisions made by the Court, especially when the decisions have been made with a five-to-four split, meaning there was no clear interpretation of the constitution by the judges. The decisions could have easily gone the other way if one of the justices had been appointed at a different time and by a different president.

Constitutional principles cannot be compared to God's commands for believers, as expressed in the Bible or in similar religious statements, because these principles reflect the views of simple mortals with their inevitable biases. Perhaps more importantly, they reflect the views of *some* mortals at the time when the document was drafted. When the randomness of the appointment of a single justice of the US Supreme Court can make a big difference in the policies of the United States, there should be something to worry about. This may be *rule of law*, but it is a rule of law that at times mystifies many. That same rule of law had allowed slavery until 1864 and legal separation between the races in some states until the 1968.

Examples of constitutional principles that are not too clear or specific, allowing them to be reinterpreted easily, abound. A good example, chosen from the current Italian Constitution, is Article 81. That article had been intended to prevent reliance on deficit financing of public spending by the Italian government when the new constitution was approved in 1948 to replace the one of 1848. The article had been pushed by Luigi Einaudi, a prominent economist and political figure who, among many important political positions that he held, was also president of Italy. The 1948 constitution was much more specific than the one of 1848 that it replaced. In the mid-1960s, when deficit financing had become fashionable and, to many economists, less sinful than in the past, because of the growing popularity of the Keynesian Revolution, the Italian Constitutional Court had reinterpreted Article 81 in a way that has not prevented the occurrence of large fiscal deficits and the accumulation of a large and worrisome public debt (in 2017, 133 percent of GDP). The Court simply classified the money obtained from the sale of public bonds as "revenue" available to finance spending. Pronto, Article 81 had been made innocuous.

Examples of too restrictive constitutional limits are also common, as found, for example, in the Brazilian Constitution of 1988. That document was legislated to prevent the recurrence of some fiscal problems that had occurred in previous years (excessive foreign borrowing by states and excessive use of "inflationary finance") and to promote specific social policies.

However, the new constitution prevented the *national* government from making important and badly needed reforms in the fiscal relations between different levels of governments, while it forced the government to allocate large amounts of national resources to specific categories of spending, creating growing fiscal difficulties for the *national* government.

Other examples of too restrictive constitutions are the Indian Constitution, which had prevented the introduction of a national sales tax while allowing Indian states to continue imposing some obstacles to trade among themselves, and the Pakistani Constitution, which has limited the scope of any sales tax imposed by the national government to only goods (excluding services) and has prevented the taxation of agricultural incomes. The Swiss Constitution sets limits to the tax rates and makes it difficult for the government to change those limits.

There would be inevitable debate among impartial observers in determining which constitution (the American or the Italian) should have more legitimacy in guiding the economic and social behavior of *modern* societies in a *globalized* world. The important point being made is that *both are the product of the time when they were written.* The US Constitution has the merit (?) of being vague on economic issues, and by being vague it is more adaptable to a modern market economy, one that is good for "capitalist development." The Italian Constitution has the defect (?) of being too specific and of giving too much power to workers.

The limitations to property rights imposed by the Italian Constitution must be compared with Edmund Burke's conservative opinion that "a law against property is a law against industry," or with Adam Smith's opinion that "the acquisition of valuable and extensive property ... necessarily requires the establishment of civil government. Where there is no property ... civil government is not so necessary" (both are cited in Landes, 1999, pp. 32 and 33, respectively). Not surprisingly, both of these statements are closer in spirit to the sentiments expressed in the US Constitution than to those in the Italian Constitution, and both reflect the political forces and the times when they were written.

If the proper economic role of the state in a market economy requires the strong protection of property rights, held by individuals and by enterprises, as much recent economic literature has argued – see Landes (1999), North and Thomas (1973), and North and Weingast (1989) – the Italian Constitution, at least in its formal declarations, is surely reluctant to assign that role to the state. It should, thus, not be surprising that economic policies and institutions in Italy, which are, as they should be, much influenced by jurists, have developed in line with the Italian Constitution. At times, they have allowed policies (such as the expropriation of land with very low or no compensation to the owners, rent controls, the occupation of privately-owned but unoccupied houses by local governments, the failure by enterprises to fire unneeded workers, and controls over interest rates. All these actions were not consistent with the principle of protection of property (see Tanzi, 2015a). This may also explain why Italy has had one of the lowest scores, in terms of "economic liberty," among the many countries assessed by the experts of the Economic Freedom Network. On the other hand, the distribution of income in Italy has not become as uneven in recent decades as it has in the United States.

In conclusion, the importance of the positive or negative role that constitutions play in determining the quality of the public sector in democratic countries with market economies cannot be exaggerated. In democratic countries, constitutions encourage, facilitate, or allow certain actions, while they prevent others on the part of the governing body and of citizens. They especially influence the behavior and the actions of public employees and the relations between national and subnational governments and with the rest of the world. At least in principle, the laws and the regulations that govern a democratic country should be consistent with the constitutional principles of that country, as interpreted by a Supreme Court. Whether they are also consistent with the principle that would be the best one to guide countries in a globalized, modern world, at a particular time, and to do so in an equitable way is a more difficult question to answer.

In recent years, there have been attempts by some countries to try to "modernize" their constitutions. The results have been questionable. These attempts have resolved some problems, while they have created others, as happened in Brazil. The revised constitutions have been at times poorly formulated and have become more complex, more specific, and, at times, more confusing. An attempt some years ago to create a constitution for the European Union, which involved two eminent European personalities (a former president of France and a former prime minister of Italy who was also a constitutional scholar), resulted in an extremely long and complex document, and the attempt was aborted.

When constitutions are subjected to frequent revisions, as has been the case in some Latin American and African countries, they tend to lose their status as reliable compasses for actions and for behavior. When they are rarely revised, they risk becoming too rigid or too anachronistic, and their interpretations by the Supreme Courts are inevitably and increasingly subjected to criticism. This has happened to some extent in the United States.

James Buchanan and Francesco Forte, the latter an Italian scholar who was also finance minister, in some of their writings argued that the economic or fiscal role of constitutions should be that of establishing *limits* to governmental action, as is presumably done by the Swiss Constitution. According to these authors, the constitutions should stress what the state cannot do, rather than what it *should* do (see Forte, 1998). These authors have favored limitations to tax rates, to levels of public spending, or to fiscal deficits. They would presumably favor the establishment of "fiscal councils" and would give strong legal powers to them.

The problem, once again, is that what the state needs to do in an economy and what the citizens expect it to do evolve with the passing of time, creating gaps between the two. What may not have been seen as essential at the time when constitutions were enacted might be seen as essential by the majority of citizens at later times, but the original rules may have made it difficult to make changes. This may be the case today with respect to laws that would allow the government to regulate the buying and wearing of weapons that have become more and more lethal. Clearly, "the right of the people to keep and bear Arms," introduced by Amendment II to the US Constitution on December 15, 1791, was highly justified. But many question whether it has the same justification in 2017.

Various kinds of "fiscal rules" have become common in various countries in recent years. They did not exist at the time when the Keynesian Revolution was in full swing. That revolution favored giving a lot of discretion to presumably wise and benevolent policymakers, especially in the conduct of fiscal policies. During that period, fiscal rules (especially the balanced-budget rule) had been seen by leading Keynesian economists, including Samuelson and Tobin, as relics of the past, because they tied the hands of governments and prevented them from pursuing desirable (countercyclical and welfare) policies. In the views of many economists, debated by others, the fiscal experiences of more recent years have led to the questioning of the wisdom of providing too much discretion to policymakers.

The basic objective of fiscal rules is often, though not always, precisely that of reducing government discretion, while playing down the potential, but now more questionable, government role in stabilizing the economy and in increasing welfare, through actions that require increases in public spending and in public debt (see Kopits, 2013). The question remains whether the fiscal limits (imposed by the fiscal rules and by the political forces that prevail at the time when the rules are imposed) should be relevant for other times and for different situations.

The Maastricht's "Stability and Growth Pact," which accompanied the creation of the European Monetary Union, might be seen as an example of such limits, imposed by a rule set by a political agreement among European governments. The Maastricht rules were opposed and have continued to be criticized by economists and individuals who want to give more discretion and more flexibility to the actions of governments, but also by individuals who want the Pact to have more force in restricting governmental behavior.

The Role of Specific Laws

While a constitution sets, or should set, general *principles* that guide a country's policies, the latter are permitted and guided by specific *laws*. The quality of the public sector is enhanced when the laws that, in a country, determine the behavior of citizens and enterprises are relatively few, are clearly written (and, thus, are not subject to conflicting interpretations or to asymmetry in their knowledge or in their use among citizens), are comprehensive in their coverage, are not in conflict among themselves, and are easily accessible and broadly known and understood by most citizens.

Difficulties arise when, in a country, the laws are many, are long, are not clearly written, do not cover all the relevant areas of economic activities, and/or provide conflicting signals to those who must obey them. Unfortunately, these difficulties have become more common than is generally realized. In most countries the Roman principle that "ignorance of the laws is no excuse" is still a guiding principle.

It has been reported by legal experts that while some European countries have relatively few (that is, relatively few *thousand*) active laws, others may have tens or even hundreds of thousands. (See, for example, Ferro et al., 1999.) It may, thus, be difficult for a normal citizen, even for an educated one, to find one's way in this legal jungle, which may contain many dark, or not fully charted, paths or spots. In countries such as the United States, laws on specific issues (for example, the relatively recent laws on the reform of the financial market, of the health sector, and some others) often contain thousands of pages and are written in a language ("legalese") that only, or mainly, highly trained and clever lawyers or accountants may be able to understand. They have increasingly been written by lawyers for lawyers, changing the "rule of law" into a "rule of lawyers."

A problem that occurs in several countries is that, when a new law is enacted, the laws that had been approved in the past, covering related areas and which are still valid, are not always carefully scrutinized and, if necessary, revised, to make sure that all the elements of the newly enacted law are consistent with the old laws. Often, this scrutiny does not take place. Given the fact that there are many existing laws and, especially, that they are not always clearly written, it is almost impossible to ascertain whether the whole legal system has remained internally consistent. Elements imbedded in past laws that are still on the books may come into conflict with the new laws. When this happens, the directives that the laws should provide to the citizens (or often to the lawyers who represent them), and to the institutions charged with implementing the programs or establishing the related regulations, get confused.

This problem could be defined as one of *legal inconsistency*. It often characterizes also the relations between national and subnational governments, or between, for example, pension and health programs, on one hand, and annual budget laws, on the other. For example, the budget law may assign a given budgetary allocation for the public health sector, but the laws that determine the performance of the public health sector may imply (or require) a higher spending level than the one allocated in the budget. (See Reviglio, 1999, for specific examples from Italy.) Zoning laws and laws dealing with the environment also suffer from this problem. At times, a law and, thus, a given institution may authorize a certain land use, but another law and another institution may prohibit it. These conflicts may lead to costly mistakes and to uncertainty about property rights and may affect negatively some market decisions. At times the conflict is discovered only after a lot of money has been spent by some private investors on particular investments. (See Tanzi, 2015a, for Italian examples.)

Another problem that has become common, especially but not only in the United States, is the aforementioned great and growing length and complexity of new laws. Like many individuals, laws have become fatter with the passing of time. To some extent they reflect the increasing complexity of new economic and social activities and the tendency of modern governments to attempt to deal with too many issues and to address too many specific problems. As mentioned, some of these new laws are thousands of pages long. Because of this characteristic, they are often voted for and approved by policymakers (members of Congress or Parliaments, ministers, and presidents) who do not have the time to read them, or, even if they had the time, might not have the specialized knowledge to understand their full context (see Tanzi, 2011).

On the issue of the length of laws, it may be worthwhile to cite the reaction of two US Supreme Court justices, Scalia and Breyer, when they were confronted with the Obama health care law. As Justice Scalia put it,

"You really want us to go through these 2700 pages? And do you expect the Court to do it?" And as Justice Breyer put it, "I haven't read every word of that … There is the mandate in the community, this is Titles I and II, the mandate, the community, preexisting condition … OK? There is bio-similarity, there is breast-feeding, there is promoting nurses and doctors to serve underserved areas, there is Class Act, etc. … So what do you propose to do other than spend a year reading all this?" These reactions were reported in newspaper articles.

This problem facilitates the insertion in the laws of words or sentences that may go unobserved during the approval process but that are important to some specific groups or individuals and that may benefit, especially, the interests that those groups represent. For example, a newspaper article dealing with the US health care law put it as follows: "The words were tucked deep into the sprawling text of President Obama's signature health care overhaul … [There] was a brief provision restricting the ability of doctors to gather data about the patients' gun use … The language [had been] pushed by the National Rifle Association in the final weeks of the 2010 debate over health care and [was] discovered only in recent days by some lawmakers and medical groups" (article by Peter Wallstein and Tom Hamburger, *Washington Post*, December 31, 2012, p. 1). That was an illuminating, but not rare, example of a growing invasion of unnoticed termites in the laws of countries. Complexity may often be a response to populist demands for "excessive" personalization of laws. But it can easily become an instrument for some groups to promote their specific interests in nontransparent ways.

As mentioned, the quality of the public sector is enhanced when: (a) the laws are written clearly and they cover the necessary areas; (b) they do not lead either the public or the public officials to conflicting interpretations; (c) their number is as small as feasible; (d) they are not in conflict among themselves; and (e) they are not so long and so complex that they make it difficult for those who are responsible for approving, enforcing, and following them to carefully read them. It should be a growing worry when the laws make it possible for some individuals to introduce in the text (often in a nontransparent way) some words that are not noted by those who must approve the laws, but that have the intent of helping those individuals, or their clients, at some point in the future. It is also a worry when those who have the responsibility to vote on the laws do so without having carefully read them.

Over the years there have been attempts by a few countries (France, Australia, Italy, and New Zealand) either to codify the existing laws or to simplify them. However, these actions, which require a lot of effort and which generate benefits only over the long run to future governments, do not get the needed political and sustained support by the current governments. It is one of the many and common cases where good policies are not introduced, or efforts are not made, because the costs are immediate and fall on the current governments, while the benefits from those operations would go to future governments. This creates an asymmetry in time in the distribution of costs and benefits among different governments of the same countries. This asymmetry has an impact on the political evaluation of the cost-benefit ratio of some actions.

Regulations and Informal Rules

In previous chapters we discussed various aspects of regulations. Laws often must be accompanied by *regulations* to give them specific content. Regulations may be legislated and thus may be laws themselves; or they may be issued by public or quasi-public agencies legally authorized to issue and to enforce regulations for citizens and enterprises in specific areas. These regulations give content to some laws. For example, in the United States, laws related to the environment are the Clean Air Act, the Clean Water Act, and the Safe Drinking Water Act. They were enacted in the 1970s when concern about the environment had become intense. Other laws specify objectives or goals to be achieved in other areas, such as the Clean Energy Act or acts related to the financial market, consumer protection, and others.

These laws specify a goal to be achieved but not how it is to be achieved. The task of promoting the objective and of monitoring and regulating particular areas (quality of water, air, etc.) was given to specific public institutions, such as the Food and Drug Administration, the Environmental Protection Agency (EPA), the Securities and Exchange Commission, the Internal Revenue Service, and several others. These institutions now have thousands of employees who study regulations to be issued to determine whether they will likely achieve the intent of the original laws. Additionally, there are regulations issued by local governments (or even by private institutions) that cover activities in areas over which those governments or institutions have some jurisdiction or control. And there are regulations issued by international organizations of which countries are members, such as the World Trade Organization the International Monetary Fund and the European Union.

The regulations that have direct economic implications cover several broad categories. They include strictly economic regulations, safety regulations (including those dealing with transportation, food, the environment, financial activities, drugs, and medical issues), informational regulations, and, increasingly, behavioral regulations. All of the regulations are likely to have some economic implications and to create benefits for some and costs for others. The regulations may specify and clarify procedures; they may elaborate on general instructions contained in laws; or, simply, they may impose behavioral requirements on actions by individuals and enterprises to make them comply with the objectives indicated by the laws. In many cases the laws that have been approved by the legislature require elaborations to increase their transparency, to give them more focus, and to make them more specific for those who will be guided by them. These elaborations may take years to complete and may lead to the creation of future regulations.

In the United States the proposed regulations ("Notices of Proposed Rulemaking") are published in the *Federal Register* to elicit public reactions and comments before they are entered in the Code of Federal Regulations (the CFR), which since 1926 has been the official register of all the US federal regulations. The CFR is divided in fifty volumes. Title 40 lists most of the environmental regulations. Other countries may have different procedures from those of the United States.

During the creation of a specific regulation by a regulatory agency, for example, the EPA, lobbying groups will try to influence the government officials who are working on the specific decision. The objective of the lobbyists and of other interested individuals is to change the regulation in an effort to make it more favorable to their clients' interests or less costly to them. In many cases the regulations are seen to be increasing costs by the enterprises and the individuals to which they apply. Therefore, the regulations will be opposed by them. Others may not consider the regulations as fully satisfying the objectives specified by the law (i.e., ensuring clean air, clean water, etc.). In the United States and in other countries regulations covering taxation, the financial market, the environment, and the pharmaceutical sector have become progressively more detailed and more numerous. They now require thousands of pages in the CFR or in similar registers.

The EPA's National Ambient Air Quality Standards (NAAQS), for example, have been given the responsibility to regulate air quality standards using available scientific evidence (from the United States and other countries) about the link that exists between air quality and illnesses and premature deaths. Using scientific and other types of knowledge other agencies are responsible for creating regulations in other areas in which the law has given specific instructions.

Regulations issued by an executive authority, or by a regulatory agency, may be complex and not easily understood by the general public. Occasionally, they may overlap with other existing regulations, creating conflicts with other regulatory agencies. In some countries regulations may not even be published or be easily available to the public, as they are in the United States. As an OECD report put it some years ago, "regulation is [today] perhaps the most pervasive form of state intervention in economic activity" (1999, p. 179), and it has been becoming progressively more so with the passing of time. This has lead, inevitably, to increasing challenges from the regulated enterprises and complaints about excessive regulation from libertarians and conservative politicians who continue to dream about a world with few limitations on the total liberty of individuals from governmental interference. See, for example Boaz, 2015.

As mentioned in an earlier chapter, intentionally or unintentionally, regulations often affect all of the basic roles of the state, and not just the role of *allocation* of resources and economic growth. They often affect the *distribution* of income that the market delivers. For example, regulations that have restricted the production of coal, because of its impact on the environment, have been blamed for increasing poverty in coal-producing regions such as West Virginia. In Europe, fishermen have complained about restrictions on fishing during particular periods of the year or on the use of some fishing nets. In particular cases, regulations can also affect aggregate demand when they change the propensity or the timing of enterprises and individuals to undertake some investments or to start new activities. Therefore, when regulations are changed, they can have an impact on the macroeconomic performance of an economy, even in the short run, and on the stabilization role of governments.

Some governments may intentionally time the introduction of particular regulations in order to influence, in directions favorable to them, the results of elections. Regulations that might be costly to some favored groups may be intentionally delayed until after the elections, while those favorable may be anticipated. Some politicians may base their political campaigns on promises to draw back existing regulations to invite the support of particular groups or regions. Obviously, changes in governments may bring important changes in attitudes and in policies vis-à-vis regulations. This is again an area in which short run benefits can bring significant long run costs, or short run costs can bring long run benefits, as with policies that deal with global warming.

There may be at work a *fundamental law of regulations*. As countries become more developed, they tend to require and to introduce more regulations. Wagner's famous law of growing public-sector activity, when countries' economies develop, may be interpreted in this way, more than in terms of public spending, as it has normally been interpreted. As countries develop, regulations tend to become more numerous, more complex, and, for some groups or for some sectors of the economy, more costly to observe.

Some countries (or some states or regions within federal countries) tend to favor having more regulations than others. For example, in Europe, France and Italy have more regulations than does the United Kingdom. In the United States, California has more regulations than does Texas. Antagonism to regulations imposed by the European Union, including, for example, the requirement for member states to indicate distances on national road signs in meters and kilometers, rather than in feet, yards, and miles, was reported (by a *Financial Times* story) to have been one of the reasons why some UK voters cast their vote in support of Brexit!

Economic development, growing urbanization, and, especially, population density, technological advances, and changes in social attitudes lead to greater actual or perceived need for more controls, by governments, on the actions of individuals and enterprises that may generate negative externalities for others. This, inevitably, creates the danger that governmental intervention may go too far and may be abused, or that it may be introduced as an excuse to excessively restrict personal freedom or to favor some groups over others. This situation may also create opportunities for corruption. Democratically enacted laws are often behind regulations, at least in democratic countries. We must recognize, though we may not wish to accept, the possibility, recognized long ago by Benito Mussolini, that "the more complicated the forms assumed by civilization, the more restricted the freedom of the individual must become" (cited in Hayek, [1944] 2007, p. 91).

Because *some* forms of regulations do not require budgetary appropriations, or may not even require formal approval by the legislature, once the regulations have been justified by broad laws, they tend to be less scrutinized by the legislators and by the *general* public. At the same time, some of the regulations tend to be *more* scrutinized by (and more influenced by the pressures of) specific lobbies. There may thus be a tendency, on the part of governments, to oversupply regulations in some areas, and to adjust and dilute others, to make them more palatable to particular groups.

The regulations that are pushed by particular groups may be opposed by other groups, which may see them as restrictions on *their* liberty or (in the case of enterprises) on their freedom of actions, resulting in higher costs and reduced profits. This has been frequently the case with environmental and financial regulations, or regulations restricting behavior such as smoking in public, generating load noises in public, or, increasingly, using some ingredients (fats and sugar) in processed foods or drinks.

The interpretation of regulations is left to the bureaucracies that must administer them and, increasingly, to the lawyers and the lobbyists of the regulated activities who specialize in and become experts on particular areas. Because of the high compensations that the latter individuals get for their lobbying activities, some of the regulated areas have been attracting to lobbyism individuals of great ability or politicians who in the past had occupied high public positions. These lobbyists are the ones that often face the less well-paid government personnel. In some sectors of the economy lawyers and lobbyists have become particularly active and influential. These activities or sectors also happen to be those that have become increasingly important in the economies of advanced countries, where they account for increasingly large shares of national income and of national profits.

Not surprisingly, some literature has identified regulations as one of the major areas in which corruption can grow. The government bureaucrats in charge of these areas often find themselves in positions where they can use and abuse their power to derive personal advantage and to provide benefits to those who directly, or indirectly (for example, through promises of well-remunerated jobs), try to bribe them (see Tanzi, 1998b). Revolving-door policies, for individuals who leave government jobs where they had been dealing with the generation or the administration of regulations, allow some of them to go to work at better-paid jobs on the other side. Regulators in subnational or local levels of governments are more easily influenced by regulated enterprises operating in those jurisdictions. The latter can contribute financially to the high costs of the elections for strategically placed local politicians. It is no surprise that corruption tends to be more frequent at the subnational level (see Tanzi, 2000b, chapter 14).

Various studies have shown that some regulations are important in promoting the public interest, while some can impose large welfare costs on the economy. It all depends on the weight of the benefits and the costs (financial and social) that the regulations impose on society. For this reason, countries should do their best to limit the introduction of regulations to only *essential* ones, when the social benefits clearly exceed the social costs. However, in a world that is becoming progressively more complex, what some individuals (and some regulatory agencies such as the EPA) see as *essential regulations*, others may see as *unnecessary* and freedom-reducing, or simply cost-increasing, ones. This conflict has appeared with increasing frequency in regulations that aim at protecting the quality of the air and water or protecting endangered species, that limit hunting activities, that protect the environment from potentially damaging contaminants, and that concern the food and drug and the energy industries.

At times the differences in opinions between opposing sides, on the need for some regulations, rest on judgments about still-debatable scientific results concerning their impact, results that are challenged by the lawyers of the regulated enterprises and of some regions or states, because the results are not considered definitive, or because the estimated social benefits from the regulations are considered too minor to justify the economic costs that they impose on the enterprises. Some think tanks or lobbyists, such as American Action Forum (AAF), produce large "estimates" of the presumed environmental burdens that regulations impose on society and the economy. Of course, some question the validity of these estimates, which tend to give more weight to the financial costs of the regulations for the enterprises and less to the benefits for society.

The problem is that even *scientific* studies often leave some uncertainty. And there is often no testing of the negative impact of some chemicals in the air and in the water. In some cases the regulatory agencies are faulted for not revealing the full evidence that has led them to justify a specific regulation, or, alternatively, for not testing for some contaminants in the air, water, or food, due to lack of resources. At the same time, the "Courts, [which] are expected to ensure the accountability of agency actions through their legal oversight role ... on matters of science policy ... do not have the expertise of the agencies" (see Pascual et al., 2013, p. 1,680). These authors concluded that their "study revealed an increasingly rigorous and substantive engagement in the courts' review of scientific challenges to the EPA's NAAQS over time," and that "the courts and agencies ... appear to work symbiotically ... on the establishment of rigorous analytical yardsticks to guide the decision process [of the NAAQS]" (ibid.). Some critics are likely to question that conclusion.

At other times the differences in judgment about particular regulations rest on the value assigned to personal liberty, against some, possibly minor, negative externalities. For example, some may object that they are not allowed to listen to the commentators of football or basketball games on a television in a restaurant, because other patrons want to eat in relative quiet. The use of cellular phones in public places, including on trains, also creates conflicts and requests for regulations. The use of cellular phones while driving has become an area of concern, because of the impact that it has on accidents. Some have been calling for strict regulations of that use, which undoubtedly others will oppose.

It has become increasingly clear that, in some areas, the absence or delay in introducing some regulations may lead to great, but delayed, costs for society. This clearly happened with the delay in regulations related to smoking in public places, which in later years led and is still leading to more cases of lung cancer and other illnesses. It may happen again with regulations related to some environmental problems, such as air and water pollution, or direct health problems, such as the excessive use of sugar in soft drinks and cereals or some fats in processed foods. The latter have been blamed for obesity in many countries and for the increasing incidence of some illnesses, such as diabetes and heart problems. In the United States life expectancy in 2016 was reported to have fallen for the first time since 1993. Recently, Mexico, the city of Philadelphia, and some other jurisdictions saw it necessary to introduce a tax on the use of sugar in soft drinks. Several cities in Europe and elsewhere have forbidden the circulation of diesel cars, because of the lead they put in the atmosphere. These regulations are liberty-reducing for some but life-lengthening for others.

Because of the dynamic character of modern societies, and because of the quickly changing nature of technological changes, it is common to find countries with anachronistic, useless, or clearly damaging regulations on some activities, while they still do not have some necessary, new regulations on other activities. Some regulations have been introduced either to protect citizens against unscrupulous sellers of some products or to protect particular workers against dangers connected with their working conditions. In a world with quickly changing technologies, it is easy to see what economic costs useless regulations, or regulations that are needed but not imposed, can impose on society.

The problem is that there is no well-organized process that attempts to keep the regulations close to some desirable or "optimal" level at a given time, while there are strong political forces, or simply inertia, that tend to retain the existing regulations or to prevent new, necessary ones from being introduced. Therefore, the use of regulations is an area of public-sector activity in which excesses and scarcity tend to coexist, both leading to suboptimal results and criticisms by some.

In recent years many countries and the European Union have been struggling to introduce useful regulations for the financial and banking sector, for the use of the information superhighway (Internet), for genetic research, for the use of new drugs, for the production of new energy, and for several other important new areas. In all of these cases there have been opposing camps, each presenting arguments for why a new regulation should or should not be introduced, or why an existing regulation should or should not be removed. And in some of these cases there are obstacles created by the multicountry or the global scope of the needed regulations. It is not surprising that regulation has become a highly contested area of government activity.

In conclusion, a high-quality public sector must have enough clear and useful rules to guide economic (and other) activities. The rules must not be so numerous, or be so vague, as (a) to give excessive power to bureaucrats; (b) to restrict normal and valuable economic activities; (c) to restrict more than necessary the economic freedom of individuals and of enterprises; or (d) to create regulatory uncertainty among those who must make economic decisions. At the same time, the regulations should not be so scarce, or be enforced in such a relaxed way, as to allow the continuation, or the acceleration, of significant economic problems.

A world with too many regulations can become stagnant and too restraining, as some European countries have been accused of having become. A world with too few regulations may not become a free and efficient world, as some claim, but may come to reflect the environment shown by movies about the American West, when the fastest guns won the short run fights, and the fastest guns were not necessarily on the good side.

In general and ideally, the rules should clearly specify what is *not* allowed, rather than require authorizations for what is allowed. The need for authorizations gives too much power to some bureaucrats who acquire a kind of monopoly power on certain actions, and often leads to acts of corruption. Unfortunately, this approach is not always practical to implement in today's world, because, from time to time, there appear new and potentially damaging products and activities that had not been anticipated by the regulations introduced in the past and, thus, have not been forbidden. Many will argue that, presumably, this is what happened in the financial sector after it was greatly liberalized in the 1990s and when monetary policy became too accommodating. The financial sector became very complex, and it became complex in ways that had not been anticipated. In the view of many experts, the complexity and the lack of needed rules played significant roles in the subprime financial crisis.

Similar issues have arisen in recent years in energy production, especially in "fracking." That activity brought significant benefits to consumers in terms of low gas and oil prices, and to workers in terms of job creation. It also created new and not yet well understood environmental costs, including potential water contamination. Similar problems are associated with other areas where bureaucratic intervention is needed but, when it comes, may not always be the optimal one. Whenever possible, the discretion of bureaucrats in interpreting old or new rules should be kept at a minimum to prevent corruption and to discourage lobbying, but again this is not always possible.

In some countries, particular activities, for example, a request for a tax incentive or an application to open a small enterprise, may require a large number of authorizations, signed by as many public employees, in many different agencies or offices. (See De Soto, 1989, and various reports by the IFC at the World Bank.) Discretion opens the possibility for some bureaucrats to extract bribes from the regulated, and for the regulated to offer bribes. And when there are no bribes, discretion may slow down economic activity, especially when bureaucrats are reluctant to make decisions for which, later, they might be criticized. This has become a problem in some countries and in some local jurisdictions.

An important, though clearly demanding and possibly unrealistic, step would be to make periodic, systematic surveys (say, every ten years) of all the existing regulations in a particular area of the economy and to create a kind of virtual "regulatory budget." That budget would aim at removing regulations that have become redundant, anachronistic, and damaging, and at adding new, necessary ones, while clarifying confusing regulations. Such a process would be inevitably costly, but if done well, could contribute to raising the overall quality of the public sector. It would be more difficult to implement in countries with various levels of governments, for example, in federations, where national and subnational governments might have conflicting powers, as in the United States, Canada, Brazil, Argentina, and several other countries. This is different from the regulatory budget that some have proposed that would fix the number of regulations. Such a budget makes no sense.

Another useful step, which has been attempted in some countries, would be the creation of a one-stop, or "single window," center, where individuals would be able to obtain all the permits and all the authorizations needed for some activities or actions. Such centers have been created in a few places and are reported to have led to the elimination of some existing regulations, as well as a reduction in corruption and in the time needed to obtain necessary authorizations. These centers integrate in one office the provision of permits and authorizations needed from one level of government, for example, municipalities. In a *unitary* country they could authorize the regulations for the whole public sector. However, in *federations* with various government levels and powers, these offices cannot provide the authorizations or the permits needed for all levels. There are also some types of regulations that would not lend themselves to such a process.

Informal Norms

In addition to the formal, constitutional principles and to the rules specified in the laws and in the regulations, the quality of the public sector is also affected by informal norms or arrangements that influence in most countries the economic behavior of individuals in the public administration and that of the public sector in general. Such norms: (a) may influence the choice of presidents, ministers, and other high-level officials; (b) may characterize appointments in the civil service; and (c) may influence contacts between the public and the private sector. These informal norms may be based on religious, social, or political relations. Being of an informal nature, and being based on cultural characteristics, they may be more difficult to change. Still, the application of the "arm's length principle" and of the rule of law to all aspects of public-sector behavior should be a goal in the search for a high-quality public sector (see Tanzi, 1995). Such principles may occasionally conflict with other objectives, such as giving some preferences to groups that have suffered from past discrimination, such as minorities, invalids, women, and others, unless these preferences are clearly specified in legislation.

Other informal rules may play an important role. One of these is punctuality, clearly an important aspect of efficiency (see Landon, 1982; Tanzi, 2015a). When authorizations and permits are necessary, it becomes important to know how quickly they could be obtained. They may involve building permits, driver's licenses, passports, authorizations to practice a given profession, and others. An efficient public sector should satisfy the punctuality requirement with respect to appointments and should keep short the time needed to obtain required permits or authorizations. This simple rule is ignored in many countries. There are places where an appointment means nothing and one may have to wait for hours to see a relevant public official, and weeks or even months to obtain required permits or authorizations. It is obvious that in these cases the public sector can become a major obstacle to the pursuit of economic efficiency. The delay in getting medical appointments and in scheduling needed medical procedures is one of the major complaints in countries that have universal public health systems. They make medical care available to everyone, but at great nonfinancial costs.

The constitution, the laws, and the regulations establish the broad legal framework within which the public sector should operate; or, putting it differently, they set the rules of the game that should determine the behavior of the public sector and the operation of the market. The importance of these rules cannot be underestimated. Over the years, several authors, including Buchanan, Alesina, von Hagen, Poterba, Tabellini, and Persson, have argued that political arrangements such as fiscal federalism and fiscal decentralization; proportional or nonproportional representation by political parties in parliaments; the frequency of elections; the choice of presidential versus nonpresidential types of governments; the role and power of the ministry of finance compared to those of spending ministries; the rules that apply to the budgetary process – for example, whether it starts with top-down macroeconomic constraints, which reflect a collective view on priorities, or whether it allows a bottom-up process, by which pressures for spending are determined through the political influence of different ministers – whether parliaments can modify the content of budgetary proposals or whether they must vote on the whole budget; whether the central bank is truly independent; whether its mandate relates only to the maintenance of price stability or involves other objectives, such as employment, financial stability, assistance in the financing of governments, and so on – all of these arrangements have a significant impact on fiscal and macroeconomic outcomes. Various situations have been modeled, often using strong assumptions and sophisticated game theories, and have also been subjected to empirical testing (see, inter alia, Tabellini and Persson, 2000; Poterba and von Hagen, 1999).

This literature, which at times has given conflicting results, cannot be reviewed here. While recognizing its importance and its potential contribution to explaining economic policy, the focus of this book is on other aspects. Political and procedural rules are more likely to affect policies, rather than the quality of the public sector or of public institutions, as they are defined in this book. It is the institutions and those who represent the institutions that confront the citizens and that implement the policies. But, of course, by changing the incentives under which policymakers and institutions operate, the political and procedural rules may affect the behavior and the quality of the institutions and of the public sector.

CHAPTER 26

The Quality of Public Institutions

The quality of the public sector may be affected by the *absence* of some essential institutions or by the *poor performance* of the existing ones. For example, in many countries, there are no institutions responsible for enforcing competition; for forcing full disclosure by financial and other institutions; for requesting the publication of good accounts on the part of enterprises whose shares are traded in the stock market; for keeping track of the outcomes from public spending; and so on. Most countries do not have fiscal councils or similar institutions that keep track, in a competent way, of fiscal developments and that assess objectively the sustainability of fiscal policy. This allows some governments to put out data on fiscal variables that are misleading. As a consequence, the public sector and the private market may function less well. Cronyism, insider information, corruption, monopoly power, absence of essential information, and other problems that to some extent exist in many countries may become more common and more damaging.

The performance of particular public institutions depends on various factors, which include but are not limited to: (a) tradition and reputation; (b) the quantity and quality of the resources available to them; (c) the discretion that the managers of the institutions have over hiring and organizational matters; (d) the clarity of their mandate; (e) their organization; (f) the incentives faced by those who operate in them; (g) the quality of the leadership and of the staff; and (h) the existence of accountability offices.

Take, for example, one of the most fundamental institutions of the public sector, the tax administration. Its performance will depend, in part, on its tradition and reputation. A tax administration that has been efficient, honest, and proud in the past is likely to value that reputation and to continue to live up to it in the future, unless it faces major, fundamental shocks. The reason is that there is inertia in reputations and in efficiency standards. By the same token, it is very difficult in the short run for a government to change a corrupt and inefficient administration into an honest and efficient one. At times countries have been forced to close corrupt administrations and to replace them with new ones in order to introduce fundamental changes, starting from scratch. This was done in Peru in the 1990s (see Tanzi, 2010b).

The performance of tax administrations will depend on the resources available to them and the freedom that their administrators have to hire capable employees, to pay competitive salaries, to invest in new technologies, to carry out necessary audits and controls of taxpayers, to fire corrupt or inefficient employees, and so on. There have been cases of tax administrations (for example, in Jamaica in the 1970s) where financial resources became so scarce that the tax administration was unable to send inspectors to the premises of taxpayers for necessary audits. There were no funds to buy gasoline for the available vehicles. There have also been cases where the tax administrations have been forced to hire incompetent or corrupt employees, because of the latter's political connections.

The clarity of the mandate – for example, the mandate to enforce fairly and objectively the tax laws as legislated by the legislative branches – is important. Day-to-day independence from political pressures is essential. When the mandate becomes unclear, either because the laws are not transparent, or because the institutions are subjected to political or other pressures that force them to accommodate the special circumstances of some politically well-connected taxpayers, problems are likely to develop. This was the case in some transition economies in the 1990s and continues to be the case in some developing countries today. Occasionally, it has also been reported to be the case in some advanced countries. Political interference may reduce the quality of the tax administrations. The organization of tax administrations to reflect the use of modern technologies and organizations is also important, and so is the set of incentives that they face.

These aspects have attracted attention in recent years from administration experts (see Shome, 2012; Shah, 2005). It should be added that the more complex the tax laws become, the more difficult it will be for a tax administration to administer them. Tax complexity has become a growing problem in many countries, in some more than in others (see Tanzi, 2013a).

If an institution is poorly organized, if good and bad performances by its employees are equally and poorly compensated, or if their managers are chosen for political reasons and not for their competence, the contributions of the institution to the quality of the public sector will be compromised. There have been attempts, in recent years, at strengthening incentives by making tax administrations politically more independent (like central banks have been assumed to be), and by negotiating explicit contracts between governments and tax administrations, contracts that specify the expected level of performance with respect to some quantitative variable, such as tax collection or returns audited. In Australia, for example, the government guarantees to the tax administration a given level of resources over a three-year-period, while the tax administration commits itself to delivering specified outcomes and quantified outputs. The ratio of the cost of collection to tax revenue may play some role in these contracts (see, for example, Highfield, 1999).

This brings into the picture two other important and related aspects of public institutions, namely: (a) the synergy among public institutions; and (b) the enforcement mechanisms. These are treated as two separate aspects, although, to a large extent, they could be considered two faces of the same coin. Like elements of an ecological system, public institutions work together and support one another. Therefore, it may not be possible to have, for example, a first-class tax administration in an environment where other relevant institutions, such as the treasury or the judiciary, or even the post office, do not function well. In countries where tax evaders are often not punished by the courts, or are punished with excessive delay, it will be more difficult to fight tax evasion. In countries where the post office does not work well, and the use of the Internet is still not common, it will be more difficult for the tax administration to be in touch with the taxpayers.

Often, similar weaknesses affect different institutions. This implies that attempting to improve just one institution, when the others need attention, may not generate the desired results. This was the experience in transition economies where, for example, the establishment of a good treasury system did not initially improve much the quality of public expenditure management systems. The budgetary process continued to produce budgets that were unrealistic for the treasury to finance or manage. In some of these cases the inevitable result was the accumulation of arrears on the part of governments toward the enterprises and, as a counterpart, the accumulation of tax arrears by the enterprises toward the government (see Potter and Diamond, 1999). In recent years the situation has improved in most of these countries.

Inter-institutional externalities or spillovers (either positive or negative) can be important factors and should be recognized. When they are negative, they must be dealt with in any attempt at improving the quality of the public sector. Perhaps, because it is obvious, this aspect has received almost no attention in the literature. For example, when the judiciary does not work well, other institutions suffer. In one recent example, the problem created by nonperforming loans of banks becomes more difficult to solve if the justice system is slow in authorizing the banks to take actions against the debtors. Similar difficulties may be created by an educational system that is not in line with a country's current economic development.

A holistic approach, one that addresses problems in different institutions at the same time, is likely to be necessary. However, such an approach, which is inevitably more demanding, must be guided by a clear and correct strategy, and by the proper sequencing of the changes required and made. If this approach requires more time to implement than the political horizon available to the government that attempts it, it is less likely that it will be fully or efficiently implemented. This is one reason why the quality of the public sector often changes only slowly over time.

The quality of the public sector will depend to a considerable extent on the existence of effective controls and enforcement mechanisms. Some of these mechanisms can operate from outside the institutions; however, others must operate within the institutions themselves, because the latter are better able to observe more directly and more closely the institutions' operations. Efficient internal auditors' offices can improve the functioning of the institutions and can provide some guarantees that the latter will not stray away from their basic mandate. But these mechanisms may not be sufficient, and the controllers may be captured by those that they should control. In other cases the enforcement mechanisms must cut across institutions. This happens when supreme audit institutions, specialized in controls and in enforcement, have the responsibility of controlling spending and revenue collection. These institutions may receive their mandate from the countries' constitutions and may act as independent bodies.

Examples of these supreme audit institutions are the General Accountability Office (GAO) in the United States, the Cour des Comptes in France, La Corte dei Conti in Italy, the General Auditors' Offices in Latin American countries, and so on. Historically, however, these audit institutions have focused too much on whether the institutions have complied with the letter of the law rather than with the spirit of it. Often, these offices have been filled with individuals with a legal, rather than economic or technical, background. Therefore, the performance of the supervised institutions *in terms of outputs and outcomes* has attracted less formal or institutional attention than whether the institutions have followed legal requirements in the uses of their budget and have satisfied existing laws. The objective of accountability is largely to provide transparency in the use of money and to reduce corruption.

Financial accountability was first introduced, in private financial accounts, in Florence in the fifteenth century by a Franciscan monk and mathematician named Luca Pacioli. He developed the concept of double accounting. At that time corruption was common in the accounts of governments, including in those of Florence and of other countries (see Waquet, 1991). Jean-Baptiste Colbert, the finance minister of Louis XIV, king of France, from 1665 to 1683, is credited with having introduced financial accountability in the public accounts of a state, France. It may have been the first attempt to separate the budget of a sovereign from that of a state (see Waquet, 1991; Soll, 2014).

While financial accountability is an important activity and a step in the right direction, it is not sufficient to promote the quality of the public sector in its most fundamental objective, that of providing the most benefits to the citizens, given a level of public spending. Accountability does not guarantee that the public money is spent in ways that generate the most value for the citizens, because money can be spent inefficiently even when the spending is accounted for and follows legitimate rules.

In recent years there has been some movement toward focusing more than in the past on *performance* and *output*, rather than, mainly, on formalities and on financial *input*. This movement has tried to assess public spending in terms of characteristics of economy, efficiency, and effectiveness. This new approach requires quantitative indicators of public-sector performance and of the full and not just of the financial cost of public-sector activities. The new approach has had its strongest expression in New Zealand and Australia, and, in modified forms, it has spread to other countries. It has encouraged changes in contractual arrangements and in organizations of public institutions.

In the countries that have tried to follow the aforementioned approach, tenure on civil service jobs has been largely abolished and many constraints, on the actions of those who run departments, have been removed. This movement has tried to eliminate the possibility of individuals continuing to receive salaries in their public-sector jobs who cannot be fired because of existing contractual rules, even when their performance does not justify the salaries that they receive.

In these new institutional arrangements, the government, *the principal*, makes contracts with a public agency, *the agent* (for example, the Australian tax administration), on what the public agency must deliver in a specified period, given its budget. The head of that agency becomes personally responsible for delivering the agreed output or outcome. If the agreed goal is not met, the contracts of the heads of the agencies may not be renewed, or other penalties, such as a reduction in bonuses or salaries or even a demotion, may be applied. Therefore, economic incentives have been linked to performance. At the same time the head of the agency has been given more discretion on the use of the available resources. The final impact of these reforms on cultures that are different from those that have prevailed in New Zealand and Australia is difficult to assess. In societies where it is culturally, legally, or politically difficult to fire government workers or to reduce their salaries, almost regardless of their performances, these reforms are difficult to fully implement.

This discussion of enforcement mechanisms and controls must be accompanied by the mention of two important points. The first is the weakness of the *cash accounting* approach, the one that has traditionally characterized the measurement of the operation of government agencies in most countries, in providing support and adequate information for good efficiency and accounting controls. The second is the measurement of consumer reactions and preferences, with respect to the services or the activities rendered by the public agencies. The quality of the government services must be related to the full cost of those services to society, and to the resources available to the agencies that generate them. The more robust are the full resources available, the better must be the public services that one would expect to be generated. Naturally, the higher is the efficiency of the public agency, the higher will also be the quality of the services.

An important question is how to measure the level of resources used. Traditionally, the fiscal accounts (and thus the budget and also the estimates of the public debt) have relied on *cash* accounting and on cash transactions. In cash accounting the cost of an operating agency, for example, a school or a public hospital, is measured by the cash that is made available to, and is used by, that agency, school, or hospital from the public budget. However, accounts based on cash transactions ignore the use of real resources, such as buildings or land, owned by the state and used by the agency, school, or hospital.

These weaknesses of cash accounting are now better recognized than they were in the past. An agency may use little cash but large amounts of public resources that are not accounted for by the public budget. The accounts may also not consider certain future costs, some of which may be of an environmental nature or in the form of future payments (pensions) promised to teachers, doctors, or others.

The need for so-called *accrual* accounting, which measures costs in a more comprehensive way than cash accounting does, is now generally recognized by experts (see Norman, 1997). However, practical difficulties with the use of accrual accounting continue to complicate and put limits on its full use. Furthermore, even accrual accounting may not take into account social costs that an activity may impose on the environment. As time passes, these costs, such as carbon in the air, discharge of dirty water in rivers and lakes, garbage generated by an activity that contaminates the soil, and so on, which, in some cases, can be high, have been receiving more attention in several countries. Calls for "green budgets" have become more frequent and more controversial for some groups.

In principle, accrual accounting provides a better measure of the true costs of public-sector (and some private) activities, because it attempts to measure more fully the use of resources by an activity. If accrual accounting is correctly and *fully* used, it allows more meaningful evaluations in assessing and comparing the costs and the outcomes of government programs, including some regulations. Cash accounting ignores the opportunity cost of using real public-sector assets when their use does not result in cash transfers (in the payment of user charges). It therefore understates, in some cases significantly, the true costs of some activities (see examples in Tanzi and Prakash, 2003). An activity that receives few cash transfers from the public budget, but uses a lot of valuable land or publicly owned buildings, is assessed to have low costs, an assessment that is obviously wrong. However, as mentioned, even accrual accounting, when used, may not take into account some important environmental and other current or future costs. With the passing of time more of these costs are being taken into account.

Another question relates to the potential role of citizens, as taxpayers and consumers of public services, in evaluating the public services. How important are the public services provided by the government for them? Some of the reforms made in a few countries in past years have made a distinction between *principal* (the government) and *agent* (a public agency). They have introduced contracts, actual or implicit, between the government and the agency. An example might be the contract between a public regulator and a natural monopoly that provides services to the public that the regulator regulates. The regulator is supposed to represent the consumers' interests. However, its direct role is ensuring the avoidance of excessive profits for the producer, rather than specifically promoting the consumer interest (including the reduction of risks). In these arrangements the direct voice of the consumer is missing. While in the private sector consumers can state their preferences in a direct way, simply by not buying some products, for public-sector services this direct expression of preference is often not available. When one needs a passport or a driver's license, there is only one place from which one can get them. The same may be the case for services rendered by public schools, public health facilities, or public transportation.

Some reforms that started a few decades ago in certain countries tried to find surrogate measures for consumer preferences in particular public services. Three such approaches might be mentioned.

In the first, some evaluation work has surveyed the views of a sample of consumers, as part of a wider exercise aimed at understanding how, for example, parents assess the education given by public schools to their children. Such exercises have tended to be partial and confined to specific sectors. They suffer from the potential weakness that those surveyed may not have the ability to judge correctly the output, and their reactions may reflect their particular biases, rather than the true quality of the services.

A second approach has been that of conducting formal consumer surveys that cover a number of different services. The World Bank and some individual countries' institutions launched initiatives in this area in past years. For example, users of public hospitals were asked to assess the quality of the services, and taxpayers were asked to give their opinions on some aspects of the tax administrations, for example, the latter's attitude vis-à-vis taxpayers' requests for assistance.

Thirdly has been the compulsory use of name badges for officials – so that consumers, through their responses, could both reward good and punish bad service by specific individuals – has also been a small, but significant, element in these consumer surveys. The use of the Internet has facilitated the responses in recent years by encouraging more evaluations.

The aforementioned are examples of how incentives are slowly being introduced in public-sector activities. In certain cases, consumers have been entitled to receive some form of compensation when the public-service providers have failed to meet required, agreed standards. It must be recognized that similar developments are being introduced in various areas of private activities (hotels, transportation, tourist services, etc.) to try to improve the efficiency of these markets.

In addition to the controls that are internal to the agencies and the institutions, and to those performed by nationwide auditing institutions, there are other institutions whose working and efficiency is an essential ingredient in the quality of the whole public sector. Among these, as mentioned earlier, the system of justice is of the greatest importance. The role of the justice system, in all its manifestations and functions, in enforcing contracts, in protecting property rights, in ensuring the safety of individuals, in keeping corruption under control, and in improving the efficiency of public institutions (and the good behavior of private ones), is fundamental. It is not an exaggeration to state that the quality of the public sector of a country and the functioning of its market depend significantly on the performance of its justice system, and that the importance of that system has grown over the years due to the increasing complexity of market activities. Unfortunately, the performance of the justice system is, in various countries, not only not as efficient as it ought to be, but it may also be inefficient in a way that is discriminatory toward individuals with fewer means.

In several countries the justice system has been in a state of crisis in recent years. Some property rights have not been protected, some contracts have not been enforced, some processes have taken years or even decades to be concluded, acts of corruption have often gone unpunished, and so on. The maxim that "justice delayed is justice denied" has qualified what happens in various countries. In some cases individuals who break the law are not punished, are punished lightly, or are not punished until years or even decades later. This reduces the deterrent effect of the punishment.

In some countries it takes many years for the government to determine whether someone accused of tax evasion ought to pay the unpaid taxes, thus increasing the propensity to evade. Furthermore, the penalties imposed are often insignificant, or tax amnesties can be expected to reduce or eliminate the penalties. In other countries the presumed equality under the law that all citizens should enjoy has been destroyed by the differing capacity and ability that the rich and the poor have to rely on the ability of able and expensive lawyers to defend them. This unequal approach to justice has compromised the fundamental concept of "equality under the law" and the importance of "rule of law."

Although knowledgeable individuals have some a priori or intuitive notion of the quality of the public sector of countries, because of their relationship and direct experience with parts of it, it would be difficult or even impossible to get objective measures of that quality. In principle one could conduct surveys of perceptions of such quality, using the same techniques adopted, for example, in some of the surveys of corruption or happiness. However, the informational requirements on the part of the respondents, to give reliable results for the whole public sector, would be extremely high, so the quality of the responses would be low and questionable. It might be easier to evaluate the quality of each of the major institutions that make up the public sector and somehow weigh their relative importance to the general quality of the public sector.

In past years some institutions and scholars began to focus on particular features that captured *some* significant aspects of the quality of public sectors. In various reports the IMF has focused on the *transparency* of fiscal policy and of fiscal institutions. This evaluation has been done against a set of general principles of fiscal transparency. The assumption is that lack of transparency is an indication of a lower quality of the public sector and that this lack of transparency promotes inefficiency and poor policies and contributes to various problems of governance. Transparency reports have started to be produced by some countries (see, for example, Government of India, 2009). If comparable and comprehensive, these reports would provide proxies for informal assessments of the quality of the public sector.

Since the 1990s, increasing attention has been paid to issues of governance and corruption in governments and in public institutions. These issues bear on the quality of the public sector. A corrupt government cannot be one of high quality, and corruption is one of the most serious termites of the state. It has been recognized that lack of transparency in the way institutions operate and lack of controls promote not only inefficiency but also corruption. There is now a large and growing literature on transparency and on corruption, and institutions such as the IMF, the World Bank, the OECD, and some national governments have been paying more attention to this termite. Some countries have created anti-corruption institutions with large amounts of power and resources to deal with corruption (see Abed and Gupta, 2002).

The debate a decade ago on the new "architecture" of the international financial system concluded that countries should become more transparent in their policymaking. More transparency would presumably mean less corruption and would imply a higher-quality and a better-performing public sector. However, much needs to be learned about these relationships. Tests of transparency may be superficial or deep, and they may or may not be followed by actions, as is the case with banks' stress tests. The Indian 2009 report on transparency did not prevent problems of corruption from becoming a major issue, in later years, in that country.

Superficial tests are not useful in understanding what is going on in public sectors that have become far more complex today than they were in the past. Deep tests require a lot of highly specialized and costly resources, and might also generate results that are easy to challenge on various grounds. As already mentioned, they must be followed by actions. An additional problem is that, in some countries, corruption has become almost legal in some cases or some aspects, because, under the pressure of lobbies, some actions that in the past would have been classified as immoral, corrupt, and illegal are no longer punished because they are not specifically forbidden by law.

Corruption on the part of both policymakers and administrators is clearly an indication that a public sector is of low quality. Some specialized institutions, such as Transparency International, have been generating corruption indexes for countries. These indexes generally measure "perceptions" or some other indirect evidence of corruption, because, almost by definition, actual acts of corruption cannot be measured, except in a few isolated cases. To some extent, and assuming that the measurements of perceptions are good indicators of the reality, these indexes can be taken as broad proxies for indicating the quality of a country's public sector. However, caution is again needed because, quite apart from the shortcomings in the indexes, a country could have a totally honest bureaucracy or even political leadership and very inefficient policies and institutions. While important, corruption is only one of various aspects of the poor quality of a public sector.

Some reports prepared in recent years by research institutions have provided estimates of bureaucratic performance and what is called "red tape" for many countries, providing still another termite that has a bearing on the quality of the public sector. Several other variables may provide information on that quality. Some of them would relate to the public sector's efficiency, some to the policies followed. For example, the relationship between spending in a given category – for example, health, education, or public investment – and the outcome of that spending – such as lives saved, successful operations performed, reduction in the incidence of certain diseases, educational achievements, or impact on growth – could be seen as an indication of efficiency.

As an indication of such a relation, on August 13, 2013, Bloomberg Net published a ranking on the efficiency of health care among countries. The ranking was in terms of spending on health care by a country and its life expectancy. The United States, which in total (public plus private) spends far more on health care, as a share of GDP, than any other country in the world, was ranked in 46th place, a ranking that would imply a very low efficiency in delivering public health *for the majority* of Americans. More significantly, it indicates the wide variances that exist in health standards and in health conditions between different classes of citizens and areas of the United States. The variances in life expectancy between some rich and some poor counties in the United States were greater than the variances between the richest and the poorest countries in the world. These variances might be taken as an indicator of the inequity of health care services in the United States, and of the inefficiency of its public health care in some areas, although other factors, such as variances in diets, in accidents, in smoking, and in homicides, clearly contributed to the results.

The variances in life expectancy in the United States are accompanied by wide variances in other areas, including education. The variances in the quality of the schools within the United States are equally surprising. The United States contains some of the top schools and some of the worst schools in the world. It would be difficult to find another OECD country with similar variances.

The quality of the public sector can be assessed only against the role that the state is expected to play. If the public sector allows the state to promote its goals in an efficient and successful way, it can be argued that the public sector is of high quality. However, the goals must be realistic, because even a very efficient public sector will be unable to deliver unrealistic goals; and if the role of the state is limited and modest, even a public sector of low quality could perform well in delivering the modest goals. In general the quality of the public sector cannot be measured by the quality of the policy outcome, although the two are obviously linked, especially over the long run. Various deficiencies, or termites, can reduce the quality of a public sector.

In general, an efficient public sector should be able to achieve the state's objectives with a minimum degree of distortion of the market, with the lowest burden of taxation on the taxpayers, with the smallest number of public employees, with the lowest use of economic resources by the public sector, and with the lowest reduction in the economic freedom of the citizens. The public sector must be transparent in its processes, and clear and specific in the outcomes that it wishes to achieve. Corruption and vested interests should play no role in the decisions made by the bureaucracy and by the political leaders. And the resources controlled by the public sector should be put to uses that maximize their *social* rate of return.

In a market economy, the public sector should be "market-augmenting," using an expression that became fashionable some years ago. It should widen the scope of the private market rather than restrict it, but not reduce worthwhile, traditional community norms. Such a public sector would pay particular attention to the protection of *legitimately* acquired property rights, to the enforcement of freely negotiated contracts, and to the safety and welfare of workers and citizens. It should do so while maintaining as much economic freedom for individual economic action as feasible, but not at the cost of ignoring the needs of less fortunate individuals.

Such a public sector could not ignore the distribution of income, especially when it becomes significantly uneven, nor especially how that distribution affects and influences the pursuit of the equity objective, an objective that has grown in importance in recent years, among the fundamental goals that a state is expected to pursue. A public sector that, through all its aspects, including minimizing distortions, facilitates the pursuit of an equitable distribution must, ceteris paribus, be deemed to be of higher quality than one that does not. However, as argued earlier, it is difficult to determine the precise (the *optimal*) role of the state in this area; and it is easy to identify disincentive effects that may be created by policies that aim at excessively redistributing income. The question is how empirically significant those effects are. The disincentive effects are more likely to be significant when the public sector is of low quality.

An important interpretation of what role the state should pursue in promoting equity was suggested by Amartya Sen (1999), who identified "development" with some definition of freedom on the part of *all* the citizens and not just of those with higher incomes. Sen and others after him have stressed that poverty can reduce the freedom of many individuals more than the payment of some taxes can reduce the freedom of richer individuals. Sen and others who share his views believe that the state has an obligation of providing access to *some* basic education and basic health *for all citizens*. He argues that the freedom of *all* citizens is important and that citizens who do not have the means to acquire the most basic goods (education, health care, food, and essential mobility) do not have much of the "freedom" that conservative writers talk so much about (see also Sen, 1999).

Sen's suggestion leads directly to a question that was asked by E. Burke two centuries ago: "What is the use of discussing man's abstract rights to food and medicine? The question relates to the method of procuring and administering them." It also leaves open some fundamental questions on the economic role of the state:

1. What should be the minimum level at which the goods and the services that Sen believes that the state should provide to the citizens are provided?
2. Who should be entitled to receive them? Everyone, or only those who cannot afford them?
3. Who should pay the taxes needed to finance the free provision of those goods and services?
4. Related to the third question, how should the tax burden be shared?

These are fundamental questions that make economic policy difficult to perfect in practice. As with many things in life, the difficulties are often found in the detailed application of policies. A high-quality public sector would facilitate, but would not guarantee, the satisfaction of Sen's objective.

Finally, the previous discussion should have made it clear that what in the last decade of the twentieth century came to be called "first generation reforms," reforms associated with policies that were promarket, did not necessarily improve the quality of the public sector, even though they might have improved the quality of public policy (see Krueger, 2000). However, those reforms did highlight the need to improve the quality of the public sector and led to the recognition of the need for particular reforms to the existing institutions. The latter were the *second-generation reforms*. Those reforms may have failed to recognize that, in a world that was becoming more globalized, and that was undergoing radical technological and social developments, the policies that were being recommended could lead to deteriorations in the income distributions and, in time, to calls on governments to give more attention to the equity objective. The remaining and third part of this book will focus on the issue of equity and on the distribution of income, issues that have attracted progressively more attention and that have been leading to populist reactions in several countries.

There should exist ... neither extreme poverty nor ... excessive wealth, for both are productive of great evil.

Plato (427 BC–347 BC)

An imbalance between rich and poor is the oldest and most fatal ailment of all republics.

Plutarch (46 AD–120 AD)

Economics is the science by which the economic elite remains the economic elite.

August Strindberg (1849 AD–1912 AD)

PART III

Focusing on Equity

CHAPTER 27

Synergy between Wealth Creation and Government Role

A distribution of wealth considered excessively uneven is not a concern limited to our age. It has been a concern for philosophers and others for a very long time, as the citations of Plato, Plutarch, and Strindberg indicate. Since the time when communities became organized enough to have some governing body, and individuals some claims to real property, wealth inequality has been a concern. In *Politica* (book V, chapter 1), Aristotle had referred to this concern, as did Plato in his works. Montesquieu, in *De L' Esprit des Lois* (1944, book V, chapters VI and VII), also referred to it. Rousseau discussed inequality at great length in his *Discourse on Inequality* (1994), and so did other philosophers, including the presumed promoter of laissez-faire, Adam Smith.

As Adam Smith put it:

> Wherever there is great property, there is great inequality ... The affluence of the rich excites the indignation of the poor, who are often both driven by want, and prompted by envy, to invade his possessions ... [The rich person] is at all times surrounded by unknown enemies ... [H]e can be protected only by the powerful arm of the civil magistrate" (1937, p. 670).

Smith concluded that "the acquisition of valuable and extensive property ... necessarily requires the establishment of civil government" (ibid.).

Writing at about the same time as Adam Smith, J. J. Rousseau believed that "property had bred inequality, conflict, and war" (see Edmonds and Eidinow, 2006, p. 138). Many socialist thinkers would come to share that view. See Woodcock 1987 on Proudhon's views. The French Revolution would follow by a few years the publication of Rousseau's and Smith's books, and the rich families in France would discover how many enemies they had, and how much they were hated by them. Revolutions would occasionally start when inequality became excessive. Hegel (1956, p. 445) commented on the role that "heavy burdens ... upon the people" and "the embarrassment of the government to procure for the Court the means of supporting luxury and extravagance" had had in leading to the French Revolution.

Thus, history teaches us that inequality, especially when it becomes extreme, can lead to great social difficulties. In the past inequality was related to the ownership of wealth, on the part of some families, while in more recent years it is more often related to incomes received by particular individuals, although wealth inequality also continues to attract attention.

Various experiments, often with tragic consequences, were attempted in the past by some governing bodies and some powerful individuals to bring equality, or more equality, in the distribution of wealth and income. Examples include efforts in France, Russia, China, Cambodia, and some other countries, including Venezuela today. The distribution of tangible wealth, and especially of land possession, had been the guiding or main preoccupation in those experiments, before income became a more-significant guiding statistic in modern times, and before other kinds of wealth (including the ownership of capital held in more liquid forms, including intellectual capital) became significant. In some way, wealth has lost the transparency than once it had.

For most economists who tend to emphasize *economic* incentives, a distribution of income that is too equal is seen as a recipe for stagnation and for excessive loss of personal initiatives and liberty. Thus, some inequality in income is required to promote efficiency. At the same time, many individuals see *excessive* inequality in income or wealth as a cause of many problems, as did Adam Smith. Therefore, the main questions should be: Is there some right balance in terms of income and wealth distribution? And how can that balance be achieved? To ignore the issue, as some economists have continued to suggest that governments should do, is not likely to be a wise choice, for both governments and for societies.

Starting at least with Adam Smith, economists could not fail to pay some attention to the issue of wealth distribution and, later, to that of income distribution. In the quotation reported earlier, Adam Smith had recognized the synergy that exists between government and wealth ownership. Next, I shall discuss other forms of synergies between the role of government and the creation of income and wealth.

During the Industrial Revolution, the English words *entrepreneur* and *entrepreneurship* were borrowed from the French verb *entreprendre*, which means "to undertake." The reason for borrowing the French word was that, by that time, the English noun *undertaker* had already taken a somewhat macabre meaning. *Entrepreneur* is defined as "[a person] who organizes, operates, and assumes the risk in a *business* venture, in the expectation of gaining a *profit*" (see *Webster's Encyclopedic Unabridged Dictionary*). Unlike the word *undertaker, entrepreneur* is definitely not a person who arranges funerals, although an undertaker can also be an entrepreneur!

According to *Webster's*, the term *entrepreneur* crossed the British channel and entered the English language around 1875–1880. That was a time of rapid transition from the old, traditional world, the world that had existed in past centuries and had seen little *economic* progress, to the new, modern, and radical world that the Industrial Revolution was creating. As a consequence of many technological discoveries and developments, the "capitalistic" organizations of large economic activities were becoming important in England and in other places. The Industrial Revolution was rapidly changing the social and economic landscape, and the relations that had existed among individuals in past centuries.

In the United States, it was the time of *The Rise of Big Business* (see Porter [1973] 1992). Entrepreneurs became important when a *laissez-faire* ideology was guiding governmental action. Some of the entrepreneurs had been acquiring enough wealth and social status to challenge and to begin to replace, in social standing and in economic positions, the traditional aristocrats whose wealth had depended mainly on land ownership. In the United States some individuals would acquire so much wealth in those decades as to be considered the richest in the world, and some, such as members of the Du Pont family, would build mansions to challenge those of the European nobles.

In a market economy, entrepreneurs aim at maximizing profits. In pursuing this goal and in their operations, they like to have as much economic flexibility and economic freedom as possible, and as society will permit. However, they also need to have some governmental assistance in their operations to better achieve their objectives and to protect their property, as Adam Smith had thought necessary. Their objectives can be more easily achieved when particular obstacles to their economic activities, obstacles that are beyond their direct control to remove, can be removed, or can be reduced in importance, by the government.

Examples of these obstacles are those imposed by the physical environment (lack of or poor roads, bridges, ports, railroads, canals, airports; reliable and cheap energy; fresh water), and obstacles imposed by strongly held traditions that may put limits to the use of some resources, and especially to the use of labor. In some societies those obstacles can impose rigid limits to business operations. At the same time, the entrepreneurs also wish to face as few obstacles as possible imposed by the government itself. Therefore, they want a friendly government that removes some obstacles for them but does not replace them with others, for example, too strong labor unions or too rigid labor and other laws. A laissez-faire government is more likely to satisfy those objectives.

Entrepreneurs want a government that not only protects their property but that is also business-friendly and that facilitates their activities, as many governments did in the second half of the nineteenth century during the laissez-faire period, at least in attitude if not always in practice. Entrepreneurs also like to operate in an environment that offers some guarantees and some protections to their activities, guarantees that only a friendly, laissez-faire government can offer. More specifically, the entrepreneurs would like to have a government that:

(a) Protects their property rights. See Pipes, 1999. Over the years, property rights, which in the past had generally been limited to the protection of *real* properties, would progressively be extended to cover various other forms of property, including *intellectual* and *intangible* properties.

(b) Protects the rights of shareholders and limits the personal liabilities of the owners and the managers of corporations. Over the years these rights were reinforced and clarified, while various limitations were imposed to the liabilities of the shareholders of corporations. When income taxes were introduced on the profits of enterprises and on personal incomes (in the United States in 1913), unrealized capital gains were not taxed, thus allowing the shareholders of corporations to accumulate wealth (especially when profits were retained and reinvested), without having to pay taxes on the growing unrealized gains. In case of bankruptcy, the liabilities of the enterprises did not become the liabilities of the shareholders or of the managers of the enterprises. The concept of *corporation* was also a relatively new concept that was very important for "capitalistic" economic development. It was a concept that underwent various modifications over the years.

(c) Allows the costs of borrowed money and the depreciation allowances to be deducted fully from the profits, before determining the taxable incomes of enterprises. Until recent years, class actions against corporations were also rare – see Rakoff (2015) – and so were responsibilities for many costs that enterprises were unloading on the environment and on future generations, especially environmental costs. There were also no consumer protection agencies.

(d) Protects legitimate contracts and intervenes when necessary to enforce contracts, not only domestically but increasingly internationally.

(e) Increases the basic education and know-how of the populations, so that the workers hired by enterprises will be more productive in their jobs and better prepared to respect existing societal rules and to apply new technologies. The intervention of the government in public education became increasingly more active as the Industrial Revolution got underway. Many young workers became literate at public expenses.

(f) Guarantees the availability and the good conditions of essential physical infrastructures (roads, canals, bridges, airports, fresh water, sewer systems, electricity, and others) in the areas where the enterprises operate.

(g) Provides basic security for the areas and the social environments in which the enterprises operate, reducing the enterprises' own costs to protect their assets and their workers from criminal elements.

(h) Guarantees to the entrepreneurs the freedom to negotiate the conditions for hiring and firing workers, for buying necessary inputs domestically and internationally, and for getting needed credit and funds from banks, shareholders, and other sources, without the need to get authorizations and permits from government offices or from other organizations, such as labor unions.

(i) Guarantees that the entrepreneurs will face and expect to continue to face a stable regulatory and legal framework.

(j) Guarantees that the enterprises will be able to retain all, or a fair share, of the profits that they make from legitimate economic activities.

(k) Guarantees that those who accumulate wealth can keep it and also pass it or most of it on to their heirs.

(l) Guarantees that the tax system will continue to have the four characteristics listed by Adam Smith: certainty, convenience, economy, and equity and continue to be light.

(m) Protects the frontiers from foreign invasions.

From contemplating this list, it is obvious that the entrepreneurs and the government are, or need to be, responsible partners and not competitors, and that there must be an implicit social contract between them: the more the government does for the enterprises, the more they will do for the government, and implicitly or indirectly for society. It is obvious that the government must share in the profits of the enterprises, because it contributes to those profits in various ways, just as the shareholders do. It is also obvious that the workers in the enterprises must also share fairly in the enterprises' revenue. Thus, managers, shareholders, the government, and workers will all be parties to an implicit contract that implies expectations and obligations from each side.

Only a *government* can satisfy some of the needs of enterprises; and, in a market economy, only enterprises and independent operators that have a minimum sense of social obligations can deliver economic growth with equity, good jobs and reasonable personal safety for workers, and protection for the environment. The income generated by the activities of the enterprises must somehow be divided fairly among the four partners: owners, managers, workers, and the government.

The aforementioned government obligations inevitably require public resources. They create expectations that part of the profits of the enterprises (and part of the compensations of those who work in the enterprises or provide capital to them) must contribute to the government's operations in the form of taxes. It follows that to guarantee that it can deliver on its share of the implicit bargain, the government must be able to impose taxes on individuals, as workers and shareholders, on the creditors that lend money to them, and on the enterprises themselves, and must establish rules to ensure that basic, essential principles are followed and respected by both enterprises and the individuals who engage in individual economic activities or work for the enterprises.

The government also needs to be an *effective, fair,* and *firm* referee between entrepreneurs, on one side, and workers and consumers, on the other side, without losing sight of both equity and efficiency considerations. The government must play its role with public spending, with occasional but rare direct interventions, with essential regulations, and also, very rarely, with specific authorizations and other less common instruments (such as subsidies and tax incentives for the enterprises, expropriation, conscription, zoning laws, assumption of contingent liabilities, and some others), which were listed in an earlier chapter.

The concept of *equitable growth*, a concept that has been mentioned with increasing frequency in recent years, is, inevitably, an important but vague concept. Growth, whether equitable or not, is normally statistically defined as an increase in the economic output over time, measured at constant market prices. There are conceptual and statistical difficulties in measuring the growth of output. Some important outputs are not even measured, for example, much of the production that takes place within a household, nor are some costs. Also, some social costs are not measured, for example, environmental degradation that often accompanies the operations of enterprises.

The output needs to be adjusted to take account of the growth of the population, so that it may be defined on a per capita basis, ideally adjusted to reflect the age structure of the population, because individuals of different ages have different economic needs. It may also be defined in relation to the number of employed workers, or in relation to the hours worked, to get a productivity-based definition. It should also take account of environmental costs. For example, some experts believe that the genuine growth rate in China, in recent decades, has been significantly lower than the officially reported one, when the environmental degradation that has accompanied that growth rate is taken into account. The same is likely to have occurred in other countries.

In spite of these qualifications, a higher growth rate is generally considered preferable to a lower growth rate. It is better to have a growing cake than one that does not grow, as long as the growth in the size of the cake is not accompanied by a lowering of its quality, or by its appropriation by only a small share of individuals who use it for just their advantage.

The aggregate concept of growth is inevitably too broad to be very informative and to be considered as the only, or the main, determinant of the change in the welfare of the citizens of a country. High growth may be accompanied by higher or lower employment; by increasing or lower shares of workers in national income; by increasing or decreasing participation of women in the workforce; by increasing or decreasing poverty rates; by increasing environmental concerns; by increasing crime rates or accidents at work; and by a distribution of the income, *among* the population and also *between* generations, that raises concerns and that is not considered equitable. A high growth rate that gives an excessive share of the gains in income to a small percentage of the population; that creates growing environmental costs; and that is too focused on the current generation may be considered less desirable than an alternative, lower growth rate that is more equitably shared and that generates fewer environmental costs.

In recent years there has been a movement, on the part of a few economists and governments, to shift the attention and the emphasis from the measurement of income to that of "happiness," assuming that happiness has the same meaning for everyone and that it can be measured (see Frey, 2008; Graham, 2011). Only time will tell whether this movement, which has involved some Nobel Prize winners in economics and has interested some governments, will acquire traction. So far Bhutan is the only country that has given official sanction to this concept, while policymakers from a few other countries have been flirting with the idea. If it is to acquire traction, governments will have to play significantly different roles than they currently do in promoting policies that presumably increase happiness, even at the cost of lower growth rates. Policies that promote a better income distribution would likely be among them.

To be *equitable*, growth must be *inclusive*, as utilitarian philosophers and economists including Bentham and Mill would have argued. It must create good jobs for most of those who want to work, and must redistribute some of the gains in total income from those with higher income to most of the population. It should be especially favorable to those who are in the lower percentiles of the income distribution, and even more to those below the poverty line, so that it can be defined as being clearly and desirably equitable, as long as the achievement of this result does not have significant negative implications for future growth or for the liberty of most and not just some richer citizens. It should also not come at the cost of high environmental degradation and should reflect the interests of both current *and* future generations.

It would be highly desirable and preferable if the aforementioned objectives could be achieved spontaneously and freely through the natural working of the market economy and without much governmental involvement, except that of ensuring that the market does not fail and is not rigged. This would require a minimum of social consciousness and community spirit, incentives not distorted by wrong economic policies, and legitimate and responsible behavior on the part of those who make economic decisions in the private sector. It would require that enterprises and also individuals pay attention to the social consequences of their economic actions, and not just to the impact on their (short run) profits or gains.

Unfortunately, for a variety of reasons, some already mentioned by Adam Smith as far back as 1759 in *The Theory of Moral Sentiments*, and, especially, in 1776 in *The Wealth of Nations*, and some connected with recent economic and policy developments, this social consciousness is often absent or not evident in the actions of enterprises and individuals. Some recent literature has even argued that *altruism* may create problems and that *greed* may be a desirable trait in those who operate in the free market. Some consider greed an incentive to greater effort. Also, some literature has argued that the main goal of private enterprises should be to maximize shareholders' (and managers'?) returns and that this objective can be satisfied more easily if taxes on profits are reduced and the wages of workers are kept as low as possible.

At times Adam Smith's concept of the "invisible hand" has been interpreted in the aforementioned terms, in the belief, by some, that maximizing shareholders' returns somehow and inevitably leads to general welfare. Excessive individualism has driven out, for many individuals, the sense of community obligations or their empathy, and, as I shall argue later, it is likely to have been a factor in making the distribution of income less even in recent decades. One should be reminded of a warning from Edmund Burke that "men are qualified for civil liberty in exact proportion to their disposition to put moral chains upon their appetite."

In more recent years, various developments have created requests on the part of an increasing share of the populations in favor of (more) governmental intervention, an intervention that would extend well beyond the limited areas associated with a minimalist state, as that concept was described in an earlier chapter. The expectation and the hope have been that the greater intervention by the government would make a significant and positive difference in promoting more socially desirable behaviors and outcomes.

Unfortunately, the experience of many countries in recent decades has indicated that the government's intervention, beyond a certain level, does not necessarily generate more welfare and more equitable growth. Rather, in some cases, it may itself create problems and distortions in the market. In more extreme cases, it may even accentuate some of the difficulties that it tries to correct. Therefore, because of the difficulty in achieving the right balance, countries may be faced with the alternative between *market failure* and *government failure* in situations where doing nothing may not appear to be a desirable option.

The optimistic and benevolent view about the role that governments can play in the economy – the view discussed in a previous chapter that had been promoted by Keynesian economics and by neoclassical economists who, after World War II, had developed what came to be called the *normative* view of the economic role of the state, a view that in some cases contributed to the creation of welfare states – received increasingly critical attention, starting late in the 1960s and accelerating in the 1970s and 1980s.

From different perspectives, that benevolent view came to be criticized by scholars associated with the School of Public Choice (of which James Buchanan and Gordon Tullock were major exponents in the United States, and Alan Peacock in the United Kingdom), and by scholars associated with the Chicago School (mostly connected with Milton Friedman, George Stigler, R. H. Coase, and some others). The work of Hayek and of other economists of the Austrian School also played some role. However, that work was in some ways distinct from that of the Chicago School, and it is a bit difficult to place the full work of Hayek and of the Austrian School, which remained less known to the general public in the United States, especially at the more popular level, even though Hayek spent many years at the University of Chicago. Some of his important works were in fact published there, and he received one of the earlier Nobel Prizes in economics while he was there.

The School of Public Choice, especially through the work of James Buchanan, drew some of its thinking from earlier writings by Swedish and Italian scholars. Recent literature has added other arguments, for example, the role that both political and administrative corruption play, to those of the aforementioned schools. In this book I refer to recent factors that may contribute to the pessimistic view of the economic role of the state as a *termite of the state*, arguing that these termites are making that role more difficult to implement at a time when, to some observers, the government role might appear more needed than in the past because of problems that have developed in the private market.

CHAPTER 28

Recent Concerns about Inequality

In many countries, but especially in Anglo-Saxon countries, the economic growth that has occurred in the last four decades has favored disproportionately a small share of the countries' populations, while workers have benefited much less because their real wages have grown little and some have lost their jobs, while some important costs, such as those for health services, for education, for access to justice, for street parking and traffic violation fines, and for some government services, have kept increasing. There is now overwhelming statistical information that supports the conclusion that the income distribution has become significantly less equal and that workers have benefitted little from growth in recent decades.

A recent study prepared at the IMF reported that, "In the United States, the share of market income captured by the richest 10 percent surged from around 30 percent in 1980 to 48 percent by 2012, while the share of the richest one-percent increased from 8 percent to 19 percent. Even more striking is the fourfold increase in the share of the richest 0.1 percent, from 2.6 percent to 10.4 percent" (IMF, 2015, pp. 38–39). In 2016, the *average* income of those in this 0.1 percent was estimated to be more than $3.7 million. The study added that, "Since 1990, inequality in the personal distribution of income has increased in most advanced economies" (ibid., p. 38), and that 'inequality in the distribution of per capita income … increased in many countries across the developing world" (ibid., p. 58). The *Economist* (November 12–18, 2016, p. 9) reported that "in real terms median male earnings are … lower [in 2016] than they were in the 1970s," while upward mobility has fallen.

Clearly, this was a global phenomenon. It seems to have started in the Anglo-Saxon countries, especially in the United Kingdom and the United States, in the 1980s and to have spread to much of the rest of the world. The utilitarian principle, that growth should benefit the majority of the population, was clearly not being satisfied. The statistical evidence, summarized by the IMF study, is now available from many sources, including

Piketty and Saez (2006); Atkinson et al. (2011); Alvaredo et al. (2013); Piketty (2014); and Milanovic (2015). The implications of that evidence have been discussed in many recent books, some listed in the references to this book.

The Gini coefficient, a statistic that is less sensitive to inequality at the lower end of the income distributions, has become larger in most countries in the last four decades, and in some it has become very high. In several countries, especially in the United States, dependent workers and the middle classes seem to have benefited very little from the growth of recent decades or from the government spending on social programs. At the same time, some evidence and some studies, especially from the United States, indicate that the *consumption* (not the income) of those in the lowest percentiles of the income distributions was helped by transfers in cash or in kind received from the governments. For example, data on the US food stamp participation by state, in September 2016, indicate that it was high. In several states, such as New Mexico and Louisiana, it exceeded 20 percent of the population. In fourteen others it exceeded 15 percent,. The data are from the USDA Supplemental Nutrition Assistance Program. Those who benefited from food stamps benefited also from several other government programs that increased their consumption, but not necessarily their cash incomes. In the US middle class individuals generally did not benefit from these programs, while some of their costs increased.

The share of income that goes to the top 1 percent or even to the top 0.1 percent of the income distributions has increased dramatically, and the concentration of *wealth* among relatively few individuals has become extraordinary. We seem to be moving in a direction in which a few individuals own much of the world wealth. At the same time there have been growing concerns about the environmental costs that have accompanied the income growth in recent decades. These concerns were reaffirmed in the 2014 UN Report of the Intergovernmental Panel on Climate Change and by more recent evidence. There have been also growing worries, on the part of many experts, that some of the costs of the recent growth were being pushed to future generations, through growing public debts, unfunded liabilities for pensions and other programs, and the deterioration of the existing infrastructure, which, especially but not only in the United States, has not been upgraded as it should have been, and will require large spending in future years.

In the United States, President Trump has declared that he plans to spend a trillion dollars on infrastructure over the next decade and to reduce taxes on capital. Other countries, including the United Kingdom, have also planned to do the same. Given the uncomfortable levels of public debt in the United States and in other countries, this spending and these tax reductions could create enormous challenges for the countries' public finances, unless they generate fast and sustained economic growth or they reduce other spending (See Tanzi, 2016b).

A question that is now being raised with growing insistence is whether the aforementioned results in terms of income distribution should be accepted as a normal outcome of the market economy or as a legitimate verdict of a free market economy, one that presumably allocates income to those who generate economic value, or whether these results would justify growing governmental intervention directed at achieving greater redistribution. The cited IMF study reported that in recent years popular support for redistribution policies has increased especially in countries, such as China, Finland, Germany, and several Eastern European countries, where the Gini coefficient has increased the most, while that support has declined in countries, such as Bulgaria, Mexico, Peru, and Ukraine, where the Gini coefficient has decreased. The evidence for the United States is more ambiguous, at least as indicated by surveys and, perhaps, by the results of the 2016 elections.

If governmental intervention is called for to deal with the growing income inequality, at what costs should that intervention take place? What instruments should the government use? And what results should it aim to achieve? Clearly, the aim should not be equality of income. Insistent calls for greater public intervention have come not only from average citizens but also from an increasing number of experts. These calls reflect the belief and the hope that governmental intervention would make the economic system, and the growth that it generates, more equitable and more sustainable, both for societies and for the environment (see Sen, 2010; Stiglitz, 2012; Lansley, 2012; Piketty, 2014; Reich, 2015; Atkinson, 2008, 2015).

As would be expected, there have been also those who have resisted and have criticized the past government's interference in the work of the private market, blaming it for some recent problems, including the financial crisis. And there are conservative politicians and some scientists who continue to deny the impact that humans are having on the environment and especially on global warming, and, together with some economists, continue to minimize the problems created by the increasing income concentration. (See, for example, the debate in the Summer 2013 issue of *The Journal of Economic Perspective*, and debates in various recent publications.)

The exponents of the latter economic point of view, called variously "market fundamentalists" or simply "conservatives" or "libertarians," have maintained that markets work or can work efficiently and are largely self-correcting if they are left alone and if they are not distorted by governmental intervention. For example, some of these exponents have blamed the intervention by the US government in the housing market for the sub-prime crisis that led to the Great Recession (see Taylor, 2009). Some have added that those who operate in a market economy, for example, those who borrowed money to buy houses before the financial crisis, should be aware of the risks that they are taking. In a market economy the market participants who generate value or make good decisions get the incomes and the rewards that they deserve. Those who do not generate value and lose must live with the losses and the consequences of their decisions. This is the ethic of a free market. It is an ethic that is inevitably amoral. It compensates winners and cannot protect losers. However, an increasing number of economists have called attention to the fact that individuals tend to be irrational and to make mistakes, or are not fully informed when they make decisions, so governmental intervention is often justified.

Conservative economists and politicians have maintained that the incomes that operators or entrepreneurs receive from their work in the market, even when those incomes are in the millions or, occasionally, in the billions of dollars, simply reflect the economic values that these individuals contribute to the national income. Without their effort, the national income would have been correspondingly lower. These economists and politicians question whether the intervention by the government in the economy, including that directed at redistributing some incomes, is needed and justified on economic or equity grounds. They are also convinced that policies aimed at income and wealth redistribution inevitably reduce the efficiency of the economy and economic growth. These policies may also change the character of individuals, making them more risk-averse and less enterprising. Therefore, over the longer run, redistributive policies cannot but fail to make *societies and economies* worse off than they would be without the policies.

If one accepts that the market works efficiently and also accepts the ethical validity of the market results, the aforementioned view and the described outcome could be justified by the traditional interpretation of the Pareto Optimum, the criterion that has dominated welfare economics for much of the past century, since Vilfredo Pareto, an Italian economist, first proposed it at the beginning of the twentieth century. The criterion states that if one group, for example, the top 1 percent of the population, is made better off by economic growth, without making the remaining 99 percent worse off (in an absolute sense), the change in the income and the wealth of the top 1 percent must be considered welfare enhancing. Obviously, it is not likely that many among the 99 percent, who may not have experienced any real growth in their average wages for a long time, would endorse that criterion. However, it must be recognized that traditionally many economists have accepted the Pareto criterion.

A theory that puts the emphasis on the *differences* in incomes, and not just on the absolute income changes, would have a more negative view of the developments of recent decades. James R. Duesenberry, who was an important economist and professor at Harvard in the 1950s and 1960s, had advanced a *relative income hypothesis* that gave more importance to the *relative*, rather than the *absolute*, incomes of individuals (see Duesenberry, 1952). The relative income hypothesis attracted some attention by economists at that time, but it was largely forgotten in later decades, in part because it conflicted with the normal interpretation given by economists to the Pareto optimum, and with the greater attention that was being paid to absolute incomes in the Keynesian countercyclical theory, at a time when the income distribution was becoming more equal.

Recent experimental, or behavioral, economics has been giving increasing importance to the psychological reactions of individuals to different choices and situations (see Lewis, 2017). Assume that a society exists in which some individuals work hard in tiring and stressful jobs, even though the jobs may not demand high skills or high formal education, and in which they earn an income that in absolute value, and adjusted for inflation, has not changed much over many years, and may have become less adequate to meet the growing costs of health needs, medical insurance, college tuition for children, emergencies to alleviate illnesses or accidents, and new gadgets (smartphones, computers, and others) that modern economies continually create and that are increasingly seen by most as necessary for an adequate living. The need for these gadgets does not reduce the need for more traditional basic goods, but purchasing these gadgets requires higher income.

Assume also that the aforementioned lower-income individuals, or at least some of them, through the television or other media outlets, have become increasingly aware that the incomes of lucky or privileged individuals – which now include bankers, hedge fund managers, successful athletes and coaches, rock stars and other performers, television personalities, managers of corporations, doctors in specialized practices, traders, innovators in Silicon Valley, successful actors, and, increasingly, even college presidents and directors of museums and charitable institutions – have, in many cases, reached millions, or, in a few extreme cases, even billions,

of dollars. Some of these individuals are splashing their incomes into buying "monster houses," expensive yachts, private planes, modern paintings
that cost tens of millions of dollars, extravagant vacations, Ferraris, Rolls-
Royces, Rolex watches, and other expensive luxury goods.

The question to be asked is: What effects do these incomes and these
consumption standards have on the psychology of less lucky persons and,
importantly, on citizens who, in spite of their lower incomes, continue to
have the power to vote in democratic countries? Can it be assumed that the
poor and the average middle class voter will be grateful to the rich individuals, because the rich individuals are not allowing their *absolute* incomes to
fall? This question merits being addressed, especially in countries that have
market economies *and* continue to have democratic governments.

In a classic article titled "Economic possibilities for our grandchildren",
first written in 1930, Keynes wrote that "the needs of human beings ... fall
into two classes – those needs which are absolute in the sense that we feel
them whatever the situation of our fellow human beings may be, and those
which are relative in the sense that we feel them only if their satisfaction
lifts us above, makes us feel superior to our fellows"; he added that "needs
of the second class ... may ... be insatiable" (in Keynes, 1933, p. 365). He
was essentially discussing the importance of absolute and relative incomes
and of what could be called *sensory needs* and *psychological needs*.

Now ask, again, how those who have not seen much increase in their
absolute income feel when they see the "insatiable needs" of the lucky ones
being satisfied to an extent that they or their children cannot even dream
of, while they are stuck in their low, current spending patterns, while new
products continually appear in the shops that they sometimes visit, and
while, perhaps, some of the cheaper products or services that they had
bought in the past at affordable prices are no longer available or are no
longer available in the areas where they live. Furthermore, as Adam Smith
observed, "poverty ... is extremely unfavorable to the rearing of children"
(1937, p. 79). Much recent research has reached a similar conclusion.

If one has been living in a modest house and has not been too dissatisfied with it in the past, and now sees houses that are ten or more times
bigger than one's own house being built down the road, it is not likely that
the individual will not be affected and will continue to feel as satisfied as
before with the house the individual lives in and with the unchanged absolute income, even if that income might still protect the individual from
cold weather and hunger.

The aforementioned example leads us to a human characteristic that is
often not admired but that for sure plays a major role in the real world in

determining welfare and attitudes toward society and policies. We could call that characteristic *envy*, although the concept is broader than the strict definition of the word *envy*. The characteristic *envy* includes feelings of inadequacy; general dissatisfaction with one's own condition; a feeling that life and societal arrangements have not been kind and fair; and a dissatisfaction with the society in which one lives and with the policymakers that make economic decisions.

This must be the feeling of many of those who belong to the middle class, made up of workers who may not have experienced any wage increases in many years or may have lost jobs that had paid a good income. As Adam Smith put it in *The Theory of Moral Sentiments* ([1969] 1976, p. 127), "There is scarce any man who does not respect more the rich and the great than the poor and the humble." Envy may be the other and uglier face of respect.

Envy is normally characterized as a defect of the human personality, and in normal situations it is definitely not an admirable quality. One should not envy those who are in better conditions or are luckier than one is. However, ignoring the moral aspect of envy in normal situations, it must be recognized that some circumstances can generate what could be considered normal or understandable *negative, psychologically based externalities* to which it would be difficult and not smart for a society not to pay attention.

A negative externality is definitely created for many hard-working but poorly paid workers when they become aware that there are individuals with very high incomes and consumption who are claiming all the country's growth in income. This happens in democratic societies that keep repeating the notion that all human beings are created equal and that there are no divine rights for some to have a privileged status. The argument that, in a market economy, high incomes are always merited is not likely to impress many of those who work hard but receive incomes barely sufficient, or often insufficient, to support a dignified lifestyle for themselves and their children.

There are increasing numbers of situations in which, because of luck at birth (what the economist R. Chetty and others have called the "birth lottery" or "birthright lottery") or luck at a later time in people's lives, or because of connections, cronyism, or abuses of the market, some individuals end up getting very large incomes and accumulating much wealth, while others, who may work as hard, are left far behind. This creates resentment on the part of the latter, especially when they do not see their situations improving over the years. It creates results that are hard to accept as simply the ethical or natural outcome of an amoral but otherwise fair market economic system. For a growing number of individuals, it is likely to generate unpleasant moral reactions, reactions that some may define, or criticize, as "class warfare." These individuals will show less respect for the market economy.

Obviously, it is silly to believe that incomes could be equalized, as Marx believed and as Lenin and Mao tried to do in Russia and China, and others have tried to do in other countries. Such attempts require the abandonment of the market system and generally lead to economic stagnation and to equality in poverty or worse. They also require the destruction of much, or the loss of all, the political and economic liberty that citizens enjoy in market economies with democratic political systems. Some significant variances in incomes are needed and must be tolerated by a market economy. These variances are associated with efficiency considerations to maintain incentives for individuals to sustain effort and to promote growth.

Thus, the issue is not replacing a market economy with central planning or with some other system to promote the objective of equality at any cost. The issue is whether *any* differences in incomes, regardless of how huge they might be, must be accepted in a market economy, especially when there are questions or doubts about the rules that have generated those differences, and when there are significant economic problems at the middle or lower end of the income distribution, problems that cannot be attributed simply or conveniently to laziness. The question is largely empirical. Must the search for more equality in a country such as the United States, where inequality has reached very high levels, necessarily lead to economic stagnation and to the loss of political liberty for the citizens, as some argue? Is there really no middle way?

In the following chapters I shall return to and defend three conclusions that have already been suggested or implied in earlier chapters.

The first is that the results of the market, in terms of the personal distribution of income, have become increasingly different and less socially desirable compared with those that would exist in a well-working market and in a country in which the *total* economic role of the state was completely neutral. This conclusion contrasts with the one still promoted in much academic literature, and especially in the work of economists who continue to trust the market and to assign to it a moral justification. According to those works, one should accept and respect the judgment of the market, a judgment that should not be changed ex post by governmental intervention, carried out with the use of taxes, spending programs, some regulations, and occasionally with other means,

The second conclusion is that the income distribution that the market generates is, in part, the consequence of the set of rules, protections, and policies that the government has established, has provided, and has allowed over many years. Without those rules and protections, the income and the distribution of income generated by the market would have been different, even if the market had worked as efficiently and as ethically as some economists assume that it does, given the existing rules.

The third conclusion is that, in the modern world, luck in its various aspects is playing an increasingly important role in generating large incomes for some individuals, and that the importance of luck has increased in modern economies because of the existence of modern technologies and government rules,that allow individuals to capitalize on it. With different technologies and different government rules, the importance of luck would be much reduced. This also raises the question of whether the government should reduce the role that luck plays in determining the disposable incomes of individuals with its tax and spending policies. In the following chapters I shall address in some detail the aforementioned conclusions.

CHAPTER 29

How Should Governments Intervene?

The view that, in the absence of the government's redistributive policies (played with taxes, spending programs, and some regulations), the income distribution that the market generates would be the same as the one that would exist if the government did not exist and the market operated optimally is naïve and not well anchored in historical developments. Many of the rules and the policies that governments have adopted over decades or even over centuries – (a) in relation to the market power that the governments have allowed private enterprises to have; (b) in the building of necessary infrastructure; (c) in foreign trade relations and operations; (d) in the operations of enterprises and banks and in their legal structures; (e) in the protection of real property; (f) in the protection, increasingly, of intellectual properties; (g) in financing fundamental research and development; (h) in the use of natural resources, including land, water, air, and minerals; (i) in financing education; (j) in limiting the liability of corporations; (k) in recognizing the legal existence of corporations; (l) in bankruptcy rules; and (m) in the creation of money by central banks and in determining access to that money from central banks – have made a great difference to the growth of countries' economies and of particular sectors, and also to the way in which the market operates and the countries' income gets created and distributed to the citizens. In some cases, governments have gone to war with other countries to protect the interests of particular industries, as, for example, they have done for the petroleum industry.

Governments have not stayed out of the way of market forces in the past and cannot be expected to stay out of the way in the future. They intervene to help and protect important national industries in various ways, and to create the ecology in which national markets operate. Inevitably, governments make mistakes, and at times they end up hurting the private sector. However, the main point here is that governments are *never* neutral in their impact on the distribution of income.

Over the years, the way governments intervene changes, but their presence is always a constant. Clearly, as was argued in an earlier chapter, and as Adam Smith stressed in his writing, communities and countries need governments; and the existence of government, *before* any intentional redistributive policies are undertaken, inevitably helps some sectors more than others and some individuals more than others, thus affecting the way incomes are created and get distributed.

To get some evidence of the aforementioned observation, all that is needed is to read some historical accounts, written by professional historians, on the role that governments and especially the US government played in assisting some enterprises or some industries in the past, when the government was more out of the way than it is today. Almost at random, three recent books, on the development of the Coca-Cola Company, the cotton industry, and the Internet, could be cited.

Bartow Elmore (2014), commenting on the incredible world success of the Coca-Cola Company – a company that was started by a small-time pharmacist in Atlanta – wrote that coke has taken advantage of global public works and has needed government interventions to succeed in world market, and pointed out that it uses almost as much water as a quarter of the world population. Furthermore, the company is an environmental threat. It has contributed to the spread of diabetes and to major recycling costs. However, the "Coca-Cola company" *with governmental assistance*, has made a lot of money for its shareholders.

Sven Beckert (2014), writing on the development of the cotton industry, argued that governmental intervention was often behind the expanding cotton industry with the financing of the infrastructure that big cotton growers and mills demanded. It is not appreciated that *public* infrastructure is often demand-driven. It is driven by the needs of the *private* sector and contributes to the profits of those industries that derive the most benefits from the publicly provided infrastructure. At other times the profits of particular sectors have benefited from the use of import duties or other kinds of import restrictions. Some of these restrictions continue to exist in most countries, including the United States, as well as in government contracts and in other areas. In the United States they were very important during the rise of big business in the period after the Civil War.

A more interesting and more modern example comes from the story behind the development and the use of the Internet. It is also in part the story behind the creation of many intellectual property rights, rights that are at the base of some of the largest incomes and fortunes in today's world. The Internet story has been told in a recent book by Andrew Keen (2015), who pointed out that the Internet has been associated with, perhaps, the greatest creation of private wealth in the world Intellectual property, often linked to the use of the Internet, has allowed some "owners" of that property, such as Zuckerberg and Gates, to become billionaires many times over, while the basic infrastructure (the Internet) has been funded with public money and has had specific public goals in mind. The intellectual property rights that have been claimed by some and have been protected by the government have generated enormous incomes, while those who have gained the most have at times ignored some basic responsibilities, according to Keen. The question of intellectual property rights is an interesting one that will require additional comments later on. On the creation and role of the Internet, the accounts in Mazzucato (2013); Brynjolfsson and McAfee (2014); and Gates (2016) are all interesting.

In all the aforementioned examples, large private incomes were made possible by government investments and by some of its current or earlier actions, including the financing of fundamental research. If the government had not been there, those incomes would not have been generated and there would be far fewer rich people today. Thus, it is disingenuous for some to argue that the incomes received by high-income individuals belong exclusively to them, and that the government has no right to claim or to claw back some of those incomes through taxes. The truth is that the government has had a lot to do with those incomes, and it should be a kind of silent shareholder in the earnings that it has made possible.

It is also disingenuous to argue that the distribution of income that the market generates is necessarily the natural, legitimate one. There is, thus, justification for the government to intervene in the economy to some extent with its redistributive policies. In this way, through taxes, society as a whole can reclaim some returns from the investment that it had financed, just as in crop-sharing arrangements that have existed in some European countries since Roman times, in which the landowners are entitled to a share of crops (in traditional arrangements, up to 50 percent) produced by tenants on their land. The relevant question is what should be the share, not whether the government has a right to some share.

If the government intervenes to change the current income distribution to make it more equitable, how should it do so? Are taxing and public spending the only, or always the right, way? If the government is to claim part of the output without other changes, as with crop-sharing arrangements, then taxing and spending may be the natural and only way, and the issue becomes the size of the share. However, if the objective is to make the income distribution that the market generates more in line with what it would be without the traditional arrangements that the government has created or made possible, there may be other and, from an efficiency point of view, possibly better ways to achieve it.

With what tools should the government intervene? At what desirable outcomes should it aim? These are important but difficult questions. They move the discussion to the difficult realm of "normative" economics, and also to economic policy. It is results and not intentions that ultimately should matter. These concerns also move the discussion back to the question of the possible existence of *termites of the state* in the current arrangements, which is the main theme of this book.

In many ways, a market economy resembles a game of soccer or of American football in that, during the game, the players are expected to follow pre-agreed rules, rules that are enforced by a presumably objective referee. The rules and the referee *both* inevitably end up influencing the results of the game. They may favor some players or some teams over others. In the market, the current government should be the referee that enforces the rules, but in some ways it and previous governments have also set the rules. The current government should enforce the current rules until they are changed, and should also follow and interpret the wishes of the past, current, and possibly future citizens, to the extent that is possible.

In today's world the rules are numerous. Increasingly, they need to be adjusted from time to time to reflect new technologies, new attitudes, and new conditions, some connected with domestic developments and some imposed by developments in international markets and by agreements reached, freely, with other countries and with international organizations. The rules indicate what private operators (individuals and enterprises) can and cannot do, within the country in which they operate, without running into legal constraints and penalties, and without committing acts of corruption. At the time of this writing, rules concerning the taxation of global activities and also about the treatment of intellectual property by other countries had become particularly important and were attracting a lot of attention. Increasingly, some market operators within countries are foreigners, a fact that creates additional difficulties, and that requires more or different formal rules on the part of *national* governments than in the past.

It is not fully appreciated the extent to which, with the passing of time, government-imposed rules have replaced the spontaneously developed social or community rules that had existed in the past and that had guided the social, commercial, or economic behavior of individuals and enterprises in what was a simpler world, one in which the word "community"

had a clearer meaning and played a larger role in guiding social and economic behavior.

In past centuries, the principles enunciated by the Ten Commandments
for Christians and Jews, and by similar guidelines or codes of conduct
for those who practiced different religions, hand, for more economically
oriented exchanges, spontaneously developed rules, such as, for example,
those imposed by the *lex mercatoria*, the law that had offered guidance
for legitimate, or accepted, behavior in economic activities (see Benson,
1989). Deviations from established economic and other principles were
expected to be punished in various ways (hell, time spent in purgatory, jail,
execution, pillory, lashes, expulsion from guilds, etc.). Often, *principles*
more than precise *rules* guided the economic relations. Some of those principles may no longer be acceptable for, or be sufficient in, modern societies
because of the likelihood that they would be differently interpreted.

Rules, now issued by modern governments, and increasingly in coordination with other governments and with international organizations, have,
to a large extent, replaced the broader *principles*, or the guidelines, that
had existed in the past. These rules are created to deal with *current* actions
and *current* perceptions of what is proper, legitimate, and necessary. The
problem is that it is difficult for specific rules to anticipate future needs and
to stipulate specific future actions that may be guided by new and unanticipated circumstances, for example, developments in synthetic biology,
in the editing of the human genome, in driverless vehicles, in the use of
drones and robots, and in several other areas.

Global and technological developments are creating situations that had
not been foreseen when the relevant official norms, which may still guide
current behavior, were created. This is happening in various technological
or biological areas, in taxation, in financial market activities, and in social
relations. For this reason new rules are, or must be, created to catch up
with new developments. Modern rules have also replaced past principles
and past forms of punishment for the violation of rules.

Interestingly, this concept was obvious to Abraham Lincoln when he
stated:

> I am not an advocate for frequent changes in laws and constitutions.
> But laws and institutions must go hand in hand with the progress of the
> human mind. As that becomes more developed, more enlightened, as
> new discoveries are made, new truths discovered and manners and opin-
> ions change, with the change of circumstances, institutions must advance
> also to keep pace with the times" (engraved on the Lincoln Memorial in
> Washington, DC).

As economies have grown and have become more developed and more advanced, they have also become more complex. As was mentioned in an earlier chapter, the geographical and social scope covered by economic transactions among parties has extended progressively, from the original, small geographical areas (the village) and the few products exchanged in the past (handmade products, natural food, and simple services such as haircuts), to the larger and larger areas and the greater number of products and services. For some transactions the geographical area now covers the whole world. Increasingly, many economic transactions now take place between individuals from different cities and from different countries, and between individuals who do not know one another, have never met, and, often, will never meet. Communications and exchanges no longer require physical contacts or physical products..

Take the financial sector as an example. There was a time when people lent their savings to relatives and to close acquaintances. Then, small, local banks appeared that were linked territorially within a particular geographic area. In that area some individuals who had temporary excess balances ("savers") deposited their money in the local banks; others, who could use the excess balances ("investors"), borrowed the money from the banks to make investments or to meet other current needs. This was a simple and easy-to-understand world. In many cases, the actors knew one another. Occasionally, when mistakes were made or unusual events occurred, that world was subjected to territorially limited financial panics and crises that could have had serious local consequences. In that world it was easy to identify the main actors, who often were individuals from the same communities, and to understand the nature of the transactions they were engaged in and the rules that guided them.

Today, the financial market has become global and is made up of participants who are very different from those of the past, and who operate in a global space and are guided by different incentives. In many cases it has become difficult to identify the savers from the investors or the investors from the consumers in need of temporary loans, or borrowers who are neither real investors nor real consumers, but who want to gamble with borrowed money. A large part of the borrowing is now directed at smoothing consumption over time, rather than at making real, productive investments, or at gambling by making bets in market activities. Trillions of dollars cross national borders on a daily basis.

"Shadow banking" – that is, the financing activities conducted outside traditional commercial banks by investment banks, equity funds, hedge funds, sovereign funds, and others – have enormously increased the scope, the complexity, the profitability, and the risks of the financial sector. "Securitization," for example, went from no use in the 1970s to an estimated $10 trillion of use before the financial crisis. Securitization, which is the aggregation of many loans (such as individual mortgages) into single financial instruments, could hide a lot of bad or misleading information on the quality of some of the underlying assets.

However, the *basic* or potentially useful function of the financial sector has remained essentially the same: *connecting those who have money to lend* (let us continue to call them "savers") with *those who want to borrow money* ("investors"). And the main risk has remained the same: liquid assets are often lent to finance illiquid activities. The thousands of specific rules that governments have created have not significantly changed that reality or reduced the risks. The function of the financial market has remained facilitating *financial transactions*, but, now, it does so in a much more complex way than in the past.

The activity or the function of the financial market is not that of *directly* producing anything, although it can help investors to make potentially productive investments, as, for example, with some of the "venture capital" or with some of those who borrow money to make real, productive investments. Yet, at least in the United States, over recent decades, this "transaction activity" has increased its share of total corporate profits from around 5 percent after World War II to around 40 percent in recent years. Huge incomes have been generated for some individuals in the financial market. Whether these incomes are really "earned and deserved" is a highly controversial question. However, they have come to be expected.

These profits have been generating enormous wealth for some individuals, derived from incomes that, in some cases, may be very close to being rents. Government policies in creating a global financial market have been instrumental in creating, for some financial operators, the possibility of earning enormous incomes. In many cases it has become more difficult to make strong arguments that these incomes represent genuine value, created in the market, that increases social welfare and, thus, that they should not be reduced by government taxes and by other policies, because they are *fully earned and deserved.*

In some cases there has been an asymmetry in time in the value created, for example, when bubbles have created incomes by increasing the resale value of houses, values that quickly disappear after the bubbles, reducing the wealth of many individuals, but leaving the original incomes in the hands of financial operators. This development can distort, for some years, the growth rates of some countries and also the fiscal accounts of some governments, because taxes were collected from virtual and temporary incomes. This clearly happened in Spain, Ireland, and some other countries before the financial crisis arrived and the bubble burst (see Tanzi, 2015c). The bubble before the financial crisis had inflated the value of newly built houses, value that vanished after the housing bubble burst, leading to many cases of foreclosure and great economic difficulties.

The determination of the "genuine" incomes generated, and of the taxes that those who operate in the financial sector and also in the global economy should pay, has become more difficult. The opportunities for abuses on the part of some of those who operate in those activities have become greater and the abuses more frequent, as almost daily reports and many books and articles on the recent financial crisis and on global tax avoidance have indicated. Some of the financial institutions have been asked by the US government to pay penalties at times in the billions of dollars for having engaged in what have been considered illegal or illegitimate activities. By December 2016, $58 billion had been paid in such penalties.

Similar trends have characterized some nonfinancial enterprises that operate globally, and especially those that perform activities linked with the use of intellectual capital. Some very large and profitable enterprises, such as Apple and Google, have been able to pay very low taxes, because of the way they have arranged their global accounts, taking advantage of legal loopholes in the tax systems, loopholes that the lobbyists for the enterprises had been able to insert in the tax laws, in the past and taking advantage of the existence of so-called tax havens. (See various articles in Pogge and Mehta, 2016.)

For many enterprises, the determination of the taxable incomes and of the tax liabilities has become a contentious issue. Tax avoidance connected with these global activities, especially with those involving some use of intellectual capital, has been estimated to amount to hundreds of billions of dollars and has been increasingly worrying the governments of many countries. This loss of public revenue has contributed to swelling the incomes of the rich and the super rich, thus increasing the Gini coefficients in many countries. Dependent workers are not the ones who benefit from these tax avoidance schemes.

Many exchanges in the modern economies involve the buying and the selling of goods and services for which the prices set in the contracts and paid by the buyers provide much less information than is assumed by price theory. The genuine value to the buyer of what has been bought is not known until the product or the service is actually used. Even standard products such as new cars may contain defects not known by the buyers, and not revealed by the sellers at the time of the transactions. Problems connected with asymmetry of information between buyers and sellers, and with the fact that those engaged in the transactions may often adhere to different codes of behavior and/or may live in different countries, have become common, raising difficult questions *about what the role of the state should be in this area.* These questions have led to debates between "market fundamentalists," on one side, and "market interventionists," on the other. The latter believe that without effective and enforced government rules and controls, abuses become common. The US Consumer Protection Agency was created because of this belief.

Another problem is that, often, the rules are not applied fairly and equally because they are not clear and lend themselves to different interpretations. They may also tend to confuse those who must follow them, and may be abused by some. Furthermore, as argued in an earlier chapter, regulations should be frequently updated and pruned of anachronisms. They rarely are. The absence of global and efficient regulators with sufficient resources and expertise contributes to some of the difficulties. This problem is now better recognized in particular sectors, such as the financial and pharmaceutical sectors, but problems continue to exist, because solutions are difficult to implement and are strongly resisted from some quarters.

How some of those who are regulated see the problem can be conveyed by citing an announcement for a seminar at the Cato Institute in Washington, DC on May 19, 2014. The title of the seminar was "Mugged by the State: When Regulators and Prosecutors Bully Citizens." The announcement stated, "The federal regulatory code has become so voluminous that it now bewilders *ordinary* citizens. The web of rules and regulations is now so vast that people can become ensnared in circumstances where they meant no harm" (italics added). The speakers were representatives of *regulated* industries. It is not likely that the lawyers of the regulated *industries* are in the same situation as the "ordinary *citizens*." Industry representatives would, of course, argue in favor of rules that promote more "civil liberties" and more "economic freedom" for the *industries*.

The issue of the complexity of the rules is clearly a universal and important one. While it justifies a concern about the rules' complexity, it does not necessarily imply that the rules should not exist, or that there should necessarily be fewer rules. Bad and unnecessary rules should clearly be eliminated, but new, necessary ones might be needed, and, when created, they should be clearly stated and objectively enforced. The proposal of the

Trump administration to replace two existing regulations with every new one introduced makes no logical sense.

National governments enact new laws that must often be accompanied by "implementing regulations." As mentioned in an earlier chapter, both the laws and the regulations often run into thousands of not-easy-to-interpret pages. It is not likely that many of those who vote for and approve them read them carefully and in their entirety. If they do, it is not likely that they fully understand them. The laws are increasingly written *by lawyers for lawyers* and use a legal language, often referred to as "legalese," that lawyers have developed. It is a language that only well trained lawyers can fully or easily understand. That language is far less clear for normal citizens than, for example, were the simple principles or instructions that, in the distant past, were written on stones and were visibly placed in public places where the average person, who could read, could easily understand them and could fear the penalties. An example is the "Hammurabi Code" written on a stone. It can be seen in the Louvre Museum in Paris.

To a significant extent, the general instructions that told citizens to follow a "morally based" behavior have been replaced by modern laws and rules that tell citizens to follow a specific and "legally accepted" behavior. In several areas (such as in the determination of tax liabilities, requests for government benefits, decisions by enterprises to follow existing regulations, and activities in the financial market), behavior that many citizens might not consider "moral" is not punishable by law, because it is not explicitly "illegal" and thus is not forbidden by an existing norm or rule. It might be immoral or questionable, but is not explicitly "illegal."

Some of these problems became evident in the financial sector during the financial crisis of 2007–2008. They are also becoming progressively more evident in the activities of some enterprises in other areas, especially in the production of energy and pharmaceutical products. The pursuit of higher profits is often facilitated by the existence of more "civil liberties," which exist when there are no rules. It continues to affect the stock market, where insider information, or more quickly obtained information, received milliseconds before some others get it, can provide illegitimate, but not necessarily or clearly illegal, advantages to some (see Lewis, 2014).

The aforementioned conflict is perhaps now most clearly perceived in the distinction that exists, and has become more marked in recent years, between "tax avoidance" and "tax evasion." In both, the ultimate objective, on the part of those who engage in these attempts, is to avoid paying taxes, or to reduce their tax payments. However, while "tax avoidance" exploits existing loopholes in the tax legislations of countries and relies on favorable interpretations of ambiguous rules, and is thus not clearly illegal and punishable, tax evasion breaks some tax rules and is thus punishable. Large enterprises, such as Apple and Starbucks, that have paid little taxes on enormous world profits have argued, with some justification, that they have been following existing laws and have not been evading taxes. The problem is the tax laws and not their behavior.

Expressions such as "inversion," "transfer prices," "patent boxes," "thin capitalization," and "double Irish" have entered the lexicon of media reporting. They reflect tax avoidance strategies used by corporations. Similar examples could be provided from several areas of the financial market or from other sectors. Once again it must be remarked that those who benefit from these interpretations are not the average workers, and that these strategies end up affecting Gini coefficients and equity.

Because of their number, their complexity, and the way in which they are now written (often requiring thousands of pages), many laws and regulations lend themselves to different interpretations by clever lawyers and accountants. Well-trained and clever individuals acquire deep knowledge of them, or of the parts that interest them. These individuals become better able to defend particular interpretations of them that are favorable to their clients. The high incomes that these activities can generate for those who engage in them have created a strong economic incentive for clever individuals to enter professions such as those of accountants, tax lawyers, investment advisors, and lobbyists, professions that have become among the best-paid activities. These individuals become very able at navigating the thick fog that often surrounds many of the regulations and the laws, and, increasingly, at influencing the drafting or the interpretation of them with their lobbying activities. Complexity creates asymmetry between the general population and the experts, in what James Buchanan called the "political market," challenging the view that in a democracy laws are equal for all citizens.

Goldman Sachs, Citibank, and other financial institutions have been frequent hiring grounds for high government positions. Increasingly, individuals in high positions in the Federal Reserve System, in the US Treasury, in the Pentagon, in central banks, in regulatory agencies, and in similar places have come from the financial market and often from particular enterprises. Some of them occasionally go back to the institutions from which they came. These people bring to their government positions the useful knowledge acquired in their previous activities and, while in their public jobs, acquire the inside, detailed expertise and knowledge of the rules and, especially, the valuable personal contacts that they can use when they go back to private-sector jobs, including those of lobbyists.

Some years ago, Senator Rockefeller, when he represented West Virginia in the US Senate, addressing the lack of enforcement of regulations in the coal industry in his state – which in one circumstance led to an environmental disaster in which thousands of West Virginians could not drink the polluted water that came out of their pipes because the water had been polluted by discharges from the coal companies – stated that the regulators are frankly in bed with the regulated.

These kinds of statements may be exaggerations and possibly reflect political biases, but they point to the existence of a real problem – the extent to which the government may have become an instrument that some vested, private interests can use for their benefits, while that use distorts the efficiency and the equity of the market, favoring a few over the many. The impact that this problem must have in the determination of some very high incomes is rather obvious. The fact that not all agree with these concerns has been made clear by the people who have been chosen to serve in the Trump administration, and by the policies that they have proposed to introduce. Time will tell how those policies will work.

The personal connections of some individuals with high-level public employees, or with politicians with public power in particular areas, have acquired great potential economic values for them. At times, the role that these connections play in market transactions or decisions make a mockery of the supposed impersonal working attributed to the market. If connections are as important in many market transactions as the financial media frequently reports, market prices (including interest rates and exchange rates) must not always play the fundamental and legitimate role attributed to them by economic theory. For some individuals, connections have become similar in value to what nobility titles used to entail in past, traditional societies. They facilitate the opening of many doors, and, for some individuals, they become roads to riches and privileges. Connections have acquired a kind of economically valuable intellectual capital, at times, more valuable in generating incomes than real property. Individuals who acquired important connections during the time they spent in high-level but often low-paying government positions are able to cash in and to earn large incomes, after leaving their official positions, by facilitating contacts with relevant public officials for private investors, or in other ways.

Good examples have come in recent years from former prime ministers of some countries and from several political figures in the United States, the United Kingdom, and other countries who had held important government positions. Some left their previous positions to go immediately, or after short intervals, into well-paid private positions, where their connections would prove useful and valuable. In a few years, some acquired considerable wealth. One must wonder if the future financial possibilities that high government positions offer are also influencing the types of individuals who are now attracted by high government positions.

These individuals essentially earn large incomes by "selling" access to individuals who have the power to make economically valuable decisions. They assume positions similar to those of the "keepers of the gate." In developing countries, the keepers of the gate are more often relatives of the powerful. Connections have become useful in those areas of today's economies in which the private market and the public sector are not separated by a firewall, and where the private market does not operate as smoothly as theory continues to claim that it does, and often requires some government collaboration, intervention, or authorization. The increase in the numbers of negative externalities and of the regulations to deal with them has widened the areas where public and private intersect. Connections are valuable in part because of the role that the government has come to play in many private decisions, and because that role can be influenced and manipulated to better fit or promote the interests of particular groups. Some enterprises can benefit from influencing policies that governments pursue, be they tax policies, trade policies, policies regarding some investments that require government authorizations, regulatory policies, or others.

The growing complexity of the economies that has accompanied the expanding regulatory and general economic role of the state has contributed to the expansion of the *lobbying industry*. This industry has become a growth industry in several countries, and especially in the United States. Lobbyists, financed by deep-pocketed billionaires, by profitable enterprises, or by representatives of some interest groups, push for new laws or for modifications of existing laws to promote what they claim to be more "civil and economic liberty." They also push for the interpretation of rules that would further benefit the industries or the activities or groups that the lobbyists represent. It is a "salami technique" that operates one slide at a time, but that, over the longer run, changes the economic landscape, generates significant benefits for some individuals or groups, and distorts the distribution of income.

Some lobbying activities have taken refuge within law and accounting firms and increasingly within think tanks, of which there are now several thousand, many of them conveniently, or strategically, located in cities such as Washington, DC and other important capitals, such as Brussels, where the European Commission is located; Paris, where the OECD is located; and Frankfurt, where the ECB is located. London, New York, and other important cities are also magnets for the location of think tanks. Some think tanks have become largely lobbying centers. They keep close contacts with both the legislative and the executive branches of governments and with significant international organizations, and send "expert witnesses" to congressional or parliamentary hearings to promote the agendas of those who finance them.

Under the mantle of doing "research," which is often financed by special interests, the think tanks push particular points of view and promote the interests of particular individuals or particular enterprises or industries. To find employment in these think tanks, it is not sufficient for an individual to be intellectually able and inquisitive, and to have a significant academic background; one must also share the specific ideological points of view of those who finance them. To a lesser extent some individuals in academia have been independently playing the same role, as a documentary, *The Inside Job*, argued.

Some observers may consider the think tanks to be genuine expressions of a vibrant, democratic process at work in a free market of ideas, as they would consider to be the large sums spent by rich individuals in financing the political campaigns of particular politicians. They are both in some sense expressions of political freedom. The problem is that the think tanks produce particular ideas *for money*. Clearly, money has entered the process of generating and promoting politically relevant ideas and is influencing the market of ideas. The more money is spent to promote particular points of view, the greater is the push for those points of view, and the brighter are the people that the money will attract to them. That is a way in which financial power may have become a more effective tool for promoting the interests of particular individuals or groups. As an aside, it may be noted that practically all the major American newspapers, today, are owned by deep-pocketed billionaires.

Some highly visible academics have been reported to have published papers that promoted points of view that were particularly favorable to the groups that had sponsored and financed their research. Perhaps, the world has always been this way, to some extent. The votes that an idea receives are influenced by the dollars that are spent on that idea. So, there is here a kind of intellectual prostitution at work. The brains rather than the bodies are hired for performing some services and for providing and generating specific results.

Often, the work of well-connected lobbyists, some nested in think tanks or with close relations with specific think tanks, succeeds in introducing what may appear to be minor changes in the wording of a draft law or a regulation, changes that may go unnoticed when the law or the regulation is passed, or when it is written, but that can bring large benefits to some. There have been reports about some of these minor changes in wording that have generated gains worth billions of dollars for particular enterprises, or even for particular individuals or families. Some of these changes have involved tax laws and regulations.

Another problem with specific legal regulations, as distinguished from general regulatory principles, is that, as was mentioned in an earlier chapter, they tend to be backward looking. They aim at correcting problems that have appeared in the recent past and that have been noted, and not those likely or anticipated to appear in the future and not yet widely noted. This happened after the Enron problem and again after the recent financial crisis. Being specific, the regulations cannot anticipate and deal with future problems and developments, as Mervyn King stressed in his recent book (2016). Like the famous Maginot Line, which was supposed to protect France from German invasion, the regulations aim at fighting the most-recent war. But their very existence stimulates attempts, by clever individuals, to go around them, by creating situations not covered by the rules and thus not forbidden by them. This has been evident both in the fiscal and in the financial area. Governments have continued to be engaged, often with limited success, in a continuous and not always successful catchup game.

With the passing of time, it has become progressively more difficult for normal citizens to keep abreast of all the rules and all the laws that are continually being created. The laws are no longer created mostly for the citizens but for the operators of specific sectors, such as the financial, health, and energy sectors. Because of the number and complexity of the norms, it has become easier for less principled individuals, and especially for those with high financial means who can hire the best experts to find ways around, or ways to bend, the existing rules. This is making the market less and less the fair and level playing field that it should be for all those who participate in it. It also raises increasing doubts about the view that all the incomes earned reflect the value created by those who receive the incomes. This is the view that makes incomes *earned* and *deserved*. If they are truly deserved, it is easier to make arguments that high incomes should not be reduced by high taxes.

If some of the aforementioned arguments are even approximately correct, the opportunities in the market are no longer equal for all those who operate in it, if they ever were, and they are not randomly distributed among the population. The "legislative inflation" has created different opportunities for the privileged few (many among the 1 percent) and for the majority (most among the 99 percent). The 1 percent, or in many cases the 0.1 percent, have the means to hire the clever experts and to have them interpret the laws and the rules in their favor. They can also hire the lobbyists, fund the think tanks, and finance the campaigns of politicians to push for laws and rules that are more favorable to them. They also have easier access to the public officials who count.

Experts and lobbyists are expensive to use, so most citizens cannot afford them unless they have a strong enough incentive to create interest groups that can act as lobbies for them, for example, those that have been created by retirees to protect their pension rights and their interests, or those created by the schoolteachers of some states to defend their employment rights and their benefits. These interest groups have their special objectives to push, objectives that may not be those of the general citizens, who individually face the classic obstacles described several decades ago by the late Mancur Olson (1965). As he explained, a common problem in democracy is that it is not worthwhile for an individual, qua individual, to spend time and effort to learn about new laws and new rules, when as an individual the power that he or she has to influence and to change them comes only from his or her single vote, which is one among millions. Rich individuals have other options. The situation risks becoming similar to one in which, in a community, there is no general police force to protect the population, but there are private guards who protect the properties of those individuals who can afford to hire them.

As a sociologist put it some years ago in an interesting book, "Democracy … is cherished chiefly as a means for the pursuit of individual and collective values … [but] it can also be conceived as a system for the protection of class privileges or for the pursuit of greed and narrow material ambitions" (see Wuthnow, 1991, p. 288). He could have added that the market can become an instrument in which money creates more bonds and more common interests among rich people. Some recent writers have argued that this has in fact happened (see Lofgren, 2015).

The basic conclusion of this chapter is that, progressively and not always transparently, the rules of the game, which should determine the way the private market and the capitalist system work in a democracy, with the passing of time have become less objective, less transparent, and less universal. Taken together with other developments, including increasing complexity and growing asymmetry in information, these developments are probably contributing to the growing income disparity that has come to characterize many countries, and especially the United States, in recent decades. The new rules of the game, and especially the results in terms of income generation and income distribution, have invited increasingly frequent questions about the fairness of the market and of the system. Some have been arguing that "the system is rigged" and have led calls for changes. The problem is that it is easier to identify the problem than to suggest concrete solutions. There are really no easy and optimal solutions.

The situation described has contributed to the rise of populism now evident in the United States and in several other countries, and also to the continued push, on the part of some groups, for more public spending and for higher taxes, especially on the rich, as well as for more regulations on some sectors of the market, especially on the financial market. The remarkable successes, first, of the book by Piketty in 2014 and, later, of Donald Trump in the 2016 US election are, from different angles, both signals of the problem discussed in this book and of its impact on the current world and on the need to bring changes.

A future that would de-emphasize specific rules and put more reliance on good general principles would seem desirable. However, such a future would be complicated by the need to agree on the principles and to create institutions, similar to Supreme Courts, that would have the difficult task of determining the adherence, on the part of the actions of citizens and enterprises, to the spirit of the principles, in the same way that Supreme Courts now determine adherence to constitutional principles. It is easy to anticipate the fights that would take place in agreeing on the principles and on the selection of the members of such institutions. There would also be the danger that the new institutions could be subjected to capture by powerful groups. Therefore, this alternative would not be without great difficulties, as we already discussed in a previous chapter.

Some might argue that the constitutions themselves would need to be changed to make them more easily adaptable and more relevant to the changing situations, as Lincoln recognized. This in turn would raise the dangers of constitutional capture by politically and economically powerful groups and of the devaluation of the constitutions themselves.

CHAPTER 30

Intellectual Property and Income Distribution

In recent decades, several important developments, some described in earlier chapters, contributed to the observed changes in the income distributions of many countries that have led to greater income inequality and, especially, to greater income concentration at the very top. Economists have been debating the causes of this development. Some have attributed the changes in the distribution of income to the globalization of the world economy that has taken place, especially since the 1980s. They have argued that globalization has had a negative impact on the real wages of industrial workers in advanced countries, and especially of those in the United States, by moving the production of many industrial products to poorer countries and by importing those products from the poorer countries into the richer countries. These products are now produced, more cheaply, by lower-paid foreign workers, often using the rich countries' own technology, supervision, designs, brand name, and, often, even capital. A significant share of the final values of the imported products is claimed by the shareholders and the managers of the multinational enterprises in the rich countries.

The location where workers live and work has contributed partly to the "birth lottery" mentioned in an earlier chapter. Similar work is higher paid in rich than in poor countries. Countries that pay low wages and that now attract much industrial production include some large ones, such as China, India, Mexico, Bangladesh, Pakistan, and Indonesia, as well as many smaller ones. This development has led to the deindustrialization of advanced countries and to the stagnation of real wages for many of the latter countries' workers. It has also, indirectly, contributed to the high incomes received by the individuals and by the enterprises in industrial countries that provide the capital, the technology, and the supervision.

Other economists – especially Piketty (2014) – have attributed the deterioration in the income distribution in recent decades to more fundamental trends such as the presumably secular, higher rate of return to wealth compared to labor, leading as a consequence to the large role that inheritance of wealth plays in market economies. In that view, once families become rich, they tend to pass the wealth to the next generations within the same families. The higher rate of return to that wealth ensures that rich families remain rich families. Piketty recommended that a significant wealth tax be imposed to correct for this trend.

The question of taxing wealth and inheritance is, of course, not a new one. Various economists of the past, including John Stuart Mill and Luigi Einaudi, had discussed this possibility (see, for example, Mill, [1900] 2004, and Einaudi, 1946). However, many of today's very rich individuals did not inherit their wealth. They acquired it themselves, as the annual lists of the world's super rich, provided by Bloomberg and by Forbes, clearly indicate. Intellectual property, rather than inherited real wealth, has often played a major role. Thus, the treatment of intellectual property merits special attention.

When some countries imposed wealth taxes, as, for example, did President Francois Mitterand in France in the 1980s, they did not achieve much with this policy. Wealth taxes have rarely, if ever, played a major role in redistributing income, because of administrative and other difficulties. In a globalized world where wealth can be owned worldwide and in various liquid forms, the use of wealth taxes is likely to be even more disappointing than in the past, when wealth was more concrete, more visible, and more concentrated geographically. Much wealth would escape to other countries and would make greater use of borrowed names than it now does, unless there were full collaboration among countries, which is not likely, or unless there were an efficient world government, which is even less likely. For a recent, skeptical view of what wealth taxation can achieve, see Zolt (2016).

Other economists and political scientists have called attention to the decline in the power of labor unions in several countries, – especially in the United States in recent decades where unionized workers are now only about 7 percent of the workforce – as a consequence of globalization and of political changes. That decline reduced the bargaining power of workers, thus shifting the effective power and responsibility for decisions on the level of wages and on the distribution of revenue within enterprises from unionized workers to managers and shareholders (see Reich, 2015). The use of robots in place of workers in industrialized countries is accentuating this trend.

In some of his writings, Paul Krugman has argued that changes in political attitudes vis-à-vis inequality in recent decades that gave more importance to efficiency and made the payment of very high incomes to individuals in some activities socially acceptable are partly to blame for the increasing inequality. Those changes in attitudes were supported by the assumption, promoted by market fundamentalists, that the market is always right and that, therefore, the incomes that individuals receive in legitimate economic activities reflect what the individuals contribute to market value. This implied that high incomes must be seen as fully deserved, even when they may reflect little effort and much luck on the part of those who receive them.

While all these developments are likely to have played some role in reducing the growth of average wages in advanced countries, and in increasing them in some low-income countries, making the income distribution more even at a global level but less even within countries, they are not likely to have been the only or the most important factors. Other factors may have been more directly, or additionally, responsible for the changes in the income distributions that occurred. I have already mentioned many of these other factors. In the rest of this book I shall address some of them more directly. In particular I shall focus on three factors:

First, the incomes associated with the production, the ownership, and the use of *intellectual property* on the part of some individuals and enterprises have become increasingly important. The market value of some of this intellectual property was magnified in recent decades by the introduction of modern communication technologies, and by the fact that, because of policy changes, individuals and enterprises could operate in markets that were much wider than in the past because they had become global, and because they were no longer limited by national borders. Thus, new technologies had operated as a kind of global multiplier that dramatically increased the market value of intellectual property.

Second, and perhaps more controversially, some individuals and some groups of individuals seem to have acquired in recent decades a growing ability to promote their *private* interests through the *influence* that they have on the actions of *public* officials, on public policies, and on the distribution of revenue within their institutions. This aspect, which some describe as *crony capitalism*, but which is broader than cronyism, was already addressed in previous chapters. Therefore, we shall not return to it. It could be mentioned that the *Economist* has developed an index that is supposed to give some quantitative dimension to aspects of cronyism in different countries.

Third, a *reduction of the progressivity of tax systems* took place in various countries, starting mainly in the United States and the United Kingdom, in the 1980s. That reduction soon spread to other countries. This reduction in effective progressivity was especially significant for incomes at very high levels and incomes gained from capital sources, the incomes that are most important for rich individuals. It happened during decades when the share of total taxes into GDP had stopped growing in all OECD countries. The peak in the tax-to-GDP levels in those countries had been reached in the 1990s, according to OECD statistics. The result was that the tax systems of most countries became less burdensome on high incomes, even though, as a consequence of the greater income concentration, the top 5 or 1 percent in the income distribution may have been paying a higher share of total taxes on *reported taxable income* than it had in earlier decades.

These three factors, and especially the first and the third, will be discussed in some detail in this and the next chapter. However, no attempt will be made to quantify the relative importance of the aforementioned factors on the income distribution, due to obvious difficulties.

We shall start with the role that the growth of intellectual capital and its various legal designations as intellectual "property" may have played in recent decades. It will be argued that: (a) the growth of various forms of intellectual capital; (b) combined with the increasing designation of it as "property"; (c) combined with government policies that, over the years, widened the definition and the scope of what could qualify as "intellectual property"; and (d) combined with new communication technologies, and especially with the Internet, made the aforementioned factors more important in generating large incomes for a relatively small number of individuals and enterprises.

Even a casual observer of the economic scene would notice that intellectual property in its various and expanding forms has been playing a growing role in the market and in generating high incomes for some individuals. It has put some of them at the top of the income distribution within a short time period, and has made some enterprises the most important players in the economic scene. New, technologically based economic giants have replaced in economic importance and in market value the great *industrial* enterprises that had dominated the past. Some of today's richest individuals in the world and some of the largest enterprises owe their positions to their ownership of intellectual *property*.

Silicon Valley and similar centers where many of the new ideas that create intellectual property are produced now host new and important enterprises that use intellectual property to produce various forms of services, often of an intangible kind. These "idea factories" have replaced the industrial centers that in earlier decades had employed millions of well-paid industrial workers. The growth of intellectual property has also changed the locations where most incomes are generated, rendering previously rich industrial areas much less rich, as described by Vance (2016, in his best-selling book).

Some of the ideas that can lead to concrete commercial applications and that can be patented or protected in other ways as intellectual property can create time-limited and, during that time, largely unregulated monopolies for those who own that intellectual property. The monopolies can produce goods and services protected by the intellectual property label, and, using modern technology, they can sell them to users in that much larger market that, because of globalization, now represents virtually *the whole world.*

Furthermore, during the times when they hold the monopoly powers that their intellectual property enjoys, there are no regulatory controls imposed by governments on the prices that these time-limited monopolies charge and on the profits that they make, as there used to be in the past and continue to be for "natural monopolies." This, for example, has allowed some drug companies to charge astronomical prices for some drugs badly needed by individuals with particular illnesses. It has also allowed some enterprises and individuals to earn extraordinary profits. These actions have been often justified by the view that the main or only goal of private enterprises is benefiting the shareholders.

Products of the fashion industry and services and products of the entertainment industry and the sporting industry have also benefited from the protection that governments give to intellectual capital, in the form of designs, brand names, trademarks, image rights, and other forms. Some fashion leaders have become billionaires exploiting trademarks that became valuable. Some of these brand names can be sold or licensed to others and can be used by other producers, allowing the fashion leaders to increase the prices of their products.

In 2004, in a rare unanimous US Supreme Court decision on a case concerning the protection of intellectual property, the late Supreme Court Justice Antonin Scalia wrote, "The opportunity to charge monopoly prices – at least for a short period – is what attracts business acumen, it induces risk-taking that produces innovation and economic growth." This was the original justification given by the US Constitution for the protection of intellectual property. Thus, the granting of time-limited monopoly status for intellectual capital creates incentives to produce more of it. That incentive is the justification for granting protection that in turn creates (temporary) monopolies and high incomes for some. However, whether it also produces economic growth has remained a more controversial question.

Because of the monopoly that intellectual capital creates in order to continue to benefit from those monopoly positions, enterprises must innovate or they must suppress potential competitors by buying the latter's patents, by challenging their patents in the courts, or by beating them in the timing when rights are acquired. Monopoly profits often give the successful enterprises the resources to continue to innovate, or to try to stop potential competitors by buying or by challenging their patents. In the United States alone there were 5,000 lawsuits filed in 2015 about the infringement of some patents.

The need to continue to innovate is common in industries such as the pharmaceutical industry, for example. The tech world is now very important, and these monopolies are largely unregulated while they have the monopoly power, unlike natural monopolies. The protection of intellectual property accorded by governmental action is a way of *increasing the cost for competitors of getting access to some knowledge* that is already available at a moment in time. At the same time, that protection is supposed to encourage the production of new "knowledge," broadly defined.

In contrast to the positions mentioned above, it should be reported that some economic historians have argued that the Industrial Revolution came during a period, in the eighteenth and nineteenth centuries, when the cost of accessing technical knowledge was being reduced by the increasing publication of that knowledge in outlets such as encyclopedias and other publications, and when "[engineers, mechanics, chemists, physicians, and natural philosophers] formed circles in which access to knowledge was the primary objective" (see Mokyr, 2002, p. 66). Mokyr reported that "by the middle of the nineteenth century, there were 1020 associations for technical and scientific knowledge in Britain with a membership of roughly 200,000" (ibid.). "In the decades after 1815, a veritable explosion of technical literature took place" (ibid., p. 71).

Today's idea factories and the granting of property status to some new knowledge, broadly defined, have created the right environment for some high-paying jobs to appear, both in the technical area but also in the fashion and the entertainment areas (see Moretti, 2013). While in the distant past, economic growth and high incomes had often been connected with the ownership of *real* assets and *real* properties, and with the exchange of available knowledge, recent economic growth in advanced countries seems to be more dependent on new knowledge that can be owned as intellectual property and that can thus exclude others from its use. At least this is true for advanced countries that cannot import technology from other countries as some developing countries can. Innovation requires new knowledge, while imitation does not.

As mentioned, some of the largest and most profitable corporations today, in the United States and in other advanced countries, are enterprises that, in their various activities and ways, use and manage intellectual capital and sell services and products that are closely linked with their intellectual property, often, but not always, held in the form of patents. These corporations are able to generate enormous profits, and incomes for their owners and for the managers of the relevant enterprises, by *excluding* others from using their intellectual knowledge.

Wikipedia has reported that in 2013, the United States Patent and Trademark Office estimated that the market value of the intellectual property in the United States was about $5 trillion and that in the European Union it was of a comparable size. Much intellectual property was also owned in Asian countries, especially in Japan, South Korea, and, increasingly, China and India. Apple, Google, Amazon, Microsoft, Facebook, Samsung, Sony, Alibaba, Canon, and other technologically oriented enterprises are now among the largest in the world. Some of these enterprises did not even exist a generation ago. Pharmaceutical companies also sell products that depend on intellectual property, held through patents and trademarks. The same is true in other economic sectors, such as the fashion and the entertainment industries, which include enterprises such as Armani, Prada, Walt Disney, and several in the movie industry. In 2015, the US Patent and Trademark Office issued 326,000 patents, and many new patents were registered in other countries, increasingly China.

IBM has been the world leader for twenty-two consecutive years in the number of patents that it gets annually. It spends about $6 billion in research and development each year, or about 6 percent of its revenue. With 7,534 patents in 2014, Korea's Samsung Electronics was second in the number of patents received, while Tokyo-based Canon Inc. was third. Many US companies are among the top twenty patent recipients. Companies such as Google, Cisco Systems, and Oracle spend about 13 percent of their revenue on R&D to keep acquiring more intellectual capital. Large producers of planes and cars also spend a lot of money to get patents. For example, Airbus gets about 6,000 patents a year. In the United States, by April 2016, there were 550,000 pending applications for patents.

Patents are not the only way to get and to protect intellectual capital. Protection of brand names, designs, packaging, and other forms of human capital, including "image rights," can be used to play a similar role as patents. As mentioned, many enterprises spend large amounts on R&D, on design, and on advertising to acquire additional intellectual property and to increase its market value. These expenses allow them to remain leaders in their fields and to continue with activities that can generate profits and that can allow them to pay large compensations to their managers, and provide dividends and capital gains to the shareholders that have invested "venture capital," or capital for expansion. Publicity expenses can increase the value of the human capital and of the brand names by increasing demand for what the enterprises sell. Large sums are spent in publicity to advertise brand names, especially by fashion-related enterprises, or to advertise new drugs in the pharmaceutical industry. Significant sums are also spent challenging others' patents. Huge compensations are often paid to the managers of the enterprises.

How large can be the compensations of the managers of some of the enterprises can be seen from a recent example. In 2015, Google hired a new finance chief from a large American bank. This person was offered a $70 million compensation package in her first year! This compensation was offered before her performance could be assessed in her new job. To get a sense of the size of that package, note that it was close to a hundred times the cash salary received by the president of the United States!

The previous discussion may give the impression that large incomes connected with intellectual property are always a direct consequence of large spending for R&D or for publicity. While that spending plays a significant role, that impression is a bit misleading. It is equally important to realize that at the noncorporate, individual level, some of the highest incomes received today by successful artists, athletes, coaches, and various other performers and entertainers, incomes that are often several or many millions of US dollars, are directly or indirectly associated with the leverage of intellectual property rights. A couple of real-life examples may help convey this point and can show how pervasive the role of intellectual property rights has become in generating some of today's very large incomes.

Highly successful football, soccer, tennis, golf, baseball, and basketball players, rock stars, and other successful individuals who perform particular cultural, artistic, entertainment, or sport activities now routinely earn incomes that place them among the top positions in the annual lists of the income tax declarations presented to the tax administrations of various countries. The reason is that "highly talented individuals can deploy their skills on a broader and worldwide market" (Piketty et al., 2011, p. 33). This was not the case a century ago or even a half-century ago, when individuals in these activities could earn good incomes but not incomes as large as in recent decades.

In an earlier chapter, it was mentioned that some of the great composers or writers of the past died poor, as probably did many of the top athletes, performers, artists, and inventors of a century ago. The reasons were that they could not transform what they produced into intellectual property and that the products or services generated from their performances could not be sold and distributed, *with government protection*, as widely as they can be today *using new technologies*. Thus, intellectual property rights and the new technologies are the two elements that have made a big difference in income creation and in income distribution.

Next, I discuss in more detail the role that intellectual property rights, including image rights, combined with modern technological developments, have played in recent years in income generation and distribution for some individuals. The developments discussed are also likely to have contributed to the perception, held by an increasing number of observers today, that the modern market economy has become less fair, at least in terms of results. The reason is that, in many cases, it seems to have created a greater disconnect than existed in the past between genuine personal *effort* and total money *rewards* for that export. The birth lottery also seems to be playing a larger role, by assigning talents or physical characteristics to some individuals that will allow them to earn large incomes.

At times, the earnings of some individuals seem to bear less and less relation to the number of hours worked, even when adjusted for talent, as the old labor theory of wages had argued that earnings should do a century ago. This has happened in a world in which traditional aristocracies are no longer expected to play the role, in the distribution of income and in social positions, that they had played, especially in Europe and in other societies, in past centuries, when aristocrats did not have to justify their standards of living and their wealth with their efforts, and when they received incomes from particular rights, including some coming exclusively from their being aristocrats.

Many citizens continue to believe that high incomes should be justified by some visible effort, perhaps with the exception of income derived from inherited wealth, which could at times be justified by the effort of one's ancestors. The rich of the past derived their positions in the distribution of income or wealth from their aristocratic status and from the inheritance of real assets (especially land and buildings) that came with it, or, increasingly, during the Industrial Revolution, from the real wealth and the occasional monopoly positions held by the enterprises that they had created and owned. Those were real assets that could be passed on to heirs.

The rich individuals of the past, while their heirs may still be rich, have been replaced to a considerable extent, at the top, by individuals who have gotten rich from the income derived from various kinds of *intellectual property rights* and from modern versions of indirect rights over real wealth, rights that tend to be less visible than was the case with the property of the past, which was more visible and more tangible. A patent right is not as visible as a steel mill or a railroad. Some individuals own the $5 trillion of property rights from intellectual property that have been estimated to exist in the United States, and equivalently large amounts in Europe and in Asia.

Some of today's rich individuals no longer control or need to *directly* control visible or tangible assets, as they did in the past. They now control assets owned, partly and indirectly, through the ownership of shares, bonds, or intellectual property. For the high incomes derived from corporations, we no longer talk about the *owners* of the enterprises, but about the enterprises' *shareholders* and their *managers*. They are the individuals whose high incomes attract attention. A look at Forbes's or Bloomberg's annual lists of the richest individuals on the planet or in the United States, or a look at the lists of the top declared taxable incomes in countries where these lists are publicly available, will confirm the importance that intellectual property, *broadly defined*, now plays in determining the incomes of many of the individuals at the upper end of the income distributions.

When individuals, some still in their twenties and who, in some cases, may even have been college dropouts, can become billionaires – because of some clever ideas that they had, ideas that today can more easily be transformed into some form of *intellectual property* that, with the help of recent technologies, can provide services (for example, those provided by Facebook or Twitter) and that, until the time when they become available, almost nobody had even thought they were needed – we should realize that we are living in a world different from that of the past.

In the past, high incomes had been associated mainly with tangible wealth gained from making and selling products, such as steel, petroleum, and cotton, from providing railroad or banking services, or from lending money. Some new *products*, as distinguished from new *services*, have also a large amount of intellectual capital associated with patents, for example, smartphones, personal computers, cameras, and similar products. Even products such as cars and planes now have a large amount of intellectual property backed up by patent rights. Soon, cars will not need the guidance of human drivers.

These new products and services benefit from the protection, provided by the government, of the intellectual capital that they contain. These new *products*, based on ideas and research developed or carried out mainly in the advanced countries, are often largely assembled by low-paid workers in poorer countries, and are sold to millions, or even billions, of individuals around the world. Because of the volume of sales, these products can bring about enormous incomes for some individuals or enterprises, due to the legal protection that governments provide, for limited numbers of years, to the owners of the intellectual property rights.

At least at the beginning, when they first appear, the new services or new products, often marvels of modern technology, might strike some observers as having questionable value for humankind (compared, for example, with the discovery of a cure for cancer or malaria, or of electricity or the steam engine). They definitely do not satisfy what could be called *basic needs*, even though many low-income individuals sooner or later end up wanting, using, and needing them. Whatever is the real, basic, or intrinsic value of these new services or products, once they have acquired large numbers of users, they generate needs for them, and high earnings for some of those who produce them. Therefore, they can enrich the individuals and the enterprises that develop and produce them.

The factors that make the individuals or the enterprises successful are: (a) the monopoly power that governments confer to the owners of the *intellectual property rights*; (b) the availability of recent communication technologies that allow the sale or the distribution of the new services to millions or even billions of individuals around the world; and (c) government policies that have made possible these developments by opening markets and by providing or facilitating the infrastructures or the new technologies.

Not all the new products or services benefiting from the protection offered to intellectual capital have a scientific or an "intellectual" base. Some have a cultural or entertainment base and are not connected with the generation of new knowledge, as "knowledge" is strictly defined. To gain an intuitive sense of some of the changes that have led to the large increases in incomes for some individuals, consider the role that intellectual property rights, broadly defined, have played in increasing the incomes of athletes or performers in nonscientific areas (music, entertainment, sports, etc.). We shall take as specific examples two of the top tennis players in the world at the time when this book was being written – Novac Djokovic, of Serbia, and Maria Sharapova, of Russia. We could have taken the example of a major entertainer, such as Lady Gaga or the late Prince, or other sports personalities, such as Serena Williams or Ronaldo.

Djokovic was born and brought up in Serbia, but he now operates, as a tennis player on a world stage. If he had been born a century earlier and had been equally good at playing tennis, his income would have been limited by the average income of his country and by the number of paying spectators that could be accommodated and were willing to buy a ticket to see him play in the tennis courts of his country, which is where he would have played exclusively. After the radio was invented and the rights to broadcast the games on the radio could be sold to radio stations in his country, this development would have allowed him to get some additional income from the broadcasts. Then, after the television came and the rights to show the game on television could be sold to television stations, and directly or indirectly to spectators outside the tennis court, his earning would have gone up further.

Some sports activities became globalized, including tennis. Top tennis players could play almost anywhere in the world, and the games could be broadcast globally. Therefore, top tennis players could play to world audiences and no longer just for their country's spectators. Because of the aforementioned developments, Djokovic's income went further up. Next came the endorsements by private companies *from around the world*. He could sell the right to use his name and his image. The companies wanted the *exclusive* (and legally protected) right to show the star's name or face on some products; to show him wearing some of their expensive watches or other items, or driving a new car; or simply to show their brand name on his shirt. Each of those developments raised the star's income, at times by very large amounts.

The same could be said about the Russian tennis star Maria Sharapova, who had the double advantage of being a top tennis player and of having the look of a fashion model. She was reported to have been the highest-earning woman athlete in the world and to have earned about $300 million in the eleven years of her playing career (see *Financial Times*, July 2/3, 2016, p. 9). As the *Financial Times* article put it, "along with her on-court earnings, she … collected endorsements" from Nike, Head, Tag Heuer, Avon, Porsche, and American Express. Much of her earnings came from the selling of her image for publicity purposes (image rights). Her earnings came to a sudden stop when she was banned from playing for having taken a banned substance. By the way, some top soccer players, such as Ronaldo and Messi, have been earning ever-larger incomes.

The described developments have the following common characteristics. First, the increase in income did not require any extra effort on Djokovic's or Sharapova's part. A labor theory of income would not explain the earnings, nor would a theory that stressed "contribution to knowledge." The increase in their incomes had the characteristic of being largely pure economic rents. Second, the increase was made possible by new technologies that had allowed the diffusion of the tennis games and the showing of the stars' performances to global audiences. Third, changes in government policies in recent decades were behind the growing diffusion of the games in the world. Fourth, the increase in their incomes depended on the protection that governments provided with their policies to the stars' performance and to the sale of their images, protection that created intellectual (?) property rights. The stars' ability and effort did not need to have changed to get the higher incomes. The stars simply were lucky to have found a policy and a technological environment that allowed them to multiply enormously their income. The *birth lottery* had not played a role except to provide them with talent, but the *time lottery* had worked very much in their favor, by making them be born at a time when their performances could attract more viewers and more value and could be protected by property rights.

The same could be said for many other high-earning individuals who engage in activities where access to performances, with government legal assistance, could be restricted to nonpaying individuals, while the performances could be distributed widely (using modern technologies) to large numbers of individuals around the world willing to pay a price. Many modern entertainers, rock stars, athletes, and others have benefited from these developments.

From the previous discussion it should be obvious that *the additional income* that some individuals receive in today's world, because of new technologies, new policies, and the protection offered by modern versions of intellectual property rights to their performances and to their images, can be a very large part of their total income. Therefore, the argument, made by some economists and by conservative politicians, that higher tax rates are not justified and that they would inevitably reduce personal effort does not have as much validity as they believe. The reason is that much of the high income is "rent," and it is not tied to extra effort. Furthermore, much of this rent has been made possible by the actions and the policies of governments. Therefore, an argument can be made that the government should be able to claim a part of that rent. Rent may be playing as large a role or even a larger role in generating high incomes as the traditional "effort" that receives so much attention by economists.

From an equity point of view, this creates an argument for justifying higher marginal tax rates *on very high incomes*, especially on the part of the income that exceeds some significant multiple of average incomes. For a proposal along that line by the author of this book, see Tanzi (2007b). Efficiency considerations might also support this conclusion. The discussion should be on the level of the marginal tax rate, and on the income level at which the high marginal tax rate would apply. It should not be on whether high tax rates are justified at high income levels for those who benefit from the government-generated rents. It could also be about which government would have the right to collect taxes, in a world in which governments are national but operations are global.

Inevitably, there may be scope for questioning the role that the government has played, especially in recent decades, in recognizing property rights for some so-called intellectual capital, broadly defined. Some of this intellectual capital does not require (large or even any) investments in the form of R&D to develop, and does not extend available knowledge in any real sense. If new knowledge were created, the 326,000 new patents issued in the United States in 2015 would have created a new world. The role of the government in protecting that capital has become very important, and some consider it also somewhat questionable.

Trade agreements today have more to do with the protection of intellectual and investment rights, broadly defined, and less with trade of real products. This has made trade agreements more controversial than they might have been in the past, when they were clearly aimed at making countries' economies more open and more efficient by removing restrictions on the movement of goods. The aim in the past was to widen the global markets and to facilitate specialization, thus increasing incomes and efficiency for the world.

In more recent years, while the protection of products made by old-style industrial workers has been reduced by the lowering of import duties, the protection of "products" and services associated with intellectual property has been implicitly increased by the extension of property rights to intellectual property. These products are not made by the cheapest producer, but by producers that have acquired the monopolies provided by patents and by other intellectual property rights. This has raised objections to recent trade agreements on the part of some countries' governments, trade unions representatives, and even some leading economists and many political figures. These objections have had an impact on some recent electoral results.

CHAPTER 31

Historical Background on Intellectual Property Rights

In past centuries, intellectual property rights did not exist. Copyrights were introduced in the seventeenth century, but they were not systematically protected until the nineteenth century. When protection for intellectual property was introduced, it was limited to narrow areas and in specific places. Patents and copyrights started to become more common in the second half of the nineteenth century, in the middle of the Industrial Revolution, when R&D appeared as a new activity. Science and technology policies by governments, including large public subsidies for some scientific projects, in areas such as atomic power, space exploration, and medical research, came in the twentieth century. Tax instruments were developed to promote R&D undertaken by private enterprises. Standard definitions of R&D were attempted by the Frascati and later by the Oslo manuals. And many countries started to spend considerable shares (up to 4.5 percent) of their GDPs in R&D activities, either publicly or privately (see Harhoff, 2016).

With the passing of time, mainly in the twentieth century, property rights were progressively extended to cover new and wider areas. Formal protection now extends beyond *patents and copyrights* to include *trademarks, brand names, industrial designs, images, plant varieties, trade dress, trade secrets, and even locations where some agriculturally based products bearing specific names (wines and spirits, olive oil, cheeses, or even bread and cherries) can be produced.* Some have even tried to patent DNA sequences.

There are continuous pressures on governments to extend that protection to cover additional areas. "Made in France," "made in China," or "made in the USA" have become normal signs to indicate the provenience of products. A theater has now the right to prevent the taking of photos of performances, or a concert hall the silent registration of music being played. Designs of products cannot be copied, and neither can some sounds. A November 9, 2015, issue of the *Economist* reported that Harley-Davidson had once sought to register the characteristic soundtrack ... of its motor-cycle. And a Bloomberg column reported on the attempt by Warner/Chappell Music to claim rights over the lyrics of the Happy Birthday song, a song that has been sung at birthday parties for more than a century (see Feldman, 2015). Without government protection, various outputs (such as sports games, songs, designs, and others) would not have acquired wings to fly, and the activities of sports or of entertainment stars would not have generated the large incomes for them that they now generate.

It should be noted and emphasized that the four ingredients in this *get-rich process* are: (a) the proprietary, "monopoly" status that the government (directly or through the courts) provides to the originators of ideas that can be patented or to the actors in particular activities; (b) the new technologies that have become available at the time when the economically relevant actions are performed; these technologies have allowed new "services" (for example, those of Facebook or LinkedIn) to be sold or distributed to millions, or the performances of athletes and artists to be broadcast to an increasingly large number of interested customers worldwide; (c) the government protection that allows the producers or the performers to appropriate the benefits, without fear of competition or imitation; and (d) government policies that have often created the technology that has allowed the distribution of the services broadly or even worldwide.

All of the aforementioned ingredients have, or have had, some government participation or input. That participation is obvious in the case of the monopoly status accorded to new intellectual output through patents or other rights. It may also have been important, but in a less obvious way, in the role that the government may have played, in the past, in financing the developing of the new technologies that have made possible the diffusion of certain outputs or services to large numbers of peoples, through radio, television, the Internet, and other means, and in the opening of frontiers that allowed the often-global distribution or diffusion of performances.

Brynjolfsson and McAfee (2014, p. 218) highlighted the role that the US government played in many important technological developments and affirmed that "it's pretty safe to say ... that hardware, software, networks, and robots would not exist in anything like the volume, variety and forms we know today without sustained government funding." Several writers have stressed that the Internet was developed mainly with government funding (see Mazzucato, 2013; Gates, 2016). Others have remarked that the Internet may have become the greatest contributor to private wealth in the history of the world. The fortunes of Gates, Zuckerberg, and others have clearly been associated with the existence of the Internet. And some writers have called attention to the fact that, after 2005, US government funding for R&D was reduced (see again Brynjolfsson and McAfeee, 2014, p. 218). Furthermore, those who own intellectual property rely on the actions of the government, through the courts, to punish those who abuse those rights.

In recent decades, especially since the 1980s, when some of the afore-mentioned developments were taking place, the tax systems have been also becoming less progressive and, definitively, more friendly toward individu-als who receive very high incomes. The highest *marginal* tax rates were sharply reduced, making it easier for individuals lucky enough to receive high incomes to keep greater proportions of the incomes received than they had kept in the earlier decades after World War II. These individuals include many of those who have gotten their incomes from the commer-cialization of activities associated with new ideas, new designs, new brand names, or performances that could be broadcast and sold in ways restricted to potential free riders. This restriction makes "intellectual output" dif-ferent from that of "pure public goods," because for the latter free access could not be and was not restricted. As I have argued, the US govern-ment has played a key role in these developments, a role that has helped make many people rich, and some *very* rich, and the income distribution less even.

In an earlier chapter it was mentioned that many of those who con-tributed to the Industrial Revolution in the eighteenth and nineteenth centuries in Great Britain, in the United States, and in various European countries, and many of the great composers, writers, and artists of that or earlier periods, had not been so lucky to have lived in the recent and more-favorable environment. They did not benefit from the modern economic role of the government in relation to their activities. As a consequence, many of them did not become rich, in spite of the extraordinary legacy that they left for humanity. Their intellectual capital could not have been transformed into government-protected intellectual *property*. The only way they could have protected it, in the case of technological inventions, was to have kept it secret as long as possible.

Until the time when intellectual capital could acquire property rights status and could benefit from government protection, "Americans saw [the] immense hoard of technology [being developed in Europe] as theirs for the asking – or for stealing" (Morris, 2012, p. 301). Morris mentions that Tench Coxe, who was Alexander Hamilton's assistant treasury secre-tary in the first US Treasury Department, "had no compunction about offering awards for stolen British textile technology and paying bounties high enough to induce [British] craftsmen to risk prison for emigrating [to the US] with trade secrets" (ibid.). He added that "the United States set out to steal whatever [technological knowledge] it could" (ibid.).

Ron Chernow, a biographer of Alexander Hamilton, put it this way: "Coxe was a well-known advocate of manufacturing and eager to raid Britain's industrial secrets" (2004, pp. 371–372). He regretted that because of Britain's pugnacious defense of its technological superiority in textiles, the United States was not, as he put it in a long letter to Hamilton, "yet in full possession of workmen, machines and secrets in the useful arts" (ibid., p. 372). "Hamilton and Coxe teamed up in a daring assault on British industrial secrets" (ibid., p. 372). For details of that "assault" see Chernow (2004, chapter 19). See also Hamilton's *Report on Manufactures*, submitted to Congress on December 5, 1791. In his report "Hamilton evoked a thriving future economy that bore scant resemblance to the static, stratified society his enemy claimed he wanted to impose" (ibid., p. 376).

Morris also comments that Japan, after World War II, and China, more recently, have been doing what the United Stated had done on a grand scale in the nineteenth century. In recent years, "China's relationship with America is much like [what was] that of the ... United States with Great Britain"; "with respect to technology, much as America did, China is stealing all it can, not only from the United States but from all Western advanced countries" (ibid., p. 302). Trade in intellectual capital over the long run tends to be a two-way street. The West had not considered it improper when, in earlier centuries, it had imported knowledge, related to the creation of paper, gunpowder, and other important discoveries, from China.

The government protection of intellectual property is a relatively recent government role. It is a role that, for some activities, came at a time when the use of intellectual capital could be sold to millions of users without, or with limited, restrictions at national frontiers, or when the money earned could be transferred across countries. Especially during the Reagan administration in the 1980s, protection of intellectual capital acquired more importance in the United States. This new government role was not a traditional one or, perhaps, even a natural one. It had to be pushed by potential beneficiaries in the private sector, for example, those in the movie industry from which President Reagan had come. These potential beneficiaries included enterprises, scientists, and prominent writers. In the nineteenth century they had included, prominently, Victor Hugo and Charles Dickens. It has been reported that Charles Dickens came to America to complain about the pirating of his work and to ask for protection of his rights.

That new government role was controversial from the beginning and has remained controversial to this day, as much economic literature indicates. It did not square with true laissez-faire ideology, nor with the free use of available knowledge, because it called for and required governmental intervention both in what constitutes intellectual property and in protecting it. It is interesting to realize that some of the individuals who want the government to "stay out of peoples' lives" are the same ones who complain the most about "intellectual piracy" and push the government to intervene and protect acquired intellectual property rights.

An important, detailed, and highly informative book written by an economist and published in the United States almost a century ago, in 1925, carrying the title of *Economics of Our Patent System*, reviewed the history of patents in England and in the United States, and the justifications for that system a century ago. The book's broad conclusions are worth reporting: "The evils connected with our patent system – industrial monopolies, suppression of patents, discouragement of invention, and economic waste [of labor and capital] – form a tremendous liability in appraising its net utility" (see Vaughan, 1925, p. 33). "A multiplicity of undesirable patents signifies useless efforts of inventors, patent examiners, lawyers, judges, etc. and the impairment of capital" (ibid., p. 224). "The patent system has within it all the elements of a state-aided lottery" (ibid., p. 225). After a detailed and lengthy review of the "evils connected with ... [t]he patent system," Vaughan's conclusion was that "in many instances the exploitation of patents in *furthering industrial monopoly* is the chief incentive to invention" (ibid., p. 249, italics added). "[The] patent system has promoted inventions, but not in the manner intended by our forefathers" (ibid., p. 249).

Vaughan's conclusion, reached in 1925, was in one aspect the same reached by Antonin Scalia a century later and reported earlier in this book. Vaughan added that "the social costs of the present patent situation – industrial monopoly, suppression of patents, discouragement of invention, and waste of human and material resources – offset considerably, if not completely, any good derived from patents" (ibid.). Obviously, today, not everyone would agree with that strong conclusion reached a century ago.

In spite of those concerns and doubts about the usefulness of many patents and of the protection of many other intellectual property rights, the US government continues to be pushed by strong vested interests to extend widely that protection. Those rights have become progressively wider, and the concept of intellectual property has been stretched to cover new and growing areas, which are hardly or not always "intellectual."

Some economists have continued to question whether that protection changes the world for the better, as some claim that it does. It is a development that has enormously extended the range and the scope of intellectual property in recent decades, both internationally and in terms of the areas of activity that it covers. In the health area intellectual property rights have created friction with various countries (India, Brazil, and others) that would have liked to use known drugs, which could be cheaply produced by those countries in their generic versions to fight debilitating diseases, if they did not have to pay astronomical royalties to those who held the patents. In some cases human lives are exchanged against corporate profits at least in the short run. Thus, available knowledge cannot be used to meet worthwhile social needs, because of legal restrictions.

More and more intellectual property has come to be protected by governmental action, including by international agreements and by the actions of international organizations, such as the World Trade Organization (WTO) and others that deal specifically with the global registration and protection of patents. The WTO has progressively extended its attention from trade in real, tangible products to trade in services, and finally to trade in "intangibles." As mentioned earlier, trade agreements among countries now deal significantly or predominantly with issues related to the protection of intellectual property and investments. There is also a lot of talk about "piracy" and about the illicit appropriation of trade secrets. Much of this new development has taken place especially since the 1980s, which was the decade when the income distribution, in several advanced countries, started to become less even. Intellectual property and the extension of its coverage are likely to have played a significant, though difficult to quantify, role in the developments in income distributions, both within and across countries.

In their daily activities individuals produce new ideas, new products, new solutions to old problems, new services, new gestures, new phrases or expressions, new behaviors, and other broadly defined new "products." These new products are to a large extent imitated, copied, mimicked, plagiarized, or used in various ways by others. Whether we do it consciously or subconsciously, and whether we are aware of it, we often copy others. Therefore, to a large extent we are the summation of all the products and all the attitudes that we have observed during our lifetime and that have influenced us, starting with the observations of our parents and siblings and of others who have been closest to us.

Closed, traditional communities generate ways of dancing, singing, producing potatoes or conserving them, making sandals, catching and cooking fish, designing a bow and arrow, making a canoe, and so on. It would have never occurred to members of these communities that these products, or the way they are made by some individual members of the community, should, or could, become exclusive properties of particular individuals, and should be protected from the use or the imitation by other members of the community, even in societies that recognized and accepted individual rights for *real* property that, by definition, cannot have unlimited or multiple uses, as is the case with public goods or knowledge. This was the way the world had existed until relatively modern times.

If, at the time the wheel was invented, there had been a system to patent it, it might have taken a longer time for vehicles to appear on the roads. Very important inventions – such as the water wheel, eyeglasses, the mechanical clock, printing, and gunpowder, some from the Middle Ages and others from later periods, including the first century of the Industrial Revolution – that have had a great impact on today's world never benefited from the protection that we now routinely accord to far more trivial "inventions." (How many of the 326,000 patents issued in the United States in 2015 were likely to be truly useful?) Yet, those important earlier inventions were made and became part of the baggage that the civilized world had available (see Landes, 1998, chapters 4 and 13).

As the *Economist* put it in an article dealing with intellectual property, "most of the wonders of the modern age ... seemed to have emerged without the help of patents" (August 8, 2015, p. 50). It is clear that the concept of intellectual *property* is the product of a society that has come to see individuals as separate elements of the society in which they live and of a world in which individuals must be given *financial* incentives to generate new ideas. Other kinds of incentives are considered less important. That society tends to give more importance to the *individual* and less to the *community* to which that individual belongs.

Just imagine the situation that would be created if all the recipes for preparing new meals could be patented by the chefs that developed them. It is in fact surprising that famous chefs have not attempted so far to get property rights for some of their new recipes. Perhaps, in the future we shall get an extension of property rights in that direction.

The assignment of property rights to some ideas and to some intangible actions – that is, to intellectual capital produced by particular individuals and enterprises, and the exclusion from the unauthorized use of that capital by others, even when that use would be possible at no cost – inevitably reduces the value to society of the intellectual capital *already available* at a moment in time. In some ways, it makes society poorer than it could be. The reason is the obvious one – a song, a musical composition, an essay, a poem, a way of producing potatoes, a dance, a phrase, a gesture, and similar other "human outputs," once they are in the public domain, can be copied or duplicated at no or at very low cost, because they have characteristics similar to those of traditional "public goods." Therefore, there must be strong and specific reasons to justify the protection that governments provide to specific individuals or enterprises when the governments allow them to get *property rights* for some of the intangible products. It is these property rights that make it possible for these individuals and enterprises to sell their intangible outputs, or copies of them, and to exclude free riders from access to them.

One such reason is the one mentioned in the US Constitution to justify *patents* and *copyrights*. As the US Constitution put it, "The Congress shall have Power … To promote the Progress of Science and useful Arts, by securing for limited Times to Authors and Inventors the exclusive Right to their respective Writings and Discoveries." Therefore, those who can get government protection for their "Writings and Discoveries" can legally exclude others from their use and can create time-limited and potentially profitable monopolies. The justification for allowing the creation of such monopolies was that this granting of temporary monopoly rights would create incentives to generate more "Writings" and more "Discoveries." The drafters of the US Constitution must have believed that the value that was lost to society by restricting access to newly created "Writings and Discoveries" would be made up, or exceeded, by the value of the newly created "Writings and Discoveries."

In the justification given by the US Constitution, we see the seed of a view that would become prevalent, especially in the 1980s and 1990s, among many economists and especially among conservative economists, and that would have a significant impact on the income distribution in the United States. It was the view that *financial* incentives (as distinguished from *societal* or *reputational* incentives) are important in determining individual performances. Some economists even define economics as the science of *individual* (financial?) incentives. These incentives presumably make individuals act, perform, and work harder than they would without them. *Collective* and *reputational* incentives received no or minimal attention. It is an open question whether a society in which *only or mainly individual* and *financial* incentives are important can be and can remain a good society in the long run.

This view became dominant and has increasingly driven public policies in recent decades. It is assumed to drive the actions of all individuals in their private-sector activities. It is the view that, in recent decades, promoted or encouraged private enterprises to start giving huge bonuses to managers. These bonuses were given to individuals who had been chosen and had been given positions and basic salaries that *expected* them (and that were justified in the first place by that expectation) to be capable of performing at high standards. These individuals had, presumably, been chosen in the belief that they would work hard and would give their best. It was thus not clear why they would need bonuses for performances that were already expected from them and were reflected in their basic compensations.

It was recently reported that performance-based compensation was part of the *new* thinking that had come to prevail in the 1980s. That thinking had been rare until that time and has continued to be less commonly accepted in continental Europe. In the United States and in some other countries it became increasingly common in the 1980s and in later years. By 2012, performance-based compensation accounted for sixty-eight of all executive contracts in the United States (see article by Peter Coy, *Bloomberg Net*, February 26, 2016).

An article by Don Cable and Freck Vermeulen (*Harvard Business Review* website, February 23, 2016) mentioned that the theory behind performance-based compensation had been first advanced in 1976 in an article by Michael Jensen and William Meckling titled "Theory of the Firm: Managerial Behavior, Agency Costs and Ownership Structure," published in the *Journal of Financial Economics*. That article had presented the view that people respond to *financial* incentives. Pay them more (regardless of their basic salary) and they will perform better. Not surprisingly, given the mood of the time, managers and many economists had bought the argument.

Three aspects of that article deserve attention. The first is that the theory seems to apply only to managers and not to normal workers. Often, the higher compensation of managers would come, to a large extent, from squeezing the wages of workers, or from cutting their numbers. This squeezing was not supposed to create disincentives among workers. Second was the timing of the article. It may have been a coincidence, but the time when the article was published was the same when other developments, such as the Laffer curve and tax theories that started arguing that capital incomes should not be taxed, or should be taxed at lower rates than income from labor, were being published. Clearly, similar winds were pushing the thinking. The third was that making the compensation of managers and shareholders dependent on short run results might introduce biases to achieve better short-term results, at times with potential long-term problems. It might, for example, lead to the taking of excessive risks.

Be that as it may, and in spite of their questionable theoretical underpinning, performance-based compensation contracts spread and, through benchmarking effects, became common. They led to overcompensation of managers, and changed dramatically the ratios of executive pay to worker pay. The American conservative administrations in the 1980s pushed this thinking also in the Bretton Woods organizations (IMF and World Bank), creating some difficulties for them. If *only* managers responded to financial incentives and not workers, it became rational to squeeze the incomes of the *workers*, while increasing those of the managers and the returns to shareholders, an objective that also became important and that was achieved. The share of labor income into GDP fell dramatically, while that of capital income increased sharply. In the United States the first fell from 64 percent in 2000 to 60 percent in 2014, and much more compared to the case in earlier years. It also fell in other major countries.

After the Great Recession, performance-based compensation started coming under some attacks, although it still remained a dominant force in the economy. In their article, Cable and Vermeulan had questioned the theoretical basis of performance-based compensation, and John Cryan, co-chief executive of Deutsche Bank, in a recent conference stated, "I have no idea why I was offered a contract with a bonus in it because I promise you I will not work any harder or any less hard in any year, in any day because someone is going to pay me more or less" (see *Financial Times*, November 25, 2015, p. 1). A table in Solimano (2016) has provided data on the ratio of average CEO compensation to average worker compensation for eighteen countries. In eleven countries – including Australia, Sweden, the United Kingdom, Japan, Austria, Denmark, and Norway – the ratio for 2012 was less than 100 and in some countries was less than 50. The large gap between the United States and the other countries does not seem to indicate that the managers of large enterprises in those other countries do not give their best effort.

This approach also highlights the importance of corporate boards and the way they are chosen in determining managers' compensations, and indirectly their influence on the distribution of income. The members of these boards are, often, chosen by the same managers whose incomes they will determine. Recently, there has been some movement to give more power to shareholders in the composition of the boards of some corporations. Excessive manager compensation ultimately reduces either the shareholders' returns or, more often, the wages of the workers. It is not difficult to imagine the reaction of those workers who have not received any wage increase for many years when they learn about the multi-million-dollar compensations of their managers, even when the corporations had not performed well (see Tanzi, 2012).

Going back to intellectual property, there has been an ongoing controversy about the empirical validity and importance of the view that the assignment of intellectual property rights leads to more genuine "discoveries," except in areas where discoveries require large private spending in R&D and to finance the work of large teams, and where the products generated by the research could be quickly and cheaply imitated and produced once the knowledge of how to make them has become known. This is the case with some drugs for which the investments to generate them and to get patents for them may run into billions of dollars. In the absence of protection to justify these large expenses (in research and in trials), the production of new drugs might slow down. Therefore, some protection might be more justified for limited areas and for special cases as long as the benefits clearly exceed the costs, which is not always obvious in the case of some new drugs that are very expensive to produce but that will benefit only a few.

Most of the important discoveries and artistic productions in the past were made without the expectations that the outputs would be legally protected. *Reputational incentives* were often as important or more important than financial incentives. There is limited evidence to support the view that the legal protection actually promotes faster progress, as there is little evidence that bonuses – for individuals who are already getting high salaries and that have been chosen for their positions on the ground that they are the most qualified and the most capable, and that they would give their best effort – improve performances. Evidence indicates that, among CEOs who get multi-million-dollar compensations, there are some high performers and some poor performers.

Many have pointed out that the detrimental cost of the creation of legally protected monopolies may easily exceed the value of what is produced because of the protection. Patents are often acquired to prevent competitors from entering a given field, rather than to genuinely protect newly discovered knowledge and use it (see Vaughan, 1925, and, more recently, Boldrin and Levine, 2008).

In the pharmaceutical sector, drug companies often buy the rights to the discoveries of other drug companies to prevent the latter from producing competitive and less expensive drugs. New drugs, produced at costs that at times run into the billions of dollars, often offer only marginal or questionable improvement over already existing drugs, or save few lives. They also require large costs in advertising (often directed more to normal citizens or potential users than to the doctors who must prescribe them). Doctors are bribed to prescribe new and more expensive drugs. Some new drugs end up having unreported serious side effects. These costs raise questions about the social benefit-cost calculations for some of these products. It is not evident that the money spent could not have been used more productively in other endeavors.

Patent lawyers have become masters at using the patent system to protect the interests and the monopoly powers of the enterprises for which they work. They have been extracting high rents from society for their work in this area. As the earlier-cited article in the *Economist* (August 8, 2015, p. 11) put it, "Studies have found that 40–90% of patents are never exploited or licensed out by their owners," but patents prevent others from entering a given field. It would be interesting to know how many of the 90,000 patents that IBM owns or the 326,000 patents issued in 2015 in the United States are useful and beneficial to society.

The bottom line is that the argument that the protection of intellectual property by governments stimulates more useful discoveries and promotes faster development that overwhelm its costs is controversial and unsettled. It is a far less controversial conclusion that patents and other intellectual property rights, including image rights, create large incomes for some lucky individuals and that, most likely, they have contributed to making the income distributions of countries less even in recent decades.

CHAPTER 32

Tax Rates, Tax Structures, and Tax Avoidance

In this chapter we focus on taxes and on the role that changes in tax rates, in tax structures, and in tax avoidance are likely to have played, in recent decades, in making the income distributions of various countries increasingly unequal. The focus will be mostly, though not exclusively, on the United States, because information is more easily available for that country and because many other countries were influenced by actions and thinking originating in the United States. Other countries also experienced similar developments, for example, the globalization of some of their economic activities, the growth of difficult-to-tax services, the globalization of financial services, and the growing problem of tax evasion associated with global activities.

Because of changing intellectual and political winds that had appeared especially in the 1970s and that pushed for lower tax rates as promoters of economic growth and of job creation, in the 1980s the (highest) marginal tax rates for income taxes were sharply reduced in many countries giving enormous benefits to those who had been exposed to those rates. Furthermore, what could be called the "architecture" of the personal income tax was also significantly changed (see Tanzi, 2012, 2014a, 2014c, for earlier descriptions of these changes). The result was much lower tax rates for the highest levels of personal income, and even larger reductions in the tax rates on those whose incomes came from capital sources. Statutory tax rates on corporate profits were also significantly reduced.

After some initial simplification of tax structures, promoted by the tax reforms of the 1980s in the United States and the United Kingdom, the complexity of tax systems started rising again, as Milton Friedman had correctly predicted at the time, because of continuing pressures from vested interests, and because of attempts by the tax administrations to catch those who evaded taxes, by making changes in the tax laws and regulations. Especially for corporations, the pressures for tax incentives and for various loopholes contributed to significantly increasing the difference between the *statutory* tax rate (which in the United States and a few other countries, though much reduced, had remained relatively high) and the *effective* tax rate

Capital incomes and tax rates on high incomes are, of course, far more important for individuals who receive high incomes and have large wealth than for average taxpayers. Complexities in tax systems can also be exploited by individuals who have high incomes and can get advice from good tax lawyers and accountants. These experts can navigate the complex laws and can find opportunities for their clients that complex tax systems often offer for "tax planning."

These high-income individuals, or high-net-worth individuals (HNWIs), find it easier than average workers to restructure the incomes that they receive to take advantage of lower rates on some income sources or in other countries. Tax planning has become increasingly important in recent decades. It involves showing more incomes in low-tax countries or in lower-tax-rate income sources. For American corporations, it also involves keeping more profits abroad. Able individuals were attracted to the tax-advising industry that assists and guides the rich taxpayers and the corporations to take advantage of existing, or newly created, tax-reducing and tax-avoiding possibilities. Within large corporations, tax experts became as important as, or even more important than, production engineers in determining corporate strategies. In these strategies the tax-reducing possibilities created by globalization became very important.

It was especially the HNWIs, including the CEOs and other managers of the corporations and successful performers in many fields, who benefited the most from the aforementioned developments, compared to normal workers, who continued to earn normal wages and to pay broadly similar taxes on those wages. Small family enterprises, which could not extract benefits from globalization and whose profits were not high, also benefited less from the new developments. In many cases, payments for fees, fines, co-payments for health services, and college tuitions became more expensive for middle class individuals during that period, because governments (especially local governments in the United States) needed more revenue and given the political climate were reluctant to raise taxes on those with high incomes. In recent years, in the United States, fees and fines have generated about one-fourth of the total revenue of local governments, according to a recent report by the Urban Institute, and some cities now collect a lot of revenue from fines and minor traffic violations.

These changes happened at a time when, for reasons described in earlier chapters, the distribution of income generated by the market was changing and was becoming less equal in many countries, and especially in the United States and other Anglo-Saxon countries. The shares of total incomes that rich individuals were receiving were increasing significantly, contributing to higher Gini coefficients. Because income taxes are one of the most important instruments available to governments for changing the market-generated income distribution, the changes in the tax systems inevitably reduced the governments' ability to deal with inequality and intensified the changes that were occurring in the market's income distributions.

Whether the reduction in tax rates on high incomes and on incomes from capital sources also made the countries' economies grow at faster rates, as some economists and representatives of some governments had argued that it would, is a more difficult question to answer. The direct evidence is that most countries' economies, including that of the United States, did not grow at faster rates in the decades after the tax rates were reduced than they had in earlier decades, as the promoter of the lower rates had predicted. But, of course, this "before and after" argument is not sufficient to conclude that the tax rate reductions did not have some positive impact on the growth rates. Other factors (such as aging and others) may have played a role in reducing the growth rates in the later years.

In addition to the changes in tax rates and in tax structures, another tax development is likely to have been at work in affecting the income distributions of several countries. This development is the connection that exists, and that has been receiving increasing attention in recent years, between the globalization of economic activities and the facility that it has created for enterprises and for some rich individuals to avoid and evade taxes through tax planning. This connection has intensified the role of tax complexity and may also have created more pressures by lobbyists to push for often small changes in the tax systems that go unnoticed but that help market operators who function globally to reduce their tax payments, making the tax systems less equitable. The now-common economic operations in multiple countries' activities, by both some HNWIs and especially by large corporations, have made it easier to use tax planning to exploit opportunities to both legally reduce tax liabilities and also to occasionally engage in explicit tax evasion. (See, for example, various papers in a recent book edited by Pogge and Mehta, 2016.)

The existence of many tax havens, the lack of harmonization of tax rates among countries, and the possibility of shifting profits (far more easily than real operations) from countries with high income tax rates to those with low, or even zero, tax rates have made it easy for some companies and for rich individuals to sharply reduce the taxes that they pay to the governments of the countries where they reside. It has been estimated that "tax avoidance by Multi-National Enterprises ... cost 100–240 billion US dollars a year globally" (OECD, 2016a, p. 8). To this must be added the tax avoidance by individuals. Both the reduction in the statutory tax rates and the tax avoidance have made it more difficult for governments to promote a more equitable after-tax income distribution.

Though not a new topic, global tax avoidance is now better understood and more studied than it was in the past. It is receiving more academic and official attention than in earlier years, when many economists believed that "tax competition" among countries was beneficial for the welfare of citizens, because it kept tax rates and tax levels low and forced governments to be more efficient. For an early discussion of this topic, in a book written as part of a large project on globalization undertaken in the first half of the 1990s by the Brookings Institution in Washington, DC, see Tanzi (1995) and OECD (1991).

The attention dedicated to this issue has grown in recent years, and so has the understanding of the issue. As indicated earlier there have also been attempts at estimating the tax revenue losses to governments of OECD and of developing countries, as a consequence of global tax avoidance and evasion. Total revenue losses at the global level have been estimated to amount to hundreds of billions, or even trillions, of US dollars. But, of course, these are guesses more than true statistical measurements. If these estimates, or guesses, are even approximately correct, it does not take much imagination, or much knowledge, to conclude that the taxes that are evaded, *mainly by high-income individuals* (either directly or through the operations of the enterprises in which they hold shares), must have been contributing significantly, in recent decades, to the growing inequality in the income distributions. The reason is simply that those who reduce the tax payments, because of global tax avoidance, are, in large part, HNWIs. They are the owners of most of the shares of the corporations that, with tax planning and tax avoidance, reduce tax payments to governments, even though some pension funds and some citizens with average incomes may own some of the shares.

Therefore, when corporations pay less in taxes, the gross incomes of those who benefit the most are the HNWIs. This makes the real (and not just the officially measured) Gini coefficients go up. The Panama Papers, in April 2016, also showed that many rich individuals evaded taxes directly and not just through the tax-evading actions of the corporations in which they owned shares.

The issues that link tax developments to changes in Gini coefficients are complex and are likely to be of varying importance among countries. They are likely to differ significantly between, for example, the United States and the United Kingdom, on one side, and Denmark and Sweden, on the other. A full and detailed treatment of those issues would require much more space than can be allocated to it in this book. However, the main lines are rather simple and can be easily summarized. In the rest of this chapter I shall attempt to describe them to show their connection with the issue of inequality and with the increase in inequality in recent decades. I shall discuss the three main issues in the same order as I presented them earlier.

Reduction in Marginal Tax Rates

The highest marginal tax rates on income taxes were dramatically reduced in most countries starting in the second half of the 1980s, as a consequence of new thinking on the role of taxes that had started to be influential in the 1970s and that affected the tax policies introduced in the 1980s and in later years. Some empirical literature on taxation in recent years has focused on the reductions in the marginal tax rates that took place, especially between the mid-1980s and the end of the 1990s. See the valuable book by Slemrod and Bakija, 2004.

Most economists would not question the conclusion that taxes and the level of tax rates play a role in some of the economic decisions of individuals and enterprises. It is easy to find examples of taxes that have had some specific impact on the economic decisions and on the behavior of economic agents, especially in relation to the supply of labor and the allocation of capital among different activities and different places. The maxim that "if you want more of something, subsidize it; and if you want less, tax it" clearly operates. However, there continues to be disagreement among experts on the empirical importance of the impact of tax rates on the labor supply, the aspect that receives most attention. For example, at the conclusion of his long and comprehensive survey of much of the relevant academic literature on this issue, Keane (2011, p. 961) concluded, "The literature is characterized by considerable controversy over the responsiveness of labor supply to changes in ... taxes." Many economists continue to not see tax rate reductions as necessarily job creators or significant growth promoters as some economists and politicians do. Some believe that in particular cases, tax rate reductions may just lead to significant macroeconomic problems when they are not accompanied by reductions in public spending.

It is important to realize that most workers are not subjected to the (highest) marginal tax rates, but, often, to significantly lower marginal rates, especially when their wages are not high and when they take advantage of various personal exemptions and tax deductions. Especially when the income distribution is highly uneven, the wages of most workers tend to be low. As Slemrod and Bakija, 2004, p. 21, put it, "[d]uring the years when the top rate was very high [in the US] it typically affected only a small fraction of 1 percent of the population; almost everyone else was in a significantly lower tax bracket." This small fraction is the one that benefited the most from the reduction in marginal tax rates in the 1980s.

Estimates for the United States that have used the IRS Statistics of Income data show that the bottom 50 percent of those who recently reported taxable income to the IRS paid only 2.4 percent of the total taxes paid, and the bottom 75 percent paid only 13 percent of the total taxes paid. Many reported no *taxable* income at all because of exemptions and deductions. On the other hand, the top 5 percent of the taxpayers, who received a very large share of the total income, paid 59.1 percent of total taxes (see De Rugy, 2013). The rest of the taxes, about 28 percent of the total, were paid by the 20 percent of the taxpayers who occupied the positions between the bottom 75 percent and the top 5 percent.

The US Tax Policy Center calculated that those in the top 0.1 percent of the population in 2016 would receive average incomes of more than $3.7 million. Naturally, given the large share of total incomes received by these individuals, they would be expected to account for a disproportionate share of total taxes. These are the individuals that would benefit the most from any future tax reduction and that benefited the most from past tax reductions. The past marginal tax rates reductions gave enormous windfalls to individuals in these income brackets.

The aforementioned statistics imply that for a large majority of taxpayers, those with lower incomes and/or with large tax deductions, the *income effect* generated by the reduction of their disposable income due to the payment of income taxes (this is the effect that is most likely to stimulate them to work harder or longer) may easily overwhelm the *substitution effect*, the one that makes leisure relatively cheaper than work. Of course, if some citizens can rely on government assistance for their consumption, an assistance that might create *poverty traps* for those looking for work, they may be able to "enjoy" (if that is the right word) the leisure of being and remaining unemployed. However, most employed workers cannot rely on such government assistance, and those who do are not employed and probably have never entered the (official) labor market. Some among them may have been active in the shadow economy, thus contributing to (unmeasured) national income, while potentially benefiting from government assistance. In this case the economy would still have benefited from their work, while tax revenue would not have.

For individuals working in jobs that pay higher wages and facing higher tax rates, the substitution effect becomes potentially more important. However, many of these individuals are likely to be dependent workers. Because of contractual arrangements or other reasons, many of them may not have the choice of deciding how many hours to work. For many of them the issue of the impact of taxes on their labor supply is of largely academic interest.

The freedom to choose whether or not to work, how much to work, and in what jobs is likely to exist for some, but it is limited to few individuals (especially second workers in households) who may depend on the assistance of other workers within the household, or those, including the self-employed, who may have enough personal assets to have the option of not working or of working less.

Some of those in the top 5 percent of the US taxpayers, who paid almost 60 percent of the total taxes paid, *might* be more affected by the substitution effect, especially those in the top 1 percent, who in 2013 paid 37.4 percent of the total taxes paid, on average taxable incomes of $370,000. Of course, many of them are not likely to be *dependent* workers but self-employed professionals in various activities or managers.

The aforementioned situation does not imply that there are no substitution effects, and that there are no effects on the labor supply and on incentives. However, it does reduce the likely magnitude of whatever substitution effect exists, making it smaller than many believe it to be and explaining Keane's 2011 conclusion. The distribution of the various marginal tax rates, among different levels of earnings, becomes important. It is not just the (highest) marginal tax rate, the one that attracts much of the attention of conservatives, that is important. To repeat, most workers are not subjected to the *highest* tax rate but to lower rates. The highest rate comes into play at a very high income level (in 2016, in the United States, for many at around $400,000). Most workers are far from earning that much money.

When we come to the truly high incomes, those in the top *1 percent* (the income levels that have attracted most attention in current discussions, and presumably the ones most affected by the highest marginal tax rate), some who are not receiving incomes from capital sources are subjected to the highest marginal tax rate (in the United States 39.6 percent at present, plus, in many states, the locally imposed income taxes). The common thinking, reinforced by the continuing popularity of the "Laffer curve" has been that these are the income levels where substitution effects must be most pronounced, leading to significant reductions in work incentive and efforts. The individuals exposed to the highest marginal tax rate might be in the part of the Laffer curve where effort and income fall, because of reactions to the high rates. For these people leisure definitely becomes relatively cheaper than work, even though, given their high earnings per hour, leisure may still be very expensive in spite of the tax effect. If one earns $200 an hour and has to pay, say, $100 in taxes, the cost of one hour of leisure is still $100, and many in the top 1 percent earn far more than $200 an hour. Furthermore, at these high income levels, other considerations are likely to come into play and to become important.

The group of high-income taxpayers is diverse and heterogeneous, and, presumably, comprises highly successful individuals. It includes individuals with different backgrounds, assets, interests, responsibilities, needs, and motivations. What they all have in common is the high income. All members of this group have achieved high economic standing, and many have achieved high social and/or professional standing. Some of them may work hard because of financial motivation. Their sole or main motivation for working hard may be money! This is the motive that receives much of the attention of economists.

Others, who may be artists, actors, athletes, writers, or successful professionals (doctors, lawyers, architects, CEOs, and others), are not likely, or are less likely, to consider money as the sole or even the most important motive for continuing to work hard. They are individuals who have achieved a reputation or a professional ranking, or are trying to establish or to maintain one. For some, or even for many of them, the *reputational motive* may be, or may have become, more important than the money income that they are earning. Their reputations in the areas in which they operate (sports, music, arts, or professional entities) give them pride and provide them with a social standing and a psychic income that may be very valuable, but that are not taxable. Once achieved, this status, and the money compensation that accompanies it, will be defended, almost regardless of tax rates. A recent empirical study has in fact reached the not-surprising conclusion that the effort elasticities of top earners are low.; these individuals are not likely to be motivated in their current activities by higher earnings (see Scherer and Werning, 2015). As Piketty et al. (2011, pp. 33–34) put it, "it somewhat strains credibility to believe that the top

1% earners ... [have] enough leeway to be able to drastically increase their tax effort."

In conclusion, it does not seem logical to assume that a higher marginal tax rate, one still within reasonable limits and somewhat lower than some of the rates that existed in the 1960s, will make high-earning individuals reduce their effort and, thus, risk compromising their reputations, their professional status, and ultimately their high incomes. To assume that a top tennis, soccer, or basketball player, a famous singer or performer, or individuals at the top of other professions will reduce his or her effort because the marginal tax rate has become higher is to think very low of human nature and of what makes individuals struggle to achieve success and high social status. In spite of what many economists seem to believe, for many individuals money is not the only index or the only measurement of success. This should be a warning about expecting too much economic impact from reductions in high tax rates.

Let us now consider the reductions in tax rates that have occurred in recent decades. I shall provide only a few examples. In the United States, the marginal tax rate was 91 percent of taxable income in the years between 1950 and 1963. It was reduced to 70 percent between 1965 and 1980, ignoring some temporary surcharges during the Vietnam War. It was reduced to 50 percent between 1981 and 1986 during the early years of the Reagan administration, and, then, to 28 percent by Reagan's "fundamental tax reform" of 1986 (see Pechman, 1987, table A-1, p. 313). To deal with growing fiscal deficits, the highest tax rate was raised, in 1993, to the current 39.6 percent rate. It was then cut to 35 percent during the second President Bush administration, and in 2013 it returned to 39.6 percent with President Obama.

To the federal tax rates must be added the income taxes levied by many local governments (both states and counties), which, in some states, can reach 10 percent of taxable income. Therefore, for some high-income taxpayers who live in the states with the highest local tax rates, the marginal tax rate on regular labor income can approach 50 percent, giving, especially for some of them, a strong incentive to move to states such as Florida or Alaska that have no local income taxes, or, for those whose US residence is not important for their professions, to even move to foreign countries that have low income tax rates, such as Singapore.

The latter is an incentive that is beyond need for discussion in this book and that has attracted attention in some states, such as New Jersey, where a billionaire who moves his or her residence to Florida may leave a significant gap in New Jersey's budget. The widening income distribution and the existence of individuals with billion-dollar incomes have created this potential tax competition problem within the United States. Some recent studies have indicated that few taxpayers actually move *for this motive*. However, if they are truly very-high-income individuals, the moves of even a few of them may still be significant for local governments.

Many other countries, and especially Anglo-Saxon countries, also reduced significantly the highest tax rates on *personal* taxable income after the 1970s. For example, from 1973 to 1992 the United Kingdom reduced the highest rate from 83 percent, in 1973, and 60 percent, in 1986, to 40 percent; Australia from 65 percent to 48 percent; Canada from 47 percent to 29 percent and then back up to 31.3 percent after 1995; Ireland from 77 percent to 52 percent (and to 48 percent after 1995); and New Zealand from 57 percent to 33 percent. Large rate reductions also took place in Japan, from 75 percent to 50 percent; in Italy, from 72 percent to 50 percent; and in other countries. (For more details, see Messere, 1993, table 10.15, p. 285; Owens and Whitehouse, 1996.)

Interestingly, the continental European countries (where the income distribution has remained more equal, in recent decades, than in Anglo-Saxon countries) did not reduce as much the marginal tax rates, except for incomes from capital sources when Scandinavian countries introduced "dual income taxes" in the 1990s. Small or insignificant changes in the tax rates on normal incomes were introduced in Belgium, Denmark, Finland, France, Germany, Luxembourg, and the Netherlands.

By 2013, the most recent year for which information was easily available, the highest marginal tax rates had been reduced in many countries. According to a report by KPMG International (2012), the marginal tax rate for all countries had fallen on average by 28.9 percent, It had fallen to 56.6 percent in Sweden, to 55.4 percent in Denmark, to 52 percent in the Netherland, and to 50 percent in several other European countries such as Austria, Belgium, and the United Kingdom, in addition to Japan. Other countries, including the United States, had lower rates. Naturally, the reduction in the marginal tax rate is only part of the story, because in different countries the income level at which the highest rate applies can also be significantly different. Spain, the United States, and Germany were the three countries with the highest income levels at which the highest tax rate applied.

The tax rate was also reduced for corporations in recent decades. In the United States it had been 52 percent of taxable profits in the 1952–1963 period. It then had been reduced, in several stages, to 46 percent. The 1986 US "fundamental tax reform" reduced the US rate to 34 percent in 1988. Many countries followed the US example and also reduced their corporate tax rates, some more significantly than the United States did. (See Messere, 1993, table 12.6, p. 341; Owens and Whitehouse, 1996.) In recent years Japan and the United States have had the highest statutory corporate tax rates, but in the United States various loopholes have reduced significantly the actual payments for many corporations. Between 1983 and 2015 the statutory average tax rate on corporate profits for twenty-eight G20 or OECD countries fell from around 50 percent to less than 30 percent.

The high US statutory tax rate has encouraged corporations and their lobbies to continue to push for various loopholes, of which there are many. It has also encouraged corporations to keep some of their profits abroad, where they remain untaxed until repatriation. The net result has been that the *statutory* tax rate on corporate profit in the United States has remained relatively high, compared with that of other countries, but the *effective* tax rate is much lower. Some large corporations, including Boeing, Verizon, Amazon, Amgen, Alphabet, Apple, IBM, Coca-Cola, and General Electric, pay effective tax rates of less than 20 percent as estimated by S&P Global Market Intelligence, and reported by Patricia Cohen in the *New York Times* (November 13, 2016, p. 21).

It would make a lot of sense to lower the statutory rate in exchange with the elimination of many loopholes, including that of not paying taxes on the trillions of dollars in profits held abroad. So far, politically this has proven impossible to do. As of March 2017 there is much talk in the United States and in the United Kingdom about reducing taxes, especially on corporations in spite of the still high fiscal deficit.

Changes in the Tax Architecture

Until 1986 it was mainly the marginal tax rates that had come under attack by conservative economists and by those who believed in the relevance of the Laffer curve. There had been less talk about the *architecture* of the income tax. The 1986 fundamental tax reform introduced by the Reagan administration had sharply reduced the marginal tax rates, but it had continued to respect the Haig-Simons principle, which had been followed by tax policy and recommended by tax experts in previous decades. That principle maintained that income is income regardless of its source, and that all income should be taxed in the same way. In practice, for administrative reasons, unrealized capital gains were always exempt from taxation. The Reagan reform had respected that principle and had tried to widen the tax base and to bring the tax rates on capital income closer to those on labor income, by reducing some tax incentives and loopholes and by lowering the marginal tax rate to bring it closer to the rate on corporate profits. A prevalent view at that time was that the highest marginal tax rate on personal income ought to be the same as, or close to the rate on corporate income.

The Haig-Simons principle was based on the view that income is essentially spending power for those who have it, and spending power does not depend on the origin of the income (see Musgrave, 1959, pp. 164–171). John Hicks, one of the earliest Nobel Prize winners, had also endorsed that principle in his definition of income. As an indication of the importance of the aforementioned principle, a lot of literature in the decades after World War II had discussed the question of how to tax "unrealized" capital gains, which were incomes that had provided spending power to some individuals but that normally had not been taxed, because of administrative and other considerations.

Starting in the late 1970s, but especially in the 1980s, the architecture of the income tax had come under attack by some influential economists (see Tanzi, 2014b). One important reason for this development was the belief that a reduction of taxes on capital incomes would increase savings and investment, thus leading to faster growth. Another was that globalization of economic activities, then underway, was opening economies to greater global influences and was making capital more mobile than it had been earlier, when the countries' economies had been closed. Globalization was making the supply of capital to a country potentially more elastic with respect to its tax rate. Capital was acquiring stronger incentives to move from countries with high tax rates to countries with low tax rates, and especially to those with no taxes, the "tax havens." Globalization was also creating incentives for some, especially small, countries to engage in *tax competition* by lowering their tax rates, or by offering other tax incentives to attract foreign capital to them.

Because, by that time, globalization and low tax rates had come to be seen as positive developments by many economists, and because equity had started to become less important as a policy objective than efficiency, there was the beginning of pressures on governments to reduce taxes, and especially to reduce the taxes on incomes from capital sources. The reason for these pressures was that capital had acquired strong incentives and new possibilities to emigrate from high-tax to low-tax jurisdictions.

The initial attacks on the Haig-Simons principle were based on largely theoretical considerations and had come from several economists, including Michael Boskin (1978); Larry Summers (1985); and Robert Lucas, 1990a, 1990b) and others. Their arguments had good economic logic.

Boskin, who at the time was an influential conservative economist, published empirical estimates that suggested that the rate of return to saving was more important than had been previously thought in determining the saving rate. In turn the country's saving rate, in an economy at full employment, largely determined the rate of investment and the economic growth for that country. Other economists argued that, if high tax rates on capital income were not reduced, in an open world, capital would move to places where it would be taxed more lightly. This would reduce the country's capital-to-labor ratios, reduce the productivity of labor, and, eventually, reduce economic growth and the real wages of workers. Therefore, the tax reduction on incomes from capital (profits, capital gains, dividends, "carried trade," etc.) could be justified as being in the workers' longer run interests. This argument complemented that made by the Laffer curve, that lower rates created incentives for citizens to work more.

The taxes on incomes from capital sources were progressively reduced, especially in the 1990s, to the point where a billionaire could remark that his average tax burden was lower than those of his secretary and his driver. During the presidential campaign in 2012, Mitt Romney was reported to have paid an average tax burden of around 12 percent on an income that amounted to many millions of dollars. The result was that as Slemrod and Bakija put in the USA, "much capital income is excluded from the personal income tax" (p. 34) and the part taxed is taxed at much lower tax rates.

A related development was that CEOs and other corporate managers learned to manipulate their total compensation packages so that a large part of them would be classified as income from capital sources, such as capital gains, rather than salary, thus reducing their tax rates, at times below those paid by the average workers in their enterprises. It is easy to see the impact that these reforms had on the psychology of industrial workers whose wages had remained stagnant for decades and who had continued to pay high rates on those wages, as well as the impact on the distribution of income.

Complexity and Global Tax Avoidance

In recent years there has been growing avoidance and evasion of taxes, by both enterprises and HNWIs, in connection with global economic activities. As globalization has intensified, tax rates have been reduced, the architecture of tax systems has been changed in many countries, and tax systems have become more complex than they need to be (see Tanzi, 2013a). See also Olmerod and Bakija on this issue.

It should be recognized that income taxation is never easy. When the income tax was first proposed as a permanent tax in the United States in the early part of the twentieth century, one of the major fiscal economists at the time, Edwin Seligman, professor of public finance at Columbia University, in a brilliant and detailed assessment of such a tax, had concluded that income taxation was pretty much a hopeless enterprise, because its administration would be too difficult to achieve (see Seligman, 1908). Supreme Court Justice Learned Hand, when he was first faced with the proposed new law, was also, reportedly, completely bewildered by its complexity and by the wording of the law. As he put it upon reading the proposed law (which had needed the approval of the US Supreme Court), words "danced before his eyes ... in a meaningless procession." Those assessments were made before the income tax laws acquired the modern characteristics that made them far more complex, and that required tens of thousands of pages of text and regulations to explicate them.

Much of the added complexity has been due to the attempt to pursue a lot of different objectives with the income tax law, in addition to that of simply collecting revenue. The more numerous have become the objectives, the greater has become the complexity of the tax. Soon after its introduction in the United States in 1913, the federal income tax ceased to be an instrument mainly used for collecting revenue. It became a tool of social engineering, used by politicians, in place of other tools, to pursue a large and continually increasing range of government objectives. In the United States, which never showed much attraction to high spending, the objectives were pursued, more than in other countries, through the income tax. Once the income tax was adopted, vested interests were encouraged to push for the introduction of special treatments of *their* worthy causes. The problem is that, in today's world, the worthy causes tend to be numerous, and they tend to grow with time.

Tax incentives, tax expenditures, special treatments of particular situations (sizes of families; ages and physical conditions of members; worthy expenses for mortgages, health care, education, travel to work, training, and purchase of tools; charitable contributions; and contributions to retirement), and others (contributions to saving accounts and incentives to work) became justifications for pushing for special tax treatment of personal income. The term "tax expenditure" was first used by Stanley Surrey, a lawyer working in the US Treasury, in 1967. In 1975, the US Congressional Budget Office required that both the executive branch and congressional agencies publish lists of tax expenditures (see Toder, 2005). Other countries have also been using tax expenditures and publishing such lists. Similar considerations entered in the taxation of enterprises for which incentives and special treatments of some expenses, such as R&D, became common.

As mentioned in an earlier chapter, in Italy the Corte dei Conti (similar to the US Accountability Office) has listed about 800 such incentives that are in use in that country. Nobody seems to have made a similar count for the United States, but it is not likely that it would generate a lower number. This situation has made income taxes increasingly complex, and complexity has made it easier for clever lawyers and accountants to exploit various tax avoidance possibilities, for lobbyists to propose what are often small and hardly noticeable changes that are increasingly more complex and more costly to administer and to comply with, and for taxpayers to evade the tax by presenting to the tax authorities misleading information (see Tanzi, 2013a, 2007a). A link has also been theorized to exist between the income tax and the underground economy (see Tanzi, 1980a).

Over recent decades, in order to deal with activities that were becoming more globalized, and with incomes originating from different jurisdictions, some additional changes were made to the countries' income taxes, making them even more complex. The complexity stimulated even more tax planning by enterprises and by rich individuals, leading to tax avoidance. The reaction by tax administrations to this development was often to introduce more rules, in an increasingly vicious cycle.

Excessive complexity is not inevitable, even though, as mentioned earlier, the income tax is a complex tax. Excessive complexity is largely, though not completely, created by those who make the laws and the rules, and by those who interpret them. It is the outcome of an often-futile attempt to reach too many objectives with a single instrument, defeating a rule that the first Nobel Prize winner in economics, Jan Tinbergen, had insisted on: to use one instrument for each objective.

Some countries, such as Denmark, Sweden, and Singapore, or economies, such as Hong Kong, have resisted the temptations to promote too many objectives with the income tax (or with other taxes) and have kept their income taxes focused on the revenue objective. Some literature has argued that the problem of complexity is a consequence of the progressive rates. That literature has argued that progressivity leads to greater pressures by vested interests for special treatments, which leads to complexity. That literature has proposed the use of flat-rate income taxes, collected from *gross* incomes. Some former socialist countries of Eastern Europe, including Russia, especially have adopted flat-rate taxes. Some problems might disappear with the use of these taxes, though not all. Complexity exists also for corporate income taxes, even though these taxes are generally proportional. The solution may be captured by a statement, frequently attributed to Keynes, that "it is better to be approximately right than precisely wrong." Income taxes have, often, tried to fit an Armani suit on every taxpayer, when the choice of a Mao tunic might have been simpler and preferable.

In relation to the issue of the growing unevenness of the income distribution, it may be worthwhile to repeat and to stress that those who have benefited disproportionately from tax avoidance and from tax rate reductions have been individuals at the top of the income distribution. The average workers have benefited much less. Tax avoidance, especially in connection with incomes from global or multicountry activities, does not have democratic characteristics. Its incidence favors the rich, just as the reduction of the highest marginal tax rate and the changes in the architecture of the tax system favored them.

I will conclude this chapter by stating unequivocally that the changes in the tax systems that have taken place in several countries, and especially in the United States and other Anglo-Saxon countries, in recent decades must have played a significant role in making the after-tax distribution of income less equitable, and in raising the observed values of the Gini coefficients. Those changes were especially damaging to those workers who did not experience wage increases but that still continued to pay significant taxes on their earned incomes and on their purchases.

CHAPTER 33

Summing Up Past Developments

The First Seven Decades of the Twentieth Century

This book has dealt with the question of how governments or, more broadly, states or public sectors have played, or attempted to play, their evolving economic roles during the last hundred or so years. Special, though not exclusive, attention has been paid to the United States, the most important and most influential country in that period. The first part of the book described how that role changed from the beginning to the middle of the last century, a period during which the economic role of governments went from one that largely reflected a laissez-faire, hands-off attitude to one in which it became more ambitious and dominant.

The new role required significantly higher public revenue to finance higher public spending, a larger and more competent bureaucracy, and an increasing number of laws and rules. The new economic role came under attack in the last three decades of the twentieth century. However, in spite of those attacks and some attempts at drawback in those years, the economic role of the state, at least in quantitative terms, has remained much larger than it had been at the beginning of the twentieth century. It has also generally become more complex.

After World War II, the redistribution of income that governments attempted to promote, across different groups of citizens (and not always, or necessarily, from richer to poorer individuals or families), grew in importance with the creation of welfare states, as did the role of stabilization of economic activities. The stabilization role had not existed in the past and had been promoted by John Maynard Keynes during the Great Depression. By the second half of the century, most governments had endorsed what came to be called the "Keynesian Revolution" and attempted to promote policies aimed at reducing the economic impact of economic cycles.

The government programs that were created to redistribute income were largely responsible for the increases in tax levels and in public spending levels that occurred especially during the second half of the century. In several countries the tax systems became also much more progressive. The allocation of resources and the stabilization of the economy were less important objectives in this context, even though stabilization may have played some role, because of the asymmetry over time in its use, and because of the view that came to prevail that a larger public sector, by creating built-in stabilizers and economic activities not linked to the cycles, would make a country's economy less exposed to recessions and depressions.

There were benefits and costs associated with the larger government involvement in the economy. Many economists and most plain citizens (more in Europe than in the United States) would probably agree that the benefits created by that involvement exceeded the costs for society as a whole. Broadly speaking, societies became institutionally more compassionate and more caring toward less fortunate members, and many members of society acquired more protections against some events that they could not control (such as old age, illnesses, illiteracy, temporary loss of jobs, or the loss of a breadwinner in families) than there were in the past, when those events would have had more serious consequences, in spite of the role that extended families and stronger community spirit had played.

Greater democratization, which led to growing shares of the populations with the right to vote (for women that right came earlier in some countries and later in others; in the United Kingdom and the United States it came in the 1920s; in Italy it came after World War II), played an important role in the change in the government role, and so did the greater proportion of the countries' populations that, during the century, moved from rural areas to large and crowded cities. These were two important determining factors that led to the expanding government role in all advanced countries. Changes in intellectual winds and other developments, such as those that occurred in Russia during the century were also important. Until the 1970s, the intellectual winds had generally pushed governments to do more for the countries' citizens.

During the twentieth century, the economies of the advanced countries had experienced great structural changes. First, growing industrialization had changed the nature of economic activities and of the market and had changed also economic relations. Industrialization had increased the number of *dependent but free* workers and had facilitated the collection of higher tax levels (by reducing informality and the atomization of activities, by concentrating the generation of income and sales in fewer but larger establishments, and by introducing on a larger scale the use of modern accounting). New, important tax instruments had been created and were increasingly used by governments to collect revenue from income taxes and from general sales taxes, especially from value-added taxes. See Tanzi, forthcoming.

The income tax and the value-added tax would account for much of the public revenue growth that occurred in many developed countries during the second half of the century. These changes, which made possible the financing of the new, expensive government programs, especially in European countries, occurred *before* the advent of the new period of globalization, and in a period when the countries' economies were still relatively closed. In those years the governments of several countries had succeeded in increasing tax burdens and in making tax systems more progressive. That experience does not suggest that when the income distribution becomes less even, governments find it easier to raise taxes or to make the tax systems more progressive. It is possible that the same forces that are making the income distribution more unequal are also making it more difficult to tax the rich. Therefore, when inequality becomes more acute, it may become more difficult to tax the rich (see Scheve and Stasavage, 2016).

There has been much controversy and a lot of econometric work that has tried to determine whether higher tax levels, as shares of GDP, and tax systems that depend more on progressive direct taxes, have a negative impact on economic growth as many believe. Unfortunately those conclusions cannot be objectively defended. For contrasting results from two good econometric studies see the paper by Arnold et al., 2011, that has concluded that higher tax burdens and tax systems that rely more on direct taxes are more damaging to economic growth, and the paper by Baiardi et al., 2017 that has not found any such correlation.

The Last Three Decades of the Twentieth Century

During the last three decades of the twentieth century, the importance of services in advanced economies grew, economies opened up to trade with other countries, and their structures changed rapidly. Multicountry activities by both multinational enterprises and increasingly individuals with high net worths or individuals with particular skills became common. A global financial market was created, new communication technologies appeared, and their use and influence spread rapidly and influenced more and more the economic activities. Internet shopping appeared and grew in importance, and together with new technologies started creating increasing

Termites of the State

challenges for many traditional jobs and activities. In many transactions the "products" exchanged lost their tangible character and become virtual.

New technologies increased the value of intellectual property, including that of various performers in several fields, who could perform in different countries and could sell their performances globally. National borders became more porous to the movement of goods, services, financial activities, intellectual property, and the performances of athletes and others. Many finished products, assembled and/or conceived in one country, started to have some of their parts produced in other countries.

By the end of the century, multicountry production of finished products, and the distribution of services sold globally by global corporations, had become common and economically very important. A large share of total trade between and among countries had become trade among related components of the same global corporations (subsidiaries or branches) operating from different countries. For tax administrations, this development created the problem of how to allocate the total values of the final products and the related incomes among the countries where the parts were produced. This allocation was important for determining the taxing rights of different countries. By this time many of the traditional jobs in large industrial enterprises in advanced countries had disappeared or had moved to developing countries, creating difficulties for workers who had held those jobs and who did not have the skills for the new jobs that were created. This was the negative side of globalization which to some extent had been ignored by government policies.

The aforementioned changes had an important impact on the countries' economic activities and on the distribution of their incomes. Generally, in advanced countries, individuals with higher levels of education and with particular skills gained, while those with lower levels of education, who had worked in traditional jobs or in the large industrial enterprises, lost, at least in relative terms. Increasingly and importantly, the changes affected the distributions of income *within* countries, making it increasingly less equal, while they made the world's income distribution more even.

For the citizens of specific countries, the fact that the changes made the *world* income distribution more equal, by increasing the growth rates of some important developing countries, especially China and India, was not important. The change in the countries' income distributions might have justified more governmental interventions, especially in markets that had become more complex and where the asymmetry in information about the value of products or services that were exchanged had become more prevalent, leading to more abuses. However, the more laissez-faire ideology that in recent decades has come to prevail in several countries has counseled against such intervention.

In recent decades the market has seemed less able to create well-paid jobs for many dependent workers in advanced countries. Consequently, income disparities, between the majority of the workers and a small minority (1 or 5 percent) of the citizens, have become increasingly large. In several countries small minorities of the populations have been appropriating many of the gains from economic growth and growing shares of total income and wealth.

People swim more easily in friendly waters. The economic waters of the 1980s and the 1990s had become very friendly for CEOs, other high level managers of large enterprises, and people with particular skills, those who could claim high wages, large bonuses, and large compensations for their work and performances. These people dared to ask for, and increasingly were able to get, what, at times, seemed absurdly high incomes and, as seen from the perspective of the workers, seemingly unjustified compensations. In the new environment, they were not as embarrassed to ask for accepting these high incomes, as they might have been in earlier decades. For example, in 2015 the *average* compensation of chief executives, for US public companies with at least $1 billion in annual revenue, was more than $19 million and the median value was $16.6 million. The lowest annual income among them was more than $12 million (see *New York Times*, May 29, 2016, pp. 8–9, BU Y). In other countries, even though they were more modest, the compensations of some managers had also become high (see Solimano, 2016).

In democratic societies where, by that time, all (or most) citizens had acquired the right to vote, and where they had been told that all people were born equal and should be entitled to equal *opportunities* in life, the growing income inequality could not be considered a desirable or normal development. It convinced many that the market system, if left to itself, might not be the admirable instrument that many economists had venerated. Some concluded that the market might have become rigged and more exposed than in the past to abuse.

After the financial crisis and the Great Recession in the new century, the economic role of governments – which starting in the 1980s had been influenced by the greater veneration of the market – came under attack and started to be seen under a different light by an increasing number of citizens and also economists. Many became convinced that the politicians who made the rules under which individuals and enterprises operated could be influenced, and were being influenced, by powerful lobbies, or that they could even be bought by rich or well-connected individuals. See Cost, 2015. Complaints about the role of cronyism, revolving-door policies, rent-seeking, corruption, and other problems became more frequent, leading, in several countries, to a worrisome rise of populist forces. Initially, some had dismissed the complaints as *class warfare*.

In the years that had followed the Great Depression of the 1930s and World War II, many governments had responded to the calls by economists and citizens for a larger government involvement in the economy by creating *welfare* states, or, as in the United States, by introducing new social programs, such as the War on Poverty. Some political forces and some individuals had always opposed governmental expansion and had continued to believe in the virtue of a small government. However, in the years after World War II the voices of these individuals had been muted or had had little echo. Starting in the 1970s, those voices acquired larger followings, especially in the United States and the United Kingdom. In those years some government activities had become less popular, and conservative economists had highlighted problems associated with too much governmental intervention. Additionally, especially in the 1970s, the economies of several countries had gone through a period of high inflation and recession at the same time.

By that time some of the costs of the social or welfare programs, in terms of high taxes, inefficiencies in public spending, horizontal inequity among beneficiaries, impact on incentives and on the personal liberty of citizens, and growing corruption, had become more evident to some observers. Those costs were being much publicized by conservative economists and politicians. The government had started to be seen in a less favorable light by increasing shares of the populations, and some had come to see it as less the solution to social and economic problems and more a potential problem. The pro-government winds of the previous decades had started to give way to pro-market enthusiasm.

The 1980s and 1990s and the first years of the new century, until the financial crisis, had become pro-market decades, and pro-market policies had started to come back, although conservative governments could not set the clock back to the time when laissez-faire had prevailed, in the early part of the twentieth century, even if they wanted to. There was too much resistance by groups that had acquired considerable political power in earlier years against the elimination of some multi-year programs, such as public pensions, public health care, and public education. However, the mood had changed, and those who believed in the work and in the results of the free market had acquired many followers.

Besides the impact that the pro-market thinking in the 1980s and later years had had on wages and incomes was the impact that it had on corporate policies that, especially in the USA and in some other Anglo-Saxon countries, had provided a corporate-based and corporate financed social benefits. Individuals working for large corporations had often received pensions and health insurance benefits. These benefits were largely slashed during the past two decades. Surveys by Bureau of Labor Statistics and by the Federal Reserve have shown that retirement benefits and health related benefits have fallen dramatically. Presumably the thinking was that the competitive system would adjust wages and higher wages would allow workers to buy protection directly from the market. See articles by Ben Steverman, 2017, and by Monique Morrissey, 2013.

While the above had been going on, market relations had become more complex; the prices of many products and services (especially in sectors that had been growing in relative importance in the economy) had become less faithful measures to the consumers of their true value; abuses in some sectors had become more frequent; and urbanization, greater population density, economic growth, and some technological developments had been creating new and growing negative externalities and greater needs to deal with them. Poverty (whether in absolute or relative terms) had remained a problem in several countries, in spite of the generous government programs that had promised to eliminate it, and in spite of the large sums that had been spent to fight poverty over the years. While in the years when the more pro-market thinking had been popular inequality had attracted less attention, in recent years economic inequality has reached levels that have not been seen since the 1920s, making it difficult to ignore.

Given the more democratic and more urban setting of recent years, and the growing role of the media, that inequality has been seen as less tolerable and more damaging than in the past. In the United States, it was shown to be associated with clearly undesirable consequences, for example, widely different life expectancies, different mortality levels at birth, different rates of incarceration, different access to educational services and to the protection of the justice system, and, increasingly, different attitudes toward some government functions in various parts of the country. For many, poverty was killing the hope for a better future, and the famed "American dream" was becoming a casualty.

In an interesting paper published in the book edited by Lilia Costabile, 2008, Samuel Bowles and Arjun Jayadev, pp. 74–94, called attention to a potentially important consequence of great inequality in countries. They provided empirical evidence from 18 countries that the more unequal is the income distribution of a country, the greater is the need for that country to allocate resources to maintain the social order. They call this relationship the enforcement–equality trade-off. As they put it, "[c]ross-national comparisons show a significant statistical association between income inequality and the fraction of the labour force that is constituted by guard labor."

For a group of 18 countries, for which they provide data on guard labor – table 3.2 on p. 82 – there seem to be a strong direct correlation between guard labor and Gini coefficients. The higher are the Ginis, the larger the proportion of the labor force diverted toward unproductive activity. It is easy to make an argument that this is a rather unproductive use of labor. If this inefficiency in the use of national resources is added to our previous argument that much of the high incomes are rents, the often made argument that inequality is important to create incentives to promote faster growth loses some of its force.

Interregional inequality in the United States is also unusually high compared with that in other advanced countries, and so is inequality in life expectancy and probably in educational achievements. See Graham and Pinto, 2017. Some data on life expectancy may help illustrate the extent to which this is a problem. The US Institute for Health Metrics and Evaluation has been collecting statistics on life expectancy for men and women among US counties. The data were reported by Bloomberg.Net.

In 1987, the average life expectancy for US men was 75.4 in the best county (Fairfax County, Virginia) and 64.6 in the worst county (Holmes County, Mississippi), a remarkable difference of 10.8 years. By 2007, the difference between these two counties had risen to 15.2 years. For women, in 1987 the difference between the two counties was 5.9 years. By 2007 it had risen to 12.5 years. These are extraordinary differences for parts of the same country. They are larger than those that exist between the richest and the poorest countries in the world, and are probably larger than those that exist between different regions of the same countries in other industrial regions.

Between 1995 and 2010 the male populations living in Washington, DC, New York City, and San Francisco enjoyed gains in life expectancy of more than 10 years, and many men living in many other counties enjoyed gains of at least 5 years. On the other hand, the male population living in Floyd County and in Perry County, in Kentucky, and in Wyoming County, in West Virginia, experienced a fall in life expectancy of between 1.7 years and 3.2 years. In twenty-five counties life expectancy fell over the 15-year period. The difference in life expectancy for males between McDowell,

West Virginia, and Fairfax County, Virginia, just 350 miles away, was an astonishing 18 years!

The female populations in Washington, DC, New York City, and San Francisco experienced gains of between 4.3 years and 5.6 years (in the Bronx, New York, the gain was 5.8 years), while the life expectancy for women in 350 counties fell, in some (especially in Oklahoma and Kentucky) by between 2 years and 3 years. In Marin County, California, women live 12 years longer than in Perry County, Kentucky. More recent reports indicate that these differences may have become more accentuated in more recent years.

There were some remarkable positive changes in particular counties. For example, in New York City, life expectancy for men increased by 12.9 years between 1987 and 2007, compared with a national average improvement of 4.3 years. In San Francisco, it increased by 10 years. In some counties, mainly in the South, life expectancy went down during that 20-year period. Similar results were experienced by women, but for them life expectancy improved less on average, and in many Southern counties it declined.

Government policy and especially the role of regulations connected with smoking and some other habits have been given a lot of credit for these improvements, especially in New York City, indicating that some government regulations can do a lot of good, for example, those associated with the use of seat belts, speed limits while driving, and smoking.

In the United States there is also great variation in upward mobility that largely parallels the statistics on life expectancy. Research by Raj Chetty, a professor of economics at Stanford, and associates has shown that the place where one lives has a lot of influence on the chance of moving from the bottom fifth to the top fifth of the income distribution. For example, it varies from 12.9 percent in San Jose to 4.5 percent in Atlanta. The research has also shown that with the passing of decades the chance that children have of earning more than their parents has fallen dramatically. Similar conclusions have been reached for several other advanced countries. A study by the McKinsey Global Institute (2016) has found that "between 2005 and 2014 real incomes for workers in advanced countries were flat and they fell. They fell for 65 to 70 percent of the households.

Gini coefficients became widely known statistics in recent years, and so did the shares of total income received by those at the top of the income distributions, as did the earnings of individuals with particularly high incomes, such as the CEOs of many banks and enterprises or the heads of hedge funds, especially when some of their incomes did not appear to be clearly deserved or earned. A report by the US Census Bureau in

September 2016 has provided the most recent data for the United States. The bottom 20 percent of households, which in mid-1975 had received 5.6 percent of all income, has seen its share fall to 3.4 percent. The richest 5 percent have seen their share go up by 6 percentage points, to 22 percent.

An increasing number of individuals have greater difficulties accepting the justification of these income shares. Comparisons between the wealth of a few individuals and that of billions of individuals have also become news items, as have the ratios of CEOs' compensations to the average wages of workers reported earlier. These data have fed increasingly populist reactions.

Except for individuals with *major*, ascertainable physical or mental handicaps, the programs of governmental assistance to the poor, created after World War II in several advanced countries including the United States, could have been directed more at making poorer individuals participate more productively in the labor market, through training and educational programs, which would have increased their economic opportunities, rather than assisting them to get some consumption support with means-tested programs. The latter created "poverty traps" and long-term dependency on the programs on the part of at least some of those who benefited from them. Some existing programs seemed to do just that, in spite of attempts aimed at reducing dependency.

In the United States there were occasional news reports of households in which no one had worked for generations, in spite of the welfare reforms of the 1990s that were supposed to eliminate these possibilities. Some individuals seemed to have become professionally (and permanently) poor. Efforts to guarantee a basic, flat cash income *for everyone while eliminating all or most of the social programs*, as was suggested in an earlier chapter, were never made or even contemplated, although the idea of providing minimum incomes to citizens has continued to attract attention in several countries.

CHAPTER 34

Why Worry about Income Distribution?

The growth of unevenness in the distribution of income in recent decades has generated much debate concerning its implications and about the economic role of government and the fairness of current market and social arrangements. There has been a heated controversy about what to do, especially about the high concentration of income and wealth at the very top of the distribution. To reduce the presumably less deserved incomes of some of those at the top, a socially concerned and well-intentioned government ought to deal with some of the factors that may have led to that concentration. It might have to modify and simplify many rules and laws (including the tax laws) that in more recent decades may have favored the better-to-do. It ought to keep income taxes effectively enough progressive to make a difference, but not so progressive as to discourage entrepreneurship and risk-taking. And it ought to pay more attention to its fundamental role of allocation, especially in creating and in maintaining, efficiently, the social and physical infrastructure that benefits everyone and that helps the economy to grow. However, while many would agree with these broad objectives, at least in principle, there would be significant disagreement on the details, and opposition to some changes by those (especially those at the top) who would lose as a result of changes.

Globalization of production, the global mobility of capital and of rich individuals, the increase in the importance of intellectual capital, the increasing protection accorded to it by the laws, and various technological developments promoted or encouraged by government policies have all contributed to making the task of improving the income distribution more difficult than it might have been a few decades ago.

One recent complication is that, in some cases, to deal with some of the problems it may no longer be sufficient to rely on the policies of *national* governments. Coordination among different countries may be more needed now than in the past. This is the case in dealing with global tax avoidance and with, for example, tax competition among countries, and in dealing with other global public goods or public "bads." That coordination remains difficult, in spite of recent talk about it at the political level, and it may be becoming more difficult. Many factors have contributed to creating the economic, social, and pro-smaller government environment that has prevailed in several countries in the past three decades. Van Creveld, a professor of history, van Creveld, 1999, has characterized that period as one of "decline of the state". It was a period in which the environment that prevailed contributed in various ways to the increase in the inequality of income. Factors that started appearing in the 1970s created a kind of perfect storm that led to a revolutionary change. Perfect storms happen when several seemingly unrelated elements come together at a given time, and combine and reinforce one another in particular, unpredictable ways.

It may be useful to mention some of the main elements that contributed to the income distributions experienced in recent decades. They were already discussed separately in previous chapters. And are listed here to highlight their synergy and their combined impact. The mid-1970s will be taken as the starting point for what became an intellectual and social revolution, that upended some of the thinking and policies that had prevailed in earlier decades.

First, there was the conservative intellectual movement, led by several able and vocal economists who identified and highlighted presumed government *failures* and market *virtues*. Toward the end of the 1970s, the government started to be seen as a problem rather than as the potential solution to some of the problems faced by citizens. The conservative message was made up of separate parts, all pointing toward more conservative and pro-market policies. In the United States the movement was promoted by economists such as Milton Friedman, F. Hayek, George Stigler, James Buchanan, Ronald Coase, Robert Mundell, Gary Becker, Arnold Harberger, Robert Lucas, and some others.

Their message was received and given a political coating and popular appeal, and was broadcast to the general public by conservative intellectuals and influential journalists. In the United States *The Wall Street Journal* in particular played a leading role, with its strong support for what came to be called the "supply-side revolution." Various think tanks – including the American Enterprise Institute in the United States, and the Institute of Economic Affairs, in England – also played a role. Important technical tools of that "revolution" were the Laffer curve, rational expectation, and the Ricardian Equivalence hypothesis. Some widely read popular books that transmitted to the wider public the antigovernment and antitax message of that revolution also played a role (see, for example, Gilder, 1981).

By the late 1970s, the supply-side revolution, and the new economic thinking that accompanied it, had acquired a strong political appeal, leading to the election of conservative governments in both the United Kingdom and the United States, and starting to influence views in several other countries. Its influence would continue to be felt in different ways and in different countries until the arrival of the financial crisis and of the Great Recession in the new century. It was the period when in Van Cleverd's term "the state declined".

Various elements had come together at approximately the same time in the late 1970s that promoted the conservative movement. They transformed the initial movement from an intellectual curiosity into, almost, a revolution. Together, they would change much of the political and social environment that many workers and citizens had become accustomed to in the previous decades. Even less conservative and some liberal governments, which still ideologically favored larger government roles, such as the Clinton administration in the United States and the Labour government of Tony Blair in the United Kingdom, would be influenced by that revolution, as indicated by increasing talks about a "Third Way" and by some of the policies that these governments introduced. (See Giddens, 1998 and Rubin, 2003.) The so-called Washington Consensus, intended to relate more to developing countries, could also be considered an offspring of the supply-side revolution.

For example, the Clinton administration was behind a major reform of welfare policies that reduced benefits to welfare recipients, and behind a major deregulation of the financial market. (See Rubin, ibid.) In Sweden, which was still perhaps the best example of a welfare state, public spending was dramatically cut in the 1990s, and major reforms were made to the pension system, the tax system, and other areas. In Italy it led to the election of the first Berlusconi government, which claimed to be a government of the center-right (see Tanzi, 2015a). Canada and Ireland sharply reduced public spending. Other countries, including Australia, Spain, New Zealand, Argentina, Chile and others were also influenced by the new thinking.

The pro-market, reduced-government revolution had the following common elements:

(a) Growing skepticism about Keynesian countercyclical policies. Keynesian policies had come under sharp attacks on the part of several

influential economists and the thinking behind "rational expectation." These policies had also been challenged by the stagflation of
the 1970s. Monetary policy started to be given more importance than
it had had during the Keynesian years.

(b)   Growing skepticism about the positive role that government pro-
      grams could play in promoting the welfare of citizens. Growing
      welfare scandals and reported abuses and inefficiencies were raising
      antagonism on the part of workers toward some of those policies.

(c)   Questions about whether policymakers were as benevolent and as
      knowledgeable as claimed, and about whether they always promoted
      the best interest of the citizens. This was a point that had been stressed
      particularly by adherents to the School of Public Choice, a school
      that had acquired more followers and more influence and had started
      publishing economic journals.

(d)   Growing faith in the operation of the market and what the market
      could achieve, if it were allowed to operate freely. In some sense this
      faith represented a return to the faith that classical economists had
      had in laissez-faire and the power of the market, a faith that had char-
      acterized economic thinking in the second half of the nineteenth cen-
      tury and the early part of the twentieth century. In recent decades this
      faith had been progressively extended, beyond national markets, to
      the world market by pro-globalization enthusiasts. Some economists
      came to believe that the invisible hand could operate globally.

(e)   A belief that a free world market would exploit countries' compar-
      ative advantage and, as a consequence, would allow much greater
      specialization for the world as a whole, and would increase produc-
      tivity and the welfare of all the world's citizens. Free trade and the
      liberalization of capital movements were enthusiastically supported,
      in spite of some doubters and continued opposition by labor unions.
      This led to the progressive elimination of many national barriers, to
      the creation of multinational enterprises, and, progressively, to the
      globalization of many economic activities and the creation of a global
      financial market. It would also lead to the movement of many indus-
      trial jobs from advanced countries to developing countries, which
      would reduce the incomes of many workers in the advanced coun-
      tries. Countries' economies became more open, and the financial
      market became capable of moving, daily, trillions of US dollars across
      national frontiers. Potential collateral damages that could arise from
      these developments *for some groups of citizens*, such as industrial work-
      ers, in some advanced countries, were largely ignored or minimized.

Examples of such damages included rapid deindustrialization, excessive borrowing, and increases in debt by governments and by the private sector that would contribute to the financial crisis of 2007. (See Mian and Sufi, 2014.)

(f) The aforementioned supply-side revolution, which brought back to prominence the role of the supply side of the economy in economic performances. That role had been minimized when the Keynesian Revolution had become popular and when it had shifted the attention of economists and of governments from the supply side of the economies to aggregate demand. This led to pushes to eliminate or to reduce structural obstacles, which was often interpreted as a need to reduce taxes, economic regulations, and the power of labor unions.

(g) The aforementioned Laffer curve, the largely *political* device that attracted the attention of economists and politicians to the role that high marginal tax rates might play in reducing incentives to work and to invest, and in reducing the potential growth of economies. The popularity of the Laffer curve, a concept that was easy to understand and to use by noneconomists and by conservative politicians, would lead to the sharp reductions in marginal tax rates that took place in several countries in the late 1980s and in the 1990s.

(h) The change in the *architecture* of the tax systems that led to the abandonment of the Haig-Simons principle of taxation, the principle that had guided the policies related to the personal income taxes in earlier decades. The new architecture led to sharp rate reductions on high incomes and especially on *incomes from capital sources*. The new architecture also increased the attraction of the value-added tax for countries that wanted to have higher public spending and thus needed higher tax revenue. The value-added tax became an important new source of revenue in most countries, including developing countries. Its introduction was resisted in the United States by both conservatives, who opposed higher tax levels, and liberals, who wanted higher taxes but on the rich. Remarkably the share of Federal receipts in the USA that in 1980–1981 had reached 19 percent of GDP would fall to 17 percent in 1994 and to 15 percent in 2010–2013. There had been practically no increases in the tax level of the USA since World War II.

(i) The privatization of many public enterprises and of various economic activities in several countries, including public pensions, infrastructure building, and some educational activities, as well as the outsourcing of many government activities, including some connected with military operations and security.

(j)   The growing faith in the role of *financial* incentives in personal effort
       that led to the introduction of, and to the growing acceptance of,
       high salaries and large bonuses in many activities. Very high com-
       pensations for individuals in top positions, except for those in top
       government positions, soon became common. Corporate managers
       and operators in financial market activities developed feelings or atti-
       tudes of entitlements to large or even enormous compensations. Even
       college and museum presidents, coaches of successful sport teams,
       and heads of large charitable institutions started commanding multi-
       million-dollar salaries.

(k)   The growing focus on short run returns to corporate and shareholder
       profits, and the reduced attention to the social responsibilities of cor-
       porations. There was even some questioning of whether corporations
       had, or should have, social responsibilities.

(l)   The growing social acceptance of large differences in compensa-
       tion between managers and workers. Financial incentives seemed to
       play a role only in promoting the productivity of managers and not
       that of workers. As a consequence the wages of workers could be
       squeezed and were often squeezed to increase corporate returns and
       the compensations of managers. Managers getting multi-million-
       dollar incomes were not embarrassed when they opposed small wage
       increases for their workers.

(m)   The weakening of the power of labor unions that in turn led to fewer
       strikes and to less negotiating power on the part of dependent work-
       ers. Union participation fell in several countries, especially in the
       United States. President Reagan and Prime Minister Thatcher played
       significant roles in this weakening of labor unions' power.

(n)   The growing belief that market results have strong ethical values, and
       that what the free market generates, in term of income levels and
       income distribution, should not be questioned or challenged by gov-
       ernment action.

(o)   The replacement of social norms with financial incentives in several
       areas, in the belief that financial incentives are more effective in gen-
       erating desirable returns (see, Sandel, 2013; Bowles, 2016).

The new thinking that became prevalent in the 1980s and 1990s, the
trend toward globalization, important technological developments, such
as the growing use of the Internet, and the reforms introduced by various
governments in those decades all contributed to changing the distribution
of income, making it less equal.

The growing income inequality has been creating a new kind of money-based aristocracy made up of individuals in the top percentiles of the income distributions. This aristocracy has acquired much of the available wealth, which can be passed on to its children. It has also been acquiring increasing influences on policies and, often non transparent but still real, privileges in society, as for example, easier access to good schools for their children and to better health care services. The more time passes, the more different the individuals who are in these groups (the rich) are likely to feel compared to how the nonrich feel, as Ernest Hemingway had observed to be the case a century ago in his famous comment on the rich. They have been separating themselves from the rest of the population, often living in exclusive conclaves.

The question that should worry all of us about the future is whether this *new* aristocracy might become a *permanent* aristocracy, one made up of individuals who, with few exceptions, come from the same families, from the same schools, and are members of the same social clubs. Such an aristocracy would be different from one made up of frequently changing rich individuals, as would exist in countries with great social mobility. A permanent aristocracy, one made of individuals who inherit the wealth, the power, the access to good schools, and the social connections that come with it, would imply a return to the past, a return to societies that were not truly democratic, and to a market that would no longer offer a free market economy. As Kaushik Basu once remarked when he was chief economist at the World Bank, "Extreme inequality is ultimately an assault on democracy." He could have added that it is also an assault on the market economy. Such an aristocracy would also have the power to prevent needed changes, including those directed at bringing improvements to income distribution. In such a society, only true revolutions would be likely to bring changes, as historical examples indicate.

It might be appropriate to conclude this book in the same way that it was opened, with a quotation from an essay by John Maynard Keynes, written in 1925, after he had returned from Russia, a period that, in terms of income distribution and other aspects, especially in the USA, had characteristics similar to those that have developed in our period. Those aspects had worried Keynes enough to lead him to believe that the institutions and the rules that prevailed at that time, would not bring an attractive future. Therefore, he felt that "we have to invent new wisdom for a new age" (published in Keynes, 1933, p. 339). The need for "new wisdom" seems evident today. It might be a serious mistake to believe that we can simply go on, with unchanged institutions and policies, and not worry about recent worrisome developments – to simply "laissez-faire," hoping for the best and believing in the power of the "invisible hand."

Following the views of de Tocqueville, some modern economists, political scientists, historians, and others have continued to maintain that democracy and economic development require mainly "equality of conditions" or "equality of opportunities" (see also the important contribution of John Rawls, 1971, and the useful survey by Roemer and Trannoy, 2016). Many of these thinkers believe that *greater* (obviously not *absolute*) equality of income is not necessary when there is equality of opportunity and conditions (see, for a recent example, McCloskey, 2015). They also believe that equal conditions or opportunities are automatically and generally provided when democratic institutions and a free market continue to exist, *regardless of the distribution of income.*

The key question is whether equality of *conditions* or *opportunities* can be, or can remain, truly equal for the children of those in the top percentiles and for those of the rest *when income inequality becomes extreme.* We definitely need to "invent new wisdom for a new age," as Keynes argued. Equality of law "that permits both rich and poor alike to sleep under the bridges at night" cannot be the answer (the quotation, from Anatole France, was cited by Paul Samuelson in an essay that resulted from a 1968 debate with George Stigler on the economic role of the state).

The "new wisdom" that Keynes was calling for in 1925 was not one that would lead to the abandonment of democratic institutions or of the market economy. He was too smart to do that especially having just returned from Russia. It was, rather, one that would allow both democracy and the market to continue to operate closer (in reality and not just in theory) to the way they should ideally operate. Keynes obviously did not believe that they were operating ideally in 1925. Do we believe that they do so now? If the answer is no, what well-designed and well-monitored policies could bring them closer to the ideal? This is the new wisdom that is needed. Wise experts, from different disciplines, should focus on generating that wisdom. A better future depends on their ability to generate the new wisdom that Keynes had called for.

Bibliography

Abed, G. T. and S. Gupta, 2002, *Governance, Corruption, and Economic Performance* (Washington, D.C.: The International Monetary Fund).

Adams, Charles, 1998, *Those Dirty Rotten Taxes: The Tax Revolts That Built America* (New York: The Free Press).

Admati, Anat and Martin Hellwig, 2013, *The Bankers' New Clothes: What Is Wrong with Banking and What to Do about It* (Princeton, NJ: Princeton University Press).

Afonso, Antonio, Ludger Schuknecht, and Vito Tanzi, 2005, "Public Sector Efficiency: An International Comparison," *Public Choice* 123, pp. 321–347.

2010, "Public Sector Efficiency: Evidence for New EU Member States and Emerging Markets," *Applied Economics* 42 (17), pp. 2147–2164.

Ahamed, Liaquat, 1999, *Lords of Finance: The Bankers Who Broke the World* (New York: The Penguin Press).

Akerlof, George A., 1970, "The Market for 'Lemons': Quality, Uncertainty and the Market Mechanism," *Quarterly Journal of Economics* 84 (3) (August), pp. 488–500.

Akerlof, George A. and Robert Shiller, 2009, *Animal Spirits: How Human Psychology Drives the Economy: And Why It Matters for Global Capitalism* (Princeton, NJ: Princeton University Press).

2015, *Phishing for Phools: The Economics of Manipulation and Deception* (Princeton, NJ: Princeton University Press).

Alesina, Alberto, 1998, "The Political Economy of Macroeconomic Stabilization and Income Inequality: Myths and Reality" in *Income Distribution and High-Quality Growth*, edited by Vito Tanzi and Ke-young Chu (Cambridge, MA: The MIT Press).

Alesina, Alberto, S. Ardagna, and F. Trebbi, 2006, "Who Adjusts and When?" The Political Economy of Reform, IMF Staff Papers, V, Special Issue, Washington, DC.

Alesina, Alberto, C. Favero, and F. Giavazzi, 2012, "The Output Effect of Fiscal Consolidation," NBER, Working Paper No. 18336 (June).

Alesina, Alberto and Francesco Passarelli, 2014, "Regulation versus Taxation," *Journal of Public Economics* 110, pp. 147–156.

Alter, Jonathan, 2006, *The Defining Moment* (New York: Simon & Schuster).

Alvaredo Facundo, Anthony B. Atkinson, Thomas Piketty, and Emmanuel Saez, 2013, "The Top 1 Percent in International and Historic Perspective," *The Journal of Economic Perspectives* 27 (3), pp. 3–20.

Amar, Akhil Reed, 2012, *America's Unwritten Constitution* (New York: Basic Books).

American Action Forum (AAF), 2016, "How Many Federal Forms Are There?" by Sam Batkins, *Insight* (April 21).

Amis, Michele, 2013, "Lo sformato legislativo," *Corriere della Sera* 8, pp. 1–2.

Ariely, Dan, 2008, *Predictably Irrational: The Hidden Forces That Shape Our Decisions* (New York: Harper Collins Publishers).

Arnold, J. M., Brys, B. Heady, C., Johansson, A. Schwellnus, C. and Vartia, L., 2011, "Tax policy for economic recovery and growth," *The Economic Journal*, 121, February, F59–F80.

Arrow, Kenneth J., 1951, *Social Choice and Individual Values* (New York: Wiley).

1974, *The Limits of Organization* (New York and London: W. W. Norton).

Arthur, W. Brian, 2015, *Complexity and the Economy* (New York: Oxford University Press).

Ashok, Vivekinan, Ilyana Kuziemko, and Ebonya Washington, 2015, "Support for Redistribution in an Age of Rising Inequality: New Stylized Facts and Some Tentative Explanations," Brookings Papers on Economic Activity, Conference Draft (March 19–20).

Aslund, Anders and Simeon Djankov, 2017, *Europe's Growth Challenge* (Oxford: Oxford University Press).

Atkinson, Anthony B., 1999, *The Economic Consequences of Rolling Back the Welfare State* (Cambridge, MA: The MIT Press).

2008, "European Union Social Policy in a Globalizing Context" in Costabile, editor, pp. 15–32.

Atkinson, Anthony B. and Gunnar Viby Mogensen, 1993, *Welfare and Work Incentives* : A North European Perspective (Oxford: Clarendon Press).

Atkinson, Anthony B., Thomas Piketty, and Emmanuel Saez, 2011, "Top Incomes in the Long Run of History," *Journal of Economic Literature* 39 (1), pp. 3–71.

Atkinson, Sir Anthony, 2015, *Inequality: What Can Be Done?* (Cambridge, MA: Harvard University Press).

Baiardi, Donatella, Paola Profeta, Riccardo Puglisi and Simona Scabrosetti, 2017, "Tax Policy and Economic Growth: Does It Really Matter?" SIEP, Working Paper, No. 718 (January).

Bailey, Martha J. and Sheldon Danziger, editors, 2015, *Legacies of the War on Povery* (New York: Russell Sage).

Barro, R. J., 1974, "Are Government Bonds Net Wealth?" *Journal of Political Economy* 82 (6), pp. 1095–1117.

Bartels, Larry, 2016, *Democracy for Realists: Why Elections Do Not Produce Responsive Government* (Princeton, NJ: Princeton University Press).

Bastiat, F., 1864, *Oeuvres Complètes*. 7 volumes (Paris: Guillaumin).

Batkins, Sam, 2016, "How Many Federal Forms Are There?" *Insight, AAF* (April 21).

Bator, Francis M., 1958, "The Anatomy of Market Failure," *The Quarterly Journal of Economics* 72 (3) (August), pp. 351–379.

1960, *The Question of Government Spending: Public Needs and Private Wants* (New York: Harper).

Beckert, Sven, 2014, *Empire of Cotton: A Global History* (New York: Vintage Books).

Beito, David T., Peter Gordon, and Alexander Taborrok, 2002, *The Voluntary City: Choice, Community and Civil Society* (Ann Arbor, MI: University of Michigan Press, The Independent Institute).

Ben-Shahar, Omri and Carl E. Schneider, 2015, *More Than You Wanted to Know: The Failure of Mandated Disclosure* (Princeton: Princeton University Press).

Benson, B. L., 1989, "The Spontaneous Evolution of Commercial Law," *Southern Economic Journal* 55 (January), pp. 664–661.

Bergh, Andreas and Magnus Enrekson, 2010, *Government Size and Implications for Growth* (Washington, DC: The American Enterprise Institute).

Bernanke, Ben S., 2015, *The Courage to Act: A Memoir of a Crisis and Its Aftermath* (New York: W. W. Norton & Company).

Bertrand, Msarienne, Matilde Bombardini, and Francesco Trebbi, 2014, "Is It Whom You Know or What You Know? An Empirical Assessment of the Lobbying Process," *The American Economic Review* 104 (12) (December), pp. 3885–3920.

Blinder, Alan, 1997, "Is Government Too Political?" *Foreign Affairs* 76 (6) (November/December), pp. 2–22.

Blundell, John and Colin Robinson, 1999, "Regulation Without the State," IEA Occasional Paper 109 (July 1999).

Boaz, David, 2015, *The Libertarian Mind: A Manifesto for Freedom* (New Yotk: Simon and Schuster).

Boldrin, Michele and David K. Levine, 2013, "The Case against Patents," *The Journal of Economic Perspectives* 27 (1) (Winter), pp. 3–22.

2008, *Against Intellectual Monopoly* (Cambridge and New York: Cambridge University Press).

Boskin, M. J., 1978, "Taxation, Saving and the Rate of Interest," *Journal of Political Economy* 86 (2), pp. S3–S28.

Bosworth, R. J. B., 2006, *Mussolini's Italy: Life Under the Facist Dictatorship, 1915–1945* (New York: The Penguin Press).

Bowers, Patricia F., 1974, *Private Choice and Public Welfare: The Economics of Public Goods* (Hinsdale, IL: Dryden Press).

Bowles, Samuel, 2016, *The Moral Economy: Why Good Incentives Are No Substitute for Good Citizens* (New Haven, CT: Yale University Press).

Bowles Samuel and Arjun Jayadev, 2008, "The Enforcement–Equality Trade-off," Chapter 3 of Lilia Costabile, editor. pp. 74–94.

Braibant, G., 1996, "Utilité et Difficultés de la Codification," *Droits* 24 (December), pp. 17–30.

Brandolini, Andrea and Nicola Rossi, 1998, "Income Distribution and Growth in Industrial Countries" in *Income Distribution and High-Quality Growth*, edited by Vito Tanzi and Ke-young Chu (Cambridge, MA: MIT Press), pp. 69–106.

Brewer, Mike, Luke Sibieta, and Liam Wren-Lewis, 2008, *Racing Away? Income Inequality and Evolution of High Incomes* (London: The Institute for Fiscal Studies Briefing Note No. 76).

Brogan, Hugh, 2006, *Alexis de Tocqueville: A Life* (New Haven, CT: Yale University Press).

Brookhiser, Richard, 2011, *James Madison* (New York: Basic Books).

Brynjolfsson, Erik and Andrew McAfee, 2014, *The Second Machine Age: Work Progress, and Prosperity in a Time of Brilliant Technologies* (New York and London: W. W. Norton & Company).

Buchan, James, 2006, *The Authentic Adam Smith: His Life and Ideas* (New York and London: W. W. Norton & Company).

Buchanan, James M. 1960, "La Scienza delle Finanze" in *Fiscal Theory and Political Economy*, edited by J. M. Buchanan (Chapel Hill, NC: The University of North Carolina), pp. 24–74.

Buchanan, James, 1975, *The Limits of Liberty: Between Anarchy and Leviathan* (Chicago, IL: The University of Chicago Press).

    1994, *Ethics and Economic Progress* (Norman, OK and London: University of Oklahoma).

Buchanan, James M. and Richard A. Musgrave, 1999, *Public Finance and Public Choice: Two Contrasting Visions of the State* (Cambridge, MA: The MIT Press).

Buchanan, James M. and Gordon Tullock, 1962, *The Calculus of Consent: Logical Foundations of Constitutional Democracy* (Ann Arbor: The University of Michigan Press).

Buchanan, Mark, 2014, "Is Inequality Approaching a Tipping Point?" *Bloomberg* (February 4).

Buchholz, Todd G., 1990, *New Ideas from Dead Economists: An Introduction to Modern Economic Thought* (New York: Plume Books).

Burke, Edmund, [1789–1790] 1987, *Reflections on the Revolution in France*, edited by J. G. A. Pocock (Indianapolis, IN and Cambridge, UK: Hackett Publishing Company).

Burtless, Gary, 2014, "Has Rising Inequality Brought Us Back to the 1920s? It Depends on How We Measure Income," The Brookings Institution (May 20).

Cable, Dan and Freek Vermeulen, 2016, "Stop Paying Executives for Performance," *Harvard Business Review*, February 23, pp. 1–12.

Campanile, Benedetta, 2016, *Vannevar Bush: Da Ingegnere a Tecnologo* (Ariccia, Italy: Aracne editrice).

Campbell, John Y., 2016, "Restoring Rational Choice: The Challenge of Consumer Financial Regulation," Richard Ely Lecture, *The American Economic Review, Papers and Proceedings* (May 16), pp. 1–30.

Costabile, Lilia, editor, 2008, *Institutions for Social Well Being* (Houndsville, Basingstoke, Hampshire and New York: Palgrave Macmillan).

Cassese, Sabino, 1998, *Lo Stato introvabile: Modernita' e arretratezza delle istituzioni italiane* (Rome: Donzelli Editore).

Castellucci, Laura, editor, 2014, *Government and the Environment: The Role of the Modern State in the Face of Global Challenges* (London and New York: Routledge).

Celli, Carlo, editor, 2013, *Economic Fascism: Primary Sources on Mussolini's Crony Capitalism* (Edinburg, VA: Axios Press).

Cepal and Oxfam, 2016, *Tributacion para un Crecimiento Inclusivo* (Santiago, Chile: Naciones Unidas).

Chernow, Ron, 2004, *Alexander Hamilton* (New York: Penguin Books).

Chetty, Raj, Nathaniel Hendren, Patrick Kline, Emmanuel Saez, and Nicholas Turner, 2014, "Is the United States a Land of Opportunity? Recent Trends in Intergenerational Mobility," Working Paper 19844, NBER (January).

Cipolla, Carlo M., 2012, *Istruzione e Sviluppo: il decline dell'alfabetismo nel mondo occidentale* (Bologna: Il Mulino).

Clark, Colin, 1964, Taxmanship, Hobart Paper 26, Institute of Economic Affairs (London).

Clarke, Peter, 2009, *Keynes: The Rise, Fall, and Return of the Twentieth Century's Most Influential Economist* (New York: Bloomsbury Press).

Clements, Benedict et al., 2013, *Energy Subsidy Reforms: Lessons and Implications* (Washington, DC: International Monetary Fund).

Clements, Benedict Ruud de Mooij, Sanjeev Gupta, and Michael Keen, editors, 2015, *Inequality and Fiscal Policy* (Washington, DC: International Monetary Fund).

Coase, R. H., 1960, "The Problem of Social Cost," *Journal of Law and Economics* 3, pp. 1–44.

1994, *Essays on Economics and Economists* (Chicago, IL: The University of Chicago Press).

Coffee, John C. Jr., 2015, *Entrepreneurial Litigation: Its Rise, Fall, and Future* (Cambridge, MA: Harvard University Press).

Cohen, Patricia, 2016, "Trump and Congress Both Want Tax Cuts. The Question Is Which Ones," *The New York Times*, Sunday, November 13, p. 21.

Collier, Paul, 2007, *The Bottom Billion: Why the Poorest Countries Are Failing and What Can Be Done About It* (New York: Oxford University Press).

Colm, Gerhard, 1955, *Essays in Public Finance and Fiscal Policy* (Oxford: Oxford University Press).

Cook, Philip J., 2007, *Paying the Tab: The Costs and Benefits of Alcohol* (Princeton, NJ: Princeton University Press).

Cost, Jay, 2015, *A Republic No More : Big Government and the Rise of Americam Political Corruption* (New York and London: Encounter Books).

Costabile, Lilia, editor, 2008, *Institutions for Social Well-Being: Alternatives for Europe* (London: Palgrave Macmillan).

Coy, Peter, 2016, "Once Upon a Time Came Negative Interest Rates," Bloomberg Net, February 19.

Cowell, Frank A., 1990, *Cheating the Government* (Cambridge, MA: MIT Press).

Cowen, Tyler, editor, 1999, *Public Goods & Market Failures: A Critical Examination* (New Brunswick, USA and London, UK: Transaction Publishers).

Cramb, Gordon, 1999, "Incentives Allow Deep Cuts in Company Tax", *Financial Times*, April 16, p. 7.

Crews, Clyde Wayne Jr., 1996, "Promise and Peril: Implementing a Regulatory Budget," Competitive Enterprise Institute (April).

2014, "Ten Thousand Commandments 2014," Competitive Enterprise Institute (July 6).

2016, "Assessing the Obama Years: OIRA and Regulatory Impact on Jobs, Wages and Economic Recovery," Competitive Enterprise Institute.

Dabla-Norris, Era, Kalpana Kochhar, Nujin Suphaphiphat, Frantisek Ricka, and Evridiki Tsounta, 2015, "Causes and Consequences of Income Inequality: A Global Perspective," IMF Staff Discussion Note (June).

Danziger, Danny and John Gillingham, 2003, *1215: The Year of Magna Carta* (New York: Simon and Schuster).

Davidson, Alastair, 1991, *The Invisible State: The Formation of the Australian State 1788–1901* (Cambridge, UK: Cambridge University Press).

Davis, Steven J. and Magnus Henrekson, 2005, "Tax Effects on Work Activity, Industry Mix and Shadow Economy Size: Evidence from Rich Country Comparisons" in *Labour Supply and Incentives to Work in Europe*, edited by Ramon Gomez-Salvador et al. (Chattenham: Edward Elgar), pp. 44–104.

De Jouvenel, Bertrand, [1952] 1990, *The Ethics of Redistribution* (Indianapolis, IN: Liberty Press).

De Rugy, Veronique, 2013, "The Tax Burden Across Varying Income Percentiles," Mercatus Center, George Mason University (August 12).

De Soto, Hernando, 1989, *The Other Path* (New York: Harper and Row).

De Tocqueville, Alexis, [1835 and 1840], 1966, *Democracy in America*, Volumes I and II (New York: Harper and Row).

1998, *Democrazia e povertà*, edited by Marino Revedin (Rome: Ideazione Editrice srl).

De Viti de Marco, 1936, *First Principles of Public Finance* (London: Jonathan Cape).

Deaton, Angus, 2013, *The Great Escape: Health, Wealth, and the Origins of Inequality* (Princeton, NJ and Oxford: Princeton University Press).

2016, "Measuring and Understanding Behavior, Welfare and Poverty," *The American Economic Review* 106 (6) (June), pp. 1221–1243.

Denton, Sally, 2015, *The Profiteers: Bechtel and the Men Who Built the World* (New York: Simon and Shuster).

Deroose, Sevaas and Dr. Christian Kastrop, editors, 2008, "The Quality of Public Finances: Findings of the Economic Policy Committee Working Group (2004–2007)," *European Economy: Occasional Papers* 37 (March) (Brussels: European Commission).

Desiderio, Giancristiano, 2003, *Morte (senza nostalgia) dell'intellettuale* (Rome: Editoriale Pantheon).

Dixit, Avinash K., 1996, *The Making of Economic Policy* (Cambridge MA: MIT Press).

Dollar, D. and A. Kray, 2002, "Growth Is Good for the Poor," *Journal of Economic Growth* 7 (4), pp. 195–225.

Dorn, Florian, 2016, "On Data and Trends in Income Inequality," *CESifo DICE REPORT Journal for Institutional Comparisons* 14 (4) (Winter), pp. 54–64.

Drennan, Matthew P., 2015, *Income Inequality: Why It Matters and Why Most Economists Didn't Notice* (New Haven, CT: Yale University Press).

Dudley, Susan E., 2013, "OMB's Reported Benefits of Regulation: Too Good to Be True?" *Regulation* 36 (2) (Summer), pp. 26–30.

Duesenberry, James S., 1952, *Income, Saving and the Theory of Consumer Behavior* (Cambridge, MA: Harvard University Press).

Dweck, Esther, 2015, "La experiencia en el desarrollo del Plan Pruriannual 2016–2019", XLII Seminario Internacional de Presupuesto Publico, Buenos Aires, 6–9 October.(Powerpoint).

Ebenstein, Alan, 2001, *Friedrich Hayek: A Biography* (New York: Palgrave).

Ebenstein, Lanny, 2007 Milton Friedman (London: Palgrave Macmillan).

2015, *The Evolution of Chicago Free Market Economics* (New York: St. Martin's Press).

The Economist Magazine, 2015, "Time to Fix Patents," August 8–15, p. 50.

Edmans, Alex and Xavier Gabaix, 2016, "Executive Compensation: A Modern Primer," *Journal of Economic Literature* LIV (4) (December), pp. 1232–1287.

Elmore, Bartow, 2014, *Citizen Coke: The Making of Coca-Cola Capitalism* (New York & London: W.W. Norton and Company).

Edmonds, David and John Eidinow, 2006, *Rousseau's Dog* (New York, NY: Harper Collins).

Edwards, Chris, 2015, "Why the Federal Government Fails," *Policy Analysis* 777, Cato Institute (July 27).

Einaudi, Luigi, 1964, *Prediche inutili* (Turin: Giulio Einaudi Editore).

1973, *Il buongoverno*, Volume I (Bari: Universale Laterza).

1946, *L'Imposta patrimoniale* (Rome: Edizione de "La Città Libera").

Ellis, Joseph J., 2002, *Founding Brothers: The Revolutionary Generation* (New York, NY: Vintage Books).

Esping-Andersen, Costa, 2008, *Trois leçons sur l'État-providence* (Paris: Editions du Seuil et la Republique des Idées).

Estache, Antonio and Danny Leipziger, editors, 2009, *Stuck in the Middle: Is Fiscal Policy Failing the Middle Class?* (Washington, DC: Brookings Institution Press).

Eurostat, European Commission, 2014, *Taxation Trends in the European Union* (Luxembourg: European Union).

Evandrou, Maria et al., 1998, *The State of Welfare: The Economics of Social Spending*, Second Edition (Oxford and New York: Oxford University Press).

Falcoff Mark and Ronald H. Dolkart, editors, 1975, *Prologue to Peron: Argentina in Depression and War, 1930–1943*.(Berkeley: University of California Press).

Faricy, Christopher G., 2015, *Welfare for the Wealthy: Parties, Social Spending, and Inequality in the United States* (Cambridge, UK and New York: Cambridge University Press).

Farnsworth, Kevin, 2012, *Social versus Corporate Welfare: Competing Needs and Interests within the Welfare State* (New York: Palgrave Macmillan).

Fatovic, Clement, 2015, *America's Founding and the Struggle Over Economic Inequality* (Kansas: University Press of Kansas).

Feldman, Noah, 2015, "'Happy Birthday' to All, Except for the Lawyers," *Bloomberg View* (September 28).

Ferguson, Niall, 2007, *The Pity of the War* (New York: Public Books).

Ferrarotti, Franco, editor, 1973, *Pareto* (Milan: Arnoldo Mondadori).

Ferro, Pasquale, Stefano Lo Fazo, and Giancarlo Salvemini, 1999, "L'Azione della pubblica amministrazione per la Competitivà Internazionale in Presenza di Vincoli di Finanza Pubblica" in *Concorrenza fiscale in una economia internazionale integrata*, edited by Massimo Bordignon and Domenico da Empoli (Milano: Franco Angeli Editore), pp. 30–45.

Fiel, 1989, *Los Costos del estado regulador* (Buenos Aires: Manantial).

Fine, Sidney, 1964, *Laissez-Faire and the General-Welfare State: A Study of Conflict in American Thought, 1865–1901* (Ann Arbor, MI:The University of Michigan Press).

Fiorentini, Riccardo and Guido Montani, 2012, *The New Global Economy: From Crisis to Supranational Integration* (Cheltenham, UK: Edward Elgar).

editors, 2015, *The European Union and Supranational Political Economy* (London and New York: Routledge).

Fischel, William, 1985, *The Economics of Zoning* (Baltimore, MD: The Johns Hopkins University Press).

Fogel, Robert William, 2000, *The Fourth Great Awakening and the Future of Egalitarianism* (Chicago: The University of Chicago Press).

Forte, Francesco, 1985, "Control of Public Spending Growth and Majority Rule" in *Public Expenditure and Government Growth*, edited by Francesco Forte and Alan Peacock (Oxford: Basil Blackwell), pp. 101–118.

editor, 1998, *Le Regole della costituzione fiscale* (Turin: Politeia, Anno 14-N), pp. 49–50.

Frankfurt, Harry G., 2015, *On Inequality* (Princeton, NJ: Princeton University Press).

Franklin, Benjamin, [1758] 1986, *The Way to Wealth* (Bedford, MA: Applewood Books).

Fraser, Steve, 2014, *The Age of Acquiescence: The Life and Death of American Resistance to Organized Wealth and Power* (New York, NY: Little Brown & Company).

Frey, Bruno S., 2008, *Happiness: A Revolution in Economics* (Cambridge, MA: MIT Press).

Friedman, Milton, 1962, *Capitalism and Freedom* (Chicago: University of Chicago Press).

Fry, Maxwell J., 1995, *Money, Interest, and Banking in Economic Development*, Second Edition (Baltimore and London: The Johns Hopkins University Press).

Furman, Jason, 2016, "The New View of Fiscal Policy and Its Application," unpublished mimeo (November).

Galbraith, John Kenneth, 1958, *The Affluent Society* (Boston, MA: Houghton Mifflin).

Gale, William G., Melissa S., F. Kearney, and Peter R. Orszag, 2015, "Would a Significant Increase in the Top Income Tax Rate Substantially Alter Income Inequality?" Economic Studies (Washington DC: The Brookings Institution), September.

Gates, Bill, Apeil 2016, "America's Secret Weapon," Reuters News Agency.Blogs Reuters.com

Geithner, Timothy F., 2014, *Stress Test: Reflection on Financial Crises* (New York: Crown Publishers).

Germino, Dante I., 1959, *The Italian Fascist Party in Power: A Study in Totalitarian Rule* (Minneapolis, MN: University of Minnesota Press).

Getty, J. Arch and Oleg V. Naumov, 2010, *The Road to Terror: Stalin and the Self-Destruction of the Bolsheviks, 1932–1939* (New Haven, CT: Yale University Press).

Giddons, Anthony, 1998, *The Third Way: The Renewal of Social Democracy* (Cambridge, UK: Polity Press).

Gilder, George, [1981] 2012, *Wealth and Poverty*, New Edition (Washington DC: Regnery Publishing, Inc.).

Gomez-Salvador, Ramon et al., editors, *Labour Supply and Incentives to Work in Europe* (Chattenham: Edward Elfgar).

Goode, Richard, 1976, *The Individual Income Tax*, Revised Edition (Washington, DC: The Brookings Institution).

Gordon, Robert J., 2015, *The Rise and Fall of American Growth: The US Standard of Living Since the Civil War* (Princeton, NJ: Princeton University Press).

Gordon, Scott, 1999, *Controlling the State: Constitutionalism from Ancient Athens to Today* (Cambridge, MA: Harvard University Press).

Gorton. Gary, 2015, "Stress for Success: A Review of Timothy Geithner's Financial Crisis Memoir," *Journal of Economic Literature* LIII (4) (December), pp. 975–995.

Government of India, 2009, *India's Financial Sector: An Assessment* (Mumbai: Reserve Bank of India).

Graeber, David, 2015, *The Utopia of Rules: Technology, Stupidity and the Secret Joy of Bureacracy* (New York, NY: Random House).

Graham, Carol, 2011, *The Pursuit of Happiness: An Economy of Well-Being* (Washington, DC: Brookings Focus Books).

Graham, Carol and Sergio Pinto, 2017, "Unequal Hopes and Lives in the US: Optimism (or lack thereof), Race, and Premature Mortality" Global Economy and Development at Brookings, Working Paper 104, June.

Graham Carol, Segio Pinto and Juhn Juneau, 2017, Brookings Report, July 24.

Grapperhaus, Ferdinand H. M. 1998, *Tax Tales from the Second Millennium* (Amsterdam: International Bureau of Fiscal Documentation).

Greenspan, Alan, 2004, "The Evolving U.S. Payment Imbalance and Its Impact on Europe and the Rest of the World," *The Cato Journal* 24 (1–2), pp. 1–12.

2007, *The Age of Turbulence: Adventures in a New World* (New York, NY: The Penguin Press).

Guy, S., 1996, "Une utopie: La codification," *Revue française de droit constitutionel* 26, pp. 273–310.

Hacker, Jacob S. and Paul Pierson, 2015, *American Amnesia: How the War on Government Led Us to Forget What Made America Prosper* (New York: Simon and Schuster).

Hamilton, Alexander, James Madison, and John Jay, [1787–1788] 1982, *The Federalist Papers* (New York, NY: Bantam Classic).

Harhoff, Dietmar, 2016, "Innovation and Taxation," Paper Presented at the 2016 Congress of the International Institute of Public Finance (IIPF), Lake Tahoe (August 9–11).

Hasanov, Fuad and Oded Izraeli, 2012, "How Much Inequality Is Necessary for Growth?" *Harvard Business Review*, January–February, 518–539.

Hawley, Ellis W., 1966, *The New Deal and the Problem of Monopoly: A Study in Economic Ambivalence* (Princeton, NJ: Princeton University Press).

Hayek, F. A. [1944] 2007, *The Road to Serfdom*, edited by Bruce Caldwell (Chicago: The University of Chicago Press).

[1960] 2011, *The Constitution of Liberty*, edited by Bruce Caldwell (Chicago: The University of Chicago Press).

1988, *The Fatal Conceit: The Errors of Socialism*, edited by W. W. Bartley III (The University of Chicago Press).

Hegel, Georg Wilhelm Friedrich, 1956, *The Philosophy of History* (New York, NY: Dover Publication, Inc.).

Heller, Walter W., 1966, *New Dimensions of Political Economy* (New York, NY: W.W. Norton and Company).

Hemming, John, 2008, *Tree of Rivers: The Story of the Amazon* (New York: Thames Hudson).

Highfield, Richard, 1999, "Tax Administration: Understanding and Using the Cost of Collection Ratio," mimeo (November).

Hill, Claire A. and Richard W. Painter, 2015, *Better Bankers, Better Banks* (Chicago, IL: University of Chicago Press).

Hines, James R. Jr. 2006, "Will Social Welfare Expenditure Survive Tax Competition?", *Oxford Review of Economic Policy* 22 (3), pp. 330–348.

Hirschman, Albert O., 1977, *The Passions and the Interests: Political Arguments for Capitalism before Its Triumph* (Princeton, NJ: Princeton University Press).

Hobbes, Thomas, [1651] 1958, *Leviathan, Parts One and Two* (New York, NY: Macmillan Publishing Company).

Hume, David, [1752] 1970, *Writings on Economics*, edited by Eugene Rotwein (Madison, WI: The University of Wisconsin Press).

IMF, 2012a, *The Economics of Public Health Care Reform in Advanced and Emerging Economies*, edited by Benedict Clements, David Coady, and Sanjeev Gupta (Washington, DC: IMF).

2012b, "Income Inequality and Fiscal Policy," IMF Staff Discussion Note SDN.12/08, Paper by Francesca Bastagli, David Coady, and Sanjeev Gupta.

2015, *Inequality and Fiscal Policy*, edited by Benedict Clements, Ruud de Mooij, Sanjeev Gupta, and Michael Keen (Washington, DC: IMF).

Institute for Health Metrics and Evaluation (US), 2011, "US County Level Life Expectancy," data put out by Alex Tanzi at Bloomberg (June 15).

Irwin, Timothy C., 2012, "Accounting Devices and Fiscal Illusions". IMF Staff Discussion Note SDN/12/02 (Washington DC, 28 March).

Istituto Bruno Leoni, 2008, *Indice delle liberalizzazioni 2008*, (Turin: Italy).

Jacob, Margaret C., 2014, *The First Knowledge Economy: Human Capital and the European Economy* (Cambrdige, UK and New York, NY: Cambridge University Press).

Jencks, Christopher, 2015, "The War on Poverty: Was It Lost?" *The New York Review of Books* LXII (6) (April 2), pp. 82–85.

Jensen, Michael and William Meckling, 1976, "Theory of the Firm: Managerial Behavior, Agency Costs and Ownership Structure," *Journal of Financial.*

Jimenez, Juan Pablo, editor, 2015, *Desigualdad, concentracion del ingreso y tributacion sibre las altas rentas en America Latina* (Santiago, Chile: Cepal).
Jones, Charles I. and Peter J. Klenow, 2016, "Beyond GDP? Welfare across Countries and Time," *The American Economic Review* 106 (9) (September), pp. 2426–2457.
The Journal of Political Perspective, Summer 2013.
Kahneman, Daniel, 1994, "New Challenges to the Rationality Assumption," *Journal of Institutional and Theoretical Economics* 150, pp. 18–36.
Kahneman, Daniel and Richard H. Thaler, 2006, "Anomalies: Utility Maximization and Experienced Utility," *Journal of Economic Perspective* 20 (1), pp. 221–234.
Kaul, Inge, P. Conceição, K. Le Goulven, and R. U. Mendoza, editors, 2003, *Providing Global Public Goods: Managing Globalization* (New York and Oxford: Oxford University Press).
Kaul, Inge and Pedro Conceição. Editors, 2006, *The New Public Finance: Responding to Global Challenges* (New York and Oxford: Oxford University Press).
Kay, John, 2015, *Other People's Money: The Real Business of Money* (New York, NY: Public Affairs).
Keane, M. P., 2011, "Labor Supply and Taxes: A Survey," *Journal of Economic Literature* 49 (4), pp. 961–1075.
Keen, Andrew, 2015, *The Internet Is Not the Answer* (New York: Atlantic Monthly Press).
Kelsey, Jane, 1997, *The New Zealand Experiment: A World Model for Structural Adjustment?* (Auckland University Press, Bridget Williams Books).
Keynes, John Maynard, 1926, *The End of Laissez-Faire* (London: Hogarth Press).
[1926] 1933, "Liberalism and Labor" in Keynes, 1933.
1933, *Essays in Persuasion* (London: Macmillan and Co., Limited).
1936, *The General Theory of Employment. Interest and Money* (London: Macmillan).
King, Mervyn, 2016, *The End of Alchemy: Money, Banking and the Future of the Global Economy* (New York: W. W. Norton and Co.).
Kinsella, Stephan, 2001, "Against Intellectual Property," *Journal of Libertarian Studies* 15 (2), pp. 1–53.
Klein, Naomi, 2014, *This Changes Everything: Capitalism versus the Climate* (New York: Simon and Shuster).
2013, *The Shock Doctrine: The Rise of Disaster Capitalism* (New York: Henry Holt and Company).
Kolm, Serge Christophe, 1985, *Le Contrat social liberal* (Paris: Presses Universitaires de France).
Kopits, George, editor, 2004, *Rules-Based Fiscal Policy in Emerging Markets: Background, Analysis, and Prospects* (New York, NY: Palgrave Macmillan).
editor, 2013, *Restoring Public Debt Sustainability: The Role of Independent Fiscal Institutions* (Oxford, UK: Oxford University Press).
Kornai, Janos, 1992, *The Socialist System: The Political Economy of Communism* (Princeton, NJ: Princeton University Press).

Kosny, Marek and Gaston Yalonetzky, 2015, "Relative Income Change and Pro-Poor Growth," *Econ Polit* 32, pp. 311–327.

Kropotkin, Pietro, [1905] 2008, *Lo Stato* (Salerno, Italy: Galzerano Editore).

KPMG International, 2012, *KPMG's Individual Income Tax and Social Security Rate Survey*, October, Publication Number 120916.

Krueger, Anne O., 2000, *Economic Policy Reform: The Second Stage* (Chicago, IL: The University of Chicago Press).

La Porta, Rafael, Florencio Lopez-Silanes, Andrei Shleifer, and Robert Vishny, 1998, "The Quality of Government." Unpublished mimeo

Lacey, A. R., 2001, *Robert Nozick* (Princeton, NJ: Princeton University Press).

Laffont, Jean-Jacques and Jean Tirole, 1993, *A Theory of Incentives in Procurement and Regulations* (Cambridge, MA: MIT Press).

Landes, David, 1983, *Revolution in Time: Clocks and the Making of the Modern World* (Cambridge, MA: Harvard University Press).

1998, *The Wealth and Poverty of Nations: Why Some Are So Rich and Some so Poor* (New York and London: W. W. Norton & Company).

Lange, Oskar and Fred M. Taylor, 1938, *On the Economic Theory of Socialism* (New York: McGraw-Hill Book Company).

Lansley, Stewart, 2012, *The Cost of Inequality: Why Economic Equality is Essential for Recovery* (London: Gibson Square).

Leoni, Bruno, 2009, *Law, Liberty and the Competitive Market*, Carlo Lottieri Editor (New Brunswick and London: Transaction Publishers).

Levy, David M. and Sandra J. Peart, 2015, "Learning from Failure: A Review of Peter Schucks's "Why Government Fails So Often: And How It Can Do Better," *Journal of Economic Literature* LIII (3) (September), pp. 667–674.

Lewis, Michael, 2010, *The Big Short: Inside the Doomsday Machine* (New York, NY: W. W. Norton & Company).

2014, *Flash Boys: A Wall Street Revolt* (New York, NY: W. W. Norton & Company).

2017, *The Undoing Project: A Friendship That Changed Out Minds* (New York, NY: W. W. Norton & Company).).

Lindert, Peter H., 2004, *Growing Public: Social Spending and Economic Growth Since the Eighteenth Century* (Cambridge, UK and New York, NY: Cambridge University Press).

Locke, John, [1690] 1980, *Second Treatise of Government*, edited by C. B. Macpherson (Indianapolis, IN and Cambridge, MA: Hackett Publishing Company, Inc.).

Lofgren, Mike, 2015, *The Deep State: The Fall of the Constitution and the Rise of the Shadow Government* (New York: Viking).

Looney, Adam and Kevin B. Moore, 2015, "Changes in the Distribution of After-Tax Wealth: Has Income Tax Policy Increased Wealth Inequality?" Finance and Economics Discussion Series 2015–058, Washington Board of Governors of the Federal Reserve System, http://dx.doi.org/10.17016/FEDS .2015.058.

Lowenstein, R., 2000, *When Genius Failed: The Rise and Fall of Long-Term Capital Management* (New York, NY: Random House).

Lucas, Robert, 1990a, "Supply Side Economics: An Analytical Review," *Oxford Economics Papers* 42, pp. 293–316.

1990b, "Why Doesn't Capital Flow from Rich to Poor Countries?" *The American Economic Review* 80, pp. 92–96.

Lustig, Nora, editor, 2001, *Shielding the Poor: Social Protection in the Developing World* (Washington, DC: The Brookings Institution and Inter-American Development Bank).

Mann, Charles C., 2011, *1493: New Revelations of the Americas Before Columbus.* (New York, NY: Alfred A. Knopf).

Malabre, Alfred L. Jr. 1994, *Lost Prophets: An Insider's History of the Modern Economists* (Boston, MA: Harvard Business School Press).

Marcuzzo, Maria Cristina, 2010, "Whose Welfare State? Beveridge versus Keynes" in *No Wealth but Life: Welfare Economics and the Welfare State in Britain, 1880–1945*, edited by R. Backhouse and T. Nishizawa (Cambridge, UK: Cambridge University Press), pp. 189–206.

Marmot, Michael, 2015, *The Health Gap: The Challenge of an Unequal World* (New York: Bloomsbury).

Martens, Karel, 2015, "Marginal Tax Rates and Income: New Time Series Evidence," National Bureau of Economic Research Working Paper No. 1971 (September).

Marx, Karl, 1906, *Capital: A Critique of Political Economy* (New York: The Modern Library, Random House, Inc.).

Maskin, Eric and Amartya Sen, 2014, *The Arrow Impossibility Theorem* (New York, NY: Columbia University Press).

Mattarella, B. G., 1994, "La Codification du droit: Reflections sur l' expérience française contemporaine," *Revue francaise de droit administrative* 10 (4) (July–August), pp. 666–685.

Mayer, Jane, 2017, *Dark Money: The Hidden History of the Billionaires Behind the Rise of the Radical Right* (New York, NY: Doubleday).

Mazower, Mark, 2012, *Governing the World: The History of an Idea* (New York, NY: Penguin).

Mazzucato, Mariana, 2013, *The Entrepreneurial State: Debunking Public vs. Private Sector Myths* (UK and US: Anthem Press).

McCloskey, Deirdre, 2015, *Bourgeois Equality: How Ideas, Not Capital or Institutions, Enriched the World* (Chicago, IL: University of Chicago Press).

McCraw, Thomas, 1980, "Regulatory Change, 1960–1979, in Historical Perspective," *Special Study on Economic Change* 5 (Joint Economic Committee, Government Printing Office).December 8, pp. 1–17.

McKinnon, Ronald I. 1973, *Money and Capital in Economic Development* (Washington, DC: Brookings Institution).

Mckinsey & Company, Mckinsey Global Institute, 2016, "Poorer Than Their Parents? Flat or Falling Incomes in Advanced Countries" (July) (McKinsey & Company).

Messere, Ken C.,1993, *Tax Policy in OECD Countries: Choices and Conflicts* (Amsterdam: IBFD Publications BV).

Mian, Atif and Amir Sufi, 2015, *House of Debt: How They (and You) Caused the Great Recession, and How We Can Prevent It from Happening Again* (Chicago and London: The University of Chicago Press).

Milanovic, Branko, 2005, *World Apart: Measuring International and Global Inequality* (Princeton, NJ: Princeton University Press).

2016, *Global Inequality: A New Approach for the Age of Globalization* (Cambridge, MA: Belknap Press of Harvard University Press)

Mill, John Stuart, 1998, *On Liberty and Other Essays*, edited by John Gray (Oxford: Oxford University Press).

[1861] 1962, *Considerations on Representative Government*, introduction by F. A. Hayek (Chicago, IL: Henry Regnery Company).

[1900] 2004, *Principles of Political Economy* (Amherst, New York: Prometheus Books).

Mingardi, Alberto, 2013, *L'intelligenza del denaro: Perché il mercato ha ragione anche quando ha torto* (Venice: Marsilio).

2015, "A Critique of Mazzucato's Entrepreneurial State," *Cato Journal* 3 (3) (Fall 2015), pp. 603–625.

Mises, Ludwig von, 2005, *The Quotable Mises*, edited by Mark Thornton (Auburn, AL: Ludwig von Mises Institute).

Mokyr, Joel, 2002, *The Gifts of Athena* (Princeton, NJ: Princeton University Press).

Mollenkamp, Carrick, Susanne Craig, Jeffrey McCracken, and John E. Hilsenrath, 2008, "Public Optimism Masked Private Scramble for Lehman," *The Wall Street Journal* (October 7), p.6.

Montesquieu, 1944, *De L'esprit des lois*, Volume I and II (Paris: Librairie Garnier Frères).

Moretti, Enrico, 2013, *The New Geography of Jobs* (Boston and New York: Mariner Books).

Morris Charles, R., 2012, *The Dawn of Innovation* (New York, NY: Public Affairs).

Morrissey, Monique, 2013, "Private-sector Pension Coverage Fell by Half over Two Decades," Econonic Policy Institute, Working Economics Blogs, January 11.

Moser, Caroline O. N., editor, 2007, *Reducing Global Poverty: The Case for Asset Accumulation* (Washington, DC: The Brookings Institution).

Moss, David A., 2002, *When All Else Fails: Government as the Ultimate Risk Manager* (Cambridge, MA: Harvard University Press).

Mueller, Dennis C., 1993, *Public Choice II*, Several Editions (Cambridge, UK and New Haven: Cambridge University Press).

Murray, Charles, 2016, *Raising the Floor: How a Universal Basic Income Can Renew our Economy and Rebuild the American Dream* (New York, NY: Public Affairs).

Musgrave, Richard, 1959, *The Theory of Public Finance* (New York: McGraw-Hill). 1969, *Fiscal Systems* (New Haven, CN: Yale University Press).

Musgrave, Richard and Alan Peacock, 1958, editors, *Classics in the Theory of Public Finance*, International Economic Association, (London: Macmillan & Co., Ltd.).

Myners, Paul, 2008, "Reform of Banking Must Begin in the Boardroom," *The Financial Times* (April 25), p. 11.

Myrdal, Gunnar, 1954, *The Political Element in the Development of Economic Theory* (New York, NY: Simon and Schuster).

1954, "The Theory of Public Finance," chapter 7 in Myrdal, 1954.

The New York Times, 2016, "C.E.O. Pay: The Rankings", Sunday, May 29. P 8.

Nicoletti, Giuseppe and Stefano Scarpetta, 2003, *Regulation, Productivity and Growth: OECD Evidence* (Paris: OECD, Economic Department).

Nitti, F. S., 1971, *Il Socialismo Cattolico* (Bari: Editori Laterza).

1972, *La Scienza delle finanze* (Bari: Editori Laterza).

Nordhaus, William, 2015, "The Pope and the Market," *The New York Review of Books* LXII (15) (October 8), pp. 30–35.

Norman, Richard, 1997, *Accounting for Government* (Victoria, NZ: University of Wellington).

North, Douglass C., 1990, *Institutions, Institutional Change and Economic Performance* (Cambridge, UK and New York: Cambridge University Press).

2005, *Understanding the Process of Economic Change* (Princeton, NJ: Princeton University Press).

North, Douglass C. and Barry Weingast, 1994, "Constitution and Commitment: The Evaluation of Institutions Governing Public Choice in Seventeenth Century England" in *Monetary and Fiscal Policy, Volume 1: Credibility*, edited by Torsten Persson and Guido Tabellini (Cambridge, MA: MIT Press), pp. 311–342.

Novak Michael, 1998, *Is There a Third Way?* (London: Institute of Economic Affairs).

Nozick, Robert, 1974, *Anarchy, State, and Utopia* (New York: Basic Books).

Obermayer, Bastian and Frederick Obermaier, 2016, *The Panama Papers: Breaking the Story of How the World's Rich and Powerful Hide Their Money* (London: Oneworld).

OECD, 2015a, "Achieving Prudent Debt Targets Using Fiscal Rules," OECD Economics Department Policy Notes No. 28 (July).

2015b, *In It Together: Why Less Inequality Benefits All* (Paris: OECD Publishing).

2016a, "OECD Secretary-General Report to G20 Finance Ministers," Shanghai, People's Republic of China (February 26–27).

2016b, "Trade in Counterfeit and Pirated Goods: Mapping the Economic Impact," Paris (April 18).

Okun, Arthiur M., 1970, *The Political Economy of Prosperity* (New York: W. W. Norton & Company, Inc.).

1975, *Efficiency and Equity: The Big Tradeoff* (Washington, DC: The Brookings Institution).

Olson, Mancur, 1965, *The Logic of Collective Action: Public Goods and the Theory of Groups* (Cambridge, MA: Harvard University Press).

1982, *The Rise and Decline of Nations: Growth, Stagflation, and Social Rigidities* (New Haven, CT: Yale University Press).

Oppenheimer, Franz, 2007, *The State* (Montreal/New York/London: Black Rose Books).

Ostry, Jonathan D, Andrew Berg, and Charalambos G. Tsangarides, 2014, "Redistribution, Inequality and Growth," IMF Staff Discussion Note (February).

O'Toole, Randall, 2007, *The Best-Laid Plans: How Government Planning Harms Your Quality of Life, Your Pocketbook, and Your Future* (Washington DC: CATO Institute).

Owens, J. and E. Whitehouse, 1996, "Tax Reform for the Twenty-first Century," *Bulletin for International Fiscal Documentation* 50 (11/12).

Palan, Ronen, Richard Murphy, and Christian Chavagneaux, 2013, *Tax Havens: How Globalization Really Works* (Cornell, NY: Cornell University Press)

Palmer, Tom G., 2012, *After the Welfare State*, (Ottawa, IL: Jameson Books, Inc.).

Pareto, Vilfredo, [1900] 1973, "La Psicologia del socialismo" in *Pareto: Un'Antologia*, edited by Franco Ferrarotti (Milan: Oscar Mondadori), pp. 139–142.

Pascual, Pasky, Wendy Wagner, and Elizabeth Fisher, 2013, "Making Method Visible: Improving the quality of Science-Based Regulation," *Michigan Journal of Environmental & Administrative Law* (Spring), pp. 429–471.

Peacock, Alan, editor, 1954, *Income Redistribution and Social Policy: A Set of Studies* (London: Jonathan Cape).

Pechman, Joseph, 1987, *Federal Tax Policy*, Fifth Edition (Washington, DC: The Brookings Institution).

Persson, Torsten and Guido Tabellini, 2003, *The Economic Effects of Constitutions* (Cambridge, MA: MIT Press).

Pigou, A. C., 1920, *The Economics of Welfare* (London: Macmillan).

Piketty, Thomas, 2014, *The Capital in the Twenty-first Century* (Cambridge, MA and New York: Harvard University Press).

2015, *The Economics of Inequality* (Cambridge, MA: Harvard University Press).

Piketty, Thomas, Emmanuel Saez, and Stefanie Stantcheva, 2011, "Optimal Taxation of Top Labor Incomes: A Tale of Three Elasticities," Working Paper 17616, NBER.

Piketty, Thomas, and E. Saez, 2006, "The Evolution of Top Incomes: A Historical and International Perspective," *AEA Papers and Proceedings* 96 (2) (May), pp. 2000–2005.

Pipes, Richard. 1999, *Liberty and Freedom* (New York, NY: Random House Inc.).

Plato, 1955 and 1974, *The Republic*, Second Edition, Revised (New York, NY: Penguin Books).

Plutarco, 2005, *Consigli per i Politici*, edited by Mario Scaffidi Abbate (Rome: Grandi Tascabili Economici Newton).

Pogge, Thomas and Krishen Mehta, editors, 2016, *Global Tax Fairness* (Oxford, UK and New York: Oxford University Press).

Polackova Brixi, Hana and Allen Schick, 2002, *Government at Risk: Contingent Liabilities and Fiscal Risk* (Washington, DC: The World Bank).

Polinsky, A. Mitchell, 2003, *An Introduction to Law and Economics*, Third Edition (New York: Aspen Publishers).

Pope Francis, 2015, *Laudato Si', Cyclical Letter* (Vatican City: Libreria Editrice Vaticana).

Pope Leone XIII, 1889, *Rerum Novarum, Rights and Duties of Capital and Labor* (Rome: Paoline).

Porter, Glenn, [1973] 1992, *The Rise of Big Business 1860–1920*, Second Edition (Arlington Heights, IL: Harlan Davidson, Inc.).

Porter Eduardo, 2016, "A Bigger Pie, but Uneven Slices," *The New York Times*, December 7, P B1.

Posner, Richard A., 1971, "Taxation by Regulation," *The Bell Journal of Economics and Management Science* 2 (1) (Spring 1971), pp. 22–50.

1981, *The Economics of Justice* (Cambridge, MA: Harvard University Press).

2010, *A Failure of Capitalism: The Crisis of '08 and the Descent into Depression* (Cambridge, MA: Harvard University Press).

Poterba, James M. and Jurgen von Hagen, editors, 1999, *Fiscal Institutions and Fiscal Performance* (Chicago and London: The University of Chicago Press).

Potter, Barry and Peter Diamond, 1999, *Guidelines for Public Expenditure Management* (Washington, DC: IMF).

Proudhon, Pierre-Joseph, 2009, *Qu'est-ce que la propriété?* (Paris: Flammarion).

Putnam, Robert D., 2000, *Bowling Alone* (New York, NY: Simon and Schuster).

2015, *Our Kids: The American Dream in Crisis* (New York, NY: Simon and Schuster).

Puviani, Amilcare, [1903] 1973, *Teoria dell'illusione finanziaria, a cura di Franco Volpi* (Milan: ISEDI).

Rajan, Raghuram G., 2010, *Fault Lines: How Hidden Fractures Still Threaten the World Economy* (Princeton, NJ: Princeton University Press).

Rawls, John, 1971, *A Theory of Justice* (Cambridge, MA: The Belknap Press).

Reich, Robert B., 2015, *Saving Capitalism: For the Many, Not the Few* (New York: Chicago: Knopf).

Reid, T. R., 2017, *A Fine Mess: A Global Quest for a Simpler, Fairer, and More Efficient Tax Systems* (New York, NY: Penguin Press).

Reinhart, Carmen M. and Kenneth S. Rogoff, *This Time Is Different: Eight Centuries of Financial Folly* (Princeton, NJ: Princeton University Press).

Rakoff, Jed S., 2015, "The Cure for Corporate Wrongdoing: Class Actions vs. Individual Prosecutions," *The New York Review of Books* (November 19), pp. 38–40.

2016, "Why You Won't Get Your Day in Court," *The New York Review of Books* LXIII (18) (September 24), pp. 4–6.

Rawls, John, 1971, *A Theory of Justice* (Cambridge, MA: Belknap Press of Harvard University Press).

Reid, T. R. 2017, *A Fine Mess: A Global Quest for a Simpler, Fairer, and More Efficient Tax System* (New York, NY: Penguin Press).

Reiley, Laura, 2016, "Farm to Fable: At Tampa Bay Farm-to-Table Restaurants, You Are Being Fed Fiction," *Tampa Bay Times* (April 13), http://tampabay.com/projects/2016/food/farm-to-fable/restaurants/.

Ricardo, David, [1817] 1973, *The Principles of Political Economy and Taxation* (New York: Everyman Library).

Ritter, Gerhard A., 1996, *Storia dello stato sociale* (Bari: Editori Laterza).

Rodota' Stefano, 2014, *Solidarietà* (Roma-Bari: Editori Laterza).

Roemer, John E., 2000, *Equality of Opportunity* (Cambridge, MA: Harvard University Press).

Roemer, John E., and Alain Trannoy, 2016, "Equality of Opportunity: Theory and Measurement," *Journal of Economic Literature* LIV (4) (December 9), pp. 1288–1332.

Rogers, John H., Chiara Scotti, and Jonathan H. Wright, 2014, "Evaluating Asset-Market Effects of Unconventional Monetary Policy: A Multi-Country Review," *Economic Policy* 80 (October), pp. 749–780.

Romer, Paul, 2015, "Mathiness in the Theory of Economic Growth," *American Economic Review: Papers and Proceedings* 105 (5), pp. 89–93.

Rousseau, Jean-Jacques, 1983, *On the Social Contract* (Indianapolis, IN: Hackett Publishing Company).

    1755, *Discourse on the Origin of Inequality* (Oxford: Oxford University Press).

    1994, *Discourse on Inequality* (Oxford: Oxford University Press).

Rubin, Robert E. and Jacob Weisberg, 2003, *In an Uncertain World: Tough Choices From Wall Street to Washington* (New York, NY: Random House).

Saez, Emmanuel, Joel Slemrod, and Seth Giertz, 2012, "The Elasticity of Taxable Income with Respect with Marginal Tax Rates: A Critical Review," *Journal of Economic Literature* 50 (1), pp. 3–50.

Samuelson Paul Anthony, 1947, *Foundations of Economic Analysis* (Cambridge, MA: Harvard University Press).

    1954, "The Pure Theory of Public Expenditure," *Review of Economics and Statistics* 36, pp. 387–389.

    1955, "Diagrammatic Exposition of a Theory of Public Expenditure," *Review of Economics and Statistics* 37, pp. 350–356.

    1958, "Aspects of Public Expenditure Theories," *Review of Economic and Statistics* 40, pp. 332–338.

    1968, "The Economic Role of Private Activity" in *A Dialogue on the Proper Economic Role of the State*, edited by George Stigler and Paul A. Samuelson, Selected Papers No. 7 (Graduate School of Business, University of Chicago), pp. 21–40.

Sandefur, Timothy, 2006, *Cornerstone of Liberty: Property Rights in Twenty-first-Century America* (Washington, DC: CATO Institute).

Sandel, Michael, J., 2012, *What Money Can't Buy: The Moral Limits of Markets* (New York, NY: Farrar, Straus and Giroux).

Sandmo, Agnar, 2003, "International Aspects of Public Goods Provision" in *Providing Global Public Goods: Managing Globalization*, edited by Inge Kaul, P. Conceição, K. Le Goulven, and R. U. Mendoza (New York and Oxford: Oxford University Press), pp. 112–130.

Schansberg, D. Eric, 1996, *How Poor Government Policy Harms the Poor* (New York: Westview Press).

Scheidel, Walter, 2017, *The Great Leveler* (Princeton, NJ: Princeton University Press).

Scherer, Florian and Ivan Werning, 2015, "The Taxation of Superstars," CESifo Working Paper 5479.

Scheve, Kenneth and David Stasavage, 2016, *Taxing the Rich: A History of Fiscal Fairness in the United States and Europe* (Princeton, NJ: Princeton University Press).

Schiavo-Campo, Salvatore, 2017, *Government Budgeting and Expenditure Management: Principles and International Practice* (New York and London: Routledge).

Schick, Allen, 1998, "Why Most Developing Countries Should Not Try New Zealand's Reforms," *The World Bank Research Observer* 13 (1) (February), pp. 123–131.

Scheidel, Walter, 2017, *The Great Leveler* (Princeton, NJ: Princeton University Press).

Schlesinger, Arthur M. Jr., 1959, *The Coming of the New Deal* (Boston, MA: Houghton Mifflin Company).

1957, *The Crisis of the Old Order* (Boston, MA: Houghton Mifflin Company).

Schon, Wolfgang, 2016, "Regulation and Taxation of the Financial Markets," Max Planck Institute for Tax Law and Public Finance, Working Paper 2016-08.

Schuck, Peter, 2014, *Why Government Fails So Often: And How It Can Do Better* (Cambridge and New York: Yale University Press).

2015, *Why Government Fails So Often: And How It Can Do Better* (New Haven, CT: Yale University Press).

Self, Peter, 1993, *Government by the Market? The Politics of Public Choice* (Boulder, CO and San Francisco, CA: Westview Press).

Seligman, Edwin, 1908, *Progressive Taxation in Theory and Practice*, Second Edition (Princeton, NJ: Princeton University Press).

Sen, Amartya, 1983, *Poverty and Famines: An Essay on Entitlement and Deprivation* (Oxford: Oxford University Press)

1987, *On Ethics & Economics* (Oxford and Malden, MA: Blackwell Publishers).

1999a, *Development as Freedom* (New York, NY: Alfred A. Knofp, Inc.).

1999b, "Economic Policy and Equity", in Tanzi, Chu and Gupta, pp. 28–43.

2010, *The Idea of Justice* (Belknap Press/Harvard University Press).

Shachar, Ayelet, 2015, *The Birthday Lottery: Citizenship and Global Inequality* (Cambridge, MA: Harvard University Press).

Shah, Anwar, editor, 2005, *Public Expenditure Analysis* (Washington, DC: The World Bank).

Shiller, Robert J., 2000, *Irrational Exuberance* (Princeton, NJ: Princeton University Press).

2008, *The Subprime Solution: How Today's Global Financial Crisis Happened, and What to Do about It* (Princeton, NJ: Princeton University Press).

Shome. Partho, 2012, *Tax Shastra: Administrative Reforms in India, United Kingdom and Brazil* (New Delhi: Business Standard Books).

Simons, Henry C., 1938, *Personal Income Taxation* (Chicago: University of Chicago Press).

Sinn, Hans-Werner, 2007, *Can Germany Be Saved? The Malaise of the World's First Welfare State* (Cambridge, MA: MIT Press).

2010, *Casino Capitalism: How the Financial Crisis Came About and What Needs to Be Done Now* (Oxford: Oxford University Press).

2014, *Euro Trap: On Bursting Bubbles, Budgets, and Beliefs* (Oxford, UK and New York: Oxford University Press).

Skaperlas, Stergios and Constantinos Syropoulos, 1995, "Gangs as Primitive States" in *The Economics of Organized Crime*, edited by Gianluca Fiorentini and Sam Prltzman (Cambridge, UK and New York: Cambridge University Press), pp. 61–76.

Skarbek, David, 2014, *The Social Order of the Underworld: How Prison Gangs Govern the American Penal System* (Oxford, UK and New York, NY: Oxford University Press).

Skidelsky, Robert, 2000, *John Maynard Keynes: Fighting for Britain, 1937–1946* (London: Macmillan).

Slemrod, Joel and Jon Bakija, *Taxing Ourselves: A Citizen's Guide to the Debate over Taxes*, Third Edition (Cambridge, MA and London, England: MIT Press).

Smith, Adam, 1937, *The Wealth of Nations* (New York: The Modern Library).

[1969] 1976. *The Theory of Moral Sentiments* (Indianapolis, IN: Liberty Classics).

Smith, Vernon L., 2008, *Rationality in Economics: Constructivist and Ecological Forms* (Cambridge, UK and New York: Cambridge University Press).

Solimano, Andres, 2016, *Global Capitalism in Disarray: Inequality, Debt and Austerity* (Oxford: Oxford University Press)

Soll, Jacop, 2014, *The Reckoning: Financial Accountability and the Making and Breaking of Nations* (London: Allen Lane).

Solomon, Howard M. 1972, *Public Welfare, Science, and Propaganda in Seventeen Century France: The Innovation of Theophraste Renaudot* (Princeton, NJ: Princeton University Press).

Sorensen, Peter Birch, editor, 1998, *Tax Policy in the Nordic Countries* (London: Macmillan Press Ltd).

Stein, Herbert, 1969, *The Fiscal Revolution in America* (Chicago and London: The University of Chicago).

Steiner, Arthur H., a 1938, *Government in Fascist Italy* (New York and London: McGraw-Hill Company, Inc.).

Steiner, Arthur H., a 1937b, 'The Constitutional Position of the Partito Nazionale Fascosta," *American Political Science Review*, 31 (April), 227–243.

Steuerle, C. Eugene, 1992, *The Tax Decade: How Taxes Came to Dominate the Public Agenda* (Washington, DC: The Urban Institute).

Steverman, Ben, 2017, " Americans' Retirement Benefits have Been Slashed", Bloomberg, www.Bloomberg.com/news/articles/2017-07-19/americans-reti...tm_source=newsletter&utm_term=170719&utm_campaign=bloombergdaily

Stewart, David O., 2007, *The Summer of 1787: The Men Who Invented the Constitution* (New York, NY: Simon and Schuster).

Stigler, George J., 1968, "The Government of the Economy" in *A Dialogue on the Proper Economic Role of the State*, edited by George J. Stigler and Paul Samuelson, Selected Paper No. 7 (Graduate School of Business, University of Chicago). Republished in Tanzi and Zee, editors, 2011.

1971, 'Theory of Economic Regulation," *The Bell Journal of Economics and Management Science* 2 (1) (Spring), pp. 137–146.

1975, *The Citizen and the State: Essays on Regulation* (Chicago and London: The University of Chicago Press).

Stiglitz, Joseph, 1989, *The Economic Role of the State* (Oxford: Basil Blackwell).

2003, *Globalization and Its Discontents* (New York and London: W. W Norton and Company).

2013, *The Price of Inequality* (New York and London: W. W. Norton and Company).

Strathern, Paul, 2002, *J. S. Mill in Ninety Minutes* (Chicago, IL: Ivan R. Dee).

Summers, Laurence, 1985, *Taxation and the Size and Composition of the Capital Stock: An Asset Price Approach* (Cambridge, MA: NBER).

Surowiecki, James, 2015, "Why the Rich Are So Much Richer," *The New York Review of Books* LXII (14) (September 24), pp. 32–36.

Suskind, Ronald, 2011, *Confidence Men: Wall Street, Washington, and the Education of a President* (New York, NY: HarperCollins Publishers).

Tabellini, Guido and Torsten Persson, 2000, *Fiscal Policy in Representative Governments* (Cambridge: The MIT Press).

Taleb, Nassim Nicholas, 2007, *The Black Swan: The Impact of the High Improbable* (New York: Random House).

Tan Lin Mei and Greg Tower, 1992, "Readability of Tax Laws: An Empirical Study in New Zealand," *Australian Tax Forum* 9 (3), pp. 355–372.

Tanner, Michael D., 2007, *Leviathan on the Right: How Big-Government Conservatism Brought Down the Republican Revolution* (Washington, DC: Cato Institute).

Tanzi, Vito, 1968, "Governments' Approaches to Income Redistribution," *National Tax Journal* 21 (4) (December), pp. 483–486.

1972, "Exclusion, Pure Public Goods and Pareto Optimality," *Public Finance* 27 (1), pp. 75–78.

1974, "Redistributing Income through the Budget in Latin America" *Banca Nazionale del Lavoro Quarterly Review*, March.

1980a, "The Underground Economy in the United States: Estimates and Implications," *Banca Nazionale del Lavoro Quarterly Review* 135 (December), pp. 427–453.

1980b, *Inflation and the Personal Income Tax* (Cambridge, UK and New York: Cambridge University Press).

1987a, "The Response of Other Countries to the U.S. Tax Reform Act," *National Tax Journal* XL (3), pp. 339–355.

1987b, "Quantitative Characteristics of the Tax Systems of Developing Countries" in *The Theory of Taxation for Developing Countries*, edited by David Newbert and Nicholas Stern (Oxford, UK and New York: Oxford University Press).

1988, "Forces That Shape Tax Policy" in *Tax Policy in the Twenty-First Century*, edited by Herbert Stein (New York: John Wiley & Sons), pp. 266–277.

1995, *Taxation in an Integrating World* (Washington, DC: The Brookings Institution).

1998a, "Corruption around the World," IMF Staff Paper (December).

1998b, "Government Role and the Efficiency of Policy Instruments" in *Public Finance in a Changing World*, edited by Peter Birch Sorensen (Houndmills and London: MacMillan Press), pp. 51–72.

2000a, "Toward a Positive Theory of Public Sector Behavior: An Interpretation of Some Italian Contributions," chapter 1 in Vito Tanzi, *Policies, Institutions and the Dark Side of Economics* (Edward Elgar).

2000b, "Rationalizing the Government Budget: Or Why Fiscal Policy Is So Difficult" in *Economic Policy Reform: The Second Stage*, edited by Anne O. Kruger (Chicago and London: The University of ChicagoPress), pp. 435–452.

2002a, "Transnational Crime and National Jurisdiction" in ISPI, National Sovereignty under Challenge (Milano: EGEA).

2002b, "Globalization and the Future of Social Protection", *Scottish Journal of Political Economy*, 49, 116–127.

2004a, "The Stability and Growth Pact: Its Role and Future," *The Cato Journal* 24 (1–2), pp. 57–70.

2005, "The Economic Role of the State in the Twenty-First Century," *The Cato Journal* 25 (3) (Fall), pp. 617–638.

2006a, "Fiscal Policy: When Theory Collides with Reality," CEPS Working Document No. 246 (June).

2006b, "Corruption and Economic Activity," Distinguished Lecture Series 26 (Cairo Egyptian Center for Economic Studies).

2007a, "Complexity and Systemic Failure" in *Transition and Beyond*, edited by Saul Estrin, Grzegorz W. Kolodko, and Milica Uvalic (London: Palgrave-MacMillan), pp. 220–246.

2007b, "Tax System Reform Can Address Unrest Over High Pay," *The Financial Times* (March 2, 2007), p. 17.

2008a, "The Future of Fiscal Federalism," *European Journal of Political Economy* 24, pp. 705–712.

2008b, *Peoples, Places and Policies: China, Japan, and Southeast Asia* (New York, NY: Jorge Pinto Books Inc.).

2010a, *Russian Bears and Somali Sharks: Transition and Other Passages* (New York, NY: Jorge Pinto Books).

2010b, *The Charm of Latina America* (New York, NY: iUniverse).

2011, *Government versus Markets: The Changing Economic Role of the State* (Cambridge, UK and London: Cambridge University Press).

2012, "Equity, Transparency and the Taxation of High Net Worth Individuals," *Asia-Pacific Tax Bulletin* 18 (4), pp. 299–307.

2013a, "Complexity in Taxation: Origin and Consequences" in *Transparencia fiscal e desenvolvimento: Homenagem ao Professor Isaias Coelho*, edited by Eurico Marcos Diniz De Santi et al. (Sao Paulo, Brazil: Fiscosoft Editor), pp. 199–236.

2013b, *Dollars, Euros, and Debt: How We Got into the Fiscal Crisis, and How We Get Out of It* (London: Palgrave Macmillan).

2014a, "The Laffer Curve Muddle" in *A Handbook of Alternative Theories of Public Economics*, edited by Francesco Forte, Ram Mudambi, and Pitro Maria Navarro (Cheltenham: Eduard Elgar), pp. 104–115.

2014b, "Tax Systems in the OECD: Recent Evolution, Competition, and Convergence" in *The Elgar Guide to Tax Systems*, edited by Emilio Albi and Jorge Martinez-Vazquez (Cheltenham: Edward Elgar), pp. 11–36.

2014c, "The Challenges of Taxing the Big," *Revista de economia mundial*, Special Issue on International Public Economics, No. 37, pp. 23–40.

2014d, "Globalization and Taxation: A Brief Historical Survey," *Rivista di diritto finanziario e scienza delle Finanze* 73 (1) (March), pp. 3–20.

2015a, *Dal Miracolo economico al declino? Una diagnosi intima* (New York, NY: Jorge Pinto Books Inc.).

2015b, "Crises, Initial Conditions and Economic Policies" in *Symposium: Structural Reforms and Fiscal Consolidations: Trade-Offs or Complements?* (Federal Ministry of Finance, March 25).

2015c, "Hayek and the Economic Role of the State: Some Comparison with Keynes' Views" in *Europe, Switzerland and the Future of Freedom, Essays in Honor of Tito Tettamanti*, edited by Konrad Hummler and Alberto Mingardi (Turin: IBLLibri), pp. 465–482.

2015d, "Fiscal and Economic Policies after the Financial Crisis," *Comparative Economic Studies* 57, pp. 243–275.

2016a, "Lakes, Oceans, and Taxes: Why the World Needs a World Tax Authority" in *Global Tax Fairness*, edited by Thomas Pogge and Krishen Mehta (Oxford UK and New York: Oxford University Press), pp. 251–264.

2016b, "Pleasant Dreams or Nightmares, in the Public Debt Scenarios?" *Ifo Schnelldienst* (May), pp. 27–36.

Forthcoming, *The Ecology of Taxation* (Cheltenham, UK and Northampton, MA: ISA).

Tanzi, Vito, J. B. Bracewell-Milnes and D. R. Myddelton, 1070, *Taxation: A Radical Approach* (London : The Institute of Economic Affairs).

Tanzi, Vito and Ke-young Chu, editors, 1998, *Income Distribution and High-Quality Growth* (Cambridge MA: MIT Press).

Tanzi, Vito, Ke-young Chu and Sanjeev Gupta, editors, 1999, *Economic Policy and Equity*, (Washington, DC: The International Monetary Fund).

Tanzi, Vito and Ludger Schuknecht, 2000, *Public Spending in the Twentieth Century* (Cambridge UK: Cambridge University Press).

Tanzi, Vito and Tej Prakash, 2003, "The Cost of Government and the Misuse of Public Assets" in *Public Finance in Developing Countries: Essays in Honor of Richard Bird*, Edited by Jorge Martinez-Vazquez and James Alm (Eduard Elgar), pp. 129–145.

Tanzi, Vito and Howell H. Zee, 2011, *Recent Developments in Public Finance Volume I: Resouce Allocation and Distribution* (Cheltenham, UK and Northampton, MA, USA: Edward Elgar Publishing Limited).

2011, *Recent Developments in Public Finance, Volume II, Stabilization and Growth* (Cheltenham, UK, and Northampton, MA, USA: Edward Elgar Publishing Limited).

Taylor, Alan, 2016, *American Revolutions, 1750–1804* (New York: W. W. Norton & Company).

Taylor, John B., 2009, *Getting Off Track: How Government Actions and Interventions Caused, Prolonged and Worsened the Financial Crisis* (Stanford, CA: Hoover Institution Press).

Thaler, Richard H. and Cass R. Sunstein, 2008, *Nudge: Improving Decisions about Health, Wealth, and Happiness*, (New Haven, CT: Yale University Press).

Thomas, Jean-Paul, 1994, *Les politiques economiques au XXe siècle* (Paris: Armand Colin).

Tobin, James and W. Allen Wallis, 1968, *Welfare Programs: An Economic Appraisal* (Washington, DC: American Enterprise Institute).

Toder, Eric, 2005, "Tax Expenditure and Tax Reform: Issues and Analysis," Proceedings of the 98th Annual Conference of the National Tax Association.

Tomasi, John, 2012, *Free Market Fairness* (Princeton, NJ: Princeton University Press).

Toso, Stefano, 2016, *Reddito di cittadinanza o reddito minimo?* (Bologna: Il Mulino).

Trvelyan, G. M. 1942, *English Social History* (New York: Longmans, Green and Co. Inc).

United Nations, 2013, *Report of the Intergovernmental Panel on Climate Change* (New York: UN).

US Council of Economic Advisers, 1962, *Economic Report of the President* (Washington, DC: United States Government Printing Office).

US Department of Health and Human Services, 2016, *Poverty in the United States: Fifty-Year Trends and Safety Net Impacts* (Washington DC: Governemtn Printing Office).

US Office of Management and Budget, 2009, *Historical Tables, Budget of the U.S. Government* (Washington, DC: US Government Printing Office).

Van Creveld, Martin, 1999, *The Rise and Decline of the State* (Cambridge and New York: Cambridge University Press).

Van Overtveldt, Johan, 2007, *The Chicago School: How the University of Chicago Assembled the Thinkers Who Revolutionized Economics and Business* (Chicago, IL: Agate Publishing).

Vance, J. D., 2016, *Hillbilly Elegy* (New York, NY: Harper Collins Publishers).

Vaughan, Floyd L., 1925, *Economics of Our Patent System* (New York: The Macmillan Company).

Vermeulen, Philip, 2014, "How Fat Is the Top Tail of the Wealth Distribution?" ECB Working Paper Series No. 1692 (July).

Wagner, Adolph, 1882, *Grundlegung der Politischen Okonomic*, Third Edition (Leipzig: C.F. Winter).

1883, *Finanzwissenschaft*, Third Edition (Leipzig: C.F. Winter).

Waldrop, M. Mitchell, 1992, *Complexity: The Emerging Science at the Edge of Order and Chaos* (New York, NY: Simon and Schuster Paperbacks).

Walvin, James, 1987, *Victorian Values* (Athens, GA: The University of Georgia Press).

Wapshott, Nicholas, 2011, *Keynes Hayek: The Clash That Defined Modern Economics* (New York: W. W. Norton and Company).

Waquet, Jean-Claude, [1984] 1991, *Corruption: Ethics and Power in Florence, 1600–1770* (University Park, PA: Pennsylvania State University Press).

Warren, Elizabeth, 2014, *A Fighting Chance*, (New York, NY: Metropolitan Books/ Henry Holt & Company).

Watson, William, 2015, *The Inequality Trap: Fighting Capitalism Instead of Poverty* (Toronto: University of Toronto).

Weber, Max, 1958, *The Protestant Ethics and the Spirit of Capitalism* (New York, NY: Charles Scribners's Sons).

West, E. G., 1976, *Adam Smith: The Man and His Works* (Indianapolis, IN: Liberty Press).

Wheen, Francis, 1999, *Karl Marx* (London: Fourth Estate).

Wicksell, Kurt, 1896, *Finanztheoretische Untersuchungen Und Das Steuerwesen Schwedens* (Germany: Jena).

Wilson, Woodrow D., 1882, *First Principles of Political Economy, with Reference to Statesmanship and the Process of Civilization* (Philadelphia, PA : Joseph Shild Nicholson).

—— 1889 [2010], *The State: Elements of Historical and Practical Politics*, Revised Edition (Boston, MA: Forgotten Books).

Winston, Clifford, 2006, "Government Failure vs. Market Failure: Micro-economics Policy Research and Government Performance," AEI-Brookings Joint Center for Regulatory Studies (Washington DC: Brookings Institution Press).

Wolfensberger, Don, 2004, "Woodrow Wilson, Congress, and the Income Tax," Woodrow Wilson International Center for Scholars, mimeo (March 16).

Woodcock, George, 1987, *Proudhon: A Biography* (Montreal and New York: Black Rose Books).

Woodward, Sir Llewellyn F.B.A., [1938] 1962, *The Age of Reform 1815–1870*, Second Edition (Oxford: Clarendon Press).

World Bank, 1997, *The State in a Changing World*, World Development Report (Washington, DC: The World Bank).

Wurman, Ilan, 2017, *A Debt Against the Living: An Introduction to Originalism* (Cambridge and New York: Cambridge University Press).

Wuthnow, Robert, editor, 1991, *Between States and Markets: The Voluntary Sector in Comparative Perspective* (Princeton, NJ: Princeton University Press).

Zingales, Luigi, 2015, "Presidential Address: Does Finance Benefit Society?" *Journal of Finance* 70 (4), pp. 1327–1363.

Zolt, Eric M., 2016, "Taxing Wealth in Developing Countries," PowerPoint (May). Presented at a Worked Bank Conference in May 2016.

Zucman, Gabriel, 2015, *The Hidden Wealth of Nations: The Scourge of Tax Havens* (Chicago, IL: University of Chicago Press).

Index

Absolute poverty, 216
Accrual accounting, 293
Administrative capability of governments, 66–68
Advertising, 116–17
The Affluent Society (Galbraith), 45
Afghanistan, legal rules in, 100
Aggregate concept of growth, 311
Aggregate demand, stabilization policies and, 239, 240
Airbus, 347
Akerlof, George A., 94, 116
Alesina, Alberto, 240–41, 286
Alibaba, 347
Allocation of resources
    in China, 188
    income redistribution versus, 220, 224
    in Italy, 188
    role of government, 187–88, 211–12
Alphabet, 377
Altruism, 312
Amazon, 347, 377
American Action Forum, 109, 126, 127, 281
American Economic Association, 99
American Enterprise Institute, 60–61, 79, 394–95
American Road and Transportation Builders Association, 234
Amgen, 377
Apple Computers, 331, 334, 347, 377
Argentina
    economic planning in, 27
    income inequality in, 221
    influence of conservatives in, 395
    regulations in, 173
Aristotle, 218, 305
Armani, 347
Arrow, Kenneth, 3, 4, 7–8, 56, 111
Asymmetry
    in exchanges, 94
    in financial sector, 330–31

in information, 108, 114–15, 148–49, 165–66, 331–32
    in stabilization policies, 62
Athletes, 204–5, 351–53
Attorneys
    implementing regulations and, 333
    intellectual property and, 366
    legal rules and, 252–53
Australia
    executive compensation in, 364
    federalism in, 284
    influence of conservatives in, 395
    marginal tax rates in, 376
    public institutions in, 291, 292
    public spending in, 121–22
    supply-side economics in, 77
    tax administration in, 289
Austria
    executive compensation in, 364
    marginal tax rates in, 376
Austrian School, 64, 69, 111, 313–14
Authorizations, 137, 144–45
Automobile industry, 115, 116

Balanced budget rules, 73
Bank of England, 113–14, 156
Bank of Italy, 5
Banks. *See* Financial institutions
Barro, Robert, 61–64
Barroso, José Manuel, 113–14
Barter, 92
Basic goods, 48
Basic minimum income, 212, 392
Basic needs, 45–46, 49, 351
Bastiat, Frederic, 210
Basu, Kaushik, 399
The Beatles, 53
Becker, Gary, 34, 85
Beckert, Sven, 325
Beethoven, Ludwig van, 203

Belgium
  marginal tax rates in, 376
  public spending in, 23, 53
  welfare policies in, 214
Bentham, Jeremy, 1, 312
Berlusconi, Silvio, 395
Bernanke, Ben, 156
"Betterment taxes," 194
Beveridge, William, 41–43
Bhutan, "happiness" in, 311–12
"Birth lottery," 341, 349, 353
Bismarck, Otto von, 20, 22, 219
"Black swans," 79
Blair, Tony, 113, 395
Bloomberg, 38, 298, 342, 350, 355–56
Bloomberg, Michael, 142
Boeing, 377
Bonuses, 82–83, 85–86
Boskin, Michael, 378–79
Brazil
  bureaucracy in, 234
  Constitution, 269–71
  corruption in, 120
  economic planning in, 27
  federalism in, 284
  income inequality in, 221
  Multiyear Plan, 234
  regulations in, 173
  welfare policies in, 212
Breyer, Stephen, 274–75
British Petroleum oil spill, 172–73
Brookings Institution, 370
Brynjolfsson, Erik, 356–57
Bubbles, 330–31
Buchanan, James
  generally, 7–8, 60–61, 394
  on constitutions, 266, 272
  on countercyclical policy, 62
  on discretion, 71
  on fiscal rules, 71–72
  on informal norms, 286
  on legal rules, 252
  on limited role of government, 85, 313–14
  on "political market," 334
  in School of Public Choice, 5, 6
  on sovereign debt, 64
Buffet, Warren, 379
Bulgaria, Gini coefficient in, 317
Bureaucracy
  legal rules and, 253–54
  public institutions and, 297–98
Bureaucratic state, 22
Burke, Edmund
  generally, 7–8
  on constitutions, 270

on income redistribution, 215, 219, 300, 312–13
on role of government, 160, 189
Bush, George W., 84–85, 375

Cable, Don, 363, 364
Cajolement. *See* Nudges
The Calculus of Consent (Buchanan), 266
Cambodia, income inequality in, 306
Cambridge University, 26–30
Cameron, David, 98
Campbell, John, 128, 156, 170
Canada
  federalism in, 284
  influence of conservatives in, 395
  marginal tax rates in, 376
  public spending in, 162
  regulations in, 173
  supply-side economics in, 77
Canon Inc., 347
"Carried trade," 87
Cash accounting, 292–93
"Casino capitalism," 84, 108, 115
Catholic socialism, 18
Catholicism, 28, 218
Cato Institute, 332
Central banks
  European Central Bank, 244
  evolution of, 35
  monetary policy and, 188
  stabilization policies and, 243, 244
  in US, 49, 188, 244
Certifications, 137, 193
Challenges to welfare policies
  administrative capability of governments
    and, 66–68
  by Austrian School, 64
  conservative challenges, 60–61, 388
  in Ireland, 60
  by Italian School, 63, 65
  libertarian challenges, 60–61
  in New Zealand, 60
  Ricardian equivalence hypothesis, 62–64
  in UK, 60, 61
  in US, 60, 61
Charity versus welfare policies, 50, 214–15
Cheap credit, 107–9
Chernow, Ron, 358
Chetty, Raj, 391
Chicago School, 62, 69, 79, 110, 313–14
China
  allocation of resources in, 188
  "fake goods" in, 149
  Food Safety Law, 149–50
  Gini coefficient in, 317
  growth in, 311, 386–87

income inequality in, 221, 227, 306, 322
intellectual property in, 347, 358
mislabeling of fish in, 149–50
Cicero, 71
Cisco Systems, 347
Citibank, 113–14, 334
Civic associations, 130, 154
Civil rights, 161
Clark, Colin, 245
Clinton, Bill, 52, 84–85, 395
Coase, Ronald, 60–61, 183–85, 313–14, 394
Coase Theorem, 121, 183–85
Coca-Cola, 325, 377
Colbert, Jean-Baptiste, 291
Colm, Gerhard, 2
Communism, 1–2
Community versus individual rights, 98
Complexity
    "crony capitalism" and, 111–12
    of exchanges, 92–94
    financial crises and, 156
    of financial instruments, 106–108
    of financial sector, 329–31
    of income tax, 379–82
    of legal rules, 329, 332–34
    normative approach to role of government
        and, 110
    of regulations, 170–72, 278
    of statutes, 274–75
    of taxation, 367–68, 379–82
Composers, 203, 349
Computer technology, 106
Confidence Men (Suskind), 9
Conscription, 136
Conservatives
    challenges to welfare policies, 60–61, 388
    common elements of beliefs, 395–98
    on government intervention, 317–18
    on growth and income redistribution, 227
    income inequality and, 394–95
    influence on liberal governments, 395
    on limited role of government, 99–100, 259
    regulations, opposition to, 160, 278
Constitutions
    overview, 265
    adaptation to change, 265–66
    in authoritarian regimes, 266–68
    in Brazil, 269–71
    Buchanan on, 266, 272
    Burke on, 270
    economics and, 270–72
    in EU (proposed), 271
    fiscal rules in, 272
    general principles, 268–69
    in India, 270

in Italy, 248–50, 266–71
in Latin America, 250, 271
majoritarianism in, 266
minority rights in, 266
modernization of, 271
Musgrave on, 266
in Pakistan, 270
problems with, 268
rule of law in, 265
Smith on, 270
in Soviet Union, 266
in Switzerland, 272
in US
    generally, 99, 250, 270
    amendment of, 250
    Bill of Rights, 43–44
    general principles, 268
    intellectual property and, 176, 193, 362
    slavery and, 249–50
    workers' rights and, 250
Consumer protection in financial
        markets, 116
Consumer protection regulations, 148–50
Contingent liabilities, 137–41
Contracts, 92–94, 308
Coolidge, Calvin, 24–25
Corporate welfare, 161
Corporations
    entrepreneurs and, 308
    income tax for, 376–77
    marginal tax rates for, 376–77
    social responsibilities of, 398
    taxation of, 161
Corporatism, 27, 231
Corruption, 120, 124, 280, 296–97
Cotton industry, 325
Countercyclical policies, 61–62, 238. *See also*
        Stabilization policies
Coxe, Tench, 357–58
Credit, ease and cheapness of, 107–9
Criminal law, 95–96, 100
Criminal organizations, 97–98
"Crony capitalism," 27, 70, 111–12, 137, 343
Cross-border externalities, 185–86
Cryan, John, 364
Current fashionable thinking, 10

Deaton, Angus, 46, 48, 227, 264
Debt. *See* Sovereign debt
Deconstruction of administrative state, 86
Defense spending
    lobbyists and, 178–79
    as public good, 175–78
    in US, 178
Deficits, 72

Democracy
   income inequality and, 400
   income redistribution and, 223
   legal rules and, 134
   regulations and, 134
   welfare policies and, 384
Demsetz, Harold, 151
Denmark
   executive compensation in, 364
   ex post income distribution in, 118
   income redistribution in, 210
   marginal tax rates in, 376
   public spending in, 122
   taxation in, 371, 381
Dependency, income redistribution and, 209–10
Dependent workers
   income inequality and, 221, 316, 387
   increase in, 384–85
   marginal tax rates for, 373
   regulations and, 23
   in US, 250
Depreciation, 308
Deregulation
   overview, 87–88
   economic freedom and, 86
   income redistribution and, 197
   potential for future crises and, 108, 109
   in US, 82
Deutsche Bank, 364
Dickens, Charles, 358–59
Direct government intervention, 32–33, 36, 230
Discretion, 71, 151–52
Dishonesty, effect on market, 79, 83
Djokovic, Novak, 351–53
Dorfman, Robert, 3
Drones as externality, 165
Drucker, Peter, 82
Duesenberry, James R., 3, 319
Du Pont, Pierre, 307
Dutch Republic, welfare policies in, 50
Dynamic scoring, 76

Eastern Europe
   Gini coefficient in, 317
   laissez faire in, 35
   taxation in, 381–82
Easy credit, 107–8
Eckstein, Otto, 2–5
Economic aristocracy, 117–18
Economic freedom
   deregulation and, 86
   economic planning and, 159
   income redistribution and, 159–60
   regulations, effect of, 130–31

Economic growth. *See* Growth
Economic planning. *See also specific country*
   overview, 25–28
   economic freedom and, 159
   Hayek on, 159
   "Economic Possibilities for our Grandchildren" (Keynes), 29
Economics. *See also specific topic*
   constitutions and, 270–72
   legal rules and, 252–53
   supply-side economics, 33, 74–78, 395, 397
Economics of Our Patent System (Vaughan), 359
The Economist, 77, 203, 343, 355–56, 361, 366
Education
   entrepreneurs and, 309
   income redistribution and, 193
   as public good, 180–81
   in US, 208
Efficient market hypothesis, 86–87
Einaudi, Luigi, 269, 342
Eisenhower, Dwight, 4, 40, 178
Elizabeth I (England), 215
Elmore, Bartow, 325
Employment
   entrepreneurs and, 309
   quotas, 145–46
   role of government, 189–90
   stabilization policies and, 237
   unemployment compensation, 237–38
"The End of Laissez Faire" (Keynes), 31–32
Energy industry, 17, 167, 283–84
Enron, 127–28, 172–73
Entertainment industry, 345, 348, 353
Entitlements, 50–51
The Entrepreneurial State (Mazzucato), 196
Entrepreneurs
   corporations and, 308
   desires of, 308–9
   education and, 309
   employment and, 309
   government, relationship with, 309–10
   historical background, 306–7
   income tax and, 308
   infrastructure and, 309
   laissez faire and, 307–8
   obstacles to, 307–8
   public resources and, 310
   referee, government as, 310
   Smith on, 307
   taxation and, 309
   in UK, 307
   in US, 307
Environmental regulations, 147, 182, 183

Envy
  income inequality and, 319–21
  poverty and, 216–18
Equitable growth, 310, 312
Esping-Anderson, Costa, 47
Ethical values of market, 398
European Central Bank, 244
European Commission, 113
European Monetary Union, 5, 69, 72, 260, 273
European Union
  Constitution (proposed), 271
  "fake goods" in, 149
  intellectual property in, 347
  mislabeling of fish in, 149–50
  occupational licensing in, 125–26
  regulations in, 276
Exchanges, 91–94
  asymmetry in, 94
  complexity of, 92–94
  contracts in, 92–94
  Friedman on, 114–15
  Hayek on, 93, 112–15
  individuals, role of, 112–13
  information in, 93, 112–13
Executive compensation
  in Australia, 364
  in Austria, 364
  bonuses, 82–83, 85–86
  in Denmark, 364
  directors, role of, 364–65
  in financial institutions, 168–69
  income inequality in, 82–83, 85–86, 105–6
  increase in, 387, 398
  intellectual property and, 348, 363–64
  in Japan, 364
  in Norway, 364
  performance-based compensation, 363–64
  in Sweden, 364
  in UK, 364
  in US, 169, 363, 364
Ex post income distribution, 118, 119
Expropriation, 136
Externalities
  balancing of, 164
  Coase Theorem and, 183–85
  correcting or reducing through regulations, 147, 281–82
  cross-border externalities, 185–86
  drones as, 165
  environmental regulations and, 182, 183
  federalism and, 183–84
  global government and, 120–21
  guns as, 165
  income inequality and, 321
  inter-institutional externalities, 290

  legal rules and, 255
  poverty and, 216–17
  public goods and, 181–82
  regulations and, 164
  smoking as, 164
  urbanization and, 91, 163–64

Facebook, 347
"Fake goods," 149
Fascism, 23, 231, 266–67
Fashion industry, 345
Federalism
  in Australia, 284
  in Brazil, 284
  in Canada, 284
  externalities and, 183–84
  legal rules and, 260
  regulations and, 125, 126, 173, 284–85
  in US, 260, 284
The Federalist Papers (Madison), 249
Fees, 142
Financial crises
  complexity and, 156
  government intervention and, 156
  Great Depression, 22, 26, 31, 253
  Great Recession, 76, 109, 318
  moral hazard and, 156–57
  Southeast Asian financial crisis (1997-1998), 109, 243–44
  2007-2008 Financial Crisis. *See* 2007-2008 Financial Crisis
Financial institutions
  executive compensation in, 168–69
  financial penalties against, 158, 169–70
  influence on governments, 113–14
  regulations and, 126, 155, 157
  rents and, 119
  sanctions against, 157
  "shadow banking," 108, 119, 242, 329–30
  "too big to fail" and, 84, 119, 168, 169
  in UK, 157
  in US, 126, 157
Financial instruments, complexity of, 106, 107, 108
Financial sector
  abuses in, 331
  asymmetry in, 330–31
  complexity of, 329–31
  function of, 330
  rents and, 330
  securitization in, 330
  "shadow financial sector," 243
  transaction activity in, 330
The Financial Times, 217, 352
Financial versus real investment, 106–7

Fine, Sidney, 18
Fines, 142
Finland
  Gini coefficient in, 317
  marginal tax rates in, 376
Fiscal councils, 72–73, 272
Fiscal drag, 61
Fiscal policy, stabilization policies and, 237
Fiscal rules, 71–72, 272
Fiscal tools, 38
Fischer, Stanley, 113–14
Fisher, Irving, 46–47
Fishing industry, 149–50
Flat taxes, 381–82
Fogel, Robert William, 67–68
Food industry, 114–15, 167
Forbes, 38, 203, 342, 350
Forte, Francesco, 272
"Fracking," 167, 283–84
France
  authorizations in, 137, 145
  Cour des Comptes, 290
  economic planning in, 27
  ex post income distribution in, 118
  "fake goods" in, 149
  financial accountability in, 291
  French Revolution, 89, 305
  income inequality in, 306
  marginal tax rates in, 376
  occupational licensing in, 125–26
  public spending in, 23–24, 53
  regulations in, 279
  wealth tax in, 342
  welfare policies in, 43, 214
France, Anatole, 400
Francis (Pope), 28, 81
Frazer Institute, 60–61, 173
Free rider problem, 175–76
Free trade, 396–97
Friedman, Milton
  generally, 7–8, 60–61, 394
  on basic minimum income, 212
  on countercyclical policy, 61–62
  on deficits, 72
  on information in exchanges, 114–15
  on irrationality, 141–42
  on Keynes, 70
  on limited role of government, 85, 313–14
  on market, 34
  on taxation, 367–68
Fundamental law of regulations, 278–79

Galbraith, John Kenneth, 3, 45–48
Gangs, 97–98
Gates, Bill, 196, 326, 356–57

Geithner, Tim, 113–14, 156
General Electric, 377
General Theory (Keynes), 46–47
Genetically modified food, 182–83
Germany
  authoritarian government in, 23
  economic planning in, 27
  "fake goods" in, 149
  Gini coefficient in, 317
  laissez faire in, 18
  marginal tax rates in, 376
  reforms in, 22
  "revolving door policies" in, 335–36
  unions in, 231
  welfare policies in, 218, 219
  welfare states in, 20
Gini, Corrado, 19
Gini coefficient. *See also specific country*
  generally, 19, 209
  changes in, 316
  income redistribution and, 219–21, 224, 317
  public spending and, 228–29
  taxation and, 368–69, 371, 382
  tax avoidance and, 331
Ginsburg, Ruth Bader, 251
Global government, 121, 260–61
Globalization
  consumer protection and, 149
  income redistribution and, 205, 385–86
  legal rules and, 261–62
  recessions and, 237
  taxation and, 378
  tax avoidance and, 369–70
  2007-2008 Financial Crisis and, 237
Global public goods, 120–21
Goldman Sachs, 113–14, 334
Goldwater, Barry, 60–61
Google, 331, 347, 348
Government failures
  causes of, 69, 73–74
  identification of, 65
  income inequality as, 225
  market failures versus, 313
  market fundamentalism and, 86
  socialism and, 73–74
Government intervention
  conservatives on, 317–18
  in cotton industry, 325
  debate regarding, 326–27
  direct government intervention, 32–33, 36, 230
  financial crises and, 156
  growth and, 313–14
  Hayek on, 226
  indirect government intervention, 33, 36, 58

Internet and, 325–26
libertarians on, 317–18
non-neutral nature of, 324
positive effects of, 324
private income, effect on, 326
referee, government as, 327
Smith on, 226, 325
2007-2008 Financial Crisis and, 156
Governments
administrative capability of, 66–68
financial institutions, influence of,
113–14
income redistribution and. *See* Income
redistribution
limited role of. *See* Limited role of
government
role of. *See* Role of government
Graeber, David, 170
Great Depression, 22, 26, 31, 253
Great Recession, 76, 109, 318.
See also 2007–2008 Financial Crisis
Great Wall of China, 136
Greece
contingent liabilities in, 140
economic problems in, 69, 106
sovereign debt in, 241
Greed, 312
"Green budgets," 293
Greenspan, Alan, 37, 84
Growth
advantages of high growth, 311
aggregate concept of, 311
in China, 311, 386–87
decline in, 227
effect of regulations on, 158–59
equitable growth, 310, 312
government intervention and, 313–14
income redistribution and, 227, 228
in India, 386–87
marginal tax rates and, 227–28, 369
regulations, effect of, 158–59, 228
relative poverty and, 226–27
role of government, 7, 189–90
social consciousness and, 312
stabilization policies and, 237
Guns as externality, 165

Hagen, Jurgen von, 286
Haig-Simons principle, 377–79, 397
Hamburger, Tom, 275
Hamilton, Alexander, 249, 357–58
Hammurabi Code, 333
Hand, Learned, 380
Hansen, Alvin, 3, 42
"Happiness," 311–12

"Happy Birthday" (song), 355–56
Harberger, Arnold, 394
Harley-Davidson, 355–56
Harvard Business Review, 363
Harvard University, 3
Hausmann, Ricardo, 325
Hawley, Ellis W., 87
Hayek, F.A.
generally, 7–8, 60–61, 394
in Austrian School, 64
on Beveridge, 42–43
on corporatism, 231
on economic planning, 26–27, 159
on government intervention, 226
on income inequality, 227
on information in exchanges, 93, 112–15
on limited role of government, 85, 259, 313–14
on stabilization policies, 189
on unions, 231
Health care
information in, 166
limited role of government and, 98
as public good, 180–81
resistance to changing policies, 222–23
in US, 208, 222–23, 298
Hegel, G.W.F., 99, 305–6
Heller, Walter, 56
Hemingway, Ernest, 399
Hicks, John, 378
High net worth individuals (HNWIs)
marginal tax rates for, 373–75
taxation of, 368
tax avoidance by, 370, 382
Hitler, Adolf, 2–3, 27
Hobbes, Thomas, 7–8, 90
Hollande, François, 113–14
Hong Kong
public spending in, 121–22
taxation in, 381
Hoover, Herbert, 24–25
Hoover Dam, 241, 256
Housing
mortgage crisis, 107–8, 116, 140–41
as public good, 180–81
Hugo, Victor, 358–59
Hull, Cordell, 25
Human capital, income redistribution and, 193
Hume, David, 71

IBM, 347, 377
"Idea factories," 344–45
"Image rights," 347–49
Immigration, 262
Implementing regulations, 333
Import duties, 15–16, 34

Incentives
  income redistribution and, 306
  intellectual property and, 362–63, 365
  in Italy, 381
  marginal tax rates and, 83
  as policy tool, 135
  public spending as disincentive, 74–75
  social norms versus, 398
  tax incentives, 135, 380–81
Income effect, 372–73
Income inequality
  generally, 205–6
  overview, 315
  in Argentina, 221
  in bonuses, 82–83, 85–86
  in Brazil, 221
  in China, 221, 227, 322
  conservatives and, 394–95
  "crony capitalism" and, 343
  debate regarding, 322
  democracy and, 400
  dependent workers and, 221, 316, 387
  economic aristocracy and, 117–18
  envy and, 319–21
  in executive compensation, 82–83, 85–86, 105–6
  ex post income distribution and, 118, 119
  externalities and, 321
  in France, 306
  Gini coefficient. *See* Gini coefficient
  as government failure, 225
  Hayek on, 227
  importance of, 393
  increase in, 316
  in India, 221, 227
  intellectual property, effect of, 343–45
  justification of, 105, 117
  Keynes on, 320
  lack of confidence caused by, 387
  legal rules and, 257, 323
  "luck" and, 321–23
  market fundamentalism and, 342–43
  middle class and, 206–7
  national governments, limitations
    of, 393–94
  negative effects on, 389
  "new aristocracy" resulting from, 399
  Pareto Welfare Criterion and, 318–19
  progressive taxes, and decline in, 343–44
  psychological effects of, 319–21
  public spending and, 228–29
  relative income hypothesis, 319
  removal of conditions of, 118–19
  role of government, 317
  in Russia, 306, 322
  "safety nets," 207–8
  Smith on, 305, 306, 320, 321

  social acceptance of, 398
  social costs of, 206, 305–6
  spending habits and, 216–17
  taxation and, 368–69, 382
  in UK, 315
  undesirable effects of market on, 322
  unions, and decline in, 342
  urbanization and, 206
  in US, 161–62, 208–9, 221, 224, 227, 315–16,
    389, 391–92
  working class and, 206–7
Income redistribution
  allocation of resources versus, 220, 224
  athletes and, 204–5
  basic minimum income, 212
  Burke on, 215, 219, 300, 312–13
  certifications and, 193
  composers and, 203
  debate regarding, 209, 219, 317
  democracy and, 223
  in Denmark, 210
  dependency and, 209–10
  deregulation and, 197
  economic freedom and, 159–60
  education and, 193
  effects on, 191–92
  explicit government actions, 192, 200–1.
    See also Public spending; Taxation
  ex post income distribution, 118, 119
  general policies, 191
  Gini coefficient and, 219–21, 224, 317
  globalization and, 205, 385–86
  growth and, 227, 228
  historical background, 209, 218–19
  human capital and, 193
  incentives and, 306
  influences on, 220–21
  infrastructure and, 192–93
  institutions responsible for, 224
  intellectual property and, 203–4
  inventors and, 203
  investment activity and, 194
  "invisible hand of government," 199
  legal rules and, 257
  limited role of government and, 98, 160–61
  market and, 37–38
  as market failure, 111
  market rules and, 194
  market versus, 191
  mechanism of, 210–11
  monetary policy and, 197
  Musgrave on, 220
  "nanny states" and, 209–10
  natural distribution in market and, 198, 326
  non-explicit government actions, 191,
    198–200

opposition to, 200
performers and, 204–5
politics and, 219, 221–22
"poverty traps" and, 209–10
prior to taxing and spending, 191, 198–200
progressive taxes and, 228
proposal regarding, 210–11
protection of property and, 193–94
public institutions and, 299
regulations and, 278
research and, 194–97
resistance to changing policies and, 222–23
role of government, 187, 189, 190, 202
specific policies, 191
taxation and, 223–24
technology and, 385–86
in US, 200
value added taxes and, 207, 211, 212
welfare policies and, 45–46, 48
in welfare states, 224, 383
Income tax
"architecture," changes in, 135, 367, 377–79
avoidance. *See* Tax avoidance
complexity of, 379–82
for corporations, 376–77
entrepreneurs and, 308
evasion, 295–96, 333–34
marginal tax rates. *See* Marginal tax rates
negative income tax, 212
progressive taxes, 52–53, 228, 343–44
reduction in, 87
revenue growth and, 385
stabilization policies and, 238
tax expenditures and, 207
in US, 19, 24–25, 208
India
Constitution, 270
corruption in, 120
growth in, 386–87
income inequality in, 221, 227
mislabeling of fish in, 149–50
Indirect government intervention, 33, 36, 58
Individualism, 89, 312–13
Individualist governments, 65
Individual versus community rights, 98
Industrial Revolution, 16–17, 346, 357
Inequality. *See* Income inequality
Informal norms, 285–86
Information
asymmetry in, 108, 114–15, 148–49,
165–66, 331–32
in exchanges, 93, 112–13
in health care, 166
legal rules and, 254–55
in new markets, 165–66
on prices, 167–68, 331–32

public institutions and, 296
Infrastructure
entrepreneurs and, 309
income redistribution and, 192–93
legal rules and, 256
limited role of government and, 96
in UK, 316–17
in US, 234, 316–17
The Inside Job (documentary), 337
Institute for Health Metrics and Evaluation, 390
Institute of Economic Affairs, 60–61, 79, 394–95
Institutions. *See* Public institutions
Intangible property, 94–95, 308
Intellectual property
overview, 341
athletes, 204–5, 351–53
attempts to extend protection of,
355–56, 359–60
attorneys and, 366
basic needs and, 351
in China, 347, 358
composers, 203, 349
discovery, effect on, 365
entertainment industry, 345, 348, 353
in EU, 347
executive compensation and, 348, 363–64
fashion industry, 345
forms of, 347–48
government protection of, 94–95, 193–94,
203–4, 308, 356, 358–60, 366
historical background, 355
"idea factories," 344–45
"image rights," 347–49
incentives and, 362–63, 365
income inequality, effect on, 343–45
income redistribution and, 193–94, 203–4
Industrial Revolution compared, 346, 357
inventors, 203
in Japan, 347, 358
laissez faire and, 359
marginal tax rates and, 353–54, 357
monopolies and, 345–47, 356, 365
patents, 347, 359, 361
in pharmaceutical industry, 365–66
piracy and, 360
rents and, 353
role of government, 354
social value of, 361–62
in South Korea, 347
technology and, 356–57
theft of, 357–58
trade agreements and, 354
traditional societies compared, 360–61
in UK, 357–58
in US, 176, 193, 204, 347, 357–58, 362
wealth creation and, 349–51

Intergovernmental Panel on Climate
  Change, 316
Inter-institutional externalities, 290
International Monetary Fund, 7, 8, 109, 113–14,
  296–97, 315–16
Internet, 325–26
Inventors, 203
Investment activity, income redistribution
  and, 194
"Invisible hand of government," 199
"Invisible hand of market," 66, 312–13
Iran hostages, 100–1
Ireland
  bubbles in, 331
  challenges to welfare policies in, 60
  contingent liabilities in, 138, 140
  famine in, 218
  influence of conservatives in, 395
  marginal tax rates in, 376
  public spending in, 121–22, 162
  supply-side economics in, 77
Irrationality
  consumer protection and, 148–49
  effect on market, 79, 83
  Friedman on, 141–42
  nudges and, 141–42
  recessions and, 236
Islam, 218
Italian School, 5–6, 63, 65, 178
Italy
  allocation of resources in, 188
  authoritarian government in, 23
  bureaucracy in, 234
  Communist Party, 1–2
  Constitution, 248–50, 266–71
  Constitutional Commission of
    Eighteen, 267–68
  corporatism in, 231
  corruption in, 120
  Corte dei Conti, 161, 234, 290, 381
  economic planning in, 27
  fascism in, 23, 231, 266–67
  financial accountability in, 291
  incentives in, 381
  influence of conservatives in, 395
  "Keynesian Revolution" in, 269
  Labor Charter of 1927, 248
  marginal tax rates in, 376
  privatization in, 33–34
  public ownership in, 135
  public spending in, 23
  regulations in, 279
  sovereign debt in, 241
  unions in, 23, 231
  welfare policies in, 214
  women's suffrage in, 20

Japan
  economic planning in, 27
  executive compensation in, 364
  "fake goods" in, 149
  intellectual property in, 347, 358
  marginal tax rates in, 376, 377
  sovereign debt in, 241
Jefferson, Thomas, 249–50
Jensen, Michael, 363
Johnson, Lyndon B., 43, 56, 58, 229
Journal of Financial Economics, 363
Jouvenel, Bertrand de, 45
Judges, legal rules and, 251
Justice systems, 295–96

Kahneman, Daniel, 79
Keen, Andrew, 325–26
"Keepers of the gate," 336
Kennedy, John F., 2–3, 55–58, 239
Keynes, John Maynard
  generally, 7–8
  on capitalism, 28–30
  on corporatism, 231
  countercyclical policy, 61–62
  decline in influence of, 86–87
  Galbraith and, 46–47
  on income inequality, 320
  on laissez faire, 31–32
  on market, 37, 38
  on "new wisdom," 399–400
  pessimism of, 28–30
  on public works, 241
  on Soviet Union, 27–30, 78
  on stabilization policies, 70–71, 189, 237
  on taxation, 245
  on unions, 230–31
  on US, 47
  on welfare states, 383
  on workers' rights, 19
"Keynesian Revolution," 2, 41, 42, 56,
  269, 383
King, Melvyn, 113–14, 156, 338
Klein, Lawrence, 42
Klein, Naomi, 29
Kornai, Janos, 26
KPMG International, 376
Krugman, Paul, 240–41, 342–43
Kuznets, Simon, 3

Lady Gaga, 351–52
Laffer Curve, 74–76, 363, 373–74, 377, 379,
  394–95, 397
Laissez faire, 15–21
  abandonment of, 43
  criticism of, 3
  in Eastern Europe, 35

energy and, 17
entrepreneurs and, 307–8
in Germany, 18
government and, 65
Industrial Revolution and, 16–17
intellectual property and, 359
Keynes on, 31–32
in Latin America, 33
resurgence of, 33–35
role of state, 15–16, 19–20
trade and, 17
in UK, 31
in US, 17–19, 30, 31
workers' rights and, 18, 19
Landis, James, 57–58
Lange, Oskar, 26
La Porta, Rafael, 263–64
Larosiere, Jacques de, 64
Latin America
    constitutions in, 250, 271
    laissez faire in, 33
    public institutions in, 290
Laudato Si' (Francis), 28, 81
Law and Economics, 183–85
Law of public expenditure growth, 51, 87
Laws. *See* Statutes
le Bon, Gustave, 28
Legal rules. *See also* Policy tools
    overview, 132, 247
    adaptation to change, 248, 259–60, 327, 328
    arbitrariness of, 247–48
    attorneys and, 252–53
    backward-looking nature of, 338
    Buchanan on, 252
    bureaucracy and, 253–54
    changes in, 251–52
    complexity of, 329, 332–34
    constitutions. *See* Constitutions
    democracy and, 134
    economics and, 252–53
    expertise required for, 257–58
    externalities and, 255
    federalism and, 260
    general principles versus, 340
    global government and, 260–61
    globalization and, 261–62
    government rules versus social
        principles, 327–28
    immigration and, 262
    income inequality and, 257, 323
    income redistribution and, 257
    inconsistent application of, 332
    individual versus community in, 262
    informal norms, 285–86
    information and, 254–55
    infrastructure and, 256

judges and, 251
market fundamentalism and, 133–34
in modern society, 248
moral rules versus, 333
national scope of, 260
in pre-modern societies, 134
problems with, 338–40
public goods and, 255
quality of public sector, 263–64
regulations. *See* Regulations
role of government, changes in, 258–59
self-regulation of market, 94, 133–34
spontaneous generation of, 133–34
stabilization policies and, 255–56
statutes. *See* Statutes
urbanization and, 254
weakness of, 70
Legitimization of market, 85–86
Lenin, V.I., 322
Leontief, Wassily, 3, 46–47
Leo XIII (Pope), 20
Lex mercatoria, 99–100, 328
Liberals
    on growth and income redistribution, 227
    regulations and, 160
Libertarians
    challenges to welfare policies, 60–61
    on government intervention, 317–18
    "libertarian paternalism," 141–42
    on limited role of government, 99–100,
        259
    regulations, opposition to, 153–54, 278
    on safety-related regulations, 147
Life expectancy, 390–91
Limited role of government
    generally, 85
    Buchanan on, 85, 313–14
    conservatives on, 99–100, 259
    criminal law and, 95–96
    Friedman on, 85, 313–14
    Hayek on, 85, 259, 313–14
    health care and, 98
    income redistribution and, 98, 160–61
    infrastructure and, 96
    libertarians on, 99–100, 259
    market fundamentalism and, 80, 159
    ministrant functions, 98–99
    nudges and, 97
    protection of property and, 94–96
    public spending and, 96
    Smith on, 99
    social contract and, 89–91
    social needs and, 96–97
    in UK, 98
    urbanization, effect of, 97
    in US, 98

Lincoln, Abraham, 328, 340
Lobbyists
  defense spending and, 178–79
  former government employees as, 113, 173
  genetically modified food and, 182–83
  power of, 336–38
  problems with, 339
  regulations and, 171, 173, 280
  restrictions on, 119
Locke, John, 7–8
Lopokova, Lydia, 27–28
Louis XIV (France), 291
Lucas, Robert, 38, 85, 160–61, 313–14,
    378–79, 394
"Luck," income inequality and, 321–23
Luxemburg, marginal tax rates in, 376

Maastricht Stability and Growth Pact, 273
Machiavelli, Niccolò, 183
Madison, James, 202, 249–50
Mafia, 97–98
Maginot Line, 338
Mandated disclosures, 127–28
Mao Zedong, 322
Marat, Jean-Paul, 160
Marginal tax rates. *See also specific country*
  for corporations, 376–77
  for dependent workers, 373
  empirical importance of, 371
  growth and, 227–28, 369
  for higher wage workers, 373
  for high net worth individuals
    (HNWIs), 373–75
  incentives and, 83
  income effect and, 372–73
  intellectual property and, 353–54, 357
  loopholes and, 377
  for lower wage workers, 372–73
  "poverty traps" and, 209–10
  reduction in, 201, 367, 371, 375–77
  reputational motive and, 374–75
  substitution effect and, 372–73
Market distortion, 167
Market-enhancing regulations, 150–51
Market failures
  government failures versus, 313
  identification of, 41, 49–50
  income redistribution as, 111
  normative approach to role of government
    and, 110–11
  public spending and, 121–22
Market fundamentalism
  generally, 39
  faith in, 78
  government failures and, 86

income inequality and, 342–43
legal rules and, 133–34
limited role of government and, 80, 159
public spending and, 35–36
regulations and, 158, 160
in UK, 35–36
in US, 35–36
Market manipulations
  overview, 226
  government correction of markets, 226, 229–30
  by individuals, 231–32
  "shadow control," 232
  "termites of the state," 232
Market-ruled society, 80–81
Marx, Karl, 218–19, 322
"Mathism," 79
Mazzucato, Mariana, 196
McAfee, Andrew, 356–57
McKinsey Global Institute, 391
Meckling, William, 363
Memoire sur le paupérisme (Tocqueville), 210
Mercantilism, 70, 123
Messi, Lionel, 352
Mexico
  economic planning in, 27
  Gini coefficient in, 317
  regulations in, 282
Microsoft, 347
Middle class, income inequality and, 206–7
Milanovic, Branko, 227
Mill, John Stuart, 147, 212, 312, 342
Minimal role of state. *See* Limited role of
    government
Minimum wages, 145–46
Ministrant functions, 98–99
"Misery index," 61
Mises, Ludwig von, 64, 70–71, 258
Mitterrand, François, 342
Modernity, problems of, 153
Modigliani, Franco, 3
Mokyr, Joel, 346
Monetary policy
  central banks and, 188
  importance of, 395–96
  income redistribution and, 197
  stabilization policies and, 238, 242, 244
Monopolies
  intellectual property and, 345–47, 356, 365
  market distortion and, 167
  natural monopolies, regulations and, 147
  "too big to fail" and, 79–80
Monopolistic governments, 65
Montesquieu, 218, 305
Moral hazard, 138, 156–57, 255–56
Moral rules versus legal rules, 333

Morris, Charles R., 357–58
Mortgage crisis, 107–8, 116, 140–41
Mundell, Robert, 394
Musgrave, Richard
  generally, 3–5, 7–8
  on constitutions, 266
  on import duties, 15–16
  on income redistribution, 220
  on public goods, 176–77
  on regulations, 278
  on role of government, 110, 162, 168, 187, 189
  in School of Public Choice, 5, 6
Mussolini, Benito, 5, 27, 248, 252,
    266–67, 279
Myrdal, Gunnar, 10, 20–21, 51–52, 64, 111, 118

"Nanny states," 209–10
Napoleon, 267–68
"National champions," 74, 245–46
National Rifle Association, 275
Natural monopolies, regulations and, 147
Negative income tax, 212
Netherlands, marginal tax rates in, 376
"New aristocracy," 399
"New wisdom," 399–400
New Zealand
  challenges to welfare policies in, 60
  influence of conservatives in, 395
  marginal tax rates in, 376
  public institutions in, 291, 292
  public ownership in, 136
  public spending in, 121–22, 162
  regulations in, 174
  supply-side economics in, 77
"Nirvana error," 151
Nitti, F.S., 28
Non-basic goods, 48
Non-basic needs, 45–46
Normative approach to role of government
  generally, 3–4, 313–14
  complexity and, 110
  market failures and, 110–11
  politics and, 111
  in US, 110
North, Douglass C., 265
Norway
  executive compensation in, 364
  public spending in, 162
  welfare policies in, 50
Nozick, Robert, 7–8, 60–61, 98
Nudges, 36, 65, 97
Nuisance regulations, 144–45

Obama, Barack, 9, 98, 196–97, 208, 275
Occupational licensing, 124–26

Occupy Wall Street, 29
Oceana (NGO), 149–50
Oil crisis, 6–7
Olson, Mancur, 71, 130, 183, 339
"On Liberty" (Mill), 147
Oracle, 347
Organization of Economic Co-operation and
    Development (OECD), 149, 241–42,
    278, 296–97
Outsourcing, 112

Pacioli, Luca, 291
Pakistan, Constitution, 270
Panama Papers, 370
Pareto, Vilfredo, 28, 37, 63, 318–19
Pareto Optimum, 217–18
Pareto Welfare Criterion, 318–19
Patents, 347, 359, 361
Paternalistic governments, 65
Paternalistic regulations, 36
Peacock, Alan, 5, 6, 60–61, 313–14
Pensions
  resistance to changing policies, 222–23
  in US, 222–23
Performance-based compensation, 363–64
Performers, 204–5
Persson, Torsten, 286
Peru, Gini coefficient in, 317
Pharmaceutical industry, 115–17, 158, 365–66
Pharmaceutical Research and Manufacturers of
    America, 171
Phillips curve, 61
Pigou, A.C., 184, 185
Piketty, Thomas, 340–42
"Piñata capitalism," 115
Piracy, 360
Plato, 302, 305
Plutarch, 218, 302
Policy tools
  overview, 142–43
  authorizations, 137, 144–45
  certifications, 137
  conscription, 136
  contingent liabilities, 137–41
  expropriation, 136
  fees and fines, 142
  nudges, 141–42. *See also* Nudges
  public ownership, 135–36
  regulations, 141. *See also* Regulations
  rezoning, 136
  tax expenditures, 135
  tax incentives, 135
  tax levels, 135
  tax structures, 135
"Political market," 334

Populism, 74, 340, 387–88
Posner, Richard A., 129, 184–85
Poterba, James M., 286
Poverty
  absolute poverty, 216
  envy and, 216–18
  externalities and, 216–17
  relative poverty, 216, 226–27
  "Poverty traps," 209–10
Prada, 347
Prices
  controls on, 145–46
  information on, 167–68, 331–32
Prince, 351–52
Privatization, 33–34, 85, 397
Production, 45
Productivity, effect of regulations on, 158–59
Progressive taxes, 52–53, 228, 343–44
Project Syndicate, 325
Property
  criminal law and, 95–96
  government protection of, 94–96, 193–94,
    202, 308
  intangible property, 94–95, 308
  intellectual property. *See* Intellectual
    property
  protection of, 94–96, 193–94, 202
  real property, 95, 308
  tangible property, 94
Protection of property, 94–96, 193–94, 202
Proudhon, Pierre-Joseph, 218–19
Psychological effects of income
    inequality, 319–21
Psychologie du Socialisme (le Bon), 28
Public assistance. *See* Welfare policies
Public employees, 232–33, 235, 291–92
Public goods
  overview, 175
  defense spending as, 175–78
  education as, 180–81
  externalities and, 181–82
  free rider problem, 175–76
  global public goods, 120–21
  health care as, 180–81
  housing as, 180–81
  legal rules and, 255
  Musgrave on, 176–77
  NASA as, 179
  public spending, necessity of, 176–77
  pure public goods, 175, 177–78
  quasi-public goods, 180–81
  research as, 179–80
  Samuelson on, 175–77
  in UK, 180
  welfare as, 181

Public institutions. *See also specific country*
  overview, 287
  accrual accounting and, 293
  audits, 290–91
  bureaucracy and, 297–98
  cash accounting and, 292–93
  corruption and, 296–97
  efficiency of, 299
  enforcement mechanisms, 289–91
  evaluation of public services, 293–95
  factors affecting, 287
  financial accountability, 291
  first-generation reforms, 300–1
  holistic approach to, 290
  income redistribution and, 299
  information and, 296
  inter-institutional externalities, 290
  justice systems, 295–96
  "market-augmenting" nature of, 299
  output, focus on, 291–92
  performance, focus on, 291–92
  recommendations regarding, 299
  role of government and, 298–300
  second-generation reforms, 300–1
  spillovers, 290
  synergy in, 289
  tax administration, 287–89
  transparency and, 296–97
  weakness in, 69–70
Public interest, 131
Public ownership, 135–36
Public private partnerships, 106, 112,
    137–38
Public sector compensation, 83, 129–30
Public spending. *See also specific country*
  apparatus responsible for, 188, 233
  as disincentive, 74–75
  Gini coefficient and, 228–29
  historical overview, 23–24, 35–36
  income inequality and, 228–29
  increases in, 384
  law of public expenditure growth, 51, 87
  limited role of government and, 96
  market failures and, 121–22
  market fundamentalism and, 35–36
  optimal level, 220
  public goods, necessity in, 176–77
  stabilization policies and, 240–41, 244
  value added taxes and, 53
  welfare policies and, 51, 53, 232–33
Public works, stabilization policies and, 241
Pure public goods, 175, 177–78
Putnam, D., 261
Puviani, Amilcare, 39, 52
Pyramids, 136

Quality of public sector, 263–64
Quantitative easing, 109, 197, 244
Quasi-fiscal regulations, 151
Quasi-public goods, 180–81

Rakoff, Jed S., 252–53
Rational expectations, 62, 86–87, 394–96
Rationing, 145–46
Reagan, Ronald, 33, 40, 59, 61, 71–72, 77, 87, 358, 375, 377–78, 398
Real property, 95, 308
Real versus financial investment, 106–7
Recessions
    overview, 236
    causes of, 236–37
    globalization and, 237
    irrationality and, 236
Redistribution of income. *See* Income redistribution
"Red tape," 124, 228, 253–54, 297–98
Referee, government as, 310, 327
Regulations. *See also specific country*
    overview, 144
    abuse of, 124
    adaptation to change, 282
    banks and, 126
    civic associations and, 130, 154
    complexity of, 170–72, 278
    conservative opposition to, 160, 278
    consumer protection regulations, 148–50
    correcting or reducing externalities through, 147
    corruption and, 124, 280
    creation of, 277
    debates regarding, 154, 170
    demand, effect on, 128–29
    democracy and, 134
    dependent workers and, 23
    deregulation
        overview, 87–88
        economic freedom and, 86
        income redistribution and, 197
        potential for future crises and, 108, 109
        in US, 82
    discretion and, 151–52
    economic freedom, effect on, 130–31
    economic impact of, 276–77
    essential regulations, 280–81
    evolution of, 123, 124
    excessive regulations, 279
    externalities and, 164, 281–82
    failure of, 171–73
    federalism and, 125, 126, 173, 284–85
    financial institutions and, 126, 155, 157
    fundamental law of, 278–79

growth, effect on, 158–59, 228
implementing regulations, 333
income redistribution and, 278
institutional reforms, 173–74
liberals and, 160
libertarian opposition to, 153–54, 278
lobbyists and, 171, 173, 280
mandated disclosures, 127–28
market-enhancing regulations, 150–51
market fundamentalism and, 158, 160
as mercantilism, 123
Musgrave on, 278
natural monopolies and, 147
negative effects of, 124, 128
"nirvana error," 151
nuisance regulations, 144–45
occupational licensing and, 124–26
opposition to, 123, 129, 153–55, 160, 170, 278, 282–83
as policy tool, 141
politics and, 278–80
productivity, effect on, 158–59
public interest and, 131
quasi-fiscal regulations, 151
recommendations regarding, 283
"red tape," 124, 228
rents and, 124–25
review of, 172, 284
safety-related regulations, 146–47
scientific studies and, 281
second-best regulations, 145–46
"single window" system, 284–85
social costs of, 282
social regulations, 146
urbanization, effect of, 130
Regulatory budget, 284
Regulatory capture, 129, 172–73
Relative income hypothesis, 319
Relative poverty, 216, 226–27
Religious trust in market, 37, 78, 396
Rent control, 145–46
Rents
    "crony capitalism" and, 112
    financial institutions and, 119
    financial sector and, 330
    intellectual property and, 353
    regulations and, 124–25
Reputational motive, 374–75
Rerum Novarum (Leo XIII), 20
Research
    income redistribution and, 194–97
    as public good, 179–80
    in US, 194–97
Rezoning, 136

Ricardian equivalence hypothesis, 62–64, 86–87, 394–95
Ricardo, David, 63
The Road to Serfdom (Hayek), 26–27
Rockefeller, Jay, 335
Role of government
  overview, 1–11
  allocation of resources, 187–88, 211–12. *See also* Allocation of resources
  Burke on, 160, 189
  employment and, 189–90
  growth and, 7, 189–90
  income inequality and, 317
  income redistribution, 187, 189, 190, 202. *See also* Income redistribution
  intellectual property and, 354
  legal rules, changes in, 258–59
  limited role. *See* Limited role of government
  Musgrave on, 110, 162, 168, 187, 189
  normative approach to
    generally, 3–4, 313–14
    complexity and, 110
    market failures and, 110–11
    politics and, 111
    in US, 110
  public institutions and, 298–300
  Samuelson on, 110, 400
  stabilization policies, 187, 189, 211–12. *See also* Stabilization policies
  tutorial role, 65, 141–42, 162, 189–90
Romney, Mitt, 379
Ronaldo, Cristiano, 351–52
Roosevelt, Franklin D., 4, 22, 24–25, 31, 43–45, 47, 48, 82, 157, 253
Roosevelt, Theodore, 18
Rousseau, Jean-Jacques, 7–8, 89, 218, 305
Rubin, Robert, 84
Rule of law, 247–48, 265
Rules. *See* Legal rules
Russia. *See also* Soviet Union
  corruption in, 120
  income inequality in, 306, 322
  taxation in, 381–82

"Safety nets," 207–8
Safety-related regulations, 146–47
Samsung Electronics, 347
Samuelson, Paul
  generally, 3, 56
  on discretion, 71
  on disincentives, 48–49
  on fiscal rules, 272
  on public goods, 175, 176–77
  on role of government, 110, 400
Sandel, Michel, 34, 80–81

Scalia, Antonin, 251, 274–75, 345, 359
Scandinavia
  labor participation in, 47
  marginal tax rates in, 376
  public spending in, 53
  regulations in, 174
  welfare policies in, 43, 214
Schlesinger, Arthur M., Jr., 32
School of Public Choice, 5–6, 62, 69, 72, 110, 313–14, 396
Schumpeter, Joseph, 111
Scienza delle Finanze (Italian School), 5–6, 63, 65, 178
Second-best regulations, 145–46
Securitization, 330
Self-regulation of market, 94, 133–34
Seligman, Edwin, 380
Sen, Amartya, 7–8, 159–60, 299–300
Seneca, 102
"Shadow banking," 108, 119, 242, 329–30
"Shadow financial sector," 243
"Shadow fiscal policy," 38–39
"Shadow governments," 202
Sharapova, Maria, 351–53
Shiller, Robert J., 116
Silicon Valley, 344–45
Simons, Henry C., 119
Singapore
  public spending in, 121–22, 162
  regulations in, 174
  taxation in, 381
Sinn, Hans-Werner, 20, 108
Slavery, 249–50, 265–66
Smith, Adam
  generally, 7–9, 12, 189
  on constitutions, 270
  on dishonesty, 79
  on entrepreneurs, 307
  on government intervention, 226, 325
  on income inequality, 305, 306, 320, 321
  individualism and, 89
  "invisible hand of market," 66, 312–13
  on limited role of government, 99
  on mercantilism, 70, 123
  on social consciousness, 312
  on specialization, 91–92
Smoking as externality, 164
Social consciousness, growth and, 312
Social contract, 89–91
Social costs of income inequality, 206
Socialism
  government failures and, 73–74
  public ownership and, 135
  types of, 28
Socialization of loss, 83–84

Social programs. *See* Welfare policies
Social regulations, 146
Social responsibilities of corporations, 398
"Soft budgets," 71, 138
Solow, Robert, 3, 56
Sony, 347
Sorensen, Theodore, 2–3
Southeast Asian financial crisis (1997-1998), 109, 243–44
South Korea
  intellectual property in, 347
  public spending in, 121–22, 162
Sovereign debt
  Buchanan on, 64
  easy credit and, 106
  in Greece, 241
  growth in, 64
  in Italy, 241
  in Japan, 241
  size of, 109
  stabilization policies and, 241–42, 244–45
Soviet Union. *See also* Russia
  Constitution, 266
  economic challenges from, 2–3
  economic planning in, 26
  Keynes on, 27–30, 78
Spain
  authoritarian government in, 23
  bubbles in, 331
  contingent liabilities in, 138
  influence of conservatives in, 395
  marginal tax rates in, 376
Specialization, 91–92
Spending. *See* Public spending
Spillovers, 290
Sputnik, 2
Stabilization policies, 55–59
  aggregate demand and, 239, 240
  asymmetry in, 62
  central banks and, 243, 244
  employment and, 237
  executive versus legislative approaches, 241
  expertise required in, 240
  fiscal policy and, 237
  growth and, 237
  Hayek on, 189
  income tax and, 238
  initial conditions and, 241–42
  Keynes on, 70–71, 189, 237
  legal rules and, 255–56
  monetary policy and, 238, 242, 244
  "national champions" and, 245–46
  problems with, 239–40
  public spending and, 240–41, 244
  public works and, 241

role of government, 187, 189, 211–12
  skepticism toward, 395–96
  sovereign debt and, 241–42, 244–45
  stimulus and, 239–40, 242
  structural policies and, 238–39
  taxation and, 56–57, 238, 240–41
  in UK, 59
  in US, 55–59
  value added taxes and, 240
Stalin, Josef, 266, 267
Standard and Poor, 106
Starbucks, 334
Statutes
  overview, 273
  complexity of, 274–75
  excessive volume of, 273
  legal inconsistency, 273–74
  length of, 274–75
  problems with, 273–75
  recommendations regarding, 275
  simplification of, 275–76
  in US, 276
"Stealth taxes," 144
Steiner, Arthur H., 267
Stigler, George, 60–61, 85, 129, 184, 313–14, 394, 400
Stimulus, 239–40, 242
"Stress tests," 108
Strikes, 19
Strindberg, August, 302
Structural policies, stabilization policies and, 238–39
Subsidies, 33
Substitution effect, 372–73
Summers, Larry, 84, 378–79
Supply-side economics, 33, 74–78, 395, 397
Surrey, Stanley, 135, 380
Suskind, Ron, 9
Sweden
  ex post income distribution in, 118
  executive compensation in, 364
  influence of conservatives in, 395
  marginal tax rates in, 376
  public spending in, 162, 190
  taxation in, 190, 371, 381
Switzerland
  Constitution, 272
  "fake goods" in, 149
  fiscal rules in, 71
  public spending in, 121–22, 162
Systemic risk, 155, 168

Tabellini, Guido, 286
Tacitus, 102

Taiwan, public spending in, 121–22
Tangible property, 94
Tanzi, Vito, 1–11
Taxation. *See also specific country*
  administration of, 287–89
  apparatus responsible for, 188, 233
  "architecture," changes in, 135, 367,
    377–79, 397
  avoidance. *See* Tax avoidance
  "betterment taxes," 194
  collection of, 188
  complexity of, 367–68, 379–82
  of corporations, 161
  efficiency of, 188
  entrepreneurs and, 309
  evasion, 295–96, 333–34
  fees and fines, 368
  flat taxes, 381–82
  Friedman on, 367–68
  Gini coefficient and, 368–69, 371, 382
  globalization and, 378
  Haig-Simons principle, 377–79
  of high net worth individuals (HNWIs), 368
  income inequality and, 368–69, 382
  income redistribution and, 223–24
  income tax. *See* Income tax
  increases in, 384
  Keynes on, 245
  loopholes, 331, 333–34
  marginal tax rates. *See* Marginal tax rates
  negative income tax, 212
  progressive taxes, 52–53, 228, 343–44
  rates, 135
  reduction of, 77, 87
  social contract and, 90–91
  social costs of, 189
  stabilization policies and, 56–57, 238, 240–41
  statutory rates versus effective rates,
    367–68, 377
  "stealth taxes," 144
  tax expenditures, 52–53, 134, 135,
    232–33, 380–81
  tax incentives, 135, 380–81
  value added taxes
    income redistribution and, 207, 211, 212
    public spending and, 53
    revenue growth and, 385
    stabilization policies and, 240
  voluntariness of, 90–91
  wealth tax, 341–42
  welfare policies and, 45, 48–49
Tax avoidance
  Gini coefficient and, 331
  globalization and, 369–70
  by high net worth individuals (HNWIs), 370, 382

rise in, 379
  tax competition, 370, 378
  tax evasion versus, 333–34
  tax havens, 369–70, 378
  tax planning, 368, 369, 381
"Taxman" (song), 53
Taylor, Fred M., 26
Ten Commandments, 79, 328
"Termites of the market," 119–20, 199
"Termites of the state," 119–20, 198, 199, 232,
  264, 314
Thatcher, Margaret, 33, 59, 64, 77, 87, 98,
  180, 398
The Theory of Moral Sentiments (Smith), 312, 321
The Theory of Public Finance (Musgrave),
  176–77, 187
Think tanks, 336–38, 394–95
"Third Way," 395
Tinbergen, Jan, 82, 381
Tobin, James, 4, 56, 272
Tocqueville, Alexis de, 7–8, 89, 210, 400
"Too big to fail"
  financial institutions and, 84, 119, 168, 169
  monopolies and, 79–80
  moral hazard and, 138, 156–57
Trade, 34
Trade agreements, 354
Traditional justice, 100
Transaction activity in financial sector, 330
Transparency, public institutions and, 296–97
Transparency International, 120, 297
Truman, Harry, 43
Trump, Donald, 129, 150, 316–17, 335, 340, 345
Tullock, Gordon, 313–14
Tutorial role of government, 65, 141–42,
  162, 189–90
2007–2008 Financial Crisis
  generally, 333
  deregulation and, 109
  easy credit and, 107–8
  globalization and, 237
  government intervention and, 156
  Southeast Asian financial crisis (1997–1998)
    compared, 243–44

Ukraine, Gini coefficient in, 317
Unemployment compensation, 237–38
Unions
  decline in, 398
  in Germany, 231
  government control of, 23
  Hayek on, 231
  historical background, 19
  importance of, 23
  income inequality and decline in, 342

in Italy, 23, 231
Keynes on, 230–31
in US, 342
United Kingdom
Beveridge Report, 41–43, 50
Brexit, 279
challenges to welfare policies in, 60, 61
economic planning in, 27
entrepreneurs in, 307
executive compensation in, 364
financial institutions in, 157
income inequality in, 315
infrastructure in, 316–17
intellectual property in, 357–58
laissez faire in, 31
limited role of government in, 98
marginal tax rates in, 376, 377
market fundamentalism in, 35–36
Poor Laws, 50
progressive taxes in, 53, 343–44
public goods in, 180
public ownership in, 135
regulations in, 279
"revolving door policies" in, 335–36
stabilization policies in, 59
supply-side economics in, 76–78, 395
taxation in, 53, 371
welfare policies in, 214, 219
welfare state in, 41–42
women's suffrage in, 20
United States
administrative capability of governments
in, 67–68
Affordable Care Act, 208, 213, 274–75
Agriculture Department, 126, 127, 194–95
Aid to Dependent Children, 207
authorizations in, 145
balanced budget rules in, 73
bureaucracy in, 233
Census Bureau, 391–92
central bank in, 49, 188, 244
challenges to welfare policies in, 60, 61
Children's Health Insurance Program, 213
Child Support Program, 213
Clean Air Act, 276
Clean Energy Act, 276
Clean Water Act, 276
Code of Federal Regulations, 126–27, 172, 277
Community Health Centers, 213
Congressional Budget Office, 72–73,
180–81, 380
Constitution
generally, 99, 250, 270
amendment of, 250
Bill of Rights, 43–44

general principles, 268
intellectual property and, 176, 193, 362
slavery and, 249–50
workers' rights and, 250
Consumer Financial Protection Bureau, 128
consumption in, 316
contingent liabilities in, 138, 140–41
corporate taxation in, 161
Council of Economic Advisors, 56
Credit Card Accountability Responsibility
and Disclosure Act of 2009, 128
Declaration of Independence, 43–44, 99
Defense Advanced Research Project Agency
(DARPA), 194–95
Defense Department, 334
defense spending in, 178
dependent workers in, 250
deregulation in, 82
Dodd-Frank Wall Street Reform and
Consumer Protection Act, 109,
126, 128
Economic Opportunity Act of 1964, 213
Economic Report of the President
(1962), 56, 71
education in, 208
entrepreneurs in, 307
Environmental Protection Agency, 183, 276,
277, 281
executive compensation in, 169, 363, 364
ex post income distribution in, 118
"fake goods" in, 149
Fannie Mae, 138, 140–41
federalism in, 260, 284
Federal Register, 126–27, 277
Federal Reserve Bank, 49, 244
Federal Reserve System, 19, 113, 334
fees and fines in, 142
financial institutions in, 126, 157
financial penalties in, 169–70
"fireside chat," 43–45, 48, 50
Food and Drug Administration, 276
food stamps, 206, 213, 221
Freddie Mac, 138, 140–41
Full Employment Act of 1948, 49
Gini coefficient in, 317, 391–92
Government Accountability Office
(GAO), 290
guns in, 165
Head Start, 213
Health and Human Services Department,
127, 213
health care in, 208, 222–23, 298
income inequality in, 161–62, 208–9, 221,
224, 227, 315–16, 389, 391–92
income redistribution in, 200

United States (*cont.*)
income tax in, 19, 24–25, 208
infrastructure in, 234, 316–17
intellectual property in, 176, 193, 204, 347, 357–58, 362
Internal Revenue Service, 276, 372
Joint Economic Committee, 2
Justice Department, 126, 169–70
"Keynesian Revolution" in, 42, 56
laissez faire in, 17–19, 30, 31
Landis Report, 57–58
life expectancy in, 390–91
limited role of government in, 98
Low Income Home Energy Assistance Program, 213
marginal tax rates in, 375–77
market fundamentalism in, 35–36
Medicaid, 166, 180–81, 213, 221
Medicare, 166, 213
"military-industrial complex" in, 178
National Aeronautics and Space Administration (NASA), 179, 194–95
National Ambient Air Quality Standards (NAAQS), 277, 281
National Institutes of Health, 194–95
National Strategic Computing Initiative, 196–97
New Deal, 4, 22, 32, 67–68, 207
normative approach to role of government in, 110
occupational licensing in, 125–26
Outdoor Recreation Review Commission, 3
Patent and Trademark Office, 347
Pension Protection Act of 2006, 128
pensions in, 222–23
populism in, 74
Progressive Era, 18, 223
progressive taxes in, 52–53, 343–44
protection of property in, 202
public ownership in, 135, 136
public spending in, 23–24, 40–41, 77–78, 190
regulations in, 173, 276, 277, 279
research in, 194–97
"revolving door policies" in, 335–36
Safe Drinking Water Act, 276
"safety nets" in, 207–8
safety-related regulations in, 146–47
"Second Bill of Rights," 43–45
Securities Act of 1933, 57
Securities and Exchange Commission, 84–85, 276
Securities Exchange Act of 1934, 57
Sixteenth Amendment, 24
slavery in, 249–50, 265–66
stabilization policies in, 55–59

statutes in, 274–75, 276
stimulus in, 239–40
Supplemental Nutrition Assistance Program, 126, 316
supply-side economics in, 76–78, 395
Supreme Court, 251, 253, 267–69
taxation in, 52–53, 190, 367, 368, 371, 380
tax expenditures in, 232–33, 380–81
tax reduction in, 77, 87
Treasury Department, 127, 334
unions in, 342
upward mobility in, 391
"War on Poverty," 43, 48, 56, 58, 229, 388
welfare policies in, 43–45, 212–14
Women, Infants and Children (WIC), 213
Universal welfare programs, 214
Upward mobility, 391
Urban Institute, 368
Urbanization
externalities and, 91, 163–64
income inequality and, 206
legal rules and, 254
limited role of government, effect on, 97
regulations, effect on, 130
U.S. Tax Foundation, 233
U.S. Tax Policy Center, 372

Value added taxes
income redistribution and, 207, 211, 212
public spending and, 53
revenue growth and, 385
stabilization policies and, 240
Vaughan, Floyd L., 359
Venice (Republic), welfare policies in, 50
Verizon, 377
Vermeulen, Freck, 363, 364
Vivaldi, Antonio, 203
Volcker, Paul, 157

Wagner, Adolph, 218, 278–79
Wallstein, Peter, 275
Wall Street Journal, 394–95
Walt Disney, 347
Wapshott, Nicholas, 42
Washington Consensus, 39, 81–82, 84–85, 230, 395
Wealth creation. *See* Entrepreneurs
The Wealth of Nations (Smith), 189, 312, 320
Wealth tax, 341–42
Weber, Max, 70, 71, 73
Weingast, Barry, 265
Welfare policies
abuses in, 214
in Belgium, 214

benefits of, 54, 384
Beveridge Report and, 41–42
in Brazil, 212
challenges to. *See* Challenges to welfare
    policies
charity versus, 50, 214–15
democracy and, 384
in Dutch Republic, 50
economic problem and, 45, 47
entitlements, 50–51
fiscal expansion and, 49
in France, 43, 214
in Germany, 218, 219
goals of, 49–50
historical background, 218
income redistribution and, 45–46, 48
in Italy, 214
in Norway, 50
opposition to, 388
public good, welfare as, 181
public spending and, 51, 53, 232–33
resistance to changing, 222–23
in Scandinavia, 43, 214
skepticism toward, 396

taxation and, 45, 48–49
tax expenditures and, 52–53
in UK, 214, 219
universal welfare programs, 214
in US, 43–45, 212–14
Welfare states
    generally, 231, 388
    in Germany, 20
    income redistribution in, 224, 383
    Keynes on, 383
    rise of, 32–33
    in UK, 41–42
Williams, Serena, 351–52
Wilson, Woodrow, 18, 24–25, 98–99
Women's suffrage, 20
Woodward, Llewellyn, 66
Workers' rights, 18, 19, 23, 250
Working class, income inequality and, 206–7
Working hours, 146
World Bank, 145, 224, 284, 294, 296–97
World Trade Organization, 34, 276, 360
Wuthnow, Robert, 339

Zuckerberg, Mark, 326, 356–57